Improving Survey Methods

This state-of-the-art volume provides insight into the recent developments in survey research. It covers topics like survey modes and response effects, bio-indicators and paradata, interviewer and survey error, mixed-mode panels, sensitive questions, conducting web surveys and access panels, coping with nonresponse, and handling missing data. The authors are leading scientists in the field and discuss the latest methods and challenges with respect to these topics.

Each of the book's eight parts starts with a brief chapter that provides a historical context along with an overview of today's most critical survey methods. Chapters in the sections focus on research applications in practice and discuss results from field studies. As such, the book will help researchers design surveys according to today's best practices.

The book's website, www.survey-methodology.de, provides additional information, statistical analyses, tables, and figures.

An indispensable reference for practicing researchers and methodologists or any professional who uses surveys in their work, this book also serves as a supplement for graduate or upper-level undergraduate courses on survey methods taught in psychology, sociology, education, economics, and business. Although the book focuses on European findings, all of the research is discussed with reference to the entire survey-methodology area, including the USA. As such, the insights in this book will apply to surveys conducted around the world.

Uwe Engel is Professor of Sociology at the University of Bremen, Germany.
Ben Jann is Professor of Sociology at the University of Bern, Switzerland.
Peter Lynn is Professor of Survey Methodology at the University of Essex, UK.
Annette Scherpenzeel is the cohort manager of the Consortium of Individual Development at Utrecht University, the Netherlands.
Patrick Sturgis is Professor of Research Methodology at the University of Southampton, UK.

| | The European Association of Methodology (EAM) serves to promote research and development of empirical research methods in the fields of the Behavioral, Social, Educational, Health, and Economic Sciences as well as in the field of Evaluation Research. Homepage: www.eam-online.org |

The purpose of the EAM book series is to advance the development and application of methodological and statistical research techniques in social and behavioral research. Each volume in the series presents cutting-edge methodological developments in a way that is accessible to a broad audience. Such books can be authored, monographs, or edited volumes.

Sponsored by the European Association of Methodology, the EAM book series is open to contributions from the Behavioral, Social, Educational, Health, and Economic Sciences. Proposals for volumes in the EAM series should include the following: (1) title; (2) authors/editors; (3) a brief description of the volume's focus and intended audience; (4) a table of contents; and (5) a timeline including planned completion date. Proposals are invited from all interested authors. Feel free to submit a proposal to one of the members of the EAM book series editorial board, by visiting the EAM website (www.eam-online.org). Members of the EAM editorial board are Manuel Ato (University of Murcia), Pamela Campanelli (Survey Consultant, UK), Edith De Leeuw (Utrecht University), and Vasja Vehovar (University of Ljubljana).

Volumes in the series include:

Engel/Jann/Lynn/Scherpenzeel/Sturgis: Improving Survey Methods: Lessons from Recent Research, 2015

Davidov/Schmidt/Billiet: Cross-Cultural Analysis: Methods and Applications, 2011

Das/Ester/Kaczmirek: Social and Behavioral Research and the Internet: Advances in Applied Methods and Research Strategies, 2011

Hox/Roberts: Handbook of Advanced Multilevel Analysis, 2011

De Leeuw/Hox/Dillman: International Handbook of Survey Methodology, 2008

Van Montfort/Oud/Satorra: Longitudinal Models in the Behavioral and Related Sciences, 2007

Improving Survey Methods

Lessons from Recent Research

Edited by

Uwe Engel, Ben Jann, Peter Lynn,
Annette Scherpenzeel, and
Patrick Sturgis

Routledge
Taylor & Francis Group

NEW YORK AND LONDON

First published 2015
by Routledge
711 Third Avenue, New York, NY 10017

and by Routledge
27 Church Road, Hove, East Sussex BN3 2FA

Routledge is an imprint of the Taylor & Francis Group, an informa business

© 2015 Taylor & Francis

Library of Congress Cataloging-in-Publication Data
A CIP record for this book has been requested.

ISBN: 978-0-415-83625-8 (hbk)
ISBN: 978-0-415-81762-2 (pbk)
ISBN: 978-1-315-75628-8 (ebk)

Typeset in Minion Pro
by Apex CoVantage, LLC

Printed and bound in the United States of America by Publishers Graphics,
LLC on sustainably sourced paper.

Contents

Preface

In responding to socio-technological change, survey research is itself changing. New ways of conducting surveys emerge and replace others. To keep step with this development, continued research and innovation on the improvement of survey methods is needed. To this end, this volume presents recent survey methodological and statistical research from different European countries. The research reported on draws on invited presentations at the first two international conferences of the Priority Programme on Survey Methodology (PPSM) of the German Research Foundation (DFG). Additional contributions come from the wider network of PPSM researchers.

The Priority Programme on Survey Methodology commenced in January 2008. Sixteen projects were undertaken over the course of the following six years. While most project sites were located within Germany, two projects included were based in Switzerland and the Netherlands. The establishment of this Program came at a time when comparable survey research networks already existed in neighboring European countries. In the United Kingdom, the UK Survey Design and Measurement Initiative was established in 2007. In the Netherlands, too, a key survey methodology/statistics research environment already existed at that time, with outstanding researchers at Utrecht University, Statistics Netherlands, the Netherlands Institute for Social Research, and Tilburg University. Additionally, a number of data collection facilities and research panels arose from networks of survey methodologists and statisticians. In the Netherlands, for instance, the Measurement and Experimentation in the Social Sciences (MESS) facility and its Longitudinal Internet Studies for the Social Sciences (LISS) panel was established in 2007. The following year in the United Kingdom, the Understanding Society Innovation Panel began collecting data. It was therefore extremely helpful for the six years of development of the Priority Programme and its own research panel to be able to benefit so strongly from the cooperation with leading social scientists from within these research networks. From a PPSM point of view, this international cooperation and collaboration has been greatly appreciated.

The Priority Programme on Survey Methodology organized three international conferences which focused on the objective of improving survey methodological practice. They took place biennially in Bremen, with the first one, in November 2009, simply titled "Improving Survey Methods".

Invited talks were given by Jelke Bethlehem (Statistics Netherlands), Don Dillman (Washington State University), and Peter Lynn (University of Essex). The second conference entitled "Advancing Survey Methods" was held two years later in November 2011. The list of invited speakers at the second conference included Edith De Leeuw and Joop Hox (Utrecht University), Annette Scherpenzeel (formerly Tilburg University, now Utrecht University), Ineke Stoop (The Netherlands Institute for Social Research), Patrick Sturgis (University of Southampton), and Vasja Vehovar (University of Ljubljana). Finally, a third conference in September 2013 addressed "Survey Methods in Future Research".

The improvement and innovation of survey methods cannot take place without statistical and methodological research *about* survey methods. Unless such research delivers insight into the potential strengths and weaknesses of a given survey method, it is not possible to fruitfully develop this method further. The present volume is about such statistical and methodological research and focuses on a wide range of areas within survey research. The chapters introduce these methods along with the empirical evidence found for them, and the scientific insights gained from this evidence. Depending on the survey method under consideration, this may be evidence from field-experimental research, quasi-experimental research, observational studies, simulation studies, or some combination of such research designs. The research questions addressed in the eight parts of the volume cover a broad range of fields of survey methodology/statistics, from survey modes and response effects, to interviewers and survey error, to asking sensitive questions, and to conducting web surveys and access panels. They expand the horizon by referring to linkages of survey data with other types of data. Furthermore, one part of the volume deals with coping with nonresponse, another with the handling of missing data. Chapter 1 provides a general introduction and overview of the research questions addressed in the present volume. Furthermore, each of the eight parts of the volume starts with a short introductory chapter to orientate the reader.

Some chapters of the volume take advantage of using the accompanying website at www.survey-methodology.de for supplementing their analyses with additional information, analyses, tables, and figures. The respective references will be given in situ.

For whom is this volume written? We hope that the volume will be of benefit to three primary audiences. First of all, it will assist applied survey researchers in designing their survey studies at a state-of-the-art level. Survey statisticians and survey methodologists, in their roles as both researchers and teachers, represent another audience. The book should also be appropriate as course reading at the advanced B.A., M.A., and Ph.D. level in university departments that offer specialized courses on survey methods to their students.

We are grateful to all authors for their excellent contributions, the always pleasant cooperation, and their mutual commitment to elaborating peer reviews of the chapters. Special thanks go to Laura Burmeister and Kim-Sarah Kleij for their excellent organizational assistance and to Katherine Bird who checked all chapters linguistically from the point of view of an English native speaker, to make final linguistic amendments when necessary.

Regarding the Priority Programme on Survey Methodology (PPSM), the financial support this programme received from the German Research Foundation (DFG) is gratefully acknowledged. Regarding the PPSM panel, special thanks go to the University of Bremen as well.

Uwe Engel, Ben Jann, Peter Lynn
Annette Scherpenzeel and Patrick Sturgis

Contributors' Affiliations

Christian Aßmann
Chair of Statistics and Econometrics/National Educational Panel Study
Otto-Friedrich-University Bamberg

Boyko Amarov
Institute of Statistics and Econometrics
Freie Universität Berlin

Katrin Auspurg
Chair of Empirical Social Research
Department of History and Sociology
University of Konstanz

Sara Bahrami
Chair of Statistics and Econometrics/National Educational Panel Study
Otto-Friedrich-University Bamberg

Wolfgang Bandilla
Survey Design and Methodology
GESIS—Leibniz Institute for the Social Sciences Mannheim

Dorothée Behr
Survey Design and Methodology
GESIS—Leibniz Institute for the Social Sciences Mannheim

Jelke Bethlehem
Faculty of Social Sciences
Leiden University and Statistics Netherlands
The Hague

Michael Braun
Survey Design and Methodology
GESIS—Leibniz Institute for the Social Sciences Mannheim

Sebastian Bredl
Department of Economics
Justus-Liebig-University Giessen

Britta Busse
Institute Labour and Economy (IAW)
University of Bremen

Roel de Jong
University of Hamburg

Edith D. De Leeuw
Department of Methodology and Statistics
Utrecht University

Andreas Diekmann
Chair of Sociology
ETH Zurich

Tobias Enderle
Survey Design and Methodology
GESIS—Leibniz Institute for the Social Sciences Mannheim

Uwe Engel
EMPAS and Social Statistics & Research Group
University of Bremen

Marek Fuchs
Institute of Sociology
Technische Universität Darmstadt

Anja S. Göritz
Department of Psychology
University of Freiburg

Hagen von Hermanni
Faculty of Education
University of Leipzig

Thomas Hinz
Chair of Empirical Social Research
Department of History and Sociology
University of Konstanz

Marc Höglinger
Chair of Sociology
ETH Zurich

Joop J. Hox
Department of Methodology & Statistics
Utrecht University

Ben Jann
Institute of Sociology
University of Bern

Lars Kaczmirek
Survey Design and Methodology
GESIS—Leibniz Institute for the Social Sciences Mannheim

Kristian Kleinke
Faculty of Sociology
University of Bielefeld

Britta Köster
EMPAS and Social Statistics & Research Group
University of Bremen

Frauke Kreuter
Maryland Population Research Center

Ivar Krumpal
Institute of Sociology
University of Leipzig

Stefan Liebig
Faculty of Sociology
University of Bielefeld

Peter Lynn
Institute for Social and Economic Research (ISER)
University of Essex

David Martin
Department of Geography and Environment
University of Southampton

Florian Meinfelder
Chair of Statistics and Econometrics/National Educational Panel Study
Otto-Friedrich-University Bamberg

Natalja Menold
Survey Design and Methodology
GESIS—Leibniz Institute for the Social Sciences Mannheim

Ralf Münnich
Chair of Economic and Social Statistics
Trier University

Andraž Petrovčič
Faculty of Social Sciences
University of Ljubljana

Susanne Rässler
Chair of Statistics and Econometrics/National Educational Panel Study
Otto-Friedrich-University Bamberg

Jost Reinecke
Faculty of Sociology
University of Bielefeld

Ulrich Rendtel
Institute of Statistics and Econometrics
Freie Universität Berlin

Carsten Sauer
Faculty of Sociology
University of Bielefeld

Annette Scherpenzeel
Consortium of Individual Development
Utrecht University

Rainer Schnell
Institute of Sociology
University of Duisburg-Essen

Chris Skinner
Department of Statistics
The London School of Economics and Political Science

Ana Slavec
Faculty of Social Sciences
University of Ljubljana

Martin Spiess
Psychological Methods
University of Hamburg

Ineke Stoop
The Netherlands Institute for Social Research/SCP

Nina Storfinger
Center for International Development and Environmental
Reasearch (ZEU)
Justus-Liebig-University Giessen

Patrick Sturgis
School of Social Sciences
University of Southampton

Malgorzata Turner
Student Data management and Analysis
University of Oxford

Vasja Vehovar
Faculty of Social Sciences
University of Ljubljana

Peter Winker
Department of Economics
Justus-Liebig-University Giessen

About the Editors

Uwe Engel is Professor of Sociology and Director of the Social Science Methods Centre at the University of Bremen, Germany. He is co-founder and coordinator of the German Priority Programme on Survey Methodology. Uwe has over 30 years of experience in survey research. In 2004 he was one of the founding members of the European Association of Methodology.

Ben Jann is Professor of Sociology at the University of Bern, Switzerland. His research interests include social science methodology, statistics, social stratification, and labor market sociology. Recent publications include papers in *Sociological Methodology, Sociological Methods & Research, Public Opinion Quarterly, the Journal of Survey Statistics and Methodology, the Stata Journal,* and the *American Sociological Review.*

Peter Lynn is Professor of Survey Methodology at the University of Essex, UK. He has over 25 years of experience in survey research and was previously Director of the Survey Methods Centre at the National Centre for Social Research (now known as NatCen Social Research). Peter was founding editor of the online journal *Survey Research Methods* and has served as vice-president of the International Association of Survey Statisticians. In 2003 the Royal Statistical Society awarded him the Guy Medal in Bronze for his contribution to survey research methods and practice.

Annette Scherpenzeel was, from 2006 to 2013, the project leader of the MESS facility for online data collection and the LISS panel at CentERdata, Tilburg University, the Netherlands. She has more than 20 years of experience in panel surveys and online interviewing. Since September 2013, she is the cohort manager of the Consortium of Individual Development at the Utrecht University.

Patrick Sturgis is Professor of Research Methodology at the University of Southampton in the UK, Director of the UK National Centre for Research Methods, and president of the European Survey Research Association (ESRA). His research interests are in the areas of survey methodology, statistical modeling, public opinion and political behavior, and public understanding of science and technology. He has published widely on measurement issues in survey methodology in journals such as *Public Opinion Quarterly, Sociological Methods and Research, the Journal of the Royal Statistical Society,* and the *Journal of Official Statistics.*

1

Improving Survey Methods

General Introduction

Uwe Engel, Ben Jann, Peter Lynn, Annette Scherpenzeel and Patrick Sturgis

1.1 INTRODUCTION

Surveys are conducted all over the world. They represent influential sources of information for public opinion formation and decision-making. Their quality should therefore be sufficient for this important function. We assume that surveys can fulfill this function only if appropriately designed and prepared to militate efficiently against the known sources of survey error (Biemer & Lyberg, 2003). Just what do these demands mean in a changing world? In responding to socio-technological change, survey research is changing itself. While new ways of conducting surveys emerge and replace others, they change the way in which people respond to survey requests and the way in which they answer survey questions. A case in point is the growing importance of web surveys, access panels, and the use of mobile communication devices like mobile phones, smartphones, and tablet PCs. Special challenges arise from the mixture of survey modes, contact modes, question and response formats.

We know that people respond differently to different implementations of survey research. Response rates, for instance, vary considerably between survey modes like face-to-face, telephone, and web. The same applies to the response behavior itself. Answers to sensitive questions are likely to be more honest if obtained in self-administered modes. Just how valid are answers if obtained in response to special techniques for asking sensitive questions? We know that individual response propensities may be affected by design features such as mixtures of contact modes, the use of prepaid incentives, and refusal conversion efforts. But what about the *effects* of such interventions on sample composition and the answering behavior of respondents? If the mixing of modes is an appropriate answer to declining response propensities and changing communication habits, what are its consequences? Do such interventions impair the comparability of survey responses and, if yes, is it possible to enhance comparability post hoc?

This all calls for continued research focus on the improvement of survey methods. To this end, the current volume presents recent methodological and statistical research from different European countries. It attends to major sources of survey error, established and emerging forms of conducting survey research, and recent approaches to meeting the challenges that they present. In this chapter, we shortly introduce these major sources of survey error, starting with the types of error encountered in the first stages of a survey, and going through the whole survey process. All chapters of this book relate to one or more of these survey design issues and the associated survey error, as we will show.

1.2 NONRESPONSE BIAS

The first and perhaps most important source of survey error is caused by nonresponse. If surveys are used to arrive at sample estimates of unknown population characteristics, these estimates should come as close as possible to the true values. Most importantly, perhaps, they should be unbiased. It is clear that a survey will fail to reach this objective if systematic unit nonresponse distorts the randomness of a sample. Therefore survey research is well-advised to pay attention to factors that impair this randomness. Response propensity modeling is a powerful approach to identify such factors and quantify their impact. Such propensities are individual response probabilities estimated with respect to auxiliary variables. Some chapters of the present volume deal with this approach (Chapters 14, 18, 20, and 21). We can use response propensities, for instance, for the computation of modified Horvitz-Thompson estimates, the assessment of nonresponse bias of mean estimates, or for weighting adjustments (Bethlehem, Cobben, & Schouten, 2011). Propensity models are useful for the identification of selective forces in recruitment processes that should actually be random processes. In terms of statistical modeling, the approach is routinely applied by means of logistic regression modeling. Somewhat more challenging, however, is the collection of the necessary auxiliary variables, since information is needed about both nonrespondents and respondents to model individual response probabilities.

Estimates of individual response probabilities crucially depend on the sets of auxiliary variables available to the survey researcher. Such variables may come from the contact process and/or population registers. Sometimes information is used that classifies places of residence of respondents by district or neighborhood information. When using contact information, a further source of variation arises out of the consideration of refusal conversion efforts. Chapter 18 discusses in this context how estimates of nonresponse bias change if the set of auxiliary variables is altered. There will generally be the tendency to use as auxiliary variables the only ones that are available in a particular context. This availability of effective auxiliary variables is discussed in Chapter 14. Available variables may not, however, represent the best choice. The situation gets even worse in cross-national research, as discussed in Chapter 29.

Another option for collecting the necessary auxiliary variables consists in exploiting the contact process that leads target persons to accept or refuse a survey invitation. For that purpose surveys collect so-called *paradata* (Chapter 25). Amongst other uses, such data can be used to detect two kinds of factors, namely factors that affect the probability of making contact with target persons and factors that shape the probability of achieving cooperation. Another option consists of the application of approaches that aim at winning over persons to a survey who initially refuse to take part. One such approach is the "basic question" approach (Bethlehem, 2009), another one the Pre-Emptive Doorstep Administration of Key Survey Items (PEDAKSI) methodology (Lynn, 2003). Such approaches seek required auxiliary variables (i.e., the required background data) not by collecting data *besides* the survey data, i.e., by *para*data, but by enlarging the body of survey data itself. Chapters 5 and 18, for instance, take advantage of this approach.

High response rates are often regarded as an indicator of sample quality. That nonresponse bias may tend to become smaller when response rates increase says something for this view. However, in view of the range of response rates typically achieved in survey research, substantial scope for nonresponse bias is likely to remain even when response rates are high. Hence high response rates alone cannot guarantee unbiased sample estimates. Typically response rates also vary across survey modes and countries. Chapter 14 discusses the former source of variation. Chapter 29 addresses the latter, presenting clear evidence from the European Social Survey and discussing possible reasons for the variation. It might accordingly be inappropriate to equate acceptable sample quality to a single overall benchmark such as a 70 percent target response rate. As Stoop notes with reference to Groves in Chapter 29, "what could be done is to shift the focus away from a blind pursuit of high response rates to an informed pursuit of high response rates (. . .)" and to consider as a criterion how balanced the response rate is across subgroups of a sample. This is, for instance, done in an approach which takes the average dispersion of individual response propensities around their mean value, i.e., around the response rate, as a building block for so-called R-indicators of "representativity" (Bethlehem et al., 2011).

1.3 INDUCING SURVEY RESPONSE

Survey designs may strive to counterbalance low or even declining response propensities by the implementation of special design features. One particularly important tool consists of the use of respondent incentives. Earlier reviews showed the effectiveness of this method for postal and interviewer-assisted surveys (e.g., Church, 1993; Engel & Schnabel, 2004; Singer, Groves, & Corning, 1999). At that time, prepaid monetary incentives turned out to be especially effective in enhancing response rates for these surveys modes. Since then, however, survey research has experienced a substantial and growing increase in the use of web surveys and volunteer panels using the web. In addition to that development, single experimental findings have suggested that the effectiveness of monetary incentives have become even stronger in recent years (Engel, Bartsch, Schnabel, & Vehre, 2012, p. 128f.). One could speculate about a growing need for incentives to motivate respondents. Will incentives become indispensable to motivate respondents in the future, maybe as an inadvertent side effect of the widespread use of volunteer web panels that pay for answers on a regular basis? Chapter 28 presents an updated review of the effectiveness of incentives. Furthermore, it expands the respective knowledge to surveys carried out on the web. Additionally in this context, Chapter 19 reports on the effect of different types of incentives on sleeper reactivation in a randomly recruited internet panel. Another incentive experiment is reported in Chapter 5 for the mobile phone mode.

An idea of growing importance in survey methodology is that of turning away from survey designs that approach all sampled households in the same manner. It is generally recommended, for instance, to let interviewers counteract possible queries and concerns of interviewees. Chapter 18 discusses the strengths of various arguments an interviewer might use to convince reluctant persons to take part in a survey. Another variant consists in offering interviews of different lengths to persons whose motivation differs accordingly. This may be accomplished by the two approaches cited above, the PEDAKSI methodology and the "basic question" approach. Meanwhile, the literature talks of "adaptive survey designs" (Bethlehem et al., 2011) to express the idea that elements of survey designs respond to situational factors in different ways. However, as shown in detail in Chapter 27, the idea of adapting the nature of the survey protocol to the circumstances of sample members in order to improve response rates did not spread to other elements of the survey process than the interview length. Instead, most other aspects of survey design and implementation remain standardized across all sample members. More recently, researchers have begun to explore the idea of treating sample subgroups differently. Interest has focused on the idea of starting data collection in a standardized way but then changing it in different ways for different sample members as fieldwork progresses. Here a distinction can be made between targeted and tailored strategies. Targeted strategies involve treating each of a limited number of sample subgroups in different ways, while tailored strategies involve treating each individual sample member differently. Chapter 27 reviews both theory and practice regarding targeted strategies to improve response rates or response balance and identifies three main categories of targeted strategies.

1.4 ENHANCING SURVEY RESPONSE OR SURVEY BALANCE?

Instead of striving for "high response rates" only, "response balance" may be a more relevant target. This is certainly an insight one can derive from the chapters on nonresponse bias and survey response inducement described in the previous paragraphs. Prepaid monetary incentives are especially known for motivating survey cooperation. However should the use of incentives be regarded as a survey method to induce survey response only? For instance, we know from a field experiment that the use of prepaid incentives can reduce the "high-education bias" of samples considerably (Vehre, Bartsch, & Engel, 2013) in comparison to reference distributions from official statistics (Microcensus). A comparable question applies to refusal conversion efforts. We know for instance from another field experiment that refusal conversion efforts do not necessarily induce response, though such efforts change sample composition systematically at the same time (Engel et al., 2012, pp. 132f. and Chapter 18).

On the whole, the preceding paragraphs suggest that it is appropriate to aim for response balance as part of targeted inducement strategies while considering possible inadvertent side effects. Chapter 4 provides evidence for one such side effect in the shape of repeatedly found cross-sectional correlations between interviewers' conversion refusal efforts and satisficing response behavior.

1.5 WEB SURVEYS, INTERNET PANELS, AND MIXED-MODE DESIGNS

A substantial proportion of survey research is now conducted over the Internet. Chapter 14 discusses three basic aspects that may complicate using the web for surveying the general population. It asks if web surveys can be used in official statistics and discusses in detail the methodological issues of under-coverage, sample selection, and nonresponse as well as some correction techniques. It highlights amongst others the really important distinction between self-selected "opt-in" panels and probability-based panels and discusses under what conditions web surveys can be used in official statistics. In that discussion the selection and recruitment mode play important roles. Probability sampling is regarded as indispensable. For web surveys probability sampling is possible by doing recruitment in a different mode. For instance, one can draw random samples from population registers to send out invitations to a web survey by mail. Another example consists in the use of random telephone sampling.

However, is it sufficient to recruit people at random? In view of differential response propensities of target persons, this is certainly not sufficient for unbiased estimates. Instead, we have to understand better who agrees to a survey request and who does not. This holds true for single surveys and for panels. There now exist two large probability panels that afford an opportunity to study the recruitment process into a panel in greater detail. In the Netherlands this is the Longitudinal Internet Studies for the Social Sciences (LISS) panel and in Germany it is the panel of the Priority Programme on Survey Methodology (PPSM). Chapter 19 describes the LISS panel in greater detail. Special attention is paid to the process of survey participation in this panel and the participation behavior after initial recruitment. The PPSM panel constitutes the basis for the propensity analysis in Chapter 18 and the response experiments in Chapter 4. A further analysis of a recruitment process into a panel is provided in Chapter 20. The analysis presented therein refers especially to the access panel of the German Federal Statistical Office.

The mixing of survey modes in a single design is an issue of substantial importance in current survey research. We can implement mixed-mode designs for recruitment to panels and we can apply it sequentially or concurrently. For instance, the PPSM panel is a mixed-mode panel, with telephone as recruitment mode and web and telephone as data collection modes. "Mixed-mode" can mean that we allocate people at random to survey modes and it can mean alternatively that people's preferences decide in which mode they like to give interviews. There exists a multiplicity of possibilities. The "mixed-mode" aspect is discussed in Chapters 3, 14, and 18.

1.6 MEASUREMENT EFFECTS

Low response rates and response rates that are unbalanced across different groups of respondents constitute a major source of bias in survey estimates. However, even if a sample is perfectly representative across all respondent groups, there can still be other sources of error. The choice of survey modes, the survey question wording and response formats, and the design of the questionnaire, for example, can all have undesirable effects on the answers of the respondents to the survey questions. Ideally, each method used to measure a substantive research concept should lead to equivalent results. That is: a question intended to measure, for example, satisfaction with work should result in about the same distribution of satisfaction across the same respondents, independent of whether it was asked by telephone, by a male or female interviewer, on paper or online, the answering scale used, and of the question translation. If this equivalence is not found, survey estimates are biased by measurement error due to the method of measurement. Hence, after designing the strategy to induce response in a survey and to attain balance in the response rates, the next step a survey researcher takes to prevent survey error is to choose or construct survey instruments and interview setups that will not affect the survey answers. The present volume focuses accordingly on response styles, mode, and response effects.

1.7 RESPONSE STYLES, MODE, AND RESPONSE EFFECTS

If it makes a difference to the distribution of responses obtained whether a question has been administered by telephone interview, face-to-face interview, web interview, or mail questionnaire, other things being equal, this can be referred to as a "mode effect". Chapter 3 deals with this type of effect. In addition, Chapter 5 focuses on one particular survey mode, namely the mobile phone mode. Another class of measurement effects arises from the ways questions are worded and response formats are styled. In this context, we talk of "response effects". Chapters 3 and 4 report recent field-experimental research on such effects. This research enlarges the relevant evidence piece by piece and focuses in particular on factors that help explain why these effects come about. Chapter 4 explores in particular the role of cognitive response styles in this regard.

Another source of variation is simply that respondents arrive at their responses to survey questions through cognitive processes that can differ in a number of important ways. Special probing techniques are then used to shed light on these internal processes. Such techniques are presented and discussed in Chapter 3, 4, and 16.

1.8 SENSITIVE TOPICS

The sensitivity of survey topics can affect response behavior in at least two ways: it can increase the likelihood of item nonresponse and it can bias answers in the direction of social desirability. The income variable is a classic example of the former, answers to questions on deviant behavior like tax fraud are likely to be prone to the latter. There are however less clear cases where it might be advisable to let respondents rate the sensitivity of survey questions explicitly. Chapter 4 reports such an analysis of *perceived* sensitivity.

Sensitive questions may be asked by special questioning techniques. The present volume evaluates two approaches to asking sensitive topics in the light of recent research findings and develops these techniques further. A first class of techniques builds random devices into the construction of a sensitive survey question. This applies to the randomized response technique and related methods. Chapters 10 and 11 deal with this class of techniques. Another approach consists in posing hypothetical questions. This method is alternatively known as the factorial survey approach, the vignette technique, and the quasi-experimental question. Chapter 12 evaluates this approach as a method for measuring sensitive issues.

1.9 INTERVIEWER EFFECTS

Despite the rise of web surveys, a large amount of data is still collected by interviewer-mediated surveys. For example, out of the 21 million quantitative interviews conducted by ADM institutes in Germany in 2012 in the private market sector of survey research, the share of interviewer-mediated (face-to-face and telephone) surveys adds up to 59 percent (ADM, 2012, p. 18). Furthermore, many important social surveys like the European Social Survey and the European Quality of Life Survey use interviewer-mediated forms of data collection. It is thus of continuing relevance to research how interviewers affect survey quality.

Answers to sensitive questions seem, for instance, less prone to be biased in the direction of social desirability if no interviewer is involved in an interview. A recent analysis, for instance, found systematically less biased answers for two item batteries if these items were asked in the web mode rather than the telephone mode (Engel, 2013). There is evidence that interviewers' background characteristics work through interview experience, expectations, and images of how to proceed in the contact situation to win over a person to an interview. Chapter 18 addresses this topic with reference to a multilevel analysis. Using a German version of IQUEST, the International Interviewer Questionnaire (De Leeuw & Hox, 2009), and additional survey questions, this analysis revealed that interviewers tend to be more successful in achieving interviews the more they believe the respondents will trust them. Interviewer attitudes also play a vital role in the contact situation. If interviewers are convinced of their ability to convince reluctant persons to take part in an interview, they prove to be more successful than interviewers who do not share this expectation (Engel et al., 2012, Chapter 9). This is in line with previous findings (Hox & De Leeuw, 2002) and represents clearly another variant of a self-fulfilling prophecy.

Chapter 7 is concerned with improving our understanding of the effect that interviewers have on the variance of survey estimates. It contributes to the body of evidence in this area by assessing whether psychological characteristics of interviewers, such as attitudes, personality, job experience, and job satisfaction are related to the magnitude of the interviewer variance component. Using data from the National Travel Survey of Great Britain, the analysis reveals a significant interviewer contribution to response variance. It also shows that the magnitude of the intra-interviewer correlation varies as a function of the interviewer characteristics, sometime substantially (Chapter 7).

It is certainly appropriate to understand interviewer effects in general as unintended side effects that arise out of interviewers' characteristics, attitudes, and behaviors. There is however a type of interviewer error that is more insidious, namely, when interviewers deliberately fabricate interviews. Survey research then needs to detect such falsifications. Chapter 8 deals with this challenging task by means of a new multivariate indicator-based method.

1.10 COMBINATION OF SURVEYS WITH OTHER TYPES OF DATA

Different methods can produce different kinds of data. To relate them in reasonable ways is quite demanding if the combination of methods is intended to mean more than a simple juxtaposition of findings produced by different methods. In the survey context it is common practice to combine survey data with paradata (Chapter 25). The same is true for geographical data. The use of bio-indicators is another example for the combination of survey data with other types of data. In the present volume the combination of surveys with non-questionnaire data is discussed in two chapters. First, Chapter 23 discusses linking surveys and administrative data. Then, Chapter 24 discusses the combination of surveys with objective measurements and observer rating.

1.11 MISSING DATA TREATMENT

Almost every survey encounters missing data. Generally this is undesirable because it reduces survey accuracy. Rather than excluding cases with missing data from an analysis, missing values are more appropriately treated via "imputation". Though missing data imputation techniques have already reached a highly sophisticated state of the art, survey research is still in need of further development. In the present volume three chapters deal with such developments. Chapter 32 reports a technique of multiple imputation for multilevel count data and Chapter 33 reports methods of robust multiple imputation. While incomplete data matrices are in general unwanted, there is one exception to this rule. In order to enlarge a questionnaire program or to reduce survey burden, one approach deliberately builds missing data into the survey design. Chapter 31 deals with such a planned, so-called split questionnaire design.

1.12 CONCLUSION

Times are changing for survey research. Those who design and carry out surveys are being presented with new challenges but also with new opportunities. These challenges and opportunities stem partly from changes in society and partly from changes in technology. Societal changes may, for example, restrict the time that people have available for participating in surveys or result in changes in the ways that people expect to communicate. Technological advances may provide a wider range of means by which researchers can sample people, contact people, administer questions, or transmit data. The chapters in this book provide ample evidence that survey methodologists are responding to these challenges. These responses relate to all components of the survey process and apply to a wide range of types of surveys. We cannot hope to have addressed all the current research issues in survey methods within the confines of a single book, but we hope that the book will be of practical use to survey researchers wanting to keep up-to-date with current issues in the field and will stimulate methodologists to strive for further advances in our knowledge of how best to carry out surveys. There is no doubt that the value of survey data is considerable, but dependent on the quality of the process by which they were collected. For that reason, continued investment in understanding and improving survey quality is not only desirable, but essential. We hope that this book makes a contribution in that direction.

REFERENCES

ADM Arbeitskreis Deutscher Markt- und Sozialforschungsinstitute. (2012). *Jahresbericht 2012*. Retrieved from www.adm-ev.de/index.php?id=jahresberichte

Bethlehem, J. (2009). *Applied survey methods. Statistical perspective*. Hoboken: Wiley.

Bethlehem, J., Cobben, F., & Schouten, B. (2011). *Handbook of nonresponse in household surveys*. Hoboken: Wiley.

Biemer, P. P., & Lyberg, L. E. (2003). *Introduction to survey quality*. Hoboken: Wiley.

Church, A. H. (1993). Estimating the effect of incentives on mail survey response rates: A meta analysis. *Public Opinion Quarterly*, 57, 26–79.

De Leeuw, E. D., & Hox, J. J. (2009). *International Interviewer Questionnaire (IQUEST). Development and scale properties*. Retrieved from http://surveymethodology.eu/media/files/warsaw/IQUESTreport.pdf

Engel, U. (2013). *Access panel and mixed-mode internet survey. PPSM Panel Report*. Retrieved from www.sozialforschung.uni-bremen.de/html/downloads.html

Engel, U., Bartsch, S., Schnabel, C., & Vehre, H. (2012). *Wissenschaftliche Umfragen. Methoden und Fehlerquellen*. Frankfurt/New York: Campus.

Engel, U., & Schnabel, C. (2004). *Markt- und Sozialforschung. Metaanalyse zum Ausschoepfungsgrad*. Retrieved from www.adm-ev.de/index.php?id=forschungsprojekte

Hox, J., & De Leeuw, E. (2002). The influence of interviewers' attitude and behavior on household survey nonresponse: An international comparison. In R. M. Groves, D. A. Dillman, J. L. Etlinge, & J. A. Roderick (Eds.), *Survey nonresponse* (pp. 103–120). New York: Wiley.

Lynn, P. (2003). PEDAKSI: Methodology for collecting data about survey non-respondents. *Quality & Quantity*, 37, 239–261.

Singer, E., Groves, R. M., & Corning, A. D. (1999). Differential incentives. Beliefs about practices, perceptions of equity, and effects on survey participation. *Public Opinion Quarterly*, 63, 251–260.

Vehre, H., Bartsch, S., & Engel, U. (2013). *The education bias in a telephone survey with incentives*. Retrieved from www.sozialforschung.uni-bremen.de/html/downloads.html

Part I

Survey Modes and Response Effects

2

Survey Modes and Response Effects

Overview and Introduction

Uwe Engel

One could argue that social data should reflect reality and not the particular methods used to collect such data. This view implies the ideal case that one and the same outcome may be obtained by different methods. This will generally not be the case. Instead, outcomes are likely to depend on researchers' decisions about how to collect data at least to some extent. If, however, different methods produce different outcomes, other things being equal, then one should be able to assess and understand this dependency. In the present section, this concerns the identification of so-called mode and response effects. Responses to survey questions may depend on the survey mode and the ways questions are worded and response formats are styled. Once identified, such effects may be used to counterbalance this dependency. This may be accomplished in quite different ways: first of all, by simply considering it when interpreting findings. An early attempt at considering this dependency quantitatively goes back to Galtung (1969, pp. 336–339, 440 ff.) who developed formulas for assessing the degree of confirmation of propositions as part of an approach to systematic replication. The conduct of statistical sensitivity analyses also affords an opportunity to assess the dependency of outcomes on systematically varied methods. Most frequently, advanced structural equation modeling like e.g. MTMM models and latent class analysis will presumably be first class (e.g. Saris, van der Veld, & Gallhofer, 2004; Biemer, 2011; Byrne, 2012, e.g. pp. 285ff.).

2.1 SURVEY MODES AND MODE EFFECTS

"Measurement" represents one of the cornerstones of survey research (De Leeuw, Hox, & Dillman, 2008, pp. 11–13). The authors identify three main sources of measurement error: the questionnaire, the respondent, and the method of data collection. Mode effects may come about with respect to recruitment/contact modes and data collection modes. Regarding the latter, "mode effects" are indicated if, other things being equal, people respond differently to the same survey questions if asked in different mode. For instance, this is likely to apply to sensitive questions if asked in a self-administered vs. interviewer-assisted mode. Answers to survey questions which affect images of social desirability on the respondent side are also likely to be affected by the involvement of interviewers in the question-answer process. Chapter 3 discusses the topic of mode effects in greater detail. Chapter 5 addresses in particular the "mobile phone" mode.

Following a description of the history of different modes of survey data collection, Chapter 3 discusses major survey modes in relation to sources of survey error. It deals in particular with the relation of survey modes to coverage error, sampling error, nonresponse error, and measurement error. Special attention is drawn to the relation of measurement error to survey mode, i.e. to the so-called "mode effects", to continue with identifying mode-specific strategies to optimize questionnaires. To quote Edith De Leeuw and Joop Hox (Chapter 3), "two prime examples of different optimizing strategies for a particular mode are a different labeling of scale points in telephone surveys and the explicit offering of a 'don't know' option in self-administered surveys". The chapter discusses both strategies and continues with a description of two related mode experiments. Both were carried out concurrently in the web and telephone mode of the Priority Programme on Survey Methodology (PPSM) panel. The first experiment compares 5pt scales where response categories were either fully labeled or only endpoint labeled. The second split ballot experiment investigates the effect of offering an explicit "don't know" (DK) and following up DK responses with a gentle probe in both web and telephone. As described in detail in Chapter 3, the experiments revealed a strong effect of different labeling options. To quote Edith De Leeuw and Joop Hox once again, "explicitly offering a 'don't know' option dramatically increases the proportion of 'don't know' answers, especially in the web mode", while "using a gentle probe after each 'don't know' response reduced the final number of non-substantive answers in both the web and the telephone interview".

Chapter 5 reports on telephone surveys using mobile phones. It discusses this mode in relation to sources of survey error: coverage, sampling, nonresponse, and measurement. Using face-to-face Eurobarometer data from ten countries as benchmarks, Busse and Fuchs present an analysis of relative coverage bias in mobile phone telephone surveys by assessing "several sociodemographic estimates simulating a landline survey (ignoring mobile-onlys) and a mobile phone survey (ignoring landline-onlys)". Concerning sampling, the authors refer to the so-called Gabler-Häder design to tackle two relevant goals: first, increasing the rate of attaining numbers of known eligibility in German mobile phone samples by number validation services and text messaging services, and second, assessing potential bias due to cell phone sharing. Concerning nonresponse, the authors determine the relative nonresponse bias for several stages of the usual contact process using the prominent basic question approach. They also explore the effectiveness of prepaid incentives. Finally, Chapter 5 addresses the topic of measurement error for mobile phone surveys.

2.2 RESPONSE EFFECTS

"Response effects" arise out of the ways questions are worded and response formats are styled. Other things being equal, such response effects are indicated if the answers to a survey question about a given subject matter differ if the way this question is designed also differs. In addition, answers to a question may be influenced by its placement in the sequence of questions in a questionnaire. Relevant topics include question order, response order, question wording, and the distinction between closed-ended vs. open-ended questions. There also exists a multiplicity of different response formats. Regarding such mode-specific response effects, Chapters 3 and 4 present experimental results which are based on data of the probability-based mixed-mode access panel of the PPSM. These experiments follow in part the lines of earlier such experiments in the field (Christian, Dillman, & Smyth, 2008) in an attempt at contributing additional knowledge about factors that may help deepening our understanding of possible response effects.

2.3 RESPONSE FORMATS

Response effects may be due to response formats for closed-ended survey questions. First of all, one has to determine the number of scale points: 4pt, 5pt, 7pt, and 11pt scales are common formats. Second, scale points have to be labeled. Here one can distinguish between two basic variants: all categories of a scale receive labels vs. only the endpoints of a scale receive labels. If in addition to the endpoints the middle category of a scale is also labeled, a third variant results. Third, the categories of a scale can be presented to respondents in one step or two steps. The latter variant applies if a scale is unfolded: for instance, first one asks if a respondent agrees or disagrees with something. Depending on this choice, one continues to the second step by asking the respondent about the extent of this agreement (if applicable) or the extent of disagreement (if applicable). In this context, middle categories of scales become the center of interest. The same is true for categories that might have equivalent functions as a neutral middle category, namely an explicit "don't know" category. In addition to the two-mode experiments described above, Chapter 4 reports the outcomes of a further experiment on four different response formats. This experiment compares the responses to a 7pt scale (only endpoints labeled), a 5pt scale (only endpoints labeled), a 5pt scale (all categories labeled), and a 4pt scale (unfolded) for the survey modes "online" and "telephone". Table A4.6 in the online appendix to Chapter 4 reports this analysis and shows how the degree of satisficing modifies the response scale formats effects involved.

2.4 QUESTION WORDINGS

Response effects may be due to the wording of survey questions. Chapter 4 presents corresponding experimental results. A first experiment reported therein compares a set of seven statements about distributive justice with respect to the opposite poles "just" vs. "unjust". In a split-ballot experiment, one random half of the sample was asked if an image of distributive justice is "just", while the other half was asked if it is "unjust". The researchers used 7pt scales. Table A4.4 in the online appendix to Chapter 4 presents the results and shows how the degree of satisficing behavior affects the strengths of the mean differences involved. Then, a similar experiment referred to a dichotomous scale. Table A4.5 in the online appendix to Chapter 4 shows whether it makes a difference to label the disagreement pole of a scale "not agree" or "refuse".

2.5 RESPONSE ORDER

The sequence in which response categories are presented to the respondent represents a further source of response effects. We can distinguish between sets of unordered or ordered categories. Regarding the former, prominent effects are the so-called "primacy" and "recency" effects. A primacy effect arises out of the tendency to prefer options at the beginning of a list of items over those at the end. Recency effects mean just the opposite. These effects are due to the tendency to choose options at the end of a list of items (Tourangeau, Rips, & Rasinski, 2000, pp. 250–251). Following Krosnick and Alwin, Tourangeau et al. (2000, p. 251) present the hypothesis that primacy effects are more likely than recency effects to arise in cases where the categories are presented visually, while the opposite is expected when the list is presented only in aural communication. Chapter 4 discusses this hypothesis with respect to experimental findings for one such mode, namely the "telephone" mode and a set of ordered categories. It explores in greater detail the modifying effects of satisficing behavior and perceived sensitivity of survey items on the strength of the response effects involved.

2.6 RESPONSE STYLES

Following Schouten and Calinescu (2013, p. 233), satisficing can be viewed as a response style, with acquiescence, primacy, and recency as special forms of satisficing. Based on interviewer ratings, Chapter 4 explores the modifying effect of satisficing response behavior on different types of response effects (as already indicated above). We also carried out a longitudinal stability analysis that casts doubt on the assumption that satisficing behavior is to be regarded as a response "style". Rather, the degree of satisficing behavior appeared to be primarily associated with the effort needed to convince reluctant persons to take part in an interview. This supports the view that satisficing depends more on situational factors than on personal factors that are more stable over time. This analysis is presented in Table A4.2 in the online appendix to Chapter 4.

Another analysis presented in Chapter 4 deals with the identification of cognitive response styles by latent class analysis. The researchers explored which scale points were used to anchor an answer and how strong cognitive anchoring is coupled with an affinity to grade an opinion. Three such styles were identified. The latent class analysis is carried out separately using 5pt and 7pt answering scales.

2.7 SPECIAL PROBES

Special probes may be placed immediately after a survey question has been asked. Both Chapters 3 and 4 take advantage of this option. As outlined above, amongst others Chapter 3 analyzes the effect of placing a gentle probe after each "don't know" response. In Chapter 4, a sequence of a meaning probe followed by a think-aloud probe is employed to investigate the practicability of respondent debriefing during an otherwise standardized telephone interview. Furthermore, Chapter 16 deals with probing questions in web surveys.

2.8 SOURCES OF SURVEY ERROR CONSIDERED SIMULTANEOUSLY

Mode effects and mode-specific response effects represent just two sources of survey error. Interviewer effects represent a further source. Nonresponse effects matter too. All of these sources contribute to the "total survey error" (Weisberg, 2005) and should thus be considered simultaneously if possible. Chapter 4 reports on such an analysis. It is a covariance analysis that compares the two different response formats "midpoint of an 11pt scale named vs. not named", namely nested within the three different survey modes "landline", "cell phone", and "web". The model also comprises response propensity scores computed beforehand (see, e.g. Tourangeau, 2004, p. 215 for the need for controlling this source of variation). The findings are related to 11pt scales on happiness and satisfaction with life. As reported in Table A4.9 in the online appendix to Chapter 4, the mean values were significantly lower in the online mode than in the two telephone modes. We observed this pattern in other mode experiments as well and interpret it as expressions of a social-desirability effect in interviewer-assisted survey modes (see Engel, 2013, for these other mode experiments). While the survey mode effects prove statistically significant with regard to both scales, the nested response scale effects do not. At the same time, two statistically significant effects indicate that the stronger the response propensity the more happiness and satisfaction with current life is reported. It is this type of finding which indicates by example the biasing effect of differential response propensities on the frequency distributions of survey variables. Finally, the degree of satisficing proves influential. As described in detail in Engel (2013), different measurement error/nonresponse error patterns emerged across the various mode/response experiments which were carried out on different types of scales and different subject matters.

REFERENCES

Biemer, P. P. (2011). *Latent class analysis of survey error*. Hoboken: Wiley.

Byrne, B. M. (2012). *Structural equation modeling with Mplus*. New York, London: Routledge.

Christian, L. M., Dillman, D. A., & Smyth, J. D. (2008). The effects of mode and format on answers to scalar questions in telephone and web surveys. In J. M. Lepkowski, C. Tucker, J. M. Brick, E. D. De Leeuw, L. Japec, P. J. Lavrakas, M. W. Link, & R. L. Sangster (Eds.), *Advances in telephone survey methodology* (pp. 250–275). Hoboken: Wiley.

De Leeuw, E. D., Hox, J. J., & Dillman, D. A. (2008). The cornerstones of survey research. In E. D. De Leeuw, J. J. Hox, & D. A. Dillman (Eds.), *International handbook of survey methodology* (pp. 1–17). New York: Erlbaum.

Engel, U. (2013): *Access Panel and Mixed-Mode Internet Survey. PPSM Panel Report* (2nd ed.). Retrieved from www.sozialforschung.uni-bremen.de/html/downloads.html

Galtung, J. (1969). *Theory and methods of social research* (Revised Ed.). Oslo: Universitetsforlaget.

Saris, W. E., van der Veld, W., & Gallhofer, I. (2004). Development and improvement of questionnaires using predictions of reliability and validity. In S. Presser, J. Rothgeb, M. P. Couper, J. T. Lessler, E. Martin, J. Martin, & E. Singer (Eds.), *Methods for testing and evaluating survey questionnaires* (pp. 275–297). Hoboken: Wiley.

Schouten, B., & Calinescu, M. (2013). Paradata as input to monitoring representativeness and measurement profiles: A case study of the Dutch Labour Force Survey. In F. Kreuter (Ed.), *Improving surveys with paradata* (pp. 231–258). Hoboken: Wiley.

Tourangeau, R. (2004). Experimental design considerations for testing and evaluating questionnaires. In S. Presser, J. Rothgeb, M. P. Couper, J. T. Lessler, E. Martin, J. Martin, & E. Singer (Eds.), *Methods for testing and evaluating survey questionnaires* (pp. 209–224). Hoboken: Wiley.

Tourangeau, R., Rips, L. J., & Rasinski, K. (2000). *The psychology of survey response*. Cambridge: Cambridge University Press.

Weisberg, H. F. (2005). *The total survey error approach*. Chicago: University of Chicago Press.

3

Survey Mode and Mode Effects

Edith D. De Leeuw and Joop J. Hox

3.1 INTRODUCTION

From the early 1930s to the 1970s, face-to-face interviews and paper mail surveys were the main modes used for survey data collection (De Heer, De Leeuw, & Van der Zouwen, 1999; De Leeuw & Collins, 1997). Face-to-face interviews were, and still are, seen as the gold standard by which other modes are compared; mail surveys were considered a low-cost, fallback method, until the work of Dillman (1978) made it respectable. By the late 1960s, telephone interviews started in the US, and they grew in popularity in the 1980s. Telephone surveys reached their zenith in the 1990s in the US, Canada, Australia, and large parts of Northern and Western Europe (Tucker & Lepkowski, 2008), and were seen as the heir apparent to the more expensive face-to-face interview; however the onset of mobile telephones posed new challenges to telephone surveys.

Technological changes in the 1980s made computer-assisted forms of data collection possible. In the US, CATI (Computer-Assisted Telephone Interviewing) was developed, while in Sweden and Holland the first forms of CAPI (Computer-Assisted Personal (face-to-face) Interviewing) were pioneered, which were soon accepted both by respondents and interviewers and supplied high-quality data (De Leeuw & Nicholls, 1996). In the Netherlands, an innovative new form of computer-assisted data collection was initiated by Saris (1991): a computer-at-home-panel, or telepanel, where respondents received a weekly questionnaire through a (at that time technologically advanced) telephone modem. This telepanel was the prototype for modern online panels, such as the LISS-panel in Holland or Knowledge Networks in the US. The 1990s also saw the emergence of a new survey mode for both panel and cross-sectional designs: web surveys (Couper, 2000, 2011; Smyth & Pearson, 2011).

Finally, a combination or mix of data collection methods grabbed increasing attention. Mixed-modes were used as early as the late 1960s (Dillman & Tarnai, 1988); at that time they included mixes of paper mail, telephone, and face-to-face surveys. But, with the onset of web surveys, mixed-mode really became a 'trending topic'. By combining several survey data collection methods into one design, these methods complement each other and the weaknesses of each individual method are compensated for (Biemer & Lyberg, 2003, Chapter 6). Mixed-mode designs have been used to reduce nonresponse and under-coverage problems, to reduce social desirability bias and interviewer effects, and to collect follow-up panel data at reasonable costs (De Leeuw, 2005). For instance, sequential mixed-mode studies, where face-to-face interviews are alternated with telephone or self-administered forms, have been used in panel studies to reduce the overall costs. Sequential mixed-mode designs are also used for nonresponse follow-up studies, where nonrespondents are approached with a different method (e.g., telephone follow-up of a mail survey). In a concurrent mixed-mode design, two or more data collection methods are implemented at the same time; for example, online surveys in combination with telephone or mail surveys for those without internet. Concurrent mixed-mode studies are standard best practice for collecting sensitive data during interviews, when a self-administered mode is embedded in interview surveys for a subset of questions to enhance privacy and reduce social desirability bias. For a detailed overview of mixed-mode designs see De Leeuw, Hox, & Dillman (2008).

3.2 SURVEY MODES: SIMILARITIES AND DISSIMILARITIES

Cornerstones of Data Collection: Survey Error and Survey Mode

In his classic handbook, Groves (1989) presents an analysis and synthesis of survey errors and differentiates between coverage error, sampling error, nonresponse error, and measurement error. For an in-depth discussion of survey errors, see Biemer (2010) and Groves and Lyberg (2010). Survey modes differ in their abilities to reduce these errors. A concise description is given below; for a detailed overview, see De Leeuw (2008).

Coverage error arises from the failure to give any chance of sample selection to some persons in the population, because they are not part of the sampling frame or sampling list used to identify members of the population.

Face-to-face interviews are the most flexible and complete method with respect to coverage, but may be difficult or costly to apply (e.g., employing enumerators and using random walk methods to select addresses). Telephone surveys may suffer from coverage error, due to unlisted numbers when telephone directories are used or by omitting mobile phones and sampling and surveying landline phones only (e.g., Mohorko, De Leeuw, & Hox, 2013; Busse & Fuchs, Chapter 5). For mail surveys, lists of potential postal addresses are needed, such as postal delivery sequence files. From the onset of internet surveys, coverage error has been a source of major concern (Couper, 2000). A main problem with internet surveys is under-coverage resulting from the 'digital divide', that is, a difference in rates of internet access among different demographic groups (such as an unequal distribution regarding age and education for those with and without internet access; for an overview, see Mohorko, De Leeuw, & Hox, 2011). A potential solution for coverage problems is a concurrent mixed-mode strategy, for instance by using a dual-frame design.

Sampling error is an error in estimation due to taking a sample instead of measuring every unit in the sampling frame. Sampling error may result in two types of errors: sampling bias and sampling variance (for an overview see Groves et al., 2000). Data collection methods differ in available sampling procedures (e.g., De Leeuw, 2008) with face-to-face surveys being most flexible. Modern telephone surveys that include mobile phones face challenges and have adopted new sampling strategies (cf. Busse & Fuchs, Chapter 5). Sampling procedures pose extra problems for internet surveys of the general population, because no general sampling frame is available. A potential solution is the formation of an internet panel, where members are sampled and recruited through a different mode for which a good sampling procedure is available (e.g., face-to-face or telephone, see Engel, Chapter 18; Scherpenzeel, Chapter 19).

Nonresponse error arises from the failure to collect data on all persons selected in the sample (e.g., because of noncontacts or refusals). If nonresponse is completely at random, this will result in increased sampling variance. Nonresponse bias will occur if the persons who respond differ on the variable of interest from those who do not respond (Couper & De Leeuw, 2003). Nonresponse has been growing in the western world (De Leeuw & De Heer, 2002), although the decline in response is more pronounced for interviews than for paper mail surveys (Hox & De Leeuw, 2002). Furthermore, web surveys yield on average a 10–11% lower response rate than comparable mail and interview surveys (Lozar Manfreda, Bosjnak, Berzelak, Haas, & Vehovar, 2008). Nonresponse rate and nonresponse bias are weakly related (Groves & Peytcheva, 2008), and researchers have put much effort into coping with nonresponse. Both general response inducement methods, such as incentives (Singer, 2002; Göritz, Chapter 28), and more mode-specific measures, such as interviewer training (e.g., Groves & Couper, 1998), targeting (Lynn, Chapter 27), and personalizations and reminder strategies (Dillman, Smyth, & Christian, 2009) have proven their effectiveness in raising response rates. Also, sequential mixed-mode surveys which use extensive follow-ups in a different mode (e.g., mail survey, followed by interview surveys) have been successful in reducing nonresponse (De Leeuw, 2005).

Measurement error, or inaccuracies in the responses, arises from (a) effects of the interviewer, (b) error due to the respondents themselves, (c) error due to wording of the questionnaire, (d) errors due to mode of data collection, and (e) interactions between error sources, such as mode and questionnaire (Groves, 1989). In the next section we discuss how survey mode influences measurement error.

Mode Effects: Measurement Error and Survey Mode

Survey modes vary along several related dimensions in how they influence measurement error (Couper, 2011). Key elements (De Leeuw, 1992, 2008) are information transmission (aurally, visually, or both), available communication channels (verbal, nonverbal, paralinguistic, and graphical), degree of interviewer impact and privacy, interactivity (help, feedback), and locus of control and pacing (respondent, interviewer, or shared). These key elements influence both the way questions can be presented (e.g., number of response options, use of showcards) and the psychological question-answer process (see Jäckle, Roberts, & Lynn, 2010; Tourangeau, Rips, & Rasinski, 2000). In addition, within each mode the introduction of technology is a potential source of differences (Fuchs, 2002). A strong feature of computer-assisted data collection is the potential to prevent errors and the ability to ask more complex questions (De Leeuw & Nicholls, 1996).

Studies into mode effects have been stimulated by major changes in data collection methods. The older studies were prompted by the onset of telephone surveys and compared face-to-face, telephone, and paper mail surveys. De Leeuw (1992) performed a meta-analysis of 67 publications reporting experimental mode comparisons and found small but consistent differences between these methods. The results suggest a dichotomy in modes with and without an interviewer: especially with sensitive questions self-administered surveys performed better, producing less social desirability in feelings and attitudes and more openness in reporting sensitive or unwanted behavior. Similar results were found in recent studies comparing interviews and web surveys: internet surveys give rise to less social desirability bias (for a detailed review, see De Leeuw & Hox, 2011; Tourangeau, Conrad, & Couper, 2013, Chapter 7). These results clearly point to the beneficial influence of reduced interviewer impact and more privacy for the respondent when asking sensitive questions (see also Jann, Chapter 9). Note that the meta-analysis by De Leeuw (1992) also finds heterogeneity of mode effects, indicating that mode effects differ across studies. Mode differences may result from multiple sources of error, such as the mode in question, the implementation, and the question wording (Couper, 2011).

In general, it is somewhat harder to get people to answer questions in mail surveys than in interview surveys, resulting in a higher amount of item missing data for self-administered mail forms (for meta-analysis, see De Leeuw, 1992). This supports the idea that interviewer probing and the interaction between respondent and interviewer is important in reducing missing data. For comparisons with web surveys, the results are less clear-cut, depending on the design of the web survey. In those cases where skipping a question or answering 'don't know' is allowed in a web survey, web surveys, like mail surveys, do result in more item missing data than comparable interviews (for a summary, see De Leeuw & Hox, 2011).

When long lists of response options are offered visually, either in self-administered modes or in face-to-face interviews using showcards, those response options presented early receive more attention, giving rise to a primacy effect. When long lists are presented only aurally, limited memory capacity makes it hard to remember all alternatives and the last heard are more often endorsed: a recency effect (Krosnick & Alwin, 1987). There is some evidence of recency effects in telephone surveys, but the results have not always been consistent (Dillman & Christian, 2005).

Social custom requires that the initiator of a conversation also is the locus of control and takes the lead, especially in telephone interviews. In face-to-face interviews, due to the mitigating effects of nonverbal communication, channel control is more evenly divided between respondent and interviewer, while in self-administered mail and web questionnaires, the respondent is in total control of the pace and time (De Leeuw, 2008). Empirical mode comparisons on this topic are rare. De Leeuw (1992) investigated reliability and consistency of answers and found more consistent answers and less random error in the mail condition where the respondent is the locus of control, and more in telephone surveys with the face-to-face survey in between. A similar result was found in an experiment by Chang and Krosnick (2009); they detected more random measurement error in telephone data then in web survey data.

Mode Effect or Question Format Effect?

The empirical mode comparisons reviewed show relatively small mode effects, with an exception for sensitive topics where self-administered mail and internet surveys produce better results. However, in experimental comparisons usually extreme care is taken to use equivalent questionnaires, while in daily practice each survey mode has different conventions and designers try to optimize questionnaires for each data collection mode (Dillman & Christian, 2005). Two prime examples of different optimizing strategies for a particular mode are a different labeling of scale points in telephone surveys and the explicit offering of a 'don't know' option in self-administered surveys.

Labeling of Scale Points

Data collection modes differ in channel capacity for communication (auditory vs. visual). Visual transmission of information through the web or on paper does not place great demands on respondents' memory capacities, since they can refer back to the text in the questionnaire, but aural transmission of information makes higher demands on memory capacity because respondents must remember all options (Christian, Dillman, & Smyth, 2008). To accommodate the limitations of auditory-channel-only modes, researchers have designed special formats for telephone interviews. To ease the cognitive burden placed on the respondent, response scales are often simplified by providing only the polar endpoint labels in telephone surveys, while in other modes advantage is taken of the visual channel and fully labeled response scales are used. Christian et al. (2008) report numerous experiments with the US student population and report that independent of scale format, respondents more often chose extreme response categories in the telephone than in the web mode, but also point out that within a single mode (be it web or interview) full vs. partial labeling influences the response distribution.

'Don't Know' Option

The presence of well-trained interviewers and the potential for optimal interviewer-respondent interaction makes it possible to probe respondents during interviews in those cases when a non-informative answer is given. In interviews it is standard good practice *not* to offer an explicit 'don't know' option and only accept a non-substantive answer after a gentle interviewer probe, to avoid that respondents satisfice or flee in a 'don't know' answer. In paper mail questionnaires respondents are always free to skip a question, which is one of the main reasons why mail surveys produce more item missing data. Regarding missing data in web surveys, much depends on the technical design. Although modern web programs now allow formats that make it possible for the respondent to skip a question, most programs still have 'mandatory response' as the default option, where respondents are required to provide a substantive answer. This may have drawbacks such as increased break-offs or satisficing (Tourangeau et al., 2013, Chapter 3). Moreover, crude measures like forcing a response are not necessary, as the advantage of web surveys is that they can be far more interactive than paper mail surveys, and more sophisticated prompts may be used for probing respondents; thereby combining the advantages of web and interview surveys (see Wine, Cominole, Heuer, & Riccobono, 2006).

To assess the relative effects of survey mode and question format we conducted two experiments in the German Priority Programme on Survey Methodology (PPSM) panel, which is a probability based mixed-mode (web and telephone) panel; for details on how this panel was established see Engel (Chapter 18).

3.3 TWO MODE EXPERIMENTS IN THE PPSM PANEL: WEB VS. TELEPHONE

Fully Labeled vs. Endpoints Only Labeled Response Options

A split ballot experiment was implemented in the PPSM panel to investigate the effect of labeling response options on the responses given. The same split ballot was conducted in the telephone and the web part of the panel, making it possible to investigate the effects of labeling within and between the two modes. Eight questions on the acceptability of advanced medical technology were used, based on earlier work on technology assessment (Steegers, Dijstelbloem, & Brom, 2008); a five-point response scale was used, ranging from 'totally agree' to 'totally disagree'; 'don't know' was not explicitly offered, but was accepted when given. Respondents were randomly assigned to a condition where response categories were either fully labeled or only endpoint labeled. Dependent variables were mean scale score (the average on the eight items in the scale), which indicates acceptability of modern technology, and extremeness which was operationalized as choosing either 1 or 5 as opposed to the middle categories.

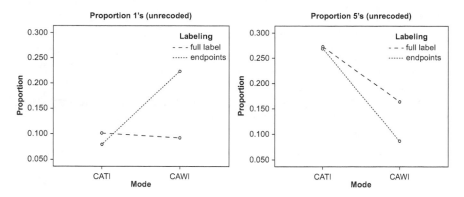

FIGURE 3.1
Proportion extreme scores (1 or 5): Primacy effect left; recency effect right

Differences in mean score of the scale are conceptually of interest: will there be a difference in the outcome on the main variable of interest in a study depending on mode and question format used? The answer is yes. More acceptance of technology was found in the web and in the endpoint only labeling condition ($p < .05$). The overall average score in the web survey was 3.17 and in the CATI survey was 2.89 (on a five-point range); in the fully labeled condition the overall average was 2.97 and in the endpoint labeling condition this was 3.08. There was a significant interaction, meaning that the effect of labeling is different in web and telephone ($p < .05$). The smallest difference was in the fully labeled condition (average web 3.01, CATI 2.94). From a robustness standpoint, fully labeling response categories is advisable.

We investigated two different forms of extreme responding: primacy and recency. Both the effects of mode and labeling and their interaction were significant ($p < .05$). As Figure 3.1 shows, there was a clear primacy effect in CAWI for endpoint labeling only, and a recency effect in CATI for both full and endpoint labeling.

Offering a 'Don't Know' Option with and without Probes

A split ballot experiment was implemented in the PPSM panel to investigate the effect of offering an explicit 'don't know' (DK) and following up DK responses with a gentle probe in both web and telephone. The same probe that was scripted for the interviewers was also programmed into the web questionnaire. Since the same split ballot was conducted in the telephone and the web part of the panel, we can compare the effects between the two modes. Six knowledge questions on the use of embryos in biomedical research were used, based on earlier work on technology assessment (Steegers et al., 2008). Response categories were Yes/No, and depending on the experimental condition 'don't know' was either explicitly offered or not. Skipping a question on the web or responding spontaneously with 'don't know' over the telephone was accepted, but all non-substantive (skip or DK) responses were followed by a gentle probe. Dependent variables were the proportion of DK responses before and after probing.

There was a significant effect ($p < .05$) of offering DK: the proportion of DK responses before probing increases dramatically in both modes. Offering DK increased the proportion of DK responses from 0.02 to 0.21 in the web survey, and from 0.05 to 0.17 in the telephone survey (interaction $p < .05$).

As Figure 3.2 shows, the proportion of DK responses drops dramatically after probing. In total, 481 probes were issued. Of these, 304 produced an informative response after the probe (63.1%). When DK was explicitly offered, 71.1% of the probes resulted in a substantive answer. When DK is not offered 47.7% of the probes resulted in a substantive answer; this difference is significant. All other effects were not significant; there is no interaction with mode, which means that probing is equally effective in both telephone and web mode. Therefore we recommend that, if for substantive reasons it is necessary to use an explicit DK option, to always follow-up with a friendly probe, not only in interviews but also in web surveys.

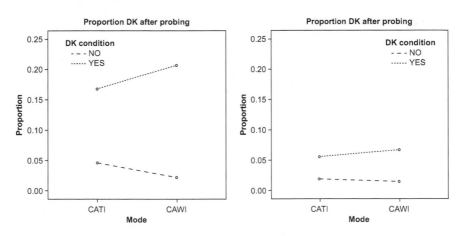

FIGURE 3.2
Proportion DK before (left) and after probing (right)

3.4 CONCLUDING REMARKS

At present, there is no dominating data collection method and all main survey modes (e.g., face-to-face interviews, telephone interviews, paper mail surveys, and web surveys) are still being used as a stand-alone method or as part of a mixed-mode design. Mixing survey modes is an increasingly used data collection approach in both cross-sectional and longitudinal surveys. Two main reasons for the increased use of mixed-mode designs are the opportunity to address coverage and nonresponse problems associated with one mode by adding a different mode to the mix, while saving costs by using less expensive modes where possible. Furthermore, international and cross-cultural surveys are becoming increasingly necessary for our global world. Still, countries greatly differ in economic and technological resources and infrastructure, which makes a mixed-mode strategy almost unavoidable. To quote Bill Blyth (2008), mixed-mode is the only fitness regime in the near future.

As mixed-mode designs become more popular in surveys, the risk that mode effects may bias the measurements is becoming an important issue. Sources of mode effects are (a) inherent characteristics associated with the mode itself (e.g., presence or absence of an interviewer), the pure mode effects, (b) the way the mode is implemented, and (c) the way the questions are formulated in each specific mode. In other words, mode effects on survey measurements in a mixed-mode design may be the result of differences in inherent characteristics of the modes used, but they can also be the result of *avoidable* differences in the wording of the questions used, or in other implementation choices.

The distinction between inherent mode effects and mode effects due to differences in question wording and implementation is illustrated by the two experiments carried out in the PPSM panel. These experiments are related to two frequently encountered differences in question wording and implementation between telephone and web surveys. The first experiment is linked to the custom of fully labeling Likert-type response scales in the visual presentation mode (web), while using endpoint labeling in the aural presentation mode (telephone). The results clearly show that there is a strong effect of different labeling options, to the extent that substantive answers (as indicated by average scores on a scale) can be affected by such decisions.

The second experiment is linked to differential implementations of 'don't know' options. First, in a telephone interview, it is tacitly assumed that a respondent may reply with 'don't know', even if the interviewer does not explicitly offer this option. In a web survey, the 'don't know' option may or may not be explicitly offered. As the results of the second experiment show, explicitly offering a 'don't know' option dramatically increases the proportion of 'don't know' answers, especially in the web mode. Second, interviewers are usually instructed to probe after a 'don't know' answer. In the second experiment, each 'don't know' answer was followed up by a friendly probe in both the telephone and the web survey. The probe in the web survey emulated the telephone interviewer and used the same script. Using a gentle probe after each 'don't know' response reduced the final number of non-substantive answers in both the web and the telephone interviews and repaired much of the damage done by including an explicit 'don't know' option.

The results of the experiments clearly demonstrate that if multiple modes are employed in a survey, it is important to pay careful attention to question wording and implementation details. Optimizing a survey towards a specific mode is generally beneficial for the quality of the data in a single mode survey. However, in a mixed-mode design, one should optimize towards the mix, by using equivalent questionnaires and implementation procedures, in order to prevent avoidable mode effects.

REFERENCES

Biemer, P. P. (2010). Total survey error: Design, implementation, and evaluation. *Public Opinion Quarterly, 74*(5), 817–848. doi:10.1093/poq/nfq058

Biemer, P. P., & Lyberg, L. E. (2003). *Introduction to survey quality.* New York: Wiley.

Blyth, B. (2008). Mixed-mode: The only 'Fitness' Regime? *International Journal of Market Research, 50*(2), 241–266.

Chang L., & Krosnick, J. A. (2009). National surveys via RDD telephone interviewing versus the internet: Comparing sample representativeness and response quality. *Public Opinion Quarterly, 73*(4), 641–678. doi:10.1093/poq/nfp075

Christian, L. M., Dillman, D. A., & Smyth, J. D. (2008). The effect of mode and format on answers to scalar questions in telephone and web surveys. In J. M. Lepkowski, C. Tucker, J. M. Brick, E. D. De Leeuw, L. Japec, P. J. Lavrakas, M. W. Link, R. L. Sangster (Eds.), *Advances in telephone survey methodology* (pp. 250–275). New York: Wiley.

Couper, M. P. (2000). Web surveys: A review of issues and approaches. *Public Opinion Quarterly, 64*(4), 464–494. doi:10.1086/318641

Couper, M. P. (2011). The future of modes of data collection. *Public Opinion Quarterly, 75*(5), 889–908. doi:10.1093/poq/nfr046

Couper, M. P., & De Leeuw, E. D. (2003) Nonresponse in cross-cultural and cross-national surveys. In J. A. Harkness, F.J.R. van de Vijver, & P. P. Mohler (Eds.), *Cross-cultural survey methods* (pp. 157–177). New York: Wiley.

De Heer, W., De Leeuw, E. D., & Van der Zouwen, J. (1999). Methodological issues in survey research: A historical review. *Bulletin de Methodologie Sociologique, 64*, 25–48.

De Leeuw, E. D. (1992). *Data quality in mail, telephone, and face-to-face surveys.* Amsterdam: TT-publikaties, Retrieved from http://edithl.home.xs4all.nl/pubs/disseddl.pdf

De Leeuw, E. D. (2005). To mix or not to mix. *Journal of Official Statistics, 21*(2), 233–255. Retrieved from www.jos.nu/Articles/article.asp

De Leeuw, E. D. (2008). Choosing the method of data collection. In E. D. De Leeuw, J. J. Hox, & D. A. Dillman (Eds.), *International handbook of survey methodology* (pp. 113–135). New York: Taylor & Francis Group, European Association of Methodology (EAM) book series.

De Leeuw, E. D., & Collins, M. (1997). Data collection methods and survey quality: An overview. In L. Lyberg, P. Biemer, M. Collins, E. De Leeuw, D. Trewin, C. Dippo, & N. Schwarz (Eds.), *Survey measurement and process quality* (pp. 199–220). New York: Wiley.

De Leeuw, E., & De Heer, W. (2002). Trends in household survey nonresponse: A longitudinal and international comparison. In R. M. Groves, D. A. Dillman, J. L. Eltinge, & R.J.A. Little (Eds.), *Survey nonresponse* (pp. 41–54). New York: Wiley.

De Leeuw, E. D., & Hox, J. J. (2011). Internet surveys as part of a mixed-mode design. In M. Das, P. Ester, & L. Kaczmirek (Eds.), *Social and behavioral research and the internet* (pp. 45–76.) New York: Taylor & Francis Group, European Association of Methodology (EAM) book series.

De Leeuw, E. D., Hox, J. J., & Dilman, D. A. (2008). Mixed-mode surveys. In E. D. De Leeuw, J. J. Hox, & D. A. Dillman (Eds.), *International handbook of survey methodology* (pp. 299–31). New York: Taylor & Francis Group, European Association of Methodology (EAM) book series.

De Leeuw, E. D., & Nicholls, W. L. II (1996). Technological innovations in data collection: Acceptance, data quality and costs. *Sociological Research Online*. Retrieved from www.socresonline.org.uk/1/4/leeuw.html

Dillman, D. A. (1978). *Mail and telephone surveys: The total design method*. New York: Wiley.

Dillman, D. A., & Christian, L. M. (2005). Survey mode as a source of instability in responses across surveys. *Field Methods, 17*, 30–52.

Dillman, D. A., Smyth, J. D., & Christian, L. M. (2009). *Internet, mail, and mixed-mode surveys, the Tailored Design Method*. New York: Wiley.

Dillman, D. A., & Tarnai, J. (1988). Administrative issues in mixed mode surveys. In R. M. Groves, P. P. Biemer, L. E. Lyberg, J. T. Massey, W. L. Nicholls II, & J. Waksberg (Eds.), *Telephone survey methodology* (pp. 509–528). New York: Wiley.

Fuchs, M. (2002). The impact of technology on interaction in computer-assisted interviews. In D. W. Maynard, H. Houtkoop-Steenstra, N. C. Schaeffer, & J.V.D. Zouwen (Eds.), *Standardization and tacit knowledge. Interaction and practice in the survey interview* (pp. 471–491). New York: Wiley.

Groves, R. M. (1989). *Survey error and survey costs*. New York: Wiley.

Groves, R. M., & Couper, M. P. (1998). *Nonresponse in household interview surveys*. New York: Wiley.

Groves, R. M., Fowler, F. J., Couper, M. P., Lepkowski, J. M., Singer, E., & Tourangeau, R. (2000). *Survey methodology* (2nd ed.). New York: Wiley.

Groves, R. M. & Lyberg, L. E. (2010). Total survey error: Past, present, and future. *Public Opinion Quarterly, 74*(5), 849–879. doi:10.1093/poq/nfq065

Groves, R. M., & Peytcheva, E. (2008). The impact of nonresponse rates on nonresponse bias. *Public Opinion Quarterly, 72*(2), 167–189. doi:10.1093/poq/nfn011

Hox, J. J., & De Leeuw, E. D. (2002). A comparison of nonresponse in mail, telephone, & face to face surveys: Applying multilevel modeling to meta-analysis. *Quality & Quantity, 28*, 329–344. (Reprinted in: David de Vaus (2002), *Social Surveys, part eleven, nonresponse error*. London: Sage, Benchmarks in Social Research Methods Series.)

Jäckle, A., Roberts, C., & Lynn, P. (2010). Assessing the effect of data collection mode on measurement. *International Statistical Review, 78*, 3–20.

Krosnick, J., & Alwin, D. A. (1987). An evaluation of a cognitive theory of response-order effects is survey measurement. *Public Opinion Quarterly, 51*(2), 201–219.

Lozar Manfreda, K., Bosjnak, M., Berzelak, J., Haas, I., Vehovar, V. (2008). Web surveys versus other survey modes: A meta-analysis comparing response rates. *International Journal of Market Research, 50*, 79–104.

Mohorko, A., De Leeuw, E., & Hox, J. (2011). Internet coverage and coverage bias in countries across Europe and over time: Background, methods, question wording and bias tables. Retrieved from www.joophox.net

Mohorko, A., De Leeuw, E., & Hox, J. (2013). Coverage bias in European telephone surveys: Developments of landline and mobile phone coverage across countries and over time. *Survey Methods: Insights from the field.* Retrieved from http://surveyinsights.org/?p=828

Saris, W. E. (1991). *Computer-assisted interviewing.* Newbury Park: Sage.

Singer, E. (2002). The use of incentives to reduce nonresponse in household surveys. In R. M. Groves, D. A. Dillman, J. L. Eltinge, & R.J.A. Little (Eds.), *Survey nonresponse* (pp. 163–177). New York: Wiley.

Smyth, J. D., & Pearson, J. E. (2011). Internet survey methods: A review of strengths, weaknesses, and innovations. In M. Das, P. Ester, & L. Kaczmirek (Eds.), *Social and behavioral research and the internet* (pp. 11–44). New York: Taylor & Francis, European Association of Methodology (EAM) book series.

Steegers, C., Dijstelbloem, H., & Brom, F.W.A. (2008). *Meer dan status alleen. Burgerperspectieven op embryo-onderzoek.* [In Dutch: Assessment and points of view of citizens on technology and embryo research]. The Hague: Rathenau-Instituut, TA rapport 0801.

Tourangeau, R., Conrad, F. G., & Couper, M. P. (2013). *The science of web surveys* (pp. 129–150). New York: Oxford University Press.

Tourangeau, R., Rips, L. J., & Rasinski, K. (2000). *The psychology of survey response.* Cambridge: Cambridge University Press.

Tucker, C. & Lepkowski, J. M. (2008). Telephone survey methods: Adapting to change. In J. M. Lepkowski, C. Tucker, J. M. Brick, E. D. De Leeuw, L. Japec, P. J. Lavrakas, M. W. Link, & R. L. Sangster (Eds.), *Advances in telephone survey methodology* (pp. 3–26). New York: Wiley.

Wine, J. S., Cominole, M. B., Heuer, R. E., & Riccobono, J. A. (2006). Challenges of designing and implementing multimode instruments. Presented at the Second International Conference on Telephone Survey Methodology, Miami, FL, January 2006. Paper available at www.rti.org/pubs/TSM2006_Wine_paper.pdf

4

Response Effects and Cognitive Involvement in Answering Survey Questions

Uwe Engel and Britta Köster

4.1 THEORY AND RESEARCH ON RESPONSE EFFECTS

Sudman, Bradburn, and Schwarz (1996) identify three different sources of response effects: effects coming from interviewers, effects produced by respondents, and effects arising from the tasks themselves. Meanwhile, though many studies on different aspects of mode and response effects have been published, there is still a need for more research (cf. Schwarz, Knäuper, Oyserman, & Stich, 2008 and De Leeuw, 2008 for recent reviews). In the following, examples of literature are listed for analyzing different aspects such as the role of interviewers (Groves & Couper, 1998; Groves & Fultz, 1985; Couper & Groves, 1992; Lyberg & Dean, 1992; De Leeuw & Hox, 1996; De Leeuw, Hox, Snijkers, & de Heer, 1997), visual aspects (Couper, Tourangeau, Conrad, & Crawford, 2004; Tourangeau, Couper, & Conrad, 2004, 2007), including optical aspects such as visual analogue scales (Couper, Tourangeau, Conrad, & Singer, 2006), response-order effects (Krosnick & Alwin, 1987; Engel, Bartsch, Schnabel, & Vehre, 2012), rating scales (Engel et al., 2012), asking sensitive questions (Jann, Jerke, & Krumpal, 2012; Krumpal, 2011; Engel et al., 2012) and mode effects (Christian, Dillman, & Smyth, 2008; Engel et al., 2012; Ye, Fulton, & Tourangeau, 2011).

Another aspect of survey questions are open-ended questions. On the one hand, these are used to receive a non-supported or less influenced picture of possible answers, without given answering options (Foddy, 1996; Willis, 2004; Christodoulou, Junghaenel, DeWalt, Rothrock, & Stone, 2008). On the other hand, open-ended questions can be used as meta-questions to receive more information on the process of gaining answers.

Two theoretical models for the cognitive process of answering rating scales and open-ended questions are offered by Sudman et al. (1996) and by Tourangeau, Rips, and Rasinski (2000). The transfer of these models into surveys and therefore their evaluation is not yet sufficiently complete. Also, the idea of using open-ended questions in terms of meta-questions is not a new one. Researchers described the usage of these questions for gaining an introspective insight into cognitive workings in the late 1970s (Nisbett & Wilson, 1977; Nisbett & Ross, 1980). Sudman et al. (1996) did not deny that the usage of meta-questions has its challenges, but in their opinion it still provides useful information about the cognitive work of respondents' memories.

As basic explanations of response effects Sudman et al. (1996) as well as Tourangeau et al. (2000) developed two different but rather comparable models. They developed essential theories to explain the work of our brain in general, the cognitive workload and interfering processes which determine the process of generating an answer.

The Question-Answer-Model by Sudman et al. (1996) describes a model with four steps within the answering process:

1. deciphering and interpreting the question,
2. looking for the answer by retrieving the information,
3. forming judgment and including answers in an appropriate answering scheme, and
4. editing the answer to fit the given context.

Sudman et al. (1996) emphasize assessments of cognitive work by comparing different think-aloud and probing strategies and their impact on answers. Tourangeau et al. (2000) enhance this four-step model to include the module "cognitive involvement". They describe four steps within this cognitive process:

1. question interpretation,
2. the search in memory for all necessary information needed to answer,
3. assessment of available information concerning its suitability in regard to different aspects (social desirability, etc.), and finally
4. formulation of answers.

Other theories of explaining response effects to be found within most research are the primacy and recency effects (elements are memorized better when they are placed at the beginning or the end of a list, cf. Sternberg,

1969), different memory models (for further information see Anderson, 2007), social desirability, response sets, and halo-effects (for a short overview see Kriz, 2000).

4.2 SATISFICING RESPONSE BEHAVIOR

While a respondent is answering questions of a survey, their cognitive involvement can differ. The cognitive involvement a respondent is willing to invest is a variable element. The theory of satisficing behavior of this cognitive involvement is another important explanation strategy that is offered on the subject of response effect. Tourangeau et al. (2000) proposed an explanation of selecting the first reasonable answer coming to mind instead of the most appropriate one, if this most reasonable answer was followed by another, more appropriate one. So, the first answer that seems to fit a question is selected if respondents' cognitive involvement is lower or if the cognitive capacities one person can provide do not allow more involvement. Krosnick (1991) describes satisficing behavior as one form of performance during formulating a response.

Observable indicators are needed to infer a respondent's cognitive involvement in the question-answering process. Weisberg (2005, p. 286), for instance, reports on three experiments which used the percentage of "don't knows" respectively "no opinion" response options in a face-to-face vs. telephone comparison. Yan and Olson (2013, p. 74f.) cite recent studies to confirm that respondents "who go through a questionnaire too quickly, . . . are more likely to exhibit satisficing response behavior". Accordingly, a relevant factor is the time spent completing a questionnaire. The authors describe an example study which relates this overall response time to the number of "primacy effects", the latter taken as an expression of satisficing response behavior (Yan & Olson, 2013, p. 86). Following Schouten and Calinescu (2013, p. 233), satisificing can be viewed as a response style, with acquiescence, primacy, and recency as special forms of satisficing "where the respondent always provides, respectively, a positive answer, the first answer on the list and the last answer on the list".

Interviewer evaluations represent another form of paradata (Olson & Parkhurst, 2013, p. 54). In the present study we especially pursued this approach to assess the degree of satisficing behavior and reluctance, respectively. Based on interviewer-ratings, the present chapter explores the modifying effect of satisficing response behavior on a response-order effect, a question-wording effect, and the response style. The online appendix to this chapter reports in addition on the influence of satisficing behavior on a scale-label effect and a special scale-format effect on response behavior. To assess the degree of satisficing response behavior, we used the following instruction: "Attempt to assess the response behavior of the respondent: Did the respondent take care in answering the question properly and conscientiously or did the respondent 'rush' through the questions, without thinking of his/her answers properly? Rate the response behavior on a scale from 1 to 7, where the 1 means that the respondent answered the questions very conscientiously and the 7 means that the respondent did not answer the questions conscientiously at all". Each interviewer had to answer this question as part of the contact protocol immediately after an interview had been conducted. In addition, we employed a standardized interviewer-rating of the effort needed to win a target person over to an interview. Here, a 7-point scale was used ranging from 1 = "immediately ready" to 7 = "ready only after investing a great deal of effort". Tables A4.1 and A4.2 in the online appendix to this chapter provide information about these ratings. There we report on the frequency distributions of these rating variables, their stability over five measurement occasions, and occasion-specific correlations between satisficing behavior and reluctance. We observed a clear pattern: a minimal stability over time is associated with consistently higher and per se substantial cross-sectional correlation between reluctance and satisficing. The more an interviewer had to invest in convincing a respondent of taking part in an interview, the more a respondent shows satisficing behavior afterwards.

4.3 DATA

The data used in this chapter stem from the access panel of the German Priority Programme on Survey Methodology (PPSM). PPSM panel members were recruited in a sequence of three selection steps. Telephone samples were utilized to recruit panel members on a probabilistic basis. Chapter 18 in this volume describes this first selection step of participating or not participating in the recruitment samples in greater detail. In the concluding part of the recruitment interviews, all respondents were asked if they were ready to join the panel. 10,077, or 70.7 percent, of the respondents answered in the affirmative. Target persons who agreed to join were then allocated to the downstream panel survey modes "telephone" and "online". This was realized at random in case both survey-mode options were offered by the respondents. Otherwise respondents were allocated to the single offered survey mode. Out of the circle of 10,077 consenting respondents, 7,347, or 72.9 percent, participated in the welcoming interview of the panel afterwards (74.2 percent in the telephone mode (cooperation rate: 86 percent) and 60.3 percent in the online mode). A detailed exposition of the panel design is given in Engel et al. (2012) and Engel (2013).

While the analyses presented below on response-order effects and response style use data from the recruitment stage, the other experiments use different PPSM panel surveys conducted afterwards, if applicable, in conjunction with the interviewer ratings of satisficing behavior and response propensity from the recruitment phase.

4.4 RESPONSE ORDER

The present section explores the modifying impact of perceived sensitivity and satisficing response behavior on the effect that the response order of a frequency scale exercises upon response behavior. As putative sensitive questions are not necessarily experienced as sensitive ones, we pursued the approach to let the respondents rate the perceived sensitivity of survey questions with respect to two subject areas: deviant behavior and health behavior. For the latter subject the meta-question was worded as follows: "I would like to come back again shortly to the health questions. How personal did you feel the questions about alcohol consumption were? On a scale from 1 to 7, the 1 means this time, that you felt the question to be not at all personal, and the 7, that you felt the question to be much too personal. With the values in between you can grade again your opinion".

The relevant survey question had been posed beforehand. Respondents had been asked to rate their own alcohol consumption on a 6-point scale. One random half of the sample received this scale starting with the lowest possible frequency, while the other half received the scale starting with the highest possible consumption frequency. The question was worded as "How often did you consume alcoholic drinks of any kind during the last 12 months?" This was followed by the two scale formats as:

Split A: never, once a month or less, two to four times per month, two to three times per week, four to six times per week, daily; don't know (last category not read to the respondent)

Split B: daily, four to six times per week, two to three times per week, two
to four times per month, once a month or less, never; don't know
(last category not read to the respondent)

Controlling for interviewer effects by a random-intercept regression
equation, the estimated mean frequency of alcohol consumption turned
out to be 2.99 in split A, while the expected mean difference to split B
was 0.69 (Table 4.1). Accordingly, the mean value in split B is estimated
to be 3.68. Thus on average a comparably higher mean estimate results if
the scale is started with the highest possible consumption category. Taking into account that the categories are read to the respondent one by
one, the finding seems to indicate that the respondent chooses from that
sequence of categories the first one that appears acceptable to him/her.
Perhaps one can consider this to be a "modified primacy" effect, keeping
in mind that the primacy vs. recency distinction actually refers to unordered sets of categories (cf. Tourangeau et al., 2000, pp. 250–254): it is not
the first category that receives special attention but the first acceptable
one. Though this interpretation would not be in line with the hypothesis
that primacy effects are more likely to arise than recency effects in cases
where the categories are presented visually, while the opposite is expected
in cases where the list is presented only in verbal communication (cf.
Tourangeau et al., 2000, p. 251; De Leeuw, 2008, p. 118f.).

TABLE 4.1

The effect of perceived sensitivity and satisficing behavior on the strength of a response-
order effect on answers to a question about the frequency of alcohol consumption

Satisficing ↓	Perceived sensitivity of a question about alcohol consumption							
	low		middle		high		all	
	b_0	b_1	b_0	b_1	b_0	b_1	b_0	b_1
1 low	2.90	0.75	3.04	0.67	3.33	0.29	3.03	0.63
2 middle	2.83	0.99	3.13	0.40	3.12	0.51	2.99	0.70
3 high	2.72	0.97	3.02	0.69	2.70	0.82	2.79	0.86
All	2.86	0.86	3.07	0.57	3.13	0.47	2.99	0.69

The table displays the estimates of effect of a linear regression with randomly varying intercepts across
a total of 184 interviewers ($N = 5,627$). The estimates are computed totally as well as conditional upon
the 3×3 combinations of sensitivity and satisficing behavior. Split variable is coded 0/1: b_0 estimates
the mean value in split group A, while b_1 estimates the mean difference to split group B. All estimates
of effect are statistically significant ($p < 0.05$). Further information is given in the online appendix to
this chapter.

It is assumed that the susceptibility to response-order effects like primacy or recency may depend on the degree of satisficing response behavior (cf. Tourangeau et al., 2000, p. 253). Read column by column, the figures in Table 4.1 indicate that in the present context the expected differences in mean values do in fact increase when the degree of satisficing response behavior increases. Overall, the expected mean differences increase from 0.63 over 0.70 to 0.86 and are particularly pronounced in cases where the question is, at the same time, also perceived as highly sensitive (0.29 vs. 0.51 vs. 0.82). This observed effect pattern makes sense: The more accurately questions are answered, the closer a response will be to the "true" value and hence the less susceptible a respondent will be to the sequence in which categories are read to the respondent in verbal communication.

At the same time, the perceived sensitivity of a survey question may play a decisive role too. In the present context this is exemplified by the figures in Table 4.1. Read in a row, the figures indicate that the expected mean differences drop when the perceived sensitivity goes up. Overall, the figures decline from 0.86 over 0.57 to 0.47, while this decline turns out to be particularly sharp in the case of a low degree of satisficing response behavior. Then the expected differences diminish from 0.75 over 0.67 to 0.29. This means that if respondents understand a question as very personal, the respondent is more accurate in understanding and evaluating possible answering options for their own situation.

While these figures reveal that mean differences across the two scale formats depend on the degree of perceived sensitivity and satisficing response behavior (as indicated by the b_1's), the mean levels themselves too are associated with both conditions. This becomes evident when comparing the b_0-entries in Table 4.1. Read column by column, they show that the level of alcohol consumption declines the higher the degree of satisficing becomes. Stated the other way round, the more one drinks on average, the lower the degree of satisficing in that respective question. The overall mean figures drop from 3.03 over 2.99 to 2.79 and turn out to be particularly pronounced in cases where the topic is perceived as highly sensitive at the same time. Then the same line of figures amounts to 3.33, 3.12, and 2.70. The mean level of alcohol consumption seems to give rise to a reason for answering the question particularly attentively.

At the same time, it holds that different mean levels of alcohol consumption are associated with different levels of sensitivity. The more one drinks on average, the more sensitively the question is perceived. Read in a row, the overall mean level is raised from 2.86 over 3.07 to 3.13 and is particularly pronounced in case of a low degree of satisficing response behavior (2.90 vs. 3.04 vs. 3.33).

4.5 QUESTION WORDING

A list of seven statements about distributive justice was used to conduct a question-wording experiment (cf. Table A4.4 in the online appendix). We asked one group about justice and the other group about injustice. The experimental factor varies, in particular the formulation "just" vs. "unjust". Table 4.2 displays the results for three such statements. If the respondents were asked "It is just if someone who keeps working hard earns more than someone who doesn't", an overall mean of 6.2 is observed. Accordingly, there is high agreement to this statement. If the same situation is inquired replacing the word "just" by "unjust", a pronounced mean difference of −1.6 is the consequence if both scales were made comparable beforehand. A significant mean difference also arises with respect to the statement "It can only be just if all people are financially equally well off". We obtain a mean value of 3.0 using the formulation "just" and a significantly higher mean in the comparison group (Table 4.2, third statement). Worth mentioning now is that the degree of satisficing behavior modifies this question-wording effect: while a low degree is associated with a weaker mean difference, the opposite is observed in case of a middle respectively high degree of satisficing response behavior. Respondents who answer the questions conscientiously are thus less susceptible to the present question-wording effect than respondents who are not answering that conscientiously. Contrary to that is the finding on the statement that it is just/unjust "if everybody gets what they need for life, even without their own effort" (Table 4.2, second statement).

TABLE 4.2

The effect of satisficing behavior on the strength of a question-wording effect on answers to statements about distributive justice

Distributive justice	Satisficing							
	high		middle		low		all	
	$\bar{x}_j$	Δ	$\bar{x}_j$	Δ	$\bar{x}_j$	Δ	$\bar{x}_j$	Δ
"hard work"	5.6	−1.4	6.4	−3.0*	6.2	−0.8*	6.2	−1.6*
"without own effort"	3.2	0.6	3.9	−0.5	3.3	0.7*	3.5	0.3
"all equally well off"	2.6	1.4*	2.9	0.3	3.0	0.5	3.0	0.6*
N	51		111		211		373	

*Sig. ($p \leq 0.05$). The table displays mean values using the "just" formulation and mean differences with respect to the comparison group. The complete table and further explanations are given in the online appendix to this chapter.

In the online appendix to this chapter the modifying impact of satisficing is additionally explored with respect to a scale-label effect in the context of a dichotomous scale (Table A4.5) as well as with respect to four different scale formats that vary the number of scale points and scale labeling (Table A4.6).

4.6 RESPONSE STYLE

A set of seven meta-questions on the recruitment interview was used to obtain respondent ratings on 7-point respectively 5-point scales as part of a relevant scale experiment. Using both the 7-point scales (1 = "do not agree at all" to 7 = "totally agree") and 5-point scales (1 = "does not apply at all" to 5 = "totally applies"), latent class analyses were computed to reveal possible response styles. Table A4.7 in the online appendix to this chapter informs about the conditional response probabilities obtained for each item and the respective item wordings. The analysis is certainly complicated by the fact that there are two basic sources of variation involved in the response probabilities: (a) differences in terms of content issues and (b) differences in the usage of the scales. This makes it difficult to separate out the former effects from the latter. It appears nevertheless possible to discern different styles of responding. One such style consists in choosing the endpoints of a scale to anchor one's response. If this is connected with the strong tendency to choose this anchor itself as one's response, the probability pattern of latent class 3 emerges. This applies equally well to both the 5-point and 7-point answering scales. If the use of endpoints as cognitive anchors is coupled with an affinity to grade one's opinion a bit more than not at all, the response style of latent class 1 arises from that. This too becomes evident in case of both the 5-point and 7-point scales. Regarding the response patterns in latent class 2, actually two such patterns can be observed. The first applies to the first two items in Table A4.7 in the online appendix to this chapter. It may be interpreted as combining the use of endpoints as cognitive anchors with a comparably stronger affinity to grade one's opinion than the level of affinity that is observed for latent classes 1 and 3: from no such affinity in class 3 over a slight tendency in class 1 to an affinity in class 2 which is a bit more pronounced. This pattern may be due to the fact that the subject matters were often answered as agreement (there were, put bluntly, no two opinions on these subjects). However, if the answers to a question cover the range of a scale more fully, a shift of the response probabilities to the middle categories of a scale can be observed. This particularly concerns the actual middle category or the category next to that middle category. Table A4.7 reveals this pattern with respect to all items except the first two. While the actual middle category is preferred in case of the 5-point scales, it is the category next to the middle category in case of the 7-point scales. An attempt at interpreting this pattern may follow two lines. On the one hand, it may simply hold that the more heterogeneous the answers to a subject matter are, the more the peak of the response probabilities shifts to the middle of a scale. This would be in accordance with a model that assumes the use of endpoints as cognitive anchors of answers. On the other hand, the observed pattern in latent class 2 may be due to the use of the middle category to anchor an answer. In telephone surveys, rating scales are normally not visualized and have to be remembered while answering. This is a cognitive task which has to be performed. To reduce the complexity of this task, respondents may pursue two opposite approaches: one part of respondents anchor their answers in the middle category, while another part chooses the endpoints of a scale for that purpose. Based on the observed response patterns in Table A4.7 alone, however, one can only speculate about which of the two interpretations for response class 2 do apply. One can build a bridge to findings of related response experiments though. These relate to 11-point scales and indicate only insignificant mean differences across two conditions: the midpoint of such a scale is named vs. not named if the scale is read to the respondent on the phone. Table A4.9 in the online appendix to this chapter reports the results. Though no direct comparability is given to the present experiment (11-point vs. 7/5-point scales, different subject matters, different statistical techniques applied), the insignificant mean differences reported in Table A4.9 seem to suggest that respondents do indeed anchor their answers in the middle category of such a scale. While it is possible that it makes a difference if the midpoint is read to the respondent or not, no significant difference is observed. Read to the respondent or not, middle categories appear to be used as cognitive anchors, resulting in very similar mean values.

Worth mentioning now is the relationship between response style and satisficing response behavior. Table A4.8 in the online appendix to this chapter informs about the relevant percentages, Table 4.3 about a corresponding multinomial logistic regression analysis. If response style 2 ("anchor: midpoint") is used as the reference category, the odds of belonging to latent class 1 ("anchor: endpoints; affinity to grade one's opinion: weak") increase with the degree of satisficing behavior, while the odds of belonging to latent class 3 ("anchor: endpoints; affinity to grade one's opinion: virtually none") decrease as satisficing increases. Stated the other way round, response style 3 is associated with the comparably highest percentage of respondents who answer the questions very conscientiously, and response style 1 with the comparably lowest such percentage. This applies

TABLE 4.3

Response style, satisficing behavior, and response propensity

	Style	5pt scales			7pt scales		
		b	b/s.e.	e^b	b	b/s.e.	e^b
Reluctance		0.20	5.43	1.2	0.09	2.76	1.1
Satisficing		0.19	3.79	1.2	0.23	4.69	1.3
Schooling	1	0.01	0.38	1.0	0.13	4.88	1.1
Gender*		−0.18	−1.72	0.8	−0.05	−0.48	1.0
Intercept		−1.61	−8.97	0.2	−1.57	−9.18	0.2
	2	Reference style			Reference style		
Reluctance		−0.07	−2.27	0.9	−0.11	−3.37	0.9
Satisficing		−0.11	−2.37	0.9	−0.01	−0.17	1.0
Schooling	3	−0.19	−7.88	0.8	−0.13	−5.27	0.9
Gender*		−0.35	−4.00	0.7	−0.42	−4.64	0.7
Intercept		1.02	7.16	2.8	0.71	4.78	2.0

*Male (vs. female). 5pt scales: $N = 2,804$ (Pseudo-$R^2 = 0.032$); 7pt scales: $N = 2,728$ (Pseudo-$R^2 = 0.029$). The table displays the estimates of a multinomial logistic regression.

to both the 5-point and 7-point scales. In addition, schooling is of relevance too: educational status increases the odds of response style 1 and decreases the odds of response style 3 (vs. style 2 respectively). Being male decreases the odds of both response styles 1 and 3. Finally we observe an interesting propensity effect on the likelihood of the different response styles. The "reluctance score" used is just the interviewer's rating of the degree of convincing effort needed to win a person over to the recruitment interview. Table 4.3 now shows that the likelihood of response style 1 is increased by the degree of such convincing efforts, while the likelihood of response style 3 is decreased. Convincing efforts do not only affect response rates but also sample composition in terms of response styles and the inherent degree of satisficing response behavior. We observe in particular that convincing efforts raise the likelihood of getting respondents into the survey who answer the survey questions not so conscientiously.

4.7 COGNITIVE DEBRIEFING IN A STANDARDIZED INTERVIEW

Open-ended meta-questions create the possibility of gaining more information on the survey content itself, as well as on the process of how information is recalled and provided for the answering process. We use the term "meta-question" (instead of "question") only to indicate that cognitive debriefing takes place by asking respondents questions about survey questions (cf. Christodoulou et al., 2008; Groves et al., 2009, pp. 263–265; Ploughman, Austin, Stefanelli, & Godwin, 2010 for expositions of cognitive debriefing respectively cognitive interviewing). We were particularly interested in examining the usability of respondent debriefing questions for standardized telephone interviews if these probes are to be employed as an integral part of such interviews. To place special probes immediately after a survey question has been asked is one possible use of such probes, as Martin (2004, pp. 161–164, 168) and Campanelli (2008, p. 193, for think-alouds) point out. For that purpose a sequence of a meaning probe and a "think-aloud" probe was built in the interview. The latter question was only asked if respondents showed no problems in answering the former question. Respondents who received this second question were asked to think aloud and relate what was going on in their heads while answering the preceding question on the meaning of the word "Finanzausgleich" (financial equalization scheme between states of the European Union). Only experienced interviewers or interviewers who were rather eloquent during interviewer briefings conducted this target. Probing was standardized and had to be noted with a tick box. Coding was done using three researchers. The reliability turned out to amount to kappa = 0.84 as to the number of codes respectively kappa = 0.79 as to code content.

The first result worth mentioning is the opportunity of extracting practical and realistic information on cognitive processes embedded into a quantitative survey. Four hundred eighty-seven respondents received the first open ended-question, of which 88 percent ($n = 429$) were able to deliver an answer. Only 189 of these respondents received the meta-question, since only selected interviewers were allocated to this task. Out of the circle of respondents who received this meta-question, 92.6 percent were able to provide an answer, 7.4 percent did not answer or gave irrelevant answers like "don't know" or told abstract stories. This demonstrates that a majority of respondents were able to express themselves well and delivered reasonable answers on both open-ended questions.

In total, 336 aspects were extracted from the answers to the meta-question, which means that on average 1.8 aspects describing the cognitive work per respondent were identified. Codes were defined by the type of cognitive task. Of the respondents, 49.2 percent interpreted the answer with "interesting aspects in general" coming to their minds while answering the open-ended question. This code implies answers like "thought about an earlier discussion with a friend", "saw a report on TV", or "am interested in politics in general". This all implies a current and daily occupation with the subject.

Of the respondents, 30.7 percent are reminded of their moral education and judge the approach to the financial crisis negatively. Examples are reactions like "people from other European countries live too excessively and we've got to pay" and "we (Germans) have to pay for lazy people from other countries". Of the respondents, 15.3 percent had clear associations and found internal pictures in their minds while answering. These pictures are, for example, "empty wallet" or "German reunion". Further, 14.8 percent told the interviewer about personal experiences (long-term episodic memory), e.g. "my life experience allows this assessment", or "I was born in 1938. When I was young we had nothing . . .", while 8.5 percent stated negative emotional reactions (e.g. "capitalistic thinking", "it has negative implications for the population"). Of the respondents, 8.5 percent had associated thoughts connected to the word "Finanzausgleich" (associations regarding the redistribution of money in the Federal Republic of Germany's 'Laenderfinanzausgleich'), e.g. "thought about Germany's 'Laenderfinanzausgleich'". Other sources of cognitive involvement were identified as follows: long-term memory tasks (5.8 percent) with answers like "based on my knowledge from life experiences", other semantic associations (5.3 percent) like associations towards Germany in general, automatisms (4.8 percent) like "just my thinking", "spontaneously, intuition", ambivalent emotional reactions (2.1 percent; "on the one hand, we are a community and need to support each other, but I don't want to pay again"), and sensitive reactions if the question of sharing the thought was too personal (e.g. "thought about your question and this is my answer") or if someone tried to impress the interviewer (e.g. "I have been interested in this topic for years and read every article and book about it"; 1.1 percent each).

4.8 CONCLUSION

It has been shown that the degree of satisficing response behavior may substantially affect the strength of response effects. The more conscientiously questions are answered, the less susceptible a respondent is to the sequence in which the categories of a frequency scale for a more or less sensitive topic are read to him/her in verbal communication. A further modifying effect is due to the perceived sensitivity in that context. Respondents who answer questions conscientiously are also less susceptible to question-wording effects than respondents who are not answering so conscientiously. This was shown in an experiment on images of distributive justice. An experiment which compared four different scale formats revealed that these formats yielded comparably less differing response distributions if the survey questions on environmental behavior were answered very conscientiously. We also found a clear relationship between the degree of satisficing behavior and response style. In this context another effect is especially worth mentioning. We observed that convincing efforts affect sample composition in terms of response styles and the inherent degree of satisficing response behavior. We observed in particular that convincing efforts raise the likelihood of getting respondents into the survey who answer survey questions not so conscientiously.

Respondent debriefing may be realized during an otherwise standardized telephone interview. This became clear from an analysis of a sequence of a meaning probe followed by a "think-aloud" probe. This finding suggests that the inclusion of open-ended meta-questions may help greatly in gaining useful information about the underlying cognitive response process, namely just in standardized survey interviews.

REFERENCES

Anderson, J. R. (2007). *Cognitive psychology and its implications* (6th ed.). New York, NY: Worth.

Campanelli, P. (2008).Testing survey questions. In E. D. De Leeuw, J. J. Hox, & D. A. Dillman (Eds.), *International handbook of survey methodology* (pp. 176–200). New York, NY: Erlbaum.

Christian, L. M., Dillman, D. A., & Smyth, J. D. (2008). The effects of mode and format on answers to scalar questions in telephone and web surveys. In J. M. Lepkowski, C. Tucker, J. M. Brick, E. D. De Leeuw, L. Japec, P. J. Lavrakas, M. W. Link, & R. L. Sangster (Eds.), *Advances in telephone survey methodology* (pp. 250–275). Hoboken, NJ: Wiley.

Christodoulou, C., Junghaenel, D. U., DeWalt, D. A., Rothrock, N., & Stone, A. A. (2008). Cognitive interviewing in the evaluation of fatigue items: Results from the patient-reported outcomes measurement information system (PROMIS). *Quality of Life Research, 17,* 1239–1246.

Couper, M. P., & Groves, R. M. (1992). The role of the interviewer in survey participation. *Survey Methodology, 18*(2), 263–277.

Couper, M. P., Tourangeau, R., Conrad, F. G., & Crawford, S. D. (2004). What they see is what we get—Response options for web surveys. *Social Science Computer Review, 22*(1), 111–127.

Couper, M. P., Tourangeau, R., Conrad, F. G., & Singer, E. (2006). Evaluating the effectiveness of visual analog scales—A web experiment. *Social Science Computer Review, 24*(2), 227–245.

De Leeuw, E. D. (2008). Choosing the method of data collection. In E. D. De Leeuw, J. J. Hox, & D. A. Dillman (Eds.), *International handbook of survey methodology* (pp. 113–135). New York, NY: Erlbaum.

De Leeuw, E. D., & Hox, J. J. (1996). The effect of the interviewer on the decision to cooperate in a survey of the elderly. In S. Laaksonen (Ed.), *International perspectives on nonresponse. Proceedings of the sixth international workshop on household survey nonresponse* (pp. 46–52). Helsinki: Statistics Finland.

De Leeuw, E. D., Hox, J. J., Snijkers, G., & De Heer, W. (1997). Interviewer opinions, attitudes and strategies regarding survey participation and their effect on response. In A. Koch & R. Porst (Eds.), *Nonresponse in survey research* (pp. 239–248). ZUMA-Nachrichten Spezial Band 4. Mannheim: ZUMA.

Engel, U. (2013). *Access panel and mixed-mode internet survey. PPSM Panel Report.* 2nd Edition. pdf file available at www.sozialforschung.uni-bremen.de

Engel, U., Bartsch, S., Schnabel, C., & Vehre, H. (2012). *Wissenschaftliche Umfragen. Methoden und Fehlerquellen.* Frankfurt: Campus Verlag.

Foddy, W. (1996). The in-depth testing of survey questions: A critical appraisal of methods. *Quality and Quantity, 30,* 361–370.

Groves, R. M., & Couper, M. P. (1998). *Nonresponse in household interview surveys.* New York, NY: Wiley.

Groves, R. M., & Fultz, N. H. (1985). Gender effects among telephone interviewers in a survey of economic attitudes. *Sociological Methods and Research, 14*(1), 31–52.

Groves, R. M., Fowler, F. J. Jr., Couper, M. P., Lepkowski, J. M., Singer, E., & Tourangeau, R. (2009). *Survey methodology* (2nd ed.). Hoboken, NJ: Wiley.

Jann, B., Jerke, J., & Krumpal, I. (2012). Asking sensitive questions using the Crosswise Model—An experimental survey measuring plagiarism. *Public Opinion Quarterly, 76*(1), 32–49.

Kriz, J. (2000). Methodenkritik. In R. Asanger, & G. Wenninger (Eds.), *Handwoerterbuch Psychologie* (pp. 454–458). Weinheim: Psychologie Verlags Union.

Krosnick, J. A. (1991). Response strategies for coping with the cognitive demands of attitude measures in surveys. *Applied Cognitive Psychology, 5,* 213–236.

Krosnick, J. A., & Alwin, D. F. (1987). An evaluation of a cognitive theory of response-order effects in survey measurements. *Public Opinion Quarterly, 51*(2), 201–219.

Krumpal, I. (2011). Determinants of social desirability bias in sensitive surveys: A literature review. *Quality and Quantity 47*(4), 2025–2047. doi:10.1007/s11135-011-9640-9

Lyberg, I., & Dean, P. (1992). *Methods for reducing nonresponse rates: A review.* Paper presented at the Annual Meeting of the American Association for Public Opinion Research. St. Petersburg.

Martin, E. (2004). Vignettes and respondent debriefing for questionnaire design and evaluation. In S. Presser, J. Rothgeb, M. P. Couper, J. T. Lessler, E. Martin, J. Martin, & E. Singer (Eds.), *Methods for testing and evaluating survey questionnaires* (pp. 149–171). Hoboken, NJ: Wiley.

Nisbett, R. E., & Ross, L. (1980). *Human shortcomings of social judgements.* Englewood Cliffs, NJ: Prentice-Hall.

Nisbett, R. E., & Wilson, T. D. (1977). Telling more than we know: Verbal reports on mental processes. *Psychological Review, 84,* 231–259.

Olson, K., & Parkhurst, B. (2013). Collecting paradata for measurement error evaluations. In F. Kreuter (Ed.), *Improving surveys with paradata* (pp. 43–72). Hoboken, NJ: Wiley.

Ploughman, M., Austin, M., Stefanelli, M., & Godwin, M. (2010). Applying cognitive debriefing to pre-test patient-reported outcomes in older people with multiple sclerosis. *Quality of Life Research, 19*(4), 483–487.

Schouten, B., Calinescu, M. (2013). Paradata as input to monitoring representativeness and measurement profiles: A case study of the Dutch Labour Force Survey. In F. Kreuter (Ed.), *Improving surveys with paradata* (pp. 231–258). Hoboken, NJ: Wiley.

Schwarz, N., Knäuper, B., Oyserman, D., & Stich, C. (2008). The psychology of asking questions. In E. D. De Leeuw, J. J. Hox, & D. A. Dillman (Eds.), *International handbook of survey methodology* (pp. 18–34). New York, NY: Lawrence Erlbaum Associates.

Sternberg, S. (1969). Memory scanning: mental processes revealed by reaction time experiments. *American Scientists, 57,* 421–457.

Sudman, S., Bradburn, N. M., & Schwarz, N. (1996). *Thinking about answers. The application of cognitive processes to survey methodology.* San Francisco, CA: Jossey-Bass.

Tourangeau, R., Couper, M. P., & Conrad, F. (2004). Spacing, position, and order— Interpretive heuristics for visual features of survey questions. *Public Opinions Quarterly, 68*(3), 368–393.

Tourangeau, R., Couper, M. P., & Conrad, F. (2007). Color, labels, and interpretive heuristics for response scales. *Public Opinions Quarterly, 71*(1), 91–112.

Tourangeau, R., Rips, L. J., & Rasinski, K. (2000). *The psychology of survey response.* Cambridge, UK: Cambridge University Press.

Weisberg, H. F. (2005). *The total survey error approach.* Chicago, IL: University of Chicago Press.

Willis, G. B. (2004). *Cognitive interviewing. A tool for improving questionnaire design.* Thousand Oaks, CA: Sage.

Yan, T., & Olson, K. (2013). Analyzing paradata to investigate measurement error. In F. Kreuter (Ed.), *Improving surveys with paradata* (pp. 73–95). Hoboken, NJ: Wiley.

Ye, C., Fulton, J., & Tourangeau, R. (2011). More positive or more extreme? A meta-analysis of mode differences in response choice. *Public Opinion Quarterly, 75*(2), 349–365.

5

Telephone Surveys Using Mobile Phones

Britta Busse and Marek Fuchs

5.1 INTRODUCTION

In recent years cell phone penetration rates have been rising all over the world (Blumberg & Luke, 2011; Carley-Baxter, Peytchev, & Black, 2010; Link, Battaglia, Frankel, Osborn, & Mokdad, 2007). In parallel to this increase in cell phone usage a widespread trend for abandoning landline telephones has been noticed (Arthur, 2004; Blumberg, Luke, Cynamon, & Frankel, 2008). Accordingly, mobile-onlys are becoming more prevalent and thus receive considerable attention in telephone survey methodology (Ehlen & Ehlen, 2007; Peytchev, Carley-Baxter, & Black, 2010; Wolter, Smith, & Blumberg, 2010). Longitudinal analyses have proven growing mobile-only rates, with currently 27 percent in the U.S. (Blumberg & Luke, 2011) and more than 50 percent in several European countries (Busse & Fuchs, 2011a).

Since high mobile-only rates have the potential of causing considerable coverage error in traditional landline telephone surveys, there is a need for examining differences between the mobile-onlys and the general population. If mobile-onlys differed significantly from the general population, neglecting this subpopulation in landline telephone surveys would induce coverage bias into estimates. Several studies have highlighted the socio-demographic characteristics of mobile-onlys: Mobile-onlys are predominantly male, young, single, living in rented dwellings in metropolitan areas and are typically earning low incomes (e.g. Blumberg & Luke, 2011; Busse & Fuchs, 2011a; Keeter, Kennedy, Clark, Tompson, & Mokrzycki, 2007; Kuusela, Callegaro, & Vehovar, 2008). Based on these findings, most authors argue that coverage bias in telephone surveys cannot be avoided as long as cell phone numbers are neglected in telephone surveys (Gabler & Ayhan,

2007; Lavrakas, Steeh, Shuttles, & Fienberg, 2007; Wolter et al., 2010). This chapter aims to highlight the methodological implications of conducting cell phone surveys, starting with coverage error considerations. In addition, we will address some new challenges and difficulties introduced into telephone survey methodology when conducting telephone surveys using cell phones and cell phone numbers in terms of sampling, nonresponse and measurement.

5.2 COVERAGE ERROR

Several studies have highlighted the need to supplement landline telephone samples with random cell phone numbers using a variety of dual frame approaches (Callegaro, Ayhan, Gabler, Häder, & Villar, 2011; Gabler & Ayhan, 2007; Kennedy, 2007; Wolter et al., 2010). However, since dual frame surveys suffer from differential nonresponse and measurement error components and are also more costly than single frame surveys, surveys using samples of cell phone numbers only (without supplemental landline telephone numbers) may become an appealing option for survey researchers once cell phone penetration has reached saturation. Consequently, we will consider the coverage error of surveys using solely cell phone numbers due to the population that cannot be reached in the cell phone frame even though they have a landline telephone number at their disposal: the landline-onlys.

So far, only a few studies assessed landline-onlys as compared to other telephone populations. Using 2001 data from a study by the European Commission, Kim and Lepkowski (2002) assessed sociodemographic variables for landline-onlys in 15 European Union member countries. Based on the results, European landline-onlys were characterized as more often living in rural areas, whereas respondents with landline and cell phone access preferred metropolitan areas. Further, landline-onlys as well as mobile-onlys were described as living more often in single-person households in contrast to users with landline and cell phone access, who live predominantly in larger households (see also Blumberg et al., 2008). Also, Kim and Lepkowski (2002) found lower incomes among landline-onlys, similar to mobile-onlys (see also Blumberg et al., 2008). According to Blumberg and colleagues (2008) landline-onlys are less often home owners compared to the population having landline and cell phone access and the share of highly educated people is lowest among landline-only households (18 percent) compared to mobile-only households (21 percent) and households with both types of telephone access (32 percent).

Using data from the Experimental Mobile Phone Panel project, which was funded by Deutsche Forschungsgemeinschaft as part of its Priority Program in Survey Methodology from 2008 through 2012 (Busse & Fuchs, 2011a; Fuchs, 2012a, 2012b), we examined coverage error of landline and cell phone sampling frames. In order to assess potential coverage bias in estimates based on samples drawn from the cell phone frame or drawn from the landline telephone frame we used Eurobarometer data. This face-to-face survey across 27 European countries provides information on cell phone and landline phone access in the general population.[1] For the analysis of coverage bias in cell phone telephone surveys we used the relative coverage bias suggested by Biemer and Lyberg (2003) and assessed several sociodemographic estimates simulating a landline survey (ignoring mobile-onlys) and a cell phone survey (ignoring landline-onlys). For the analysis presented here we selected 10 European countries known to differ with respect to landline telephone and cell phone prevalence rates.

Results (see Table 5.1) indicate clear differences across the selected countries. Countries like Finland, the Czech Republic, Estonia or Hungary, which have a high proportion of mobile-onlys (50 percent at least) and a landline telephone rate of less than 50 percent, are prone to higher coverage bias in landline telephone surveys than in surveys conducted in the cell phone frame. Sweden is an example for high landline telephone and high cell phone coverage. Here the largest relative coverage bias is rather small (0.04 in the cell phone frame) because landline telephone surveys as well as cell phone surveys yield an almost perfect coverage.

Other countries like Germany, Luxembourg, Greece and Croatia exhibit mobile-only rates of less than 20 percent and still have a high landline telephone coverage (80 percent and over) while cell phone coverage is still not universal. Consequently, estimates computed based on cell phone surveys have to compete against estimates from landline telephone surveys with rather small coverage bias. However, overall countries from this group yield lower relative coverage bias for estimates based on landline telephone surveys.

Turkey exhibits a rather low landline telephone coverage (54 percent in 2011) and at the same time a considerably high cell phone penetration rate (85 percent) which jointly results in a mobile-only rate of above 40 percent. When assessing the landline frame in terms of relative coverage bias we detected a strong underrepresentation of rural populations and an overrepresentation of married persons. By contrast, the respective relative coverage bias in the cell phone frame was smaller by far. For education, results suggested no coverage bias for the landline frame while in the cell phone frame people who obtained their highest educational degree at age 20 or over were overrepresented substantially.

TABLE 5.1

Relative coverage bias in the cell phone and landline telephone frame in the first half of 2011

	Sex (male)		Age (18 to 24)		Age at highest educational degree (20+)		Marital status (married)		Type of community (rural)	
	RCB mobile phone survey	RCB landline phone survey	RCB mobile phone survey	RCB landline phone survey	RCB mobile phone survey	RCB landline phone survey	RCB mobile phone survey	RCB landline phone survey	RCB mobile phone survey	RCB landline phone survey
Germany	**0.05**	-0.03	**0.14**	-0.10	**0.08**	0.04	**-0.05**	0.04	-0.02	0.02
Luxembourg	**0.01**	0.00	0.05	**-0.15**	0.02	**0.04**	0.00	**0.03**	0.00	**0.04**
Sweden	0.00	0.00	**0.04**	0.01	0.00	**-0.01**	**-0.02**	0.01	**-0.01**	0.00
Czech Republic	0.01	**-0.03**	0.03	-0.03	0.03	**0.77**	-0.02	**0.14**	0.00	**-0.18**
Estonia	0.01	**-0.11**	0.07	**-0.31**	0.03	**0.14**	-0.02	**0.32**	0.00	**-0.13**
Hungary	0.02	**-0.07**	0.09	**-0.35**	0.13	**0.23**	-0.03	**0.30**	-0.06	**-0.08**
Finland	0.00	**-0.15**	0.01	**-0.75**	0.01	**0.06**	0.00	**0.64**	**-0.02**	0.01
Greece	**0.05**	-0.03	**0.12**	-0.10	**0.12**	0.04	**-0.15**	0.04	**-0.07**	0.02
Turkey	**0.09**	-0.07	0.04	**-0.09**	**0.14**	0.00	-0.06	**0.21**	0.00	**-0.36**
Croatia	**0.06**	-0.02	**0.21**	-0.11	0.07	**0.10**	**-0.12**	0.07	**-0.07**	0.02

Note: Calculated with Eurobarometer data from the first half-year of 2011 (weighted to compensate for nonresponse error). Figures in bold indicate that they are larger in size (ignoring algebraic signs) than the respective value for estimates based on the other sampling frame.

With respect to the countries assessed we conclude that telephone surveys conducted in the cell phone frame alone are not yet sufficiently inclusive. Even though in some countries the relative coverage bias of the cell phone frame is less extensive compared to the landline telephone frame, for the majority of countries the picture is less unambiguous. Thus, for the time being, we agree with Kalsbeek and Agans (2008), Gabler and Ayhan (2007) and others, who suggest a dual frame sample design for telephone surveys.

5.3 SAMPLING

The dual frame approach requires independent samples from the landline telephone frame as well as from the cell phone frame. These two components are then combined using design weights in order to adjust for differential selection probabilities. The random digit dialing (RDD) method for landline telephone samples in the U.S. was originally developed by Mitofsky (1970) and Waksberg (1978) and since then has been advanced and adapted to changes in the telecommunications sector (Casady & Lepkowski, 1999). Its main purpose is the inclusion of telephone numbers not listed in telephone directories or similar registers (Brick & Tucker, 2007). In order to boost hit rates a list-assisted approach (e.g. Casady & Lepkowski, 1993) has been developed (see also Brick, Judkins, Montaquila, & Morganstein, 2002). In Germany, the so-called Gabler-Häder design follows a slightly different approach. Here, a pool of all presumed working landline telephone numbers (listed and non-listed) is built, which serves as a sampling frame for samples stratified by region and other known variables (Gabler & Häder, 1999).

RDD sampling methods have been adapted for cell phone numbers. However, country-specific characteristics of the cell phone numbering system led to a variety of problems and drawbacks. For instance, the area code of cell phone numbers in the U.S. that originally carried regional information concerning the cell phone owner's residence has become unreliable (due to the regional portability of the numbers) and is no longer used for stratification purposes (Christian, Dimock, & Keeter, 2009). Also, telephone numbers originally connecting to a cell phone may have been ported to a landline telephone (AAPOR Cell Phone Task Force, 2010), requiring screener questions to distinguish landline and cell phone connections.

In Germany, Gabler and Häder (2009) developed a procedure to generate an inclusive cell phone frame (see also Häder, Häder, & Kühne, 2012). Even though this procedure is considerably inclusive (only a small fraction of all presumably existing cell phone numbers is not covered by this frame), a noteworthy portion of cell phone numbers drawn from this frame for a survey remains unknown eligible even after extensive fieldwork efforts. This is mostly due to ambiguous voice mail and operator messages, as well as extensive instances of ring-no-answer. The high proportion of numbers of unknown eligibility affects the computation of response rates (conservative formulas considering numbers of unknown eligibility yield rather low response rates) and results in more call attempts, extended field phases and ultimately in higher costs for cell phone surveys (Buskirk, Callegaro, & Rao, 2009; Callegaro et al., 2007; Schneiderat & Schlinzig, 2009a). In order to determine the eligibility of a randomly selected cell phone number prior to fieldwork, Kunz and Fuchs (2012) experimented with two different number validation methods (for a similar approach see Struminskaya et al., 2011):

- *Number validation services* provide verification in real time by performing a Home Location Register (HLR) lookup resulting in a validation code which indicates the current status of a cell phone number.
- *Text messaging services* can be used for sending bulk messages via the internet to cell phone numbers. Detailed delivery status codes and reason codes in case of failed delivery can be used for pre-call validation.

Both methods provide codes which enable the researcher to distinguish between technically valid and invalid cell phone numbers as well as numbers which are temporarily inactive. The authors compared the efficiency of screening conditions based on these codes in an experimental setting. With the help of final disposition codes known from the fieldwork, the return codes from either HLR look-up or bulk text message services were verified. Results suggested that both methods were effective means to increase the rate of numbers of known eligibility in German cell phone samples. Consequently the interviewers' workload, the number of call attempts, the overall call duration and the survey costs were reduced when using these methods to screen out cell phone numbers prior to the fieldwork. At the same time contact and interview rates were increased (Kunz & Fuchs, 2012).

Key to the design weighting of surveys including cell phones is the assumption that a cell phone is a personal device that is used only by one person (the cell phone "owner"). Thus, respondent selection procedures (e.g. birthday method or Kish method) are typically not implemented in cell phone surveys. However, some studies have demonstrated that cell phone sharing (usage of a cell phone by more than one person) does occur. Brick, Edwards, and Lee (2007) implemented a question asking for cell phone sharing in screening interviews conducted in mobile-only households yielding 8 percent cell phone sharers. Similarly, Tucker, Brick, and Meekins (2007) used a secondary analysis of the 2004 Current Population Survey to identify 66 percent of mobile-only households with more than one adult resident as cell phone sharing households. Link and colleagues (2007) found sharing rates ranging from 11 to 17 percent across U.S. states. In addition, Carley-Baxter and colleagues (2010) found a 15 percent sharing rate among mobile-onlys and 11 percent among people who also have landline telephone access. People sharing their cell phones are more often married, of Hispanic origin and living in households with five members or more compared to respondents not sharing their cell phones (Tucker et al., 2007). Also, multi-person households were more prone to cell phone sharing than single-person households (Carley-Baxter et al., 2010).

The heterogeneity of cell phone sharing rates reported above results from differences in the populations studied but also from the absence of a joint definition for cell phone sharing. Link and colleagues (2007) for instance defined cell phone sharing as using the cell phone jointly for at least one-third of the time. Tucker and colleagues (2007) asked: "How many of the cell phone numbers are answered by more than one household member?" which does not define a quantitative threshold for joint usage, but implicates a restriction to household members. By contrast, Schneiderat and Schlinzig (2009b) required sharing partners to "always" use the cell phone jointly which yielded a sharing rate of 3 percent in the general cell phone population in Germany (Schneiderat & Schlinzig, 2009b).

In the 2010 recruitment study for the Experimental Mobile Phone Panel ($n = 1,579$; Fuchs, 2012a) we distinguished two types of cell phone sharing: Passive sharing occurs when a cell phone that is proprietary to the intended respondent is actually answered also by another person within or outside the household who may or may not have an own cell phone. Active sharing denotes a behavior where an intended respondent does not only answer incoming calls on his or her own cell phone but also on another person's cell phone. When combining the responses for the categories "always", "most of the time" and "seldom", 44 percent of respondents reported passive cell phone sharing and 46 percent active cell phone sharing.

In order to assess a potential bias due to sharing we compared sociodemographic characteristics for sharing and non-sharing respondents. We found active sharers to be younger, higher educated, more often currently not working and more often married. Respondents engaging in passive sharing only turned out to be less often employed and more often married.

Respondents reporting both types of cell phone sharing were significantly younger, more often not working, more often living in households with an income greater than €2,000 and more often married (see Busse & Fuchs, 2013). Over all, results were in line with Tucker and colleagues (2007) and suggested that neglecting the sharing population in cell phone surveys carries the potential for bias.

In an advanced discussion of cell phone sharing Wolter and colleagues (2010) state: "A cell-phone survey must work with and recognize the links that exist between the population of SUs [sampling units] and the population of RUs [reporting units = every eligible user of the contacted cell phone]" (p. 206). Consequently, it is necessary to adapt the fieldwork procedures of cell phone surveys in order to accommodate cell phone sharing. In line with this reasoning, Brick, Brick and colleagues (2007) suggested the implementation of a respondent selection procedure in cell phone surveys in case cell phone sharing occurs. However, any respondent selection procedure may cause additional response burden and potentially lead to higher refusal rates. Whether the reduced selection bias outweighs bias due to higher nonresponse when implementing a respondent selection procedure needs to be determined. In the meantime a correctional weighting factor accounting for active and passive cell phone sharing may be included in the design weighting of dual frame samples (Busse & Fuchs, 2011a).

5.4 NONRESPONSE

Over the course of the past decades declining response rates have severely affected survey quality (De Leeuw & de Heer, 2002; Groves, 2006; Groves & Peytcheva, 2008; Holbrook, Krosnick, & Pfent, 2008). Thus, high response rates are not to be expected in cell phone surveys. However, when assessing response rates in cell phone surveys in contrast to landline telephone surveys it is necessary to take a country-specific point of view, as there are differences in the cell phone payment plans across countries. In the U.S. cell phone surveys are known to yield lower response rates compared to landline telephone surveys (Link et al., 2007; Steeh, 2004) with refusals being the main source for nonresponse in cell phone surveys (Brick, Brick et al., 2007). One potential explanation for more refusals in the cell phone surveys could stem from the costs of the survey call for the respondent (in the U.S. the called party is also charged for a call). Only recently, Oldendick and Lambries (2011) argued that the emerging unlimited minute plans allow U.S. cell phone users to call and to receive calls on their cell phones at virtually no cost (Oldendick & Lambries, 2011). This change in payment plans might also be an explanation for the higher cell phone survey response rate reported by Carley-Baxter and colleagues (2010) in a recent study.

However, other factors also contribute to higher nonresponse in cell phone surveys. Kennedy (2010) examined response propensities in cell phone surveys with regard to mechanisms known from landline telephone surveys (e.g. social integration, civic engagement or interest in the survey topic) and mechanisms specifically related to cell phones (e.g. costs of the call, cell phone usage patterns or attendance of strangers). Results suggest that response propensities in cell phone surveys are considerably higher for frequent cell phone users and for mobile-onlys. Device related and social psychological factors influence cooperation rates, but not contact rates (Kennedy, 2010).

In Germany (where taking cell phone calls is free of charge for the called party) Schneiderat and Schlinzig (2009a) found higher response rates in the cell phone sample than in the landline sample in their 2008 dual frame telephone survey. The authors ascribe this to a so-called "novelty effect" since in 2008 cell phone surveys were rarely conducted in Germany. Thus, taking a survey on a cell phone might have appealed to respondents as new and interesting at that point in time. Nevertheless, it is arguable whether response rates will still be higher nowadays since German research institutes have adopted cell phone survey calls as a regular survey method and the German association of market research institutes has adopted dual frame surveys as a state-of-the-art method. Recent experiences in the Experimental Mobile Phone Panel (Fuchs, 2012a) suggest rather low response rates, similar to landline surveys.

However, high nonresponse rates do not necessarily imply a threat to data quality. The impact of nonresponse on nonresponse bias is only expected in case responding and nonresponding sample members differ significantly from each other with respect to the estimate considered (Groves, 2006; Heerwegh, Abts, & Loosveldt, 2007; Peytchev, Riley, Rosen, Murphy, & Lindblad, 2010).

To examine nonresponse bias in the Experimental Mobile Phone Panel, the "Basic Question Procedure" by Kersten and Bethlehem (1984) was implemented. In case of a refusal a few sociodemographic questions were asked: highest educational degree, employment status and year of birth. In addition, interviewers were advised to record the respondent's gender. In case interviewees refused to answer the basic questions (hard refusal), the interviewers estimated the age category (below age 40, age 40 to age 60, above age 60) and recorded the respondent's gender. This approach allowed us to distinguish between nonresponse bias arising from noncontact and nonresponse biases arising from refusals.

We calculated relative nonresponse bias for several stages of the contact process: (1) persons contacted as compared to the general cell phone population (impact of noncontact), (2) respondents who answered the basic questions compared to all contacted persons (impact of strict refusals), and (3) respondents who started the interview compared to respondents who answered the basic questions (impact of soft refusals). We found the most severe nonresponse bias stemmed from noncontact (see Table 5.2). Interestingly, the nonresponse bias components caused by noncontact and nonresponse of later stages counteract each other to a certain extent. For middle-aged and older respondents the nonresponse bias arising from noncontact is counteracted by the nonresponse bias of the following stage.

To further examine field procedures counteracting nonresponse in cell phone surveys an experiment was conducted in the fifth wave of the

TABLE 5.2

Stagewise observation of relative nonresponse bias (stage 1 to 3) in the Experimental Mobile Phone Panel recruitment study 2010

	General mobile phone population 2008 [%]	Contacted respondents (stage 1)	Respondents who answered the basic questions (stage 2)	Respondents who completed the interview (stage 3)
Gender				
Male	51	5.0*	7.6*	2.7
Female	49	−5.3*	−8.8*	−3.7
Age group				
< 40	37	13.4*	10.0*	−3.6
40–60	43	10.0*	−11.9*	3.2
> 60	20	−47.6*	14.7*	2.9
Employment status				
Working	60	n/a	27.9*	−0.1
Not working	40	n/a	−41.2*	0.3
Highest level of education				
Student	4	n/a	−66.2*	0.7
No exam	1	n/a	−54.2*	6.5
Primary school	26	n/a	−32.7*	−3.7
Secondary school	36	n/a	−3.9*	−1.8
High school entrance certificate	33	n/a	40.3*	2.7

Note: Calculated with data from the "Experimental Mobile Phone Panel"; χ^2-goodness of fit test compared to the previous stage.

Experimental Mobile Phone Panel. We tested the impact of sending text message announcements a few days prior to the beginning of the field phase and also the impact of sending prepaid incentives via text message a few minutes prior to the first contact attempt (a voucher that respondents could redeem at various popular online stores). Finally, we sent a text message to all nonrespondents after the end of the field phase providing a link to a mobile web questionnaire containing core questions from the survey instrument of wave five (Busse & Fuchs, 2011b).

Results suggested the effectiveness of the prepaid incentives. Survey cooperation was significantly increased and consequently also the response rate for this experimental subsample. The contact rate was not influenced by either the incentive or by the text message announcement. Further, the text message did not foster survey cooperation. Concerning the mode switch to a mobile web core questionnaire offered to nonrespondents, results were not encouraging. Of the group invited to complete the mobile web questionnaire only 5 percent accessed the questionnaire and 4 percent finished the survey.

5.5 MEASUREMENT

Even though cell phone surveys resemble landline telephone surveys with respect to several mode characteristics, differential measurement error differences in the administration of landline and mobile telephone surveys may have the potential to affect measurement error (Lynn & Kaminska, 2012). When calling respondents on their landline telephone they will be reached at home. Similarly, in cell phone surveys most respondents are also reached at home, however a considerable portion of respondents are away from home when answering the survey call. According to Kennedy (2010) 35 percent of cell phone respondents were not at home (see also Häder, Lehnhoff, & Mardian, 2010). Similarly, in the Experimental Mobile Phone Panel (Fuchs, 2012a) about one-third of respondents in the recruitment interviews as well as in the panel waves were not at home. While landline telephone surveys are answered at home, where only friends or relatives could listen to the answers, in cell phone interviews conducted in public places strangers can listen to (and judge) the respondents' answers, which may make respondents feel uncomfortable (Häder & Kühne, 2009; Kennedy, 2010; Lavrakas et al., 2007).

Also technical problems specific to cell phone interviews like consumed accumulators, insufficient network coverage or voice quality issues may affect data quality (Häder & Kühne, 2009; Kennedy, 2010; Tucker & Lepkowski, 2008). Finally, a cell phone is considered a personal device by some respondents (Lynn & Kaminska, 2012). For them a survey call on their cell phone may be considered an intrusion into their privacy, which has the potential to influence cooperation and the answers provided (Busse & Fuchs, 2011b).

However, so far there is little consistent evidence that these factors actually cause differential measurement error: While some studies suggest more pronounced social desirability distortion in cell phone surveys, others point in the opposite direction (Brick, Brick et al., 2007; Häder & Kühne, 2009). For attitude questions, some studies found significantly more positive responses (Häder & Kühne, 2009; Kennedy, 2010) while others did not (Kennedy & Everett, 2011). Also, Witt, ZuWallack, and Conrey (2009) found no significant differences in item nonresponse across the two telephone survey modes. Even though Kennedy (2010) as well as Häder and Kühne (2009) indicate slightly higher break-off rates in the cell phone surveys, there were no differences detected regarding response order effects (Kennedy, 2007; Häder & Kühne, 2009), response latency and scale effects (Häder & Kühne, 2009). Thus, Häder and Kühne (2009) as well as Kennedy (2010) conclude that responses in cell phone surveys are as reliable as in landline telephone surveys.

Over all, methodological research concerning cell phone surveys is still in its infancy—at least when compared to the decades of methods research on landline telephone surveys. Thus, more research is definitely needed.

NOTE

1. Further details concerning the methodology and the weighting procedures used to compensate for nonresponse error in the Eurobarometer data can be found in Busse and Fuchs (2012), where the contribution of no-phones and cell phones to the overall coverage error in landline telephone samples is assessed.

REFERENCES

AAPOR Cell Phone Task Force. (2010). *New considerations for survey researchers when planning and conducting RDD telephone surveys in the U.S.: With respondents reached via cell phone numbers.* American Association of Public Opinion Research.

Arthur, A. (2004). *Are landline phones losing ground?* New York, NY: Mediamark Research Inc.

Biemer, P., & Lyberg, L. (2003). *Introduction to survey quality.* Hoboken, NJ: Wiley.

Blumberg, S. J., & Luke, J. V. (2011). *Wireless substitution: Early release of estimates from the National Health Interview Survey, January 2007–June 2010.* National Center for Health Statistics.

Blumberg, S. J., Luke, J. V., Cynamon, M. L., & Frankel, M. R. (2008). Recent trends in household telephone coverage in the United States. In J. M. Lepkowski, C. Tucker, J. M. Brick, E. De Leeuw, L. Japec, P. J. Lavrakas, M. W. Link, & R. L. Sangster (Eds.), *Advances in telephone survey methodology* (pp. 56–86). Hoboken, NJ: Wiley.

Brick, J. M., Brick, P. D., Dipko, S., Presser, S., Tucker, C., & Yuan, Y. (2007). Cell phone survey feasibility in the U.S.: Sampling and calling cell numbers versus landline numbers. *Public Opinion Quarterly, 71*(1), 23–39.

Brick, J. M., Edwards, S. W., & Lee, S. (2007). Sampling telephone numbers and weighting in the California Health Interview Survey Cell Phone Pilot Study. *Public Opinion Quarterly, 71*(5), 793–813.

Brick, J. M., Judkins, D., Montaquila, J. M., & Morganstein, D. (2002). Two-phase list-assisted RDD Sampling. *Journal of Official Statistics, 18*(2), 203–215.

Brick, J. M., & Tucker, C. (2007). Mitofsky-Waksberg. Learning from the past. *Public Opinion Quarterly, 71*(5), 703–716.

Buskirk, T. D., Callegaro, M., & Rao, K. (2009). "N the Network?": Using internet resources for predicting cell phone number status. *Social Science Computer Review, 28*(3), 271–286.

Busse, B., & Fuchs, M. (2011a). *One cell phone = one person? Findings from two studies addressing consequences of cell phone sharing for sampling in cell phone surveys.* Paper presented at the NTTS Conferences on New Techniques and Technologies for Statistics in Brussels, Belgium.

Busse, B., & Fuchs, M. (2011b). *Panel attrition in a cell phone panel survey. Can incentives, text message announcements and switching to mobile web help?* Paper presented at the 2nd international PPSM conference in Bremen, Germany.

Busse, B., & Fuchs, M. (2012). The components of landline telephone survey coverage bias. The relative importance of no-phone and mobile only populations. *Quality & Quantity, 46*(4), 1209–1225.

Busse, B., & Fuchs, M. (2013). Prevalence of cell phone sharing. *Survey methods: Insights from the field,* 1–15. Retrieved from http://surveyinsights.org/?p=1019

Callegaro, M., Ayhan, O., Gabler, S., Häder, S., & Villar, A. (2011). *Combining landline and cell phone samples. A dual frame approach.* Mannheim: GESIS.

Callegaro, M., Steeh, C., Buskirk, T., Vehovar, V., Kuusela, V., & Piekarski, L. (2007). Fitting disposition codes to cell phone surveys: Experiences from studies in Finland, Slovenia, and the United States. *Journal of the Royal Statistical Society, Series A, 170*(3), 647–670.

Carley-Baxter, L., Peytchev, A., & Black, M. C. (2010). Comparison of cell phone and landline surveys: A design perspective. *Field Methods, 22*(1), 3–15.

Casady, R. J., & Lepkowski, J. M. (1993). Stratified telephone survey designs. *Survey methodology, 19*(1), 103–113.

Casady, R. J., & Lepkowski, J. M. (1999). Telephone sampling. In P.S. Levy, & S. Lemeshow (Eds.), *Sampling of populations: Methods and applications* (pp. 455–487). New York, NY: Wiley.

Christian L., Dimock, M., & Keeter, S. (2009). *Accurately locating where wireless respondents live requires more than a phone number.* Retrieved from http://pewresearch.org/pubs/1278/cell-phones-geographic-sampling-problems (2013.08.20).

De Leeuw, E. D., & De Heer, W. (2002). Trends in household survey nonresponse: A longitudinal and international comparison. In R. M. Groves, D. A. Dillman, J. L. Eltinge, & R.J.A. Little (Eds.), *Survey Nonresponse* (pp. 41–54). New York, NY: Wiley.

Ehlen, J., & Ehlen, P. (2007). Cellular-only substitution in the United States as lifestyle adoption. Implications for telephone survey coverage. *Public Opinion Quarterly, 71*(5), 717–733.

Fuchs, M. (2012a). *Nonresponse and panel attrition in a cell phone panel survey.* Paper presented at the Federal Committee on Statistical Methodology Research Conference in Washington, D.C.

Fuchs, M. (2012b). Der Einsatz von Mobiltelefonen in der Umfrageforschung. Methoden zur Verbesserung der Datenqualitaet. In F. Faulbaum, M. Stahl, & E. Wiegand (Eds.), *Qualitaetssicherung in der Umfrageforschung. Neue Herausforderungen fuer die Markt- und Sozialforschung* (pp. 51–73). Wiesbaden: Springer VS.

Gabler, S., & Ayhan, O. (2007). Gewichtung bei Erhebungen im Festnetz und ueber Mobilfunk: Ein Dual Frame Ansatz. *ZUMA Nachrichten Spezial, 13,* 39–46.

Gabler, S., & Häder, S. (1999). Erfahrungen bei Aufbau eines Auswahlrahmens für Telefonstichproben in Deutschland. *ZUMA Nachrichten, 44,* 45–61.

Gabler, S., & Häder, S. (2009). Die Kombination von Mobilfunk- und Festnetzstichproben in Deutschland. In M. Weichbold, J. Bacher, & C. Wolf (Eds.), *Umfrageforschung. Herausforderungen und Grenzen* (pp. 239–252). Meppel: Krips b.v.

Groves, R. M. (2006). Nonresponse rates and nonresponse bias in household surveys. *Public Opinion Quarterly, 70*(5), 646–675.

Groves, R. M., & Peytcheva, E. (2008). The impact of nonresponse rates on nonresponse bias. *Public Opinion Quarterly, 72*(2), 167–189.

Häder, S., Häder, M., & Kühne, M. (2012). *Telephone surveys in Europe. Research and practice.* Heidelberg: Springer.

Häder, M., & Kühne, M. (2009). Theoretischer Rahmen und Untersuchungsdesign. In M. Häder, & S. Häder (Eds.), *Telefonbefragungen ueber das Mobilfunknetz. Konzept, Design und Umsetzung einer Strategie zur Datenerhebung* (pp. 165–174). Wiesbaden: VS-Verlag.

Häder, S., Lehnhoff, I., & Mardian, E. (2010). Cell phone surveys: Empirical findings from a research project. *Ask – research & methods, 19*(1), 3–19.

Heerwegh, D., Abts, K., & Loosveldt, G. (2007). Minimizing survey refusal and noncontact rates: Do our efforts pay off? *Survey Research Methods, 1*(1), 3–10.

Holbrook, A. L., Krosnick, J. A., & Pfent, A. (2008). The causes and consequences of response rates in surveys by the news media and government contractor survey research firms. In J. M. Lepkowski, C. Tucker, J. M. Brick, E. D. De Leeuw, L. Japec, P. J. Lavrakas, M. W. Link, & R. L. Sangster (Eds.), *Advances in telephone survey methodology* (pp. 499–678). Hoboken, NJ: Wiley.

Kalsbeek, W. D., & Agans, R. P. (2008). Sampling and weighting in household telephone surveys. In J. M. Lepkowski, C. Tucker, J. M. Brick, E. De Leeuw, L. Japec, P. J. Lavrakas, M. W. Link, & R. L. Sangster (Eds.), *Advances in telephone survey methodology* (pp. 29–55). Hoboken, NJ: Wiley.

Keeter, S., Kennedy, C., Clark, A., Tompson, T., & Mokrzycki, M. (2007). What's missing from national landline RDD surveys?: The impact of the growing cell-only population. *Public Opinion Quarterly, 71*(5), 772–792.

Kennedy, C. (2007). *Assessing measurement error in landline and cell phone RDD surveys.* Paper presented at the conference of Midwest Association for Public Opinion Research in Chicago, Illinois.

Kennedy, C. (2010). *Nonresponse and measurement error in cell phone surveys.* Doctoral thesis, University of Michigan, Michigan.

Kennedy, C., & Everett, S. E. (2011). Use of cognitive shortcuts in landline and cell phone surveys. *Public Opinion Quarterly, 75*(2), 336–348.

Kersten, H.M.P., & Bethlehem, J. (1984). Exploring and reducing the nonresponse bias by asking the basic question. *Statistical Journal of the United Nations, 2*(4), 369–380.

Kim, S. W., & Lepkowski, J. M. (2002). *Telephone household non-coverage and mobile telephones.* Paper presented at the AAPOR conference in St. Pete Beach, Florida.

Kunz, T., & Fuchs, M. (2012). Improving RDD cell phone samples. Evaluation of different pre-call valication methods. *Journal of Official Statistics, 28*(3), 373–394.

Kuusela, V., Callegaro, M., & Vehovar, V. (2008). The influence of mobile telephones on telephone surveys. In J. M. Lepkowski, C. Tucker, J. M. Brick, E. De Leeuw, L. Japec, P. J. Lavrakas, M. W. Link, & R. L. Sangster (Eds.), *Advances in telephone survey methodology* (pp.87–112). Hoboken, NJ: Wiley.

Lavrakas, P. J., Steeh, C., Shuttles, C., & Fienberg, H. (2007). The state of surveying cell phone numbers in the United States: 2007 and beyond. *Public Opinion Quarterly, 71*(5), 840–854.

Link, M. W., Battaglia, M. P., Frankel, M., Osborn, L., & Mokdad, A. H. (2007). Reaching the U.S. cell phone generation. Comparison of cell phone survey results with an ongoing landline telephone survey. *Public Opinion Quarterly, 71*(5), 814–839.

Lynn, P., & Kaminska, O. (2012). Factors affecting measurement error in cell phone interviews. In S. Häder, M. Häder, & M. Kühne (Eds.), *Telephone surveys in Europe. Research and practice* (pp. 211–228). Heidelberg: Springer.

Mitofsky, W. (1970). *Sampling of telephone households.* Unpublished manuscript, New York.

Oldendick, R. W., & Lambries, D. M. (2011). *Incentives for cell only users: What difference do they make?* Survey Practice report. Retrieved from http://surveypractice.wordpress.com/2011/02/14/cell-phone-incentives/

Peytchev, A., Carley-Baxter, L. R., & Black, M. C. (2010). Coverage bias in variances, associations, and total error from exclusion of the cell phone only population in the United States. *Social Science Computer Review, 28*(3), 287–302.

Peytchev, A., Riley, S., Rosen, J., Murphy, J., & Lindblad, M. (2010). Reduction of nonresponse bias in surveys through case prioritization. *Survey Research Methods, 4*(1), 21–29.

Schneiderat, G., & Schlinzig, T. (2009a). Teilnahmebereitschaft und Teilnahmeverhalten bei Telefonumfragen in der Allgemeinbevoelkerung über das Mobilfunknetz. In M. Häder, & S. Häder (Eds.), *Telefonbefragungen ueber das Mobilfunknetz. Konzept, Design und Umsetzung einer Strategie zur Datenerhebung* (pp. 83–97). Wiesbaden, Germany: VS.

Schneiderat, G., & Schlinzig, T. (2009b). Der Pretest und Vorstudien. In M. Häder, & S. Häder (Eds.), *Telefonbefragungen über das Mobilfunknetz. Konzept, Design und Umsetzung einer Strategie zur Datenerhebung* (pp. 145–164). Wiesbaden, Germany: VS.

Steeh, C. (2004). *A new era for telephone surveys.* Paper presented at the AAPOR conference in Phoenix, Arizona.

Struminskaya, B., Kaczmirek, L., Schaurer, I., Bandilla, W., Gabler, S., & Häder, S. (2011). Identifying non-working numbers in cell phone RDD samples via HLR-Lookup technology. *Survey Practice, 4*(4).

Tucker, C., Brick, J. M., & Meekins, B. (2007). Household telephone service and usage patterns in the United States in 2004: Implications for telephone samples. *Public Opinion Quarterly, 71*(1), 3–22.

Tucker, C., & Lepkowski, J. M. (2008). Telephone survey methods: adapting to change. In J. M. Lepkowski, C. Tucker, J. M. Brick, E. D. De Leeuw, L. Japec, P. J. Lavrakas, M. W. Link, & R. L. Sangster (Eds.), *Advances in telephone survey methodology* (pp. 3–26). Hoboken, NJ: Wiley.

Waksberg, J. (1978). Sampling methods for random digit dialing. *Journal of the American Statistical Association, 73*(361), 40–46.

Witt, L., ZuWallack, R., & Conrey, F. (2009). *Out and About: An evaluation of data quality in cell phone surveys.* Paper presented at the AAPOR conference in Hollywood, Florida.

Wolter, K. M., Smith, P., & Blumberg, S. J. (2010). Statistical foundations of cell-phone surveys. *Survey Methodology, 36*(2), 203–215.

Part II

Interviewers and Survey Error

6

Interviewers and Survey Error

Overview and Introduction

Patrick Sturgis

Despite the recent advent of a diverse range of technological innovations which have transformed the options available to survey designers, face-to-face interviews are still considered the gold standard for the conduct of random household sample surveys. This is because they generally achieve considerably higher contact and cooperation rates compared to other modes, as well as providing greater control over respondent selection, yielding a concomitantly lower risk of nonresponse bias in survey estimates. Face-to-face interview surveys are also able to collect more, and more complex, information from respondents with, as a general rule, lower levels of measurement error than self-completion and other interview modes. All of these desirable features can be attributed to the input of survey interviewers, who act as the key intermediaries between survey designers and sampled households (Campanelli, Sturgis, & Purdon, 1997).

Interviewers have been shown to deploy a range of skills, attributes, and abilities to locate and contact household members, persuade sampled individuals to provide an interview, read questions, present show cards and other accompanying materials, and answer respondent queries and requests for clarification (Groves & Couper, 1998). It is ironic, then, that these very features—which give face-to-face interviews their superior edge over alternative modes—are also the source of various kinds of random and systematic errors. Understanding how these errors emanate from the behavior and characteristics of interviewers is, therefore, an important focus of methodological investigation, because it enables the development and implementation of strategies to mitigate them and, thereby, increase the quality of survey outputs. The chapters in this section focus on two very different kinds of interviewer-induced error; one which can be characterized as unintentional on the part of interviewers, the other quite deliberate.

In their chapter, Turner, Sturgis, Martin, and Skinner address the question of how interviewers' behavior during the interview can affect the efficiency of survey estimates. These kinds of interviewer-induced measurement errors are thought to arise through interviewers diverting from the questions as they are written, not following the interviewer instructions (relating, for example, to probing and show cards), and 'helping' respondents to understand and formulate responses to difficult questions (Kish, 1962; Schnell & Kreuter, 2005). Although these practices will generally result in systematic differences between the true population value and the survey estimate, in the vast majority of cases external criteria are not available to allow their characterization as biases in this manner. It is more straightforward, however, to determine the combined effects of these idiosyncrasies of individual interviewer behavior on the precision of estimates.

Because each interviewer will tend to divert from standardized procedures in the same way over repeated interviews (e.g. he or she always provides the same clarification for an ambiguously worded question), the end result is an increase in within-interviewer homogeneity of responses (Mahalanobis, 1946). This introduces an additional source of variability into the population estimator, resulting in larger standard errors. Existing studies have been inconclusive about the cause of this kind of interviewer effect, with some contending that it results from differential nonresponse bias across interviewer assignments (West & Olson, 2010). Turner and colleagues employ data from a survey of interviewers linked to face-to-face interview data to assess whether and to what extent interviewer characteristics such as personality, attitudes toward interviewing, and experience are related to the magnitude of interviewer variance. They find that although these characteristics appear to influence the size of the interviewer variance component, the effects are generally rather small and do not produce a compelling overall pattern which fits prior expectations regarding the likely direction of effects.

While the errors which form the focus of Turner et al.'s chapter are essentially unintentional on the part of interviewers, the chapter of Menold, Winker, Storfinder, and Bredl focuses on situations where interviewers deliberately fabricate survey data. Although it is believed that such behavior is rare in high quality household surveys, it is clear that even a small proportion of fabricated data can have a strong detrimental effect on the accuracy of survey estimates.

The primary means of detecting (and deterring) interviewer fabrication is for the survey agency to call back on a sample of households that are recorded as having provided interviews to check that an interview was indeed conducted. However, unless a large sample of interviewed households is checked in this way, this strategy is prone to a high false-negative rate. And large samples are, of course, expensive. In their chapter, Menold and colleagues propose a new multivariate indicator method for detecting likely fabrications based on the substantive content and statistical properties of real and fabricated data. The proposed method can be used for more efficient selection of cases to call back on, increasing the frequency with which fabricated cases are identified at considerably lower cost.

Although more and more surveys are now being conducted online, a trend which is sure to continue and grow in the future, face-to-face interview surveys will remain the core mode by which high quality random surveys are undertaken for some considerable time yet. It is, therefore, essential that the survey research community continues to investigate how interviewer characteristics and behavior are related to the accuracy of survey estimates. The chapters in this section make important contributions to this endeavor.

REFERENCES

Campanelli, P., Sturgis, P., & Purdon, S. (1997). *Can you hear me knocking: An investigation into the impact of interviewers on survey response rates.* London: S.C.P.R.

Groves, R. M., & Couper, M. P. (1998). *Nonresponse in household interview surveys.* New York: Wiley.

Kish, L. (1962). Studies of interviewer variance for attitudinal variables. *Journal of the American Statistical Association, 57*(297), 92–115.

Mahalanobis, P. C. (1946). Recent experiments in statistical sampling in the Indian Statistical Institute. *Journal of the Royal Statistics Society, 109,* 325–378.

Schnell, R., & Kreuter, F. (2005). Separating interviewer and sampling point effects. *Journal of Official Statistics, 21*(3), 389–410.

West, B. T., & Olson, K. (2010). How much of interviewer variance is really nonresponse error variance? *Public Opinion Quarterly, 74*(5), 1004–1026.

7

Can Interviewer Personality, Attitudes and Experience Explain the Design Effect in Face-to-Face Surveys?

Malgorzata Turner, Patrick Sturgis, David Martin and Chris Skinner

7.1 INTRODUCTION

This chapter is concerned with improving our understanding of the effect that interviewers have on the variance of survey estimates. This so-called 'interviewer effect' is believed to arise through idiosyncrasies in the way that interviewers administer questionnaires. For instance, an interviewer may always make the same mistake in reading a particular question, or they may 'help' respondents to understand an unclear or ambiguous question, while other interviewers do not. These behavioral tendencies induce a dependency between responses within interviewers, which manifests in the form of larger standard errors for population inference (Hansen, Hurwitz, Marks, & Maurdlin, 1951; Kish, 1962). However, there is as yet little in the way of direct evidence to support the contention that the effect arises as the result of interviewer behavior. Some scholars have argued that the apparent interviewer effect is actually a result of differential nonresponse across interviewer assignments (West & Olson, 2010). That is to say, variance estimates differ across interviewers because the groups of people they have interviewed are actually different (due to nonresponse), rather than because of the way they were interviewed. We contribute to the body of evidence in this area by assessing whether psychological characteristics of interviewers, such as attitudes, personality, job experience and job satisfaction are related to the magnitude of the interviewer variance component. If they are, we can be more confident that interviewers are, at least in part, the cause of the interviewer variance component. This, in turn, has implications for improving survey practice. The chapter is structured as follows. The first section describes in more detail the ways in which interviewers are thought to contribute to the survey design effect and how this quantity can be calculated. This is followed by a description of the data, the measures to be used and the analysis strategy. The results are then set out and we conclude with a consideration of the implications of our findings for survey practice.

7.2 THE INTERVIEWER DESIGN EFFECT

The term 'design effect' (DEFF) refers to the part of the variance of survey estimates which arises as a result of complex design features such as stratification and clustering (Kish, 1965). Complex designs generally result in standard errors which are different from what would be obtained using a simple random sample (SRS) of the same size (Heeringa & Liu, 1998). Clustering, or multistage sampling, generally results in larger variances than would be obtained in a simple random sample of the same size, because individuals living in the same geographical area tend to be more similar to one another than are individuals in the general population. This internal homogeneity gives rise to a design effect, because we underestimate the true magnitude of population variance in survey outcomes. The design effect due to clustering can be expressed as:

$$DEFF_{cluster} = 1 + \rho_{cluster}(m - 1) \tag{7.1}$$

where $\rho_{cluster}$ or '*rho*' is the intra-class correlation coefficient and m is the average number of units within the primary sampling units (PSU). For a binary variable, *rho* is equivalent to the probability that two randomly drawn units from the same cluster will have the same value. An implication of equation 7.1 is that the design effect will be smaller as the number of within-cluster units approaches zero, holding *rho* constant. By the same token, however, if the number of within cluster units is large, the design effect could be substantial, even for small values of *rho* (Sturgis, 2004). Although the design effect due to clustering usually relates to geographical clusters, it applies equally to any situation in which observations made on lower level units are not independent within higher level units. A common situation which gives rise to this type of hierarchical dependence is when respondents are clustered within interviewers.

Research into the interviewer design effect to date has focused primarily on how different types of question may be differentially prone to interviewer effects (O'Muircheartaigh & Campanelli, 1998; Davis & Scott 1995; Schnell & Kreuter, 2005). These studies have found that questions which require more input from the interviewer, such as the use of show-cards and probing, are prone to larger interviewer effects. Additionally, sensitive questions, nonfactual questions and open questions appear to be more prone to interviewer effects. Existing research has also examined the effect of interviewer characteristics on the magnitude of the design effect. These studies have tended to focus on easily observable demographic characteristics such as gender and age (Hox, 1994; Pickery, Loosveldt, & Carton, 2001) which are often available on administrative databases. These studies have found that demographic characteristics do appear to be predictive of interviewer variance. For instance, O'Muircheartaigh and Campanelli (1998) found interviewer age and gender to be significant predictors of the magnitude of interviewer variance for a number of survey outcomes. Davis and Scott (1995) found a significant association for interviewer gender and ethnicity. Brunton-Smith, Sturgis, and Williams (2012) found that other measures of interviewing skill seem to be important, with interviewers possessing the poorest response rate records also having the largest variance components across a range of survey outcomes. These authors concluded that this association arises due to a common underlying cause and speculated that the common cause is likely to derive from psychological characteristics of interviewers, such as attitudes, personality and beliefs. For example, interviewers who score highly on the 'conscientiousness' personality dimension may stick more rigidly to the questionnaire script and instructions, thereby producing smaller within-interviewer correlations on survey outcomes. However, while interviewer personality and beliefs are pointed to as the underlying causal factor, these authors were not able to assess this empirically because they did not have access to measures of psychological variables in their data. The study presented here addresses this shortcoming by making use of measures of interviewer personality, attitudes and beliefs to assess whether these variables are associated with the magnitude of the interviewer effect.

7.3 DATA

Our analyses are based on the National Travel Survey (NTS) of Great Britain. The NTS covers the whole of Great Britain[1] but the dataset used in this study is limited to cases for England only, because the area-level information that we include as controls in the statistical models is not collected consistently across the constituent countries. The NTS employs a multistage, stratified sample design with continuous data collection via CAPI. The dataset we use combines seven years of NTS data (2002–2008). The continuous nature of the data collection produces a 'natural' cross-classification of interviewers and primary sampling units (PSU), because interviewers work in different PSUs over the course of the year and from one year to the next. The NTS data were linked to the Middle Super Output Area (MSOA) level of UK neighborhood statistics (Martin, 2001). Information about the characteristics of MSOAs was then linked from the 2001 census. Data on interviewers comes from two different sources. The first is administrative information held by the data collection agency (NatCen) such as age, gender and an indicator of which NTS administrations the interviewer had worked on. The second is a survey of all NatCen interviewers which was conducted in 2008. The dataset contains 40,244 cases at the household level and 70,645 cases at the individual level. Analysis samples are sometimes smaller than this because not all interviewers who worked on the NTS between 2002 and 2008 took part in the interviewer survey and also because some questions were only administered to a random subset of the sample.

7.4 MEASURES

Thirteen survey variables were selected for decomposition of the interviewer effect by observed interviewer characteristics. These questions require respondents to assess how long (in minutes) it would take to: walk to the nearest bus stop; walk to the nearest tube/metro; walk to the nearest railway station; get to the nearest railway station by bus; and how long the most recent walk the respondent had done took to complete. They also ask them to rate: the provision of cycle lanes; the condition of pavements; satisfaction with bus services; reliability of bus services; frequency of local bus services; reliability of the tube/metro; and frequency of the tube/metro.

The variance in these thirteen items was partitioned across six different measures of interviewer characteristics. These were:

1. Experience of working on the NTS;
2. Level of reported satisfaction with pay;
3. Attitude to accepting a refusal from potential respondents;

4. Score on a measure of communication skills;
5. Score on a (shortened) measure of the 'conscientiousness' dimension of the Big Five personality inventory; and
6. Score on a (shortened) measure of the 'extroversion' dimension of the Big Five personality inventory (Goldberg, 1990).

Interviewers were divided into either two (attitude to refusal, satisfaction with pay) or four (NTS experience, communication skills, conscientiousness and extroversion) approximately equal-sized groups on each of the six characteristics, because the modeling strategy we employ requires categorical measures in order to partition the interviewer variance component.

Existing theory regarding how these characteristics might influence the magnitude of interviewer variance is not sufficiently well developed to set out clear *a priori* hypotheses. However, our expectation is that larger interviewer variance components will be found in subgroups which: have less experience of working on the NTS, are less satisfied with their pay, are more willing to accept a refusal from reluctant respondents, have worse communication skills, are less conscientious and are more extroverted.

7.5 ANALYSIS

Estimation of the interviewer effect in face-to-face surveys generally faces a major obstacle: It is standard in most sample designs for a single interviewer to be allocated to a particular area/PSU. Where this is the case, it is not possible to partition the design effect into its area and interviewer components because the two are completely confounded. One way of overcoming this problem is to use an interpenetrated sample design, in which respondents are randomly assigned to interviewers (Mahalanobis, 1946). However, this is expensive and complex to implement and can be criticized for lacking generality to standard survey contexts. A more tractable approach is to use a sample design which provides a 'natural' overlap between interviewers and areas over time, in conjunction with statistical control to account for non-random allocation of respondents to interviewers (Hox, 1994). This is the approach that we adopt here. As we noted in the data description section, the NTS provides a natural crossing of interviewers and areas over time due to the continuous nature of its data collection. Following

Brunton-Smith et al. (2012), we use a cross-classified multilevel model with complex level 2 variance terms. The cross-classified model is appropriate when lower level units are nested within more than one classification at the same, higher level. The cross-classified model can be extended to incorporate random effects for a higher level variable in a hierarchically nested model (Goldstein, 2003). In the context of survey design effects, this allows estimation of the area and interviewer effects, and also partitioning of the interviewer effect as a function of measured interviewer characteristics. The model has the form:

$$y_{i(j,k)} = \alpha + u_j + v_k + e_{i(j,k)} \tag{7.2}$$

where $y_{i(j,k)}$ is a response on item y of the ith respondent in the j/k^{th} interviewer combination expressed as the sample mean value α, two random error terms express the area (u_j) and interviewer effect (v_k) and the respondent-specific residual, $e_{i(j,k)}$. These error terms are assumed to be independent and identically distributed (IID) with zero means and variances σj^2, σk^2 and $\sigma^2_{i(j,k)}$. The model in equation (7.2) can be easily extended to include covariates at the respondent, interviewer and area levels in order to control for differences in the sample composition between interviewers. The interviewer variance component can be expressed as:

$$\rho_{int} = \frac{\sigma^2_k}{\sigma^2_j + \sigma^2_k + \sigma^2_{i(j,k)}} \tag{7.3}$$

The null model with a complex level 2 variance term partitions σ^2_{0k} between two (or more) mutually exclusive interviewer groups. For example, if we wish to estimate the interviewer variance separately for groups defined by their score on a binary variable x, the model takes the form:

$$y_{i(j,k)} = \alpha + u_j + v_{1k} x = 1_k + v_{2k} x = 2_k + e_{i(j,k)} \tag{7.4}$$

Then the interviewer variance for the two groups can be expressed as the variance-covariance diagonal matrix Ωv:

$$\begin{bmatrix} v_{1k} \\ v_{2k} \end{bmatrix} \sim N(0, \Omega_v) : \Omega_v = \begin{bmatrix} \sigma^2_{1k} & 0 \\ 0 & \sigma^2_{2k} \end{bmatrix} \tag{7.5}$$

where σ^2_{1k} is the interviewer variance for interviewers for whom $x = 1$ and σ^2_{2k} is the interviewer variance for interviewers for whom $x = 2$. The covariances in equation (7.5) are set to 0 because the interviewer groups are mutually exclusive. All models were estimated using MLwiN version 2.13 using the Monte Carlo Markov Chain (MCMC) estimator (Rasbash, Steele, Browne, & Goldstein, 2009).

A range of respondent and area-level covariates were included as fixed effects to control for differences in sample composition across interviewer assignments. The respondent covariates were: age, gender, employment status, marital status and ethnicity and the interviewer covariates were gender and age. Area-level controls were included by linking a range of socioeconomic measures of areas (MSOA) from the 2001 census (see Brunton-Smith, 2008).

7.6 RESULTS

Unconditional variance components models revealed that, for all thirteen items the interviewer effect is greater than 0 although considerably smaller than the area component. This contrasts with previous studies (e.g. O'Muircheartaigh & Campanelli, 1998) which found the interviewer contribution to be relatively larger and is likely to be a result of the focus of the NTS on local travel conditions and amenities which are strongly area-dependent. Across the thirteen items, interviewers were responsible for an average of 4.6% of the total design effect. Similar values for the proportion of interviewer-related variance were reported by Lipps (2007) and Brunton-Smith et al. (2012). When covariates were included, the interviewer and area variance components decreased, although, as we would expect, the interviewer-related variance was less affected than the area variance following the introduction of area-level controls. The next step was to include random effects for the interviewer characteristic variables. Limitations of space mean that it is not possible to present the full set of parameter estimates for all thirteen survey outcomes by each interviewer characteristic. Instead, by way of illustration, we present the full model for a single variable, 'railway station' (time taken to walk to the nearest station), in Table 7.1. Summary statistics of key parameters for the full models are presented in Table 7.2.

The results of Model 1 in Table 7.1 show that, across all interviewers, the interviewer variance component is 8.651, which is significantly different from 0 at the 99% level of confidence. This equates to an intra-interviewer correlation of 1.85%. Introduction of the interviewer level random effects in Model 2 shows that this breaks down as variances of 13.098 for those

TABLE 7.1

Cross-classified multilevel model with level 2 random effects for the 'railway station' variable by the 'satisfaction with pay' interviewer-level variable

	Model 1 (random intercept)	Model 2 (with complex level 2 variance)
Interviewer variance (σ^2_k)	8.651 (1.209)	
satisfied with pay (σ^2_{1k})		4.955 (1.123)
not satisfied with pay (σ^2_{2k})		13.098 (2.144)
Area variance (σ^2_j)	303.756 (8.489)	303.806 (8.269)
Residual variance ($\sigma^2_{i(j,k)}$)	167.965 (1.435)	167.955 (1.433)
Intra-interviewer correlation	1.8%	
satisfied with pay		1%
not satisfied with pay		2.7%
DIC	259940	259928
Interviewers	398	398
MSOA	3603	3603
Respondents	32223	32223

Note: Models include area and respondent covariates.

who are not satisfied with their pay and 4.955 for those who are satisfied with their pay. Expressed as intra-interviewer correlations, Model 2 shows that interviewers who are satisfied with their pay contribute 1% of the total variance for this item while for those who are not satisfied with their pay the corresponding figure is 2.7%. In absolute terms, then, this represents a small difference. However, using equation (7.1) which takes account of the number of within-cluster units, and assuming an average annual workload of fifteen achieved interviews, we can see that interviewers who are satisfied with their pay produce a 14% increase in the variance for this item, compared to a 38% increase for dissatisfied interviewers.

Turning now to the overall pattern of results, Table 7.2 presents the intra-interviewer correlations for all groups defined by the six observed interviewer characteristics. Across all thirteen items, interviewers who are satisfied with their pay contribute an average of 3.5%, while those who are not satisfied introduce an average of 4.7% of the total variance. On nine items, interviewers who were not satisfied with their pay introduced more variance than their counterparts, which suggests that the general pattern is for less satisfied interviewers to introduce more variability, as expected. This overall pattern is, however, rather variable across the thirteen items,

TABLE 7.2

Intra-interviewer correlations for thirteen NTS items (columns) by six interviewer characteristics (rows)

Interviewer characteristics	station by bus	tube by bus	bus stop bus	tube	railway	walk	bus frequency	bus reliability	cycle lanes	pavements	bus provision	tube reliability	tube frequency	mean
satisfaction with pay														
satisfied	4.2%	6.9%	0.6%	2.5%	1.0%	1.8%	4.5%	2.8%	4.6%	4.0%	2.8%	4.5%	5.8%	3.5%
not satisfied	4.6%	12.0%	0.1%	1.9%	2.7%	2.1%	3.6%	4.0%	10.2%	3.0%	3.0%	6.2%	8.2%	4.7%
experience on survey														
1 administration	0.9%	6.8%	0.0%	3.5%	0.1%	2.7%	3.6%	7.6%	9.1%	9.6%	7.6%	7.8%	10.8%	5.4%
2 to 3	6.5%	4.0%	0.1%	1.0%	3.6%	2.0%	4.5%	4.8%	13.4%	1.1%	2.6%	7.9%	12.0%	4.9%
4 to 5	5.4%	18.3%	0.1%	28.9%	1.8%	2.4%	4.8%	3.5%	7.8%	7.2%	2.9%	4.6%	4.6%	7.1%
6 + administrations	3.0%	12.2%	6.0%	2.8%	1.1%	1.5%	3.4%	2.5%	6.1%	3.1%	2.6%	3.9%	5.2%	4.1%
attitude to accepting refusal														
more willing	6.7%	11.2%	0.5%	2.5%	1.0%	2.0%	4.0%	3.8%	10.3%	4.8%	3.2%	5.1%	7.1%	4.8%
less willing	2.8%	6.6%	0.2%	1.5%	2.6%	2.0%	4.2%	3.2%	4.5%	2.4%	2.8%	5.6%	7.1%	3.5%
communication skills														
poor	6.7%	14.8%	0.0%	0.4%	1.5%	1.9%	4.2%	4.2%	7.7%	4.5%	1.6%	4.2%	7.3%	4.5%
average	4.0%	8.4%	0.3%	3.3%	1.1%	2.2%	3.7%	2.4%	13.5%	5.3%	2.1%	3.4%	6.3%	4.3%
good	4.0%	17.0%	0.1%	8.0%	1.5%	2.0%	5.3%	5.0%	2.0%	3.3%	4.6%	8.6%	7.9%	5.3%
very good	2.8%	2.8%	0.7%	0.7%	3.2%	1.7%	3.7%	2.4%	5.8%	2.1%	3.2%	5.8%	6.7%	3.2%
conscientiousness														
1 = low	12.6%	3.2%	0.4%	1.3%	14.5%	1.3%	4.3%	3.4%	4.8%	1.9%	2.4%	6.5%	9.2%	5.1%
2	5.7%	17.6%	0.7%	12.0%	3.6%	2.1%	3.8%	4.0%	1.9%	1.1%	4.1%	3.2%	4.3%	4.9%
3	7.6%	12.5%	0.4%	1.4%	4.1%	1.6%	3.5%	1.6%	12.3%	5.2%	1.9%	3.4%	7.4%	4.8%
4 = high	11.1%	12.9%	0.1%	6.3%	7.6%	1.9%	4.9%	4.3%	8.8%	6.3%	3.4%	7.3%	5.5%	6.2%
extroversion														
1 = low	12.4%	13.2%	0.7%	0.9%	7.9%	2.3%	3.1%	3.2%	6.2%	4.2%	2.3%	5.2%	8.2%	5.4%
2	12.2%	13.7%	0.8%	4.1%	5.3%	1.1%	6.0%	2.4%	10.3%	7.4%	1.8%	5.5%	6.0%	5.9%
3	6.1%	18.0%	0.2%	10.5%	6.5%	1.7%	3.2%	4.2%	11.5%	0.9%	2.5%	5.3%	7.2%	6.0%
4 = high	7.1%	3.1%	0.1%	7.8%	8.8%	2.0%	4.4%	4.4%	1.1%	2.7%	4.3%	4.9%	5.6%	4.3%

with several showing no real difference and others revealing a more substantial divergence. There is a particularly large differential between groups for the 'tube station by bus' variable; those who are not satisfied with their pay introduce twice as much variance (12%) for this question compared to interviewers who are satisfied with their pay (6.9%). For dissatisfied interviewers, this equates to a substantial (168%) increase in the variance for this item (for an annual estimate, assuming an average workload of fifteen interviews).

For the measure of prior experience working on the NTS, the most experienced group does, as expected, have the lowest average intra-interviewer correlation across the thirteen items, although this is only by a small amount and the group with the largest contribution is those with the second highest number (4–5) of previous NTS administrations. As with the satisfaction with pay measure, the magnitude of the difference is highly variable across items, with no clear pattern in the rank ordering across experience groups. Thus, although there is evidence that the interviewer contribution to the variance of these items does vary according to previous experience of working on the survey, it is not reasonable to conclude that greater experience results in less response variability. On the attitudinal variables the pattern is somewhat clearer and in line with theoretical expectations; interviewers who are less willing to accept a refusal and who rate themselves as having better communication skills have lower mean values of *rho* across the thirteen items. On eight items, interviewers who are less willing to accept a refusal have a lower value of *rho*, although on only one item (provision of cycle lanes in local area) is the difference particularly notable. Similarly, on eight items interviewers with the best communication skills have a lower value of *rho* than those with the poorest self-rated communication skills.

For the two personality measures, no clear patterns emerge and no support is found for the *a priori* expectations. Indeed, interviewers with the highest scores on the conscientiousness dimension have the highest mean value of *rho*, while those with the highest score on extroversion have the lowest value of *rho*, across the thirteen items, which is in the opposite direction to what we anticipated at the outset. However, these average figures cover a large degree of heterogeneity in the direction and magnitude of differences between groups and across items. For these items on these dimensions, there is little evidence to suggest that interviewer personality makes an important contribution to the interviewer variance component.

Overall, these findings exhibit a pattern which is consistent with that observed by Brunton-Smith et al. (2012), who found that the magnitude of the difference in the interviewer variance component across interviewer groups (defined by historical level of success in achieving contact and cooperation) varied substantially over the survey variables considered, although with a notable minority of items revealing substantial differences.

7.7 CONCLUSIONS

It has long been acknowledged that interviewers are an important source of error in surveys. Although the majority of recent research attention has focused on the role of interviewers in the generation of nonresponse bias, researchers have also begun to focus in greater detail on the mechanisms which underpin the interviewer contribution to response variance. Interviewers are thought to increase the variance of survey estimators through idiosyncrasies in the way that they administer questions which, when combined across the total pool of interviewers, manifests in the form of a within-interviewer dependency in survey outcomes. While there is a good deal of evidence to suggest that this intra-interviewer correlation (*rho*) is caused by interviewers departing in various ways from the standardized interview protocol, it is also possible that at least part of this phenomenon is due to differential nonresponse across interviewer assignments (West & Olson, 2010). Because these different potential sources of the same error have rather contrasting implications for how survey managers might seek to reduce it, it is important that researchers come to a better understanding of exactly how these errors do in fact arise. This has been the objective of the present chapter. We have sought to shed additional light on the question of how interviewer-related response variance arises by evaluating the degree to which it varies across a range of more psychologically oriented interviewer characteristics. The rationale underpinning our approach is that we should expect the idiosyncratic behaviors which are thought to result in interviewer-related response variance to themselves be caused by deeper-seated psychological dispositions such as attitudes, personality and beliefs.

While several studies have evaluated the effect of interviewer characteristics on survey outcomes, these have tended to focus on a limited range of demographic characteristics such as age and gender. Additionally, they have mostly estimated the effect of these characteristics on the mean, rather than the variance of survey outcomes. In this study, we have evaluated the extent to which the interviewer variance component differs across a range of more psychologically oriented measures of interviewer characteristics, including survey experience, satisfaction with pay, attitudes toward interviewing, self-rated communication skills and two dimensions of the Big Five personality inventory. Our results show that, across the thirteen survey outcomes considered, a significant interviewer contribution to response variance was evident. The average magnitude of this effect, at 4.6%, is consistent with the findings of existing studies (Lipps, 2007; Brunton-Smith et al., 2012). We also found that the magnitude of the intra-interviewer correlation varied as a function of the interviewer characteristics, sometimes substantially. For instance, interviewers with between four and five previous NTS administrations had a *rho* value of 28.9% on one item, compared to an average of 2.4% for interviewers with different levels of experience on the survey. On another item, interviewers with the lowest score on the conscientiousness personality dimension had a *rho* value of 14.5% compared with an average of 5.1% for the remaining interviewers. However, such large effects were an exception to the more general pattern of small or no differences between interviewer groups. Furthermore, although there was some evidence that the magnitude of *rho* tended to be higher for certain interviewer characteristics, such as for interviewers who were less satisfied with their pay, this evidence was generally quite weak and it was difficult to detect any clear or consistent pattern to explain between-group differences where they did emerge.

This pattern of weak findings is consistent with those of other studies which have used measures of interviewer attitudes and personality to predict success in obtaining contact and cooperation (Groves & Couper, 1998; Jäckle, Lynn, Sinibaldi, & Tipping, 2011). However, before concluding that psychological variables of this type are not important in the generation of survey errors, it should be acknowledged that these measures are based on single items or shortened versions of larger batteries and are, therefore, likely to be subject to attenuation due to random error when they are used as predictors in statistical models. Another limitation to the robustness of our findings here is the rather limited range and quite specific substantive focus of the survey questions we have examined. In other words, the NTS questions focus on rather mundane matters of transport infrastructure and may not be particularly susceptible to personality-related interviewer effects while questions of a more personal and sensitive nature are. These speculations point toward some potentially fruitful avenues for future research in this important area.

NOTE

1. Excluding Scottish Islands and Isles of Scilly (2.2% of GB addresses).

BIBLIOGRAPHY

Brunton-Smith, I. (2008). *Local areas and fear of criminal victimization: Applying multilevel models to the British Crime Survey.* University of Surrey.

Brunton-Smith, I., Sturgis, P., & Williams, J. (2012). Is success in obtaining contact and cooperation correlated with the magnitude of interviewer variance? *Public Opinion Quarterly, 76*(2), 265–286. doi:10.1093/poq/nfr067

Davis, P., & Scott, A. (1995). The effect of interviewer variance on domain comparisons. *Survey Methodology, 21*(2), 99–106.

Goldberg, L. (1990). An alternative "description of personality": The big-five factor structure. *Journal of Personality and Social Psychology, 59*(6), 1216–29.

Goldstein, H. (2003). *Multilevel statistical models.* London: Edward Arnold.

Groves, R., & Couper, M. (1998). *Nonresponse in household interview surveys. Wiley series in probability and statistics. Survey methodology section.* New York, Chichester: Wiley.

Groves, R. M. (2004a). *Survey methodology (Wiley series in survey methodology)* (pp. xix, 424). Hoboken, NJ: Wiley. Retrieved from www.loc.gov/catdir/toc/wiley041/2004044064.html

Groves, R. M. (2004b). *Survey errors and survey costs* (pp. xxi, 590). New Jersey: Wiley.

Groves, R. M., & Heeringa, S. G. (2006). Responsive design for household surveys: Tool for actively controlling survey errors and costs. *Journal of the Royal Statistical Society: Series A (Statistics in Society), 169*(3), 439–457.

Hansen, M., Hurwitz, W., Marks, E., & Maurdlin, P. (1951). Response errors in surveys. *Journal of the American Statistical Association, 46*(254), 147–190.

Heeringa, S. G., & Liu, J. (1998). Complex sample design effects and inference in mental health survey data. *International Journal of Methods in Psychiatric Research, 7*(1), 56–65.

Hox, J. (1994). Hierarchical regression models for interviewer and respondent effects. *Sociological Methods and Research, 22*(3), 300–318.

Jäckle, A., Lynn, P., Sinibaldi, J., & Tipping, S. (2011). The effect of interviewer personality, skills and attitudes on respondent co-operation with face-to-face surveys. *Survey Research Methods, 7*(1), 1–15.

Kish, L. (1962). Studies of interviewer variance for attitudinal variables. *Journal of the American Statistical Association, 57*, 92–115.

Kish, L. (1965). *Survey Sampling.* New York: Wiley.

Lipps, O. (2007). Interviewer and respondent survey quality effects in a CATI Panel. *Bulletin de Méthodologie Sociologique, 95*(1), 5–25.

Mahalanobis, P. C. (1946). Recent experiments in statistical sampling in the Indian Statistical Institute. *Journal of the Royal Statistics Society, 109*, 325–378.

Martin, D. (2001). *Geography for the 2001 Census in England and Wales.* Department of Geography. University of Southampton.

O'Muircheartaigh, C., & Campanelli, P. (1998). The relative impact of interviewer effects and sample design effects on survey precision. *Journal of the Royal Statistical Society, Series A*(161), 63–77.

Pickery, J., Loosveldt, G., & Carton, A. (2001). The effects of interviewer and respondent characteristics on response behavior in panel surveys: A multilevel approach. *Sociological Methods and Research, 29*, 509–523.

Rasbash, J., & Goldstein, H. (1994). Efficient analysis of mixed hierarchical and cross-classified random structures using a multilevel model. *Journal of Educational and Behavioral Statistics, 19*(4), 337–350.

Rasbash, J., Steele, F., Browne, W., & Goldstein, H. (2009). *A user's guide to MLwiN. Version 2.10.* University of Bristol: Centre for Multilevel Modeling.

Schnell, R., & Kreuter, F. (2005). Separating interviewer and sampling-point effects. *Journal of Official Statistics, 21*(3), 389–410.

Sturgis, P. (2004). The effect of coding error on time use surveys estimates. *Journal of Official Statistics, 20*(3), 467–480.

West, B. T., & Olson, K. (2010). How much of interviewer variance is really nonresponse error variance? *Public Opinion Quarterly, 74*(5), 1004–1026.

8

Interviewers' Falsifications in Face-to-Face Surveys

Impact, Reasons, Detection and Prevention

Natalja Menold, Peter Winker, Nina Storfinger and Sebastian Bredl

8.1 INTRODUCTION

The face-to-face survey mode is broadly used in national and cross-cultural surveys to achieve high survey participation and data quality. The interviewer has been seen as a key factor responsible for the positive effects of the face-to-face survey mode. However, the interviewer is also a source of systematic and non-systematic errors, which decrease the quality of survey data. A perfect interviewer has been often thought of as a "machine", which implements accurately all standards and instructions prescribed by the survey organization. However, such understanding neglects interviewers' needs, motives, abilities and personality and is rather unrealistic, thus falsifications by interviewers are inevitable in surveys.

We consider an issue of survey methodology to be the prevention and detection of interviewers' misconduct behavior, and focus in this chapter on falsifications of survey data, referred to as interview falsifications.[1] Falsifications of interviews, be it partially or entirely, represent an extreme form of interviewers' deviation from prescribed survey standards. As the probably more common undocumented substitution, it might result from difficulties in contacting sampled units and obtaining their cooperation. In the case of partial falsifications, interviewers collect basic data, e.g. some household or demographic information, from a sampled unit during a so-called "short interview" (Koch, 1995). Using this basic data, the interviewer fabricates the remaining interview data. An entirely fabricated interview does not even make use of such a "short interview".

Only a small amount of documented evidence exists in the literature about the prevalence of interview falsifications. Overall, in surveys using high standards and well-established control procedures, the prevalence of falsified interviews in face-to-face surveys is reported to be quite low (cf. AAPOR, 2003). According to a few authors, falsifications may constitute between 1% and 5% of the interviews (Biemer & Stokes, 1989; Case, 1971; Koch, 1995). Using randomly selected re-interview samples, 0.2% of all interviews could be identified as fabricated in a study for the U.S. Census Bureau (Hood & Bushery, 1997, p. 823). It might be reasonable to assume that the prevalence reported in the literature may be underestimated, especially for surveys on sensitive topics (Turner, Gribbe, Al-Tayyip & Chromy, 2002) or surveys conducted in developing countries (Bredl, Winker & Kötschau, 2012). A further reason might be due to underreporting of identified falsifications by survey agencies and scientists in order not to raise doubts about data quality.

Even a quite small number of undetected interview falsifications may seriously affect the results of multivariate analyses (Schraepler & Wagner, 2003). The authors have demonstrated that the inclusion of fabricated SOEP (German Socio-Economic Panel) data in a multivariate regression reduced the estimated effect of training on log gross wages by approximately 80%, even though the proportion of fabricated interviews was less than 2.5%. Consequently, methods which help to detect data falsification are of crucial importance for survey research. In the next section we provide a review of the literature regarding existing methods to detect interviewers' falsifications. A new multivariate indicator-based method is presented in the third section, which is founded on differences between real and falsified data. Some concluding remarks are provided in the final section.

8.2 LITERATURE REVIEW REGARDING METHODS FOR IDENTIFICATION OF INTERVIEWERS' FALSIFICATIONS

Given the risk of falsifications and the devastating impact on data quality that falsifications might have, it is certainly recommended to use appropriate methods for the identification of falsifications in surveys. However, detection of fabricated interviews is not a simple task, which might to some extent explain the low reported prevalence of the problem.

A commonly used control procedure consists in sending postcards to find out whether an interview has taken place. For surveys using addresses or individuals as the sample frame, the most reliable tool for identifying falsified interviews is re-interviewing the person who should have been interviewed (cf. Forsman & Schreiner, 1991). During the re-interview, a supervisor verifies that an interview actually took place during the field period and was conducted properly. Both re-interview and sending post-cards can have problems in detecting falsified interviews, due to the low willingness of participants to respond, memory problems and the limited amount of information that can be confirmed (Hauck, 1969; cf. Bredl, Storfinger & Menold, 2013). Furthermore, re-interviewing every survey participant is far too costly. In surveys conducted by the U.S. Census Bureau, for instance, the re-interview sample only makes up 2%–10% of the survey participants (Bushery, Reichert, Albright & Rossiter, 1999).

For conducting re-interviews more effectively, the question is how to best select the subsample for re-interviews. The limited empirical evidence on the issue suggests that re-interview samples focusing on "at risk" interviewers (an expression coined by Hood & Bushery, 1997) are more effective than random re-interview samples. "At risk" interviewers are those who seem to be more likely than others to have committed falsification given the data quality they produced. For interviewers' control, metadata were used in surveys to identify suspicious interviewers, for example, by their implausible success rates (Turner et al., 2002), or by time-stamps in computer-assisted interviews (Bushery et al., 1999; Murphy, Baxter, Eyerman, Cunningham & Kennet, 2004). In addition to metadata, which represent a rather limited database and are associated with certain requirements, e.g. computer assistance for data collection, interview data itself can be used for identification of interviewers "at risk". In this regard it is important to have an idea in which ways falsified and honestly collected data differ.

Two approaches might be used to distinguish between falsified and real data. The first method concentrates on specific responses to survey questions. We call this method "content-related". Several studies conducted in Germany (Hippler, 1979; Reuband, 1990; Schnell, 1991) systematically compared real and false data in order to see how they differ in terms of their content. For a subsample of existing survey data, false data were produced in these studies by students or researchers playing the role of falsifiers. The falsified data were then compared with the real survey data. Prior to the falsifying task, some basic information about real survey participants had been provided to the falsifiers, as would be the case in partial falsifications as described above. The results show that falsifiers were often able to produce opinion and behavior-related data that did not significantly differ from the real data. Hence, falsifiers' precision in predicting responses of real respondents may depend on the topic of falsification, for example, whether it is a matter of behavior, opinions or facts, as well as which basic information about respondents is known to falsifiers (Hippler, 1979). The chances of identifying "at risk" interviewers solely on the basis of this type of content-related information appear limited and will largely depend on the specific questionnaire used.

The second type of difference between real and falsified data concerns response behavior and response patterns. We call the corresponding indicators "formal". For example, Schraepler and Wagner (2005) examined the share of item nonresponse, extreme responding and variance in responding in order to identify (*a priori* known) falsifiers in the SOEP. They report a higher discriminatory power of this method, a result confirmed by Bredl et al. (2012) in a multivariate approach using the share of item nonresponse, the share of extreme answers, the frequency of the checked option "others" in semi-open-ended questions and patterns in first digits of metric data. A more detailed description of potential indicators and their use in a new method for identification of falsifications will be provided in the next section. Before moving on, the current usage of specific survey methods dealing with the risk of falsifications will be illustrated referring to four recent case studies (GfK, SNR, Pairfam, PIAAC).

Market research is particularly interested in the easy and automatic evaluation of data quality. For this purpose, the GfK developed software called ALBERTA that checks the consistency of the data (see Hülser, 2013). ALBERTA uses (1) interview variance analysis, which assumes that interviewers who falsify data produce lower variance in item batteries than real respondents; (2) internal checks of consistency, which identify item sets filled out randomly and item sets filled out by straight-lining and (3) identification of doubled interviews, which is based on the distances between the interviews.

In a study on 1,200 German residents conducted by 81 interviewers, ALBERTA identified 2% of interviews likely to have been faked and one suspicious interviewer was found. It is not possible to differentiate between interviewers as falsifiers and respondents who do not carefully respond to the survey questions. Nevertheless, at least some data of low quality—produced by falsifiers or inaccurate respondents—can be automatically identified by ALBERTA.

Slavec and Vehovar (2013) deal with falsifications in the Slovenian National Readership Survey (NRS). NRS is a commercial CAPI survey, which collects data on readership for Slovenian newspapers and magazines. The University of Ljubljana conducted re-interviews in different survey rounds from 2007 to 2010 applying an extended control method consisting of several steps. High cooperation rates (90%) were obtained by this sophisticated method. On average, 3%–4% of re-interviewed individuals reported that they had not been interviewed before or that they had been interviewed by phone. Next, checking nonrespondents of NRS revealed a low validity of contact outcomes, which are documented by the interviewers. A majority of cases classified as noncontact or with unknown eligibility could be contacted and classified as eligible cases and 20% of them reported not having refused survey participation, highlighting the relevance of falsifications of unit nonresponse outcomes.

A striking example of falsifications of social network data is reported by Brüderl, Huyer-May and Schmiedeberg (2013) in the context of the German Family Panel (pairfam). It is shown that a substantial number of interviewers (labeled "fraudulent") seem to avoid generating large networks in order to save time, while other interviewers (labeled "diligent") rather aim at generating large networks. The fraudulent behavior appears rational given that interviewers are paid per interview. The authors used a jackknife method to identify the 5% of interviewers having the strongest impact on the intra-class correlation coefficient. For this subgroup, the mean size of the network was 1.62 as compared to 4.30 for the full sample. Two conclusions might be drawn: social network data are particularly prone to interviewers' falsifications, and resampling methods such as the jackknife or bootstrap might be valid instruments to identify influential observations which might be linked to such falsifications.

Massing, Ackermann, Martin, Zabal and Rammstedt (2013) discuss how to motivate and monitor interviewers working for the German Programme for the International Assessment of Adult Competencies (PIAAC). A central goal of the PIAAC—which is also called PISA for adults—is to provide a cross-sectional dataset about adults' key competencies. PIAAC differs from a typical social survey in that respondents are asked not only to provide sociodemographic or attitude information, but also to fulfill numerous psychological knowledge and skill tests. The average time of CAPI interviews amounts to 1:45 hours. Despite these difficulties of survey realization response rates of 50% or higher are required by the OECD to acknowledge a national study as valid. An extended control procedure was used including re-interviews with 10% of each interviewer's finalized cases, tape recordings of interviewer interaction during the interviews and checking metadata for outcome plausibility. If an interviewer was identified as suspect, all her/his cases were controlled. These extended controls did not indicate any falsifications. The PIAAC team also conducted an extended interviewer training program to prevent falsifications. In doing so, a close contact between the researchers and interviewers was established, which is a key factor for task performance according to Vroom (1964) and Gwartney (2013).

8.3 A NEW MULTIVARIATE INDICATOR-BASED METHOD

While methods suggested in survey methodology for data-driven identification of interviewers "at risk" rely mainly on the analysis of single indicators, Bredl et al. (2012) propose a multivariate method for identifying "at risk" interviewers. The main idea of this method, outlined in more detail below, is to separate the falsifiers from the honest interviewers by means of a multivariate combination of several indicators. Assuming that falsifiers are similar regarding the answer pattern produced in all their interviews, a cluster analysis is useful for splitting interviewers into two groups or clusters. Thereby, the additional information content of several content-related and formal indicators can be exploited. Ideally, one cluster contains only the honest interviewers and the second cluster only the falsifiers. In this case—or a situation close to it—re-interviewing only the interviewers in the "falsifiercluster" might result in a very efficient outcome if almost all "at risk" interviewers are indeed cheaters.

Let us first discuss a possible set of indicators for a multivariate analysis before turning to more details about the clustering procedure and some results. Starting with the indicators found in literature, Menold, Winker, Storfinger and Kemper (2013) and Menold and Kemper (2013) developed and evaluated numerous content-related and formal indicators with respect to their power to distinguish between real and falsified data. To this end, besides using a dataset with identified falsifications, a similar approach to experimental data generation as that used by Reuband (1990) and Schnell (1991) was applied. This second approach is based on both real and falsified data being collected during experimental studies, which—in our case—were conducted mainly with students as interviewers and falsifiers. However, in one pretest setting, we also considered data generated by professional interviewers.

The results of the analysis for both real and experimental data showed that most formal indicators exhibit substantial power in predicting whether data are real or fabricated (Menold & Kemper, 2013). An overview of several formal indicators is given in Table 8.1. From the table it can be inferred that most indicators could be calculated for a broad set of survey questionnaires, while some require particular data structures, e.g. filter questions, which might not always be present. Obviously, in those cases the corresponding indicator cannot be used in real applications. In addition, the results from the analysis of indicators revealed that the performance of content-related differences depends on the information

TABLE 8.1

Overview about some formal indicators

Indicator	Description
Semi-Open	Frequency of usage of "others, please specify" in semi-open-ended questions included in the questionnaire
Open	Frequency for providing responses to open-ended questions
Filter	Frequency of skipping of questions with help of a filter question
Item Non-Response	Frequency of item non-response
Extreme Responding Style	Frequency in endorsement of most extreme responses on the rating scales, e.g. "1" and "5" on a five-point rating scale
Acquiescent Responding Style	Frequency of agreement responses in differently pooled rating scales regardless of item direction
Non-Differentiation	Averaged standard deviation of responses across all items in multi-item sets
Rounding	Frequency with which rounded answers were given to numerical open questions, i.e. about minutes spent watching television (rounded numbers here are: 30, 60, 90, 120 etc.), body-mass-information and income/payment information
Primacy	Frequency of how often the first two categories were chosen in a list of nominal response categories, presented visually
Recency	Frequency of how often the last category was chosen in answers to orally presented questions.

available to the falsifiers about the persons whose answers are to be falsified. This restricts the usability of content-related indicators for detection purposes, since surveyors do not have control over what information is available to a falsifier, for example, after a short interview. However, some content-related indicators were found to be powerful. In particular, indicators which were constructed using fictive information included in response alternatives showed high explanatory power. An example is asking whether certain newspapers are read and including fictive newspapers in the list of response alternatives, which are then selected more often by falsifiers than by real respondents (Menold et al., 2013). Adding this type of questions to a survey might help to increase the discriminatory power of indicator-based identification methods such as the one discussed in this chapter.

Once a suitable set of indicators has been chosen, i.e. indicators which can be constructed for the given questionnaire and which have exhibited some discriminatory power in past research, a cluster analysis can be used to split the sample of interviewers into two parts, a "falsifiercluster" and a cluster containing the supposedly honest interviewers. The performance of a given cluster assignment is assessed based on the fraction of correctly assigned interviewers as well as the share of misclassifications. As is typical in statistical analyses, two different types of error could be expected. The first one refers to the case where honest interviewers are assigned to the "cheatercluster"; this is what we call "false alarms". The second error applies to the more fatal case of when cheaters remain undetected because they are assigned to the "honestcluster". It has to be taken into account that an evaluation of this error rate is only feasible in the experimental setting or for datasets such as the one used by Bredl et al. (2012), where the cheating interviewers were known beforehand.

We report some results based on a setting where both real and falsified data were collected within an experiment. For the experiment, $N = 78$ students were recruited. In a first phase, they each completed about 10 real face-to-face interviews. In order to make sure that all interviews were actually conducted, they were tape recorded and all recordings were controlled. In a second step, the interviewers had to produce fabricated survey data in the lab. Thereby, the students obtained some basic information about one of the real respondents (of course, from a person interviewed by someone else) and had to complete the questionnaire. In this way, we obtained a dataset of $N = 710$ falsified interviews corresponding to each of the $N = 710$ real interviews.

Using formal indicators listed in Table 8.1 and three content-related indicators (for a full list, see Menold et al., 2013), different cluster procedures were considered. Besides a standard hierarchical procedure, namely Ward's method (Ward, 1963; applied in Storfinger & Winker, 2011 and also in Menold et al., 2013), a heuristic optimization approach based on threshold accepting was examined. For the latter, one of the two resulting clusters comprised 70 interviewers including 61 falsifiers, i.e. 78% of all falsifiers in the sample, while the other cluster had 86 elements including 69 honest interviewers, i.e. 88% of all honest interviewers. By removing an indicator that did not contribute substantially to discriminatory power in this experiment (INR), the shares of correctly classified honest interviewers (92%) and falsifiers (82%) could be slightly increased (Menold et al., 2013). In addition, the results were in line with the findings by Bredl et al. (2012) that the multivariate procedure delivers superior results in terms of a high share of detected falsifiers and a low share of false alarms compared to the analysis of single indicators.

Besides the reduction of false alarms, the multivariate identification method should also aim at minimizing the number of undetected falsifiers.

Identifying more cheaters might be possible when allowing for more than one "cheatercluster". First experiments with specific indicators resulted in two "cheaterclusters" and one "honestcluster" and in a substantial increase in the share of correctly assigned falsifiers.

A second idea for minimizing the share of undetected falsifiers is based on the assumption of different "cheatertypes". A comparison of cheaters detected by the proposed multivariate method with cheaters not detected revealed significant differences concerning falsifiers' motivations. Undetected falsifiers made a bigger effort to produce "good" falsifications and attached higher importance to remaining undetected as a falsifier. The subjective probability to be detected was also assessed as lower by the undetected falsifiers than by revealed cheaters. Hence, we suppose that the group of falsifiers itself may contain different types of cheaters and we recommend to allow for different motivations and strategies for falsification in order to identify all falsifiers in the dataset.

8.4 CONCLUSIONS AND OUTLOOK

In a typical setting of face-to-face interviews in a survey, the interviews are conducted by interviewers recruited by survey institutes which themselves are engaged by the researchers. *A priori*, it is not obvious how the quality of this process can be guaranteed due to the obvious agency problems. However, there exist a number of instruments which can be used in this context to enhance data quality and reduce the risk of interviewers' falsifications. To this end, much care has to be given to the overall setup, the motivation of interviewers, the supervision during the field phase, the payment structure, etc. However, the risk of interview falsifications can hardly be excluded unless the researchers conduct all interviews themselves. Although reports on falsifications by interviewers are still rare in literature, existing case studies indicate that the risk might become substantial in some settings. Thus, it is recommended to pay particular attention to potential interview falsifications.

Experimental evidence shows that data resulting from actual interviews and falsifications differ not only with regard to their actual content, but also with regard to some statistical properties. This finding can be exploited to construct data-based methods for the identification of possible falsifications in survey data. Again, these methods cannot guarantee to identify all cases of interview falsifications. Nevertheless, they can be quite helpful in improving survey quality and for deterring potential falsifiers. Therefore, it is suggested to use the multivariate method presented in this chapter for identifying "at risk" interviewers and to focus re-interviews and other methods for ensuring data quality on this preselected subsample.

Summing up, falsifications in surveys should be on the agenda of researchers relying on survey data as well as of survey institutes. Application of existing methods and further development of additional tools both for preventing and for detecting interview falsifications should receive high priority on the research agenda given the devastating impact a low share of interviews not conducted according to the rules of the survey might have on the qualitative outcome of a research project. Furthermore, instruments might be developed to generate interviewer-based metadata which in the future might allow researchers to identify data collected by interviewers who have been detected as cheaters in some other context.

NOTE

1. This chapter summarizes findings from our own work within the context of the Priority Programme on Survey Methodology (PPSM), conducted within the project "Identification of Falsification in Survey Data" (IFIS, WI 2024/4–1, ME 3538/2–1). It also refers to results presented at the international workshop "Interviewers' Deviant Behaviour— Reasons, Detection, Prevention", organized in October 2011 within the project. We would like to thank our entire project team, involved on different project stages, in particular, Michael Blohm, Gesine Güllner, Christoph J. Kemper, Marie K. Opper, Rolf Porst and Viktoria Trofimow.

REFERENCES

AAPOR. (2003). Interviewer falsification in survey research: Current best methods for prevention, detection and repair of its effects. Retrieved from www.aapor.org/pdfs/falsification.pdf

Biemer, P., & Stokes, S. (1989). The optimal design of quality control samples to detect interviewer cheating. *Journal of Official Statistics*, 5(1), 23–39.

Bredl, S., Storfinger, N., & Menold, N. (2013). A literature review of methods to detect fabricated survey data. In P. Winker, N. Menold, & R. Porst (Eds.), *Survey standardization and interviewers' deviations—Impact, reasons, detection and prevention* (pp. 3–24). Frankfurt: Peter Lang.

Bredl, S., Winker, P., & Kötschau, K. (2012). A statistical approach to detect interviewer falsification of survey data. *Survey methodology*, 38(1), 1–10.

Brüderl, J., Huyer-May, B., & Schmiedeberg, C. (2013). Interviewer behavior and the quality of social network data. In P. Winker, N. Menold, & R. Porst (Eds.), *Survey standardization and interviewers' deviations—Impact, reasons, detection and prevention* (pp. 147–160). Frankfurt: Peter Lang.

Bushery, J. M., Reichert, J. W., Albright, K. A., & Rossiter, J. C. (1999). Using date and time stamps to detect interviewer falsification. *Proceedings of the Survey Research*

Methods Section, ASA, (9), 316–320. Retrieved from www.amstat.org/sections/srms/proceedings/papers/1999_053.pdf

Case, P. (1971).How to catch interviewer errors. *Journal of Advertising Research, 11*(2), 39–43.

Forsman, G., & Schreiner, I. (1991). The design and analysis of re-interview: An overview. In P. B. Biemer, R. M. Groves, L. E. Lyberg, N. A. Mathiowetz, & S. Sudman (Eds.), *Measurement errors in surveys* (pp. 279–301). New York: Wiley.

Gwartney, P. (2013). Mischief versus mistakes: Motivating interviewers to not deviate. In P. Winker, N. Menold, & R. Porst (Eds.), *Survey standardization and interviewers' deviations–Impact, reasons, detection and prevention* (pp. 195–215). Frankfurt: Peter Lang.

Hauck, M. (1969). Is survey postcard verification effective? *Public Opinion Quarterly, 33*(1), 117–120.

Hippler, H.-J. (1979). Untersuchung zur "Qualitaet" absichtlich gefaelschter Interviews. *ZUMA-Arbeitspapier,* 1–30.

Hood, C. C., & Bushery, J. M. (1997). Getting more bang from the re-interview buck: Identifying "at risk" interviewers. *Proceedings of the Survey Research Methods Section, ASA,* (27), 820–824. Retrieved from www.amstat.org/sections/srms/Proceedings/

Hülser, O. (2013). Automatic interview control in ad hoc market research studies. In P. Winker, N. Menold, & R. Porst (Eds.), *Survey standardization and interviewers' deviations—Impact, reasons, detection and prevention* (pp. 103–116). Frankfurt: Peter Lang.

Koch, A. (1995). Gefaelschte Interviews: Ergebnisse der Interviewerkontrolle beim ALLBUS 1994. *ZUMA-Nachrichten, 36,* 89–105.

Massing, N., Ackermann, D., Martin, S., Zabal, A., & Rammstedt, B. (2013). Controlling interviewers' work in PIAAC—the Programme for the International Assessment of Adult Competencies. In P. Winker, N. Menold, & R. Porst (Eds.), *Survey standardization and interviewers' deviations—Impact, reasons, detection and prevention* (pp. 117–130). Frankfurt: Peter Lang.

Menold, N., & Kemper, C. (2013). How do real and falsified data differ? Psychology of survey response as a source of falsification indicators in face-to-face surveys. *Journal of International Public Opinion Research.* doi:10.1093/ijpor/edt017

Menold, N., Winker, P., Storfinger, N., & Kemper, C. J. (2013). Development of a method for ex-post identification of falsifications in survey data. In P. Winker, N. Menold, & R. Porst (Eds.), *Survey standardization and interviewers' deviations—Impact, reasons, detection and prevention* (pp. 25–47). Frankfurt: Peter Lang.

Murphy, J., Baxter, R., Eyerman, J., Cunningham, D., & Kennet, J. (2004). A system for detecting interviewer falsification. *American Association for Public Opinion Research 59th Annual Conference,* 4968–4975.

Reuband, K.-H. (1990). Interviews, die keine sind: "Erfolge" und "Misserfolge" beim Faelschen von Interviews. *Koelner Zeitschrift fuer Soziologie und Sozialpsychologie, 42*(4), 706–733.

Schnell, R. (1991). Der Einfluss gefaelschter Interviews auf Survey-Ergebnisse. *Zeitschrift fuer Soziologie, 20*(1), 25–35.

Schraepler, J.-P., & Wagner, G. G. (2003). Identification, characteristics and impact of faked interviews in surveys—An analysis by means of genuine fakes in the raw data of SOEP, *IZA Discussion Paper Series, 969.*

Schraepler, J.-P., & Wagner, G. G. (2005). Characteristics and impact of faked interviews in surveys—An analysis of genuine fakes in the raw data of SOEP, *Allgemeines Statistisches Archiv, 89,* 7–20.

Slavec, A., & Vehovar, V. (2013). Detecting interviewer's deviant behaviour in the Slovenian National Readership Survey. In P. Winker, N. Menold, & R. Porst (Eds.), *Survey standardization and interviewers' deviations—Impact, reasons, detection and prevention* (pp. 131–144). Frankfurt: Peter Lang.

Storfinger, N., & Winker P. (2011). Robustness of clustering methods for identification of potential falsifications in survey data. *Discussion Paper 57.* Giessen: ZEU.

Turner, C., Gribble, J., Al-Tayyip, A., & Chromy, J. (2002). Falsification in epidemiologic surveys: Detection and remediation (Prepublication Draft). *Technical Papers on Health and Behavior Measurement, No. 53.* Washington DC: Research Triangle Institute.

Vroom, V. H. (1964). *Work and motivation.* New York: Wiley.

Ward, J. H. (1963). Hierarchical grouping to optimize an objective function. *Journal of the American Statistical Association 58*(301), 236–244.

Part III

Asking Sensitive Questions

9

Asking Sensitive Questions

Overview and Introduction

Ben Jann

Asking sensitive questions has been a salient challenge to survey research ever since Allen Barton published his polemic comment on "Asking the Embarrassing Question" in the *Public Opinion Quarterly* in 1958. Barton illustrated a number of sensitive question techniques that were used by survey researchers at the time, using the question "Did you kill your wife?" as an example. Baton's comment made quite clear that there is little hope that these techniques could, in fact, improve the measurement of sensitive topics. The techniques presented by Barton can be classified into different groups. Some techniques tried to reduce the sensitivity of the question by suggesting that there is nothing special about killing one's wife ("The Casual Approach" or "The Everybody Approach") or tried to establish a special "atmosphere" in the interview situation, facilitating respondents' disclosure of information on taboo topics ("The Kinsey Technique"). Other techniques tried to elicit more valid answers by increasing the anonymity of the question-and-answer process ("The Numbered Card" or "The Sealed Ballot Technique") or tried to gain an estimate of sensitive behavior through indirect information ("The 'Other' People Approach" or "The Projective Technique"). The first two approaches are problematic because they may, in fact, increase measurement reactivity instead of reducing it. The latter two are problematic because the induced anonymity may not be credible or the validity of the collected indirect information cannot be taken as granted.

But what exactly is the difficulty with sensitive questions? First, at a fundamental level, asking sensitive questions is about requesting information from respondents they are not willing to provide. Traditionally, such resistance is conquered by means of threat or torture, from thumbscrews in medieval Europe to waterboarding in Guantánamo. Fortunately, such approaches do not belong to the toolbox of survey researchers. Yet the challenge of overcoming respondents' resistance remains.

Second, validation studies—that is, studies in which respondents' self-reports are compared to "true" values known from a secondary source—indicate that many respondents indeed do not accurately answer sensitive questions. For example, Locander, Sudman, and Bradburn (1976) report about 50% and 30% false answers for questions regarding driving under influence and bankruptcy, respectively; van der Heijden, van Gils, Bouts, and Hox (2000) found 75% or more false answers for questions on welfare and unemployment benefit fraud; and in a study by Wolter and Preisendörfer (2013), 42.5% of respondents who were convicted by a court for minor offenses denied it.

Third, different forms of measurement error might occur in surveys on sensitive topics. On the one hand, there may be "unit nonresponse," where respondents refuse to take part in a survey due to the perceived sensitivity of the survey theme or break-off interviews after being confronted with a sensitive question, or "item nonresponse," where respondents deny answering individual sensitive questions. Both unit and item nonresponse lead to selectivity bias in survey estimates, unless nonresponse behavior is independent from respondents' sensitive characteristics (which usually cannot be assumed). On the other hand, respondents might misreport, providing false answers to sensitive questions, which leads to social desirability bias if the misreporting is systematic. A distinction is often made between socially undesirable variables (e.g. deviant behavior), where respondents tend to under-report (i.e. provide values that are lower than the "true" values), and socially desirable variables (e.g. voter turnout), where respondents tend to overreport. However, the direction of social desirability bias might also vary by context and subpopulation.

Fourth, different types and degrees of sensitivity exist, implying various consequences for the nature and magnitude of expected measurement errors. Tourangeau and Yan (2007) distinguish three basic types of sensitive questions. Questions can be intrusive in the sense that they are generally perceived as an invasion of privacy (e.g. questions about "taboo" topics). For such questions one would not necessarily expect a high degree of misreporting, however, rates of unit and item nonresponse can be high (e.g. questions on personal income). Furthermore, sensitive questions can involve a threat of disclosure (e.g. questions on criminal behavior). To evade sanctions from third parties, respondents will likely misreport such questions, denying any relation to the sensitive behavior at hand, but levels of nonresponse might be low since refusing to answer could be interpreted as an admission of guilt. Yet, the degree of misreporting can strongly depend on the interview setting, the survey sponsor, and the credibility of confidentiality assurances. Finally, a "question is sensitive when it asks for a socially undesirable answer, when it asks, in effect, that the respondent admit he or she has violated a social norm" (Tourangeau & Yan, 2007, p. 860). In general, for such questions one would expect the answers of respondents to be biased in the direction of the social norm. A difficulty, however, is that social norms may be context-specific and heterogeneous. A classic example is males overreporting, and females underreporting the number of previous sexual partners.

Fifth, a distinction can be made between active misreporting (or other-deception), when respondents explicitly lie about their behavior or deliberately engage in impression management, and passive misreporting (or self-deception), when respondents are not, in fact, aware of their misreporting. In the first case, there is a difference between the respondent's private beliefs and the public answer. Sensitive question techniques geared at such types of questions must try to eliminate the respondent's motive for deliberate misreporting (e.g. by increasing anonymity). In the second case, however, such techniques cannot work because private beliefs and public answer coincide.

Given the complexity of the topic, many different measurement approaches have been developed since Barton's comment in 1958 (a survey of which can be found in Tourangeau & Yan, 2007). An important step forward was made in 1965 when Stanley Warner demonstrated that it is possible to guarantee perfect anonymity to respondents by design, while still being able to retrieve valid population estimates from their answers. The approach proposed by Warner is called the Randomized Response Technique (RRT); it works, in essence, by misclassifying respondents' answers in a random fashion, so that the link between a given answer and the true value of the sensitive characteristic is broken at the individual level. Warner's proposal initiated a diverse research agenda on RRTs, leading to many variants and improvements. Yet, "35 years of research have not led to a consensus or a description of best practices," as noted by Lensvelt-Mulders, Hox, van der Heijden, and Maas (2005, p. 323) in their meta-analysis of the literature on RRTs, a statement that appears still true after ten additional years of research. The failure in methodological convergence may have many causes, one of which is that we cannot expect a single method to work well for all types of sensitive questions. Another potential cause is that much of the literature on RRTs pays too little attention to the details of practical implementation and the psychology of respondents.

Chapter 10 in this volume therefore presents research on an important practical element of RRTs: the randomizing device. Diekmann and

Höglinger suggest a novel device that can be used in almost any survey situation and ingeniously takes advantage of the psychology of respondents. The randomizing device is the first digit of the street address of someone the respondent knows. First digits of street addresses are approximately distributed according to Benford's law, with low digits more likely than high digits. Since most respondents are not aware of this, perceived privacy protection can be increased without sacrificing statistical efficiency, a feature that Diekmann and Höglinger call the "Benford illusion."

Chapter 11 proceeds by providing an overview of RRTs. Krumpal and coauthors present various RRT schemes suggested in the literature. Furthermore, they present the Crosswise Model (CM), a relatively new variant of the RRT that appears to overcome some important deficiencies of many other RRT schemes. The CM seems especially well-suited for application in general population surveys due to the simple implementation and the low cognitive burden imposed on respondents. Finally, Krumpal et al. also review the literature on the Item Count Technique (also known as the "List Experiment").

The basic assertion behind the techniques described in Chapters 10 and 11 is that respondents are more willing to provide truthful answers if they are guaranteed anonymity. Such an assertion only makes sense if respondents are assumed to be aware of their misreporting. In Chapter 12, the last chapter of this section, Auspurg and coauthors present research on an alternative data collection strategy that can at least in part identify social-desirability bias in situations where respondents are not fully aware of the process by which they edit their answers. The technique is called the Factorial Survey (FS) and is well known in social sciences as a method to measure social norms. In their chapter, Auspurg et al. first survey methodological findings with respect to the implementation of FSs and then provide an empirical example illustrating how FSs can be used to reveal social-desirability bias.

Although the chapters in this section do not provide a definitive solution for how to ask sensitive questions, they do highlight important aspects, describe some recent developments, and provide an overview of the methodological literature in the field.

REFERENCES

Barton, A. H. (1958). Asking the embarrassing question. *The Public Opinion Quarterly, 22*, 67–68.

Lensvelt-Mulders, G.J.L.M., Hox, J. J., van der Heijden, P.G.M., & Maas, C.J.M. (2005). Meta-analysis of Randomized Response Research. Thirty-five years of validation. *Sociological Methods and Research, 33*, 319–348.

Locander, W., Sudman, S., & Bradburn, N. (1976). An investigation of interview method, threat and response distortion. *Journal of the American Statistical Association, 71,* 269–275.

Tourangeau, R., & Yan, T. (2007). Sensitive questions in surveys. *Psychological Bulletin, 133,* 859–883.

van der Heijden, P.G.M., van Gils, G., Bouts, J., & Hox, J. J. (2000). A comparison of randomized response, computer-assisted self-interview, and face-to-face direct questioning. Eliciting sensitive information in the context of welfare and unemployment benefit. *Sociological Methods and Research, 28,* 505–537.

Warner, S. L. (1965). Randomized response: A survey technique for eliminating evasive answer bias. *Journal of the American Statistical Association, 60,* 63–69.

Wolter, F., & Preisendörfer, P. (2013). Asking sensitive questions: An evaluation of the Randomized Response Technique vs. Direct Questioning using individual validation data. *Sociological Methods and Research, 42,* 321–353.

10

A New Randomizing Device for the RRT Using Benford's Law

An Application in an Online Survey

Andreas Diekmann and Marc Höglinger

10.1 INTRODUCTION

A crucial feature of any implementation of the Randomized Response Technique (RRT) is the randomizing device. It determines whether or not a particular respondent is required to answer a sensitive question and, consequently, protects respondents' privacy. Respondents' cooperation and compliance with the RRT procedure hinge heavily on the device's ease of use, its trustworthiness, and its availability. Dice, a box with colored balls, a spinner, or cards have frequently been used in face-to-face interviews. But these are difficult to use in paper-and-pencil, online, or telephone surveys because no interviewer is present to provide them to respondents. More commonly, available objects that can be used as randomizing devices, such as coins, are preferable but might still be out of some respondents' immediate reach. This may lead to RRT break-offs or noncompliance and, as a consequence, invalid measurement. A solution to this problem of availability is to avoid physical randomizing devices and to use questions instead. However, such "randomizing questions" have so far rarely been used, as the range of suitable questions is very restricted.

In this chapter, we present a new randomizing device originally proposed in Diekmann (2012). It uses a "randomizing question" and comprises several desirable properties. Besides its ease of use and its applicability in all survey situations, it allows for increasing the statistical efficiency of the RRT without jeopardizing respondents' perceived privacy protection. For the latter, the method makes use of Benford's law and takes advantage of respondents' misperception of the properties of Benford-distributed numbers such as, in our example, house numbers. We show how this method can be implemented and we present results of its first large-scale empirical evaluation in an online survey on student cheating. Furthermore, we will discuss the important difference between respondents' objective privacy protection in RRT designs and their subjectively perceived privacy protection.

10.2 THE RANDOMIZED RESPONSE TECHNIQUE (RRT)

The Randomized Response Technique (RRT) is a well-known method to elicit more valid answers to sensitive questions in surveys (originally Warner, 1965; for an overview see Fox & Tracy, 1986 and Krumpal, Jann, Auspurg, & Hermanni, Chapter 11). It provides complete concealment of respondents' answers by introducing a systematic random error which inhibits any inference of admittance or non-admittance of sensitive behavior from an individual response. This is achieved by a randomizing device such as two dice. In the case of the unrelated-question RRT variant (Horvitz, Shah, & Simmons, 1967; Greenberg, Abul-Ela, Simmons, & Horvitz, 1969), which serves in the following as exemplary case, the randomizing device determines whether a particular respondent has to answer either a sensitive or a non-sensitive question. Respondents could, for instance, be instructed to throw two dice and answer the sensitive question "Have you ever cheated on your taxes?" if their sum is 2 to 8 and to answer the non-sensitive question "Is your mother's birthday in the months of January through June?" if their sum is 9 to 12. Since only the respondent knows the outcome of the dice throw, no one else is able to infer whether the response given is actually related to the sensitive behavior or not. Accordingly, respondents do not have to fear negative consequences of any kind by admitting a sensitive behavior and should feel free to answer truthfully.

Estimating the Prevalence of Sensitive Behavior with the RRT

Even though individual responses are completely concealed, the prevalence of the sensitive behavior can be consistently estimated in the aggregate. The researcher simply takes into account that the observed "yes" responses are not only generated by respondents answering "yes" to the sensitive question but also by respondents answering "yes" to the non-sensitive question. Let p be the probability that respondents are instructed to answer the sensitive question and $1 - p$ the probability for answering the non-sensitive question whose answer distribution $P(yes|nonsens.quest.)$ is known. The share of observed "yes" answers is defined as

$$P(yes\ observed) = p * P(yes|sens.quest.) + (1 - p) * P(yes|nonsens.quest.) \quad (10.1)$$

By rearranging the equation, we get the share of respondents answering "yes" to the sensitive question, and, hence, the prevalence of the sensitive behavior under the condition that respondents complied to the RRT instructions:

$$P(yes|sens.quest.) = \frac{P(yes\ observed) - (1 - p) * P(yes|nonsens.quest.)}{p} \quad (10.2)$$

The variance of the RRT estimator is then given by (e.g., Fox & Tracy, 1986, p. 19):

$$var(P(yes|sens.quest.)) = \frac{P(yes\ observed) * (1 - P(yes\ observed))}{n * p^2} \quad (10.3)$$

The variance is inversely related to p^2, hence the lower the probability that respondents have to answer the sensitive question, the higher the variance of the estimator of the sensitive behavior. Respondents' privacy protection comes at the cost of a lower statistical efficiency of the RRT estimator.

The RRT Randomizing Device and Its Requirements

The RRT randomizing device serves to introduce randomness into the answering process of survey respondents and, therefore, is the central part of any RRT implementation. The principal requirements a randomizing device has to meet are ease of use, trustworthiness, and availability. Ease of use means that respondents are able to carry out the randomization quickly and without too much effort. Throwing two dice, for instance, does not have to be explained and takes only seconds if dice are readily available.

Trustworthiness regarding the randomizing device means that respondents understand that the outcome of the randomization procedure is truly random and that they believe that the outcome is not detectable by somebody else. The first aspect of trustworthiness, understanding, is assured for well-known randomizing procedures such as throwing dice, flipping a coin, or drawing a card from a deck. Nevertheless, true randomness may be put into question if uncommon or novel random devices are used, such as picking numbers on a screen or using digits of a phone number.

Randomness may also be put into question when the outcome distribution is susceptible to manipulation. This is the case with most "virtual" randomizing devices implemented in online surveys, such as digital coins, dice, or spinners (see Peeters, Lensvelt-Mulders, & Lasthuizen, 2010; Coutts & Jann, 2011 for implementations).

The second aspect of trustworthiness, confidence in the undetectability of the outcome, is often an issue when the RRT is used in interviewer-administered surveys. Respondents might suspect that the interviewer is somehow able to observe the outcome of the randomization procedure. Twenty percent of respondents instructed to draw colored chips from a box in an RRT survey indicated they believed the interviewer knew which chip they would draw—making RRT pointless for these respondents (Wiseman, Moriarty, & Schafer, 1975). A similar issue arises with virtual randomizing devices in online surveys whose outcome might be suspected of being traceable. Undetectability, furthermore, might be questioned when respondents' answers to "randomizing questions" are used in place of a physical randomizing device. A randomizing question, that is, a question which serves as a randomizing device, may be asked if the distribution of a particular attribute in the surveyed population is known. For instance, the number of persons whose birthday falls in a particular month of the year ("If your birthday is between January and March, please answer the following question:. . . . If your birthday is between April and December, please answer the following question:. . . ."). However, responses to randomizing questions of this type are still detectable in principle if they refer to respondents themselves or to their relatives and, thus, raise suspicion.

Availability, finally, means that the randomizing device should be within respondents' reach during the survey. Availability is guaranteed if an interviewer is present to hand over the randomizing device or if the randomizing device is sent out together with a paper-and-pencil questionnaire. In online and telephone surveys, however, the use of a physical randomizing device is almost always problematic. Dice or cards, for instance, are rarely within respondents' reach. Sending these devices to respondents in advance works in some situations (see de Jong, Pieters, & Fox, 2010 for an example), yet it is costly and still does not guarantee that respondents have the device actually at hand when they answer the survey. The same holds for more common devices such as coins or banknotes. Even though they are available to all respondents in principle, having to get up from the computer to get one's wallet leads some respondents to skip the randomization procedure. The only safe strategy for self-administered and telephone surveys regarding availability is—in our view—to avoid any physical randomizing device and to use what we call a "randomizing question".

Questions on birthdays or other known demographics have been used frequently as non-sensitive questions in the unrelated-question RRT design (Horvitz et al., 1967). But they have rarely been used as a randomizing device for the first step in the RRT procedure to determine whether the sensitive or the non-sensitive question has to be answered. In one of the few early RRT studies that applied such a randomizing question, Brown (1975, as cited in Fox & Tracy, 1986, p. 61f.) used a demographic question on respondents' mothers' dates of birth in order to determine whether a sensitive or a non-sensitive question had to be answered subsequently. Besides the apparent advantage of availability in all survey situations the use of a randomizing question also entails some caveats. Detectability has already been mentioned. In addition, it is usually difficult to find one or more suitable randomizing questions as the set of possible questions with known response distribution in the surveyed population is usually very restricted.

Respondents' Objective and Subjectively Perceived Privacy Protection

The core rationale underlying the RRT is that respondents understand that their answers remain totally concealed and that thus admitting sensitive behavior bears no risk at all. Respondents' privacy protection is supposed to lead to more truthful answers and hence to an increase in data validity. Because the deterministic link between individual survey response and admittance of a sensitive behavior is broken by introducing randomness into the answering process, respondents' protection is guaranteed in all RRT designs. Nonetheless, a probabilistic link between individual response and sensitive behavior remains. The strength of the probabilistic link depends on the particular RRT design and on the true prevalence of the sensitive behavior under question. The researcher directly influences it by defining the RRT design parameter p, the probability with which respondents have to answer the sensitive question. A higher p increases the correlation between the individual response and the admittance of sensitive behavior. As a consequence, "respondents' jeopardy" (Fox & Tracy, 1986, p. 32), defined as $P(\text{sens.behavior}|\text{yes answer})$, the probability that a respondent giving a "yes" response actually admitted the sensitive behavior under question, increases.[1]

However, the choice of p not only influences respondents' jeopardy or—conversely—respondents' privacy but also the variance of the RRT estimator as shown in the preceding section. From this fact originates the researcher's dilemma in choosing an appropriate p for an RRT design: on the one hand, p should be low in order to provide a high level of privacy protection to respondents; on the other hand, p should be as high as possible in order to obtain an efficient estimator (see Lensvelt-Mulders, Hox, & van der Heijden, 2005 for statistical implications of the choice of RRT design parameters).

Yet, as Moriarty and Wiseman (1976) already pointed out, it is essential to distinguish between the objective p of an RRT design, and p and the privacy protection as perceived by respondents. Only the latter affects respondents' trust as well as compliance and, as a consequence, the validity of measurements obtained through the RRT. Even though a correlation between the objective value of p and respondents' perceived privacy protection may be expected, there is virtually no knowledge about this empirical relation. Studies on the effect of different values of p on respondents' trust in the RRT, on perceived privacy protection, and on data validity are almost nonexistent and the RRT literature gives no empirically grounded advice on which p to choose. A study by Soeken and Macready (1982) is the only exception known to us. They found a slight decrease in respondents' perceived privacy protection with increasing p and a statistically significantly lower perceived protection for $p = .91$ compared to values of $p \leq .84$.

10.3 BENFORD RRT: A NEW RANDOMIZING DEVICE USING BENFORD'S LAW

In this section we present Benford RRT, a new randomizing device (originally suggested in Diekmann, 2012), which fulfills the stated requirements of a good RRT randomizing device. At the core of Benford RRT lies a randomizing question on the first digit of an acquaintance's address house number. First digits of house numbers follow, as we will show in the next section, a known distribution, namely the Benford distribution. This fact can be used to obtain a suitable randomizing device that is applicable in all circumstances. Furthermore, we show how Benford RRT increases the efficiency of the RRT estimator by exploiting the divergence between respondents' objective privacy protection and their subjectively perceived privacy protection. This divergence is particularly high in the case of Benford RRT due to the "Benford illusion", the substantial misperception of the frequency of Benford distributed numbers.

Benford's Law of First Digits

First digits of many real-life data follow a particular distribution with low digits (i.e., "1") occurring more often than larger digits (i.e., "9"). This fact has been discovered and the distribution formalized by Newcomb (1881) and later Benford (1938). It is nowadays widely known as Benford's law. Benford's law states that the probabilities of first digits d = 1, 2, . . . , 9 are

$$P(d) = \log_{10}(1 + 1/d) \qquad (10.4)$$

First digits of the population of countries, the size of lakes, numbers in tax declarations or in newspaper articles, and many other data have all been shown to follow this distribution (e.g., Diekmann, 2012).

In principle, all of these data sources could be used as a randomizing device for Benford RRT. The empirical fit to the Newcomb-Benford distribution should in any case be carefully tested, as the preconditions which produce Benford-distributed first digits might not be fulfilled. For instance, the first digits of numbers in the Bible do follow a Benford distribution, with the exception of the digit 7, which is overrepresented (Hüngerbühler, 2007). Benford (1938) already hypothesized that first digits of house numbers follow a Benford distribution and found supporting evidence using the American Men of Science directory. Diekmann (2012) examined the same, using the Swiss telephone directory. Figure 10.1 shows

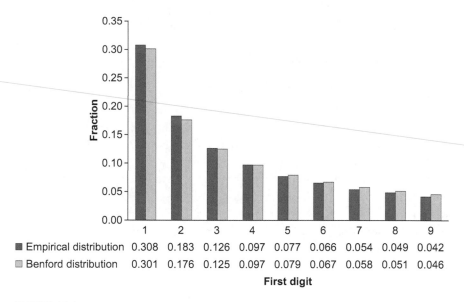

	1	2	3	4	5	6	7	8	9
■ Empirical distribution	0.308	0.183	0.126	0.097	0.077	0.066	0.054	0.049	0.042
▨ Benford distribution	0.301	0.176	0.125	0.097	0.079	0.067	0.058	0.051	0.046

First digit

FIGURE 10.1

Comparison of the empirical distribution of first digits of house numbers from the Swiss phone directory (TwixTel34, $N \approx 3$ million) with the Benford distribution. Numbers compiled by Stefan Wehrli.

that the empirical distribution of first digits of house numbers of Swiss addresses almost perfectly fits the Benford distribution, hence, obeys Benford's law. In a subsequent test, respondents of a general population survey were asked to indicate the house number of an acquaintance. The distribution of the first digits of house numbers generated through this process was in line with the theoretical Benford distribution (Diekmann, 2012). This gives empirical support to the assumption that first digits of house numbers of acquaintances generated by survey respondents approximately follow the Benford distribution.

Implementing Benford RRT

Benford RRT uses a question on the first digit of the house number of an acquaintance's address as a randomizing question. It can be implemented as follows (see also Figure 10.2):

> *Please think of an acquaintance of yours whose address you know. Now take the first digit of this person's house number.*
>
> *If this digit is 1 to 5, please answer the following question: Have you ever cheated on your taxes?*
>
> *If this digit is 6 to 9, please answer this question: Is your mother's birthday in the months of January through June?*

In this example of an unrelated-question RRT design, the first digit of the house number determines whether a respondent subsequently has to answer a sensitive or a non-sensitive question. p is defined as .78 by choosing the range of digits $\{1, 2, 3, 4, 5\}$ leading to the sensitive question and $\{6, 7, 8, 9\}$ to the non-sensitive question; but, of course, other values are possible.

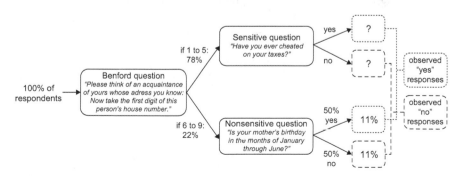

FIGURE 10.2
Benford RRT in the unrelated-question RRT design.

As first digits of house numbers follow the Benford distribution, a question on the first digit of a randomly chosen address's house number becomes a naturally occurring randomizing device with a known outcome distribution without the need for any physical artifact such as dice or coins. This makes it suitable for any survey situation.

The "Benford Illusion"

The use of a Benford question as randomizing device for the RRT bears the additional advantage that respondents usually underestimate the probability of the occurrence of Benford-distributed low digits because they typically assume a rather uniform distribution. Survey respondents, when explicitly asked, substantially underestimated the probability of the occurrence of the first digits 1 to 4 in house numbers by .09 with a subjective estimate of 0.61 ($N = 295$; Diekmann, 2012). By making use of that misperception—the Benford illusion—the tradeoff between statistical efficiency and respondents' perceived privacy protection in RRT designs is relaxed. A higher probability p that respondents are instructed to answer the sensitive question may be chosen without provoking respondents' privacy concerns because respondents' subjectively perceived p is substantially lower than the objective p.

The idea that a good randomizing device for the RRT should bear the property that respondents perceive p as smaller than the objective p, was originally brought up by Moriarty and Wiseman (1976). They investigated respondents' perception of p for different randomizing devices and found that using two dice had the desired property. Respondents heavily underestimated the outcome probability of a throw of two dice being 4 to 10 by .13 with a median perceived probability of .70; a misperception bias that is similar in magnitude to the one of Benford RRT. In this sense, Benford RRT can be seen as a substitute for the throw of two dice in interview situations where no interviewer is present to provide respondents with dice.

10.4 AN APPLICATION IN A SURVEY ON STUDENT CHEATING

Data and Design

We implemented Benford RRT in an online student survey on exam cheating and plagiarism at two major Swiss universities (Höglinger, Jann, and Diekmann, 2014a). All students enrolled at the two institutions were contacted via their official university email address in spring 2011. Out of a total of 19,410 students, 6,494 completed the survey, resulting in a response rate of 33% (RR1; AAPOR, 2011). Two hundred and one respondents who partially completed, i.e., reached the part of the questionnaire with the sensitive questions, are also included in the following analyses. Respondents who had neither sat an exam nor submitted a paper (386), or who had poor German language skills (230), as well as 67 respondents with incomplete data have been excluded, leaving us with a sample of 6,012 observations. The subsequent analyses are, furthermore, restricted to 1,001 respondents who were surveyed in direct questioning mode and 994 surveyed using Benford RRT.

Survey respondents were asked five sensitive questions about their own cheating behavior, using either direct questioning, Benford RRT, or one of four other RRT variants, which will not be discussed here. Assignment to one of these sensitive question techniques was randomized. The wording of the sensitive questions was identical in all conditions. Benford RRT was implemented in an unrelated-question RRT design as presented in the preceding section. Half of the respondents were directed to the sensitive question with probability $p = .70$, the other half with $p = .78$. This allowed the investigation of whether a different p has any effect on respondents' admittance of sensitive behavior or on their perceived privacy protection. The unrelated non-sensitive questions consisted of five questions on respondents' mothers' dates of birth, with answer distributions of $P(yes|nonsens.\ quest.) \cong .5$ (see endnote 2 for the question wording).[2] Their order was randomized to offset any effects of a particular unrelated question.

Results

In order to evaluate Benford RRT, in the following section we compare prevalence estimates of respondents' admittance of sensitive behavior resulting from Benford RRT and from direct questioning (DQ). Assuming that respondents only falsely deny but never falsely admit a sensitive behavior, higher prevalence estimates are interpreted as a result of more respondents answering truthfully. According to this "more-is-better assumption", which is the basis of all comparative RRT studies (e.g., Lensvelt-Mulders, Hox, van der Heijden, & Maas, 2005), higher prevalence estimates of one method indicate its superior validity. Due to the experimental design, i.e., the fact that respondents were randomly assigned to either Benford RRT or direct questioning, differences in prevalence estimates can be interpreted as causal effects of the particular sensitive question technique. RRT point estimates and standard errors are calculated using a generalization of the formulae from the first section to the case where different values of p and P(yes|nonsens.quest.) for subgroups of respondents are used. The procedure is implemented in the Stata module rreg (Jann, 2008).

Figure 10.3 presents comparisons of prevalence estimates for the five surveyed sensitive cheating behaviors between direct questioning (DQ) and Benford RRT. In the left panel, prevalence point estimates with 95% confidence intervals specified by the lines on both sides of the point estimates are depicted. Estimates range from 17.8% of students admitting having copied in an exam to 1.5% of students admitting partial paper plagiarism. Clearly discernible is the pattern of estimates resulting from Benford RRT

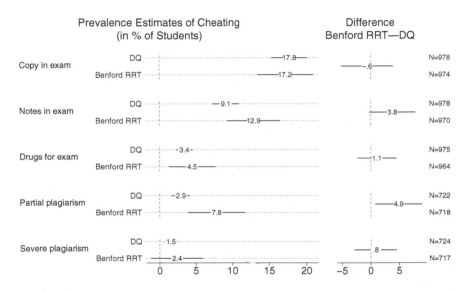

FIGURE 10.3

Comparison of prevalence estimates of cheating between direct questioning (DQ) and Benford RRT. Lines indicate 95% CIs.* N varies between the different items because questions on cheating in exams have been asked only of respondents who sat in at least one exam; questions on plagiarism only of respondents who have handed in a paper.

*Wording of the sensitive questions (translated from German):

Copy in exam: "In your studies, have you ever copied from other students during an exam?"

Notes in exam: "In your studies, have you ever used illicit crib notes in an exam (including notes on mobile phones, calculators, or similar)?"

Drugs for exam: "In your studies, have you ever used prescription drugs to enhance your performance in an exam?"

Partial plagiarism: "In your studies, have you ever handed in a paper containing a passage deliberately taken from someone else's work without citing the original?"

Severe plagiarism: "In your studies, have you ever had someone else write a large part of a submitted paper for you or have you handed in someone else's paper as your own?"

being higher than the corresponding DQ estimates except for the first item, "copy in exam", where the Benford RRT estimate is marginally lower by 0.6 [−5.0; 3.9] percentage points. Note that confidence intervals for Benford RRT estimates are considerably larger than for DQ, which is due to the RRT's inherently lower statistical efficiency.

Differences between Benford RRT and DQ estimates are portrayed in the right panel of Figure 10.3. If confidence intervals do not include the zero line, prevalence estimates between Benford RRT and DQ differ significantly at the 95% level. Results show a significant difference only for one out of the five sensitive items, namely "partial plagiarism", where the Benford RRT estimate is 4.9 [.8; 9.0] percentage points higher than the DQ estimate. For the item "notes in exam" the Benford RRT estimate is 3.8 [−.2; 7.8] percentage points higher than the DQ estimate; but with a p-value of .06 the difference just misses the conventional significance level.

Further analysis showed that the survey break-off rate for Benford RRT was almost twice as high as for direct questioning but remained with 2.2% of respondents within an acceptable level. Considering that answering the sensitive questions took respondents 175 seconds with Benford RRT and only 53 seconds with DQ, this is no surprise. Respondents' self-stated trust in the survey's anonymity and privacy protection measures was lower for Benford RRT (73% do trust) than for DQ (81%).[3] The RRT procedure seems, initially, to intensify privacy concerns among respondents. However, the risk of disclosure, i.e., the risk that any respondents' cheating behavior will be exposed because of the survey, is considered lower in the case of Benford RRT (79% see no risk) compared to DQ (71%).[4]

Finally, we compared prevalence estimates and respondents' perceived privacy protection for Benford RRT designs with different levels of privacy protection, i.e., with different values of p, the probability with which respondents are instructed to answer the sensitive question. Using $p = .70$ and $p = .78$, results showed no significant differences in prevalence estimates and no discernible pattern of one RRT design performing systematically differently from the other (see detailed results in the online appendix). Furthermore, respondents' assessment of anonymity and privacy protection, as well as risk of disclosure, did not differ between the two conditions. Choosing $p = .78$ instead of $p = .70$ had clearly no effect on prevalence estimates or respondents' perception of privacy. Yet, the choice of p affects statistical efficiency. Therefore, $p = .78$ is the preferred choice for an implementation of the Benford RRT. Possibly, even a higher p than $p = .78$ could be chosen without affecting respondents' privacy and data validity.

10.5 CONCLUSIONS

In this chapter we have introduced Benford RRT, a new randomizing device for the RRT based on Benford's law, and have presented results of an empirical evaluation of the method. The new randomizing device uses a randomizing question and does not need any physical artifact. Therefore, it is particularly suitable for self-administered surveys and telephone surveys. In addition, it allows for increasing the statistical efficiency of the RRT without jeopardizing respondents' perceived privacy protection by taking advantage of the Benford illusion, namely, respondents' misperception of Benford-distributed first digits.

Benford RRT performed well in our online survey on student cheating behavior. In one out of five items it generated a higher, and, under the more-is-better assumption, a more valid, estimate of sensitive behavior than direct questioning. A second item estimate was substantially higher, but with $p = .06$ missed conventional significance levels. No Benford RRT estimate was substantially lower than the DQ estimates, and all Benford RRT estimates were positive and meaningful. In contrast to other RRT online implementations (see, for instance, Coutts, Jann, Krumpal, & Näher, 2011; Coutts & Jann, 2011; Peeters, 2006), the problem of severely negatively biased or even negative estimates did not arise in our implementation of Benford RRT. It should be noted, however, that a new RRT variant, the Crosswise Model (Yu, Tian, & Tang, 2008), which was also implemented in our study, performed even better than Benford RRT and seems to be another well-performing, promising method to survey sensitive questions (see Höglinger, Jann, & Diekmann, 2014b).

Results also showed that an increase of the probability p with which respondents are instructed to answer the sensitive question by .08 to $p = .78$ had no effect on estimates nor on respondents' perceived privacy protection. Thus, it is safe to choose p as high as $p = .78$ when implementing Benford RRT. Future studies should address in more detail how far p can be increased without endangering data validity. It remains unclear, though, whether a decrease or increase of p within a reasonable range has no effect on respondents' perceived privacy protection in other RRT designs or whether this is somehow related to the Benford illusion, a special property of Benford RRT. Results suggest, in any case, that respondents' perception of privacy protection is mainly driven by other design considerations than the mere choice of p.

Whether the increase in more truthful answers achieved through Benford RRT justifies the additional burden put on respondents and the need for bigger sample sizes in order to compensate for the RRT's lower statistical efficiency depends on two things: the sensitivity of the topic surveyed and whether a sizeable respondent sample is actually available. If an implementation of the RRT is considered, however, Benford RRT seems to be a well-performing RRT variant that is easily implemented not only, but particularly, in survey situations where no interviewer is present.

ACKNOWLEDGEMENT

We thank Ben Jann for his support in the design and conduct of this study as well as for valuable suggestions on improving the manuscript.

FUNDING

This research was supported by a grant from the German Research Foundation, DI 292/5 to Andreas Diekmann.

NOTES

1. There are several other, more sophisticated measures of privacy protection for RRT designs suggested in the literature (for some early works see Lanke, 1975; Leysieffer & Warner, 1976; Greenberg, Kuebler, Abernathy, & Horvitz, 1977).
2. The wording of the unrelated questions was as follows (translated from German):
   Is your mother's birthday in the months of January through June?
   Is your mother's birthday in an even-numbered month? (Feb., Apr., Jun., Aug., Oct., Dec.)
   Is your mother's birthday in the first half of the month? (from 1st to 15th)
   Is your mother's birthday on an even-numbered day? (2nd, 4th, 6th, etc. of the month)
   Is your mother's birth year even-numbered? (Please, consider 0 as an even number.)
3. Wording of the question: "Please be honest: How much do you trust our measures for guaranteeing survey participants' anonymity and privacy protection?" Response categories "very much" and "quite a bit" have been coded as respondent does trust; response categories "partly", "rather not", and "not at all" as respondent does not trust.
4. Wording of the question: "In your opinion, how likely is it that it can be traced back to a particular respondent whether they carried out one of the surveyed sensitive behaviors (copying in exam, crib notes, plagiarism, etc.)?" Response categories "impossible" and "very unlikely" have been coded as respondent sees no risk; response categories "rather unlikely", "rather likely", and "very likely" as respondent sees a risk.

BIBLIOGRAPHY

AAPOR. (2011). *Standard definitions. Final dispositions of case codes and outcome rates for surveys.* (7th ed.). Lenexa, Kansas: AAPOR—The American Association for Public Opinion Research.

Benford, F. (1938). The law of anomalous numbers. *Proceedings of the American Philosophical Society, 78*(4), 551–572.

Coutts, E., & Jann, B. (2011). Sensitive questions in online surveys: Experimental results for the Randomized Response Technique (RRT) and the Unmatched Count Technique (UCT). *Sociological Methods & Research, 40*(1), 169–193. doi:10.1177/0049124110390768

Coutts, E., Jann, B., Krumpal, I., & Näher, A.-F. (2011). Plagiarism in student papers: Prevalence estimates using special techniques for sensitive questions. *Journal of Economics and Statistics, 231*(56), 749–760.

de Jong, M. G., Pieters, R., & Fox, J.-P. (2010). Reducing social desirability bias through item randomized response: An application to measure underreported desires. *Journal of Marketing Research, 47*(1), 14–27. doi:10.1509/jmkr.47.1.14

Diekmann, A. (2012). Making use of "Benford's law" for the Randomized Response Technique. *Sociological Methods & Research, 41*(2), 325–334. doi:10.1177/0049124112452525

Fox, J. A., & Tracy, P. E. (1986). *Randomized response: A method for sensitive surveys.* Newbury Park, CA: Sage.

Greenberg, B. G., Abul-Ela, A.-L.A., Simmons, W. R., & Horvitz, D. G. (1969). The unrelated question randomized response model: Theoretical framework. *Journal of the American Statistical Association, 64*, 520–539.

Greenberg, B. G., Kuebler, R. R., Abernathy, J. R., & Horvitz, D. G. (1977). Respondent hazards in the unrelated question randomized response model. *Journal of Statistical Planning and Inference, 1*(1), 53–60. doi:10.1016/0378-3758(77)90005-2

Höglinger, M., Jann, B., & Diekmann, A. (2014a). Online-Survey on "Exams and written papers". Documentation. ETH Zurich and University of Bern.

Höglinger, M., Jann, B., & Diekmann, A. (2014b). Sensitive questions in online surveys: An experimental evaluation of the Randomized Response Technique and the Crosswise Model. Working Paper. ETH Zurich and University of Bern.

Horvitz, D. G., Shah, B. V., & Simmons, W. R. (1967). The unrelated question randomized response model. *Proceedings in the Social Science Section, American Statistical Association*, 65–72.

Hüngerbühler, N. (2007). Benfords Gesetz ueber fuehrende Ziffern: Wie die Mathematik Steuersuendern das Fuerchten lehrt. In EducETH (Ed.). Retrieved from www.educ.ethz.ch/unt/um/mathe/ana/benford/Benford_Fuehrende_Ziffern.pdf

Jann, B. (2008). Rrreg: Stata module to estimate linear probability model for randomized response data. *Statistical Software Components S456962*: Boston College Department of Economics.

Lanke, J. (1975). On the choice of the unrelated question in Simmons' version of randomized response. *Journal of the American Statistical Association, 70*(349), 80–83. doi:10.1080/01621459.1975.10480265

Lensvelt-Mulders, G.J.L.M., Hox, J. J., & van der Heijden, P.G.M. (2005). How to improve the efficiency of randomised response designs. *Quality & Quantity, 39*(3), 253–265.

Lensvelt-Mulders, G.J.L.M., Hox, J. J., van der Heijden, P.G.M., & Maas, C.J.M. (2005). Meta-analysis of randomized response research: Thirty-five years of validation. *Sociological Methods & Research, 33*(3), 319–348. doi:10.1177/0049124104268664

Leysieffer, F. W., & Warner, S. L. (1976). Respondent jeopardy and optimal designs in randomized response models. *Journal of the American Statistical Association, 71*(355), 649–656. doi:10.2307/2285595

Moriarty, M., & Wiseman, F. (1976). *On the choice of a randomization technique with the randomized response model.* Paper presented at the Proceedings of the Social Statistics Section, American Statistical Association.

Newcomb, S. (1881). Note on the frequency of use of the different digits in natural numbers. *American Journal of Mathematics, 4*(1/4).

Peeters, C.F.W. (2006). *Measuring politically sensitive behavior. Using probability theory in the form of randomized response to estimate prevalence and incidence of misbehavior in the public sphere: A test on integrity violations.* Amsterdam: Faculty of Social Sciences, Vrije Universiteit Amsterdam.

Peeters, C.F.W., Lensvelt-Mulders, G.J.L., & Lasthuizen, K. (2010). A note on a simple and practical randomized response framework for eliciting sensitive dichotomous and quantitative information. *Sociological Methods & Research, 39*(2), 283–296. doi:10.1177/0049124110378099

Soeken, K. L., & Macready, G. B. (1982). Respondents' perceived protection when using randomized response. *Psychological Bulletin, 92*(2), 487–489. doi:10.1037/0033-2909.92.2.487

Warner, S. L. (1965). Randomized-response: A survey technique for eliminating evasive answer bias. *Journal of the American Statistical Association, 60*(309), 63–69.

Wiseman, F., Moriarty, M., & Schafer, M. (1975). Estimating public opinion with the randomized response model. *The Public Opinion Quarterly, 39*(4), 507–513.

Yu, J.-W., Tian, G.-L., & Tang, M.-L. (2008). Two new models for survey sampling with sensitive characteristics: Design and analysis. *Metrika, 67*(3), 251–263.

11

Asking Sensitive Questions

A Critical Account of the Randomized Response Technique and Related Methods

Ivar Krumpal, Ben Jann, Katrin Auspurg and Hagen von Hermanni

11.1 INTRODUCTION

In surveys, self-reports on sensitive issues (e.g. sexual behavior, personal health, illicit drug use, income, or attitudes towards minorities) are often distorted by social desirability bias because respondents are inclined to engage in impression management or self-deception. More specifically, respondents tend to systematically overreport socially desirable attributes and underreport socially undesirable ones. In an interview situation, they answer in accordance with perceived social norms or even refuse to answer the sensitive questions at all (Krumpal, 2013). Both can seriously bias survey estimates of sensitive characteristics. Different data collection strategies, so-called dejeopardizing techniques (Lee, 1993, p. 82) or indirect methods (Tourangeau & Yan, 2007, p. 871), have been proposed to elicit sensitive information from survey respondents and to attenuate the problem of social desirability bias in self-reports.

The common principle underlying these techniques is to anonymize answers at the individual level, making it impossible to determine a respondent's true status with respect to the sensitive characteristic under consideration. In this chapter, we will discuss the following "indirect methods": the randomized response technique (RRT), a recent variant of the RRT called the crosswise model (CM), and the item count technique (ICT).

11.2 THE RANDOMIZED RESPONSE TECHNIQUE (RRT)

All RRT schemes rely on a simple principle: in the question-and-answer process, respondents use a randomizing device (e.g. coins or dice) to obscure the meaning of an answer communicated to the interviewer. The crucial point is that the outcome of the randomizing device remains private information of the respondent. For example, in the forced-response design (Boruch, 1971) the respondent might be requested to throw three coins without telling the results to the interviewer. The respondent is then instructed to answer "yes" if the result is tails three times ($p_1 = 0.5^3 = 0.125$), to answer "no" if the result is heads three times ($p_2 = 0.5^3 = 0.125$), or to give a truthful answer to the sensitive question ("yes" or "no") if the result is a mixture of heads and tails ($1 - p_1 - p_2 = 0.750$); (see Diagram c in Figure 11.1). Since the link between a given answer and the respondent's true status is only probabilistic, nothing definite about the respondent's true status can be inferred from a given answer. However, since the probability distribution of the randomizing design is known, the prevalence of the sensitive characteristic can be estimated on the basis of probability theory: The expected value λ of an observed "yes" answer given the described RRT design can be written as $\lambda = p_1 + (1 - p_1 - p_2)\pi$, where π is the unknown population rate of subjects with the sensitive characteristic. Solving for π yields $\pi = (\lambda - p_1)/(1 - p_1 - p_2)$. An estimate $\hat{\pi}$ of the population proportion of the sensitive characteristic can then be obtained by substituting λ with its estimate $\hat{\lambda}$, which is simply the proportion of "yes" answers observed in the sample.

Establishing a probabilistic relationship between the observed answers and the unobserved true scores is the fundamental principle underlying the various RRT designs that have been developed over the last 50 years (see Figure 11.1). The most popular ones are (in chronological order): (1) Warner's (1965) original method, in which the randomizing device decides whether the sensitive question or its negation is to be answered;[1] (2) the unrelated question technique, in which the randomizing device decides whether the sensitive question or an unrelated nonsensitive question, whose distribution is known or estimated, is to be answered (Horvitz, Shah, & Simmons, 1967; Greenberg, Abul-Ela, Simmons, & Horvitz, 1969; Greenberg, Kuebler, Abernathy, & Horvitz, 1971; Moors, 1971); (3) the forced response technique, in which the randomizing

a) Warner's RRT

sensitive question — π → yes; $1-\pi$ → no

RANDOM: p → sensitive question; $1-p$ → negated sensitive question

negated sensitive question — $1-\pi$ → yes; π → no

$$\hat{\pi} = \frac{\hat{\lambda} + p - 1}{2p - 1}, \quad \widehat{\mathrm{Var}}(\hat{\pi}) = \frac{\hat{\lambda}(1 - \hat{\lambda})}{(n-1)(2p-1)^2}$$

b) Unrelated Question RRT (π^u known)

sensitive question — π → yes; $1-\pi$ → no

RANDOM: p → sensitive question; $1-p$ → nonsensitive question

nonsensitive question — π^u → yes; $1-\pi^u$ → no

$$\hat{\pi} = \frac{\hat{\lambda} - (1-p)\pi^u}{p}, \quad \widehat{\mathrm{Var}}(\hat{\pi}) = \frac{\hat{\lambda}(1 - \hat{\lambda})}{(n-1)p^2}$$

c) Forced-Response RRT

sensitive question — π → yes; $1-\pi$ → no

RANDOM: $1 - p_1 - p_2$ → sensitive question; p_1 → yes; p_2 → no

$$\hat{\pi} = \frac{\hat{\lambda} - p_1}{1 - p_1 - p_2}, \quad \widehat{\mathrm{Var}}(\hat{\pi}) = \frac{\hat{\lambda}(1 - \hat{\lambda})}{(n-1)(1-p_1-p_2)^2}$$

d) Kuk's RRT

sensitive question — π → RANDOM 1; $1-\pi$ → RANDOM 2

RANDOM 1 — p_1 → red; $1-p_1$ → blue

RANDOM 2 — p_2 → red; $1-p_2$ → blue

$$\hat{\pi} = \frac{\hat{\lambda} - p_2}{p_1 - p_2}, \quad \widehat{\mathrm{Var}}(\hat{\pi}) = \frac{\hat{\lambda}(1 - \hat{\lambda})}{(n-1)(p_1-p_2)^2}$$

e) Mangat's RRT

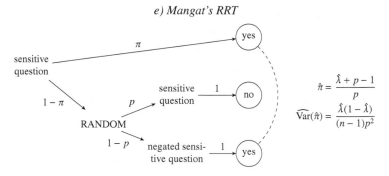

sensitive question — π → yes; $1-\pi$ → RANDOM

RANDOM: p → sensitive question → 1 → no; $1-p$ → negated sensitive question → 1 → yes

$$\hat{\pi} = \frac{\hat{\lambda} + p - 1}{p}$$

$$\widehat{\mathrm{Var}}(\hat{\pi}) = \frac{\hat{\lambda}(1 - \hat{\lambda})}{(n-1)p^2}$$

($\hat{\lambda}$ is the sample proportion of answer "yes" or "red"; n is the sample size)

FIGURE 11.1
Various RRT schemes

device decides whether the sensitive question is to be answered or a direct "yes" or "no" answer is to be given (Boruch, 1971); (4) Kuk's (1990) "two packs of cards" technique, in which the respondent draws one card each from two decks with different proportions of red and blue cards and names the interviewer only the color from the first (second) deck in case the answer to the sensitive question is yes (no); (5) Mangat's (1994) technique, in which respondents answer "yes" if the sensitive attribute applies and follow Warner's RRT otherwise. Besides the measurement of dichotomous sensitive variables, RRT schemes have also been developed for quantitative sensitive characteristics (Himmelfarb & Edgell, 1980; Gjestvang & Singh, 2007). Useful overviews comparing different RRT designs (with respect to their statistical power or details of implementation) can be found in Fox and Tracy (1986), Chaudhuri and Mukerjee (1988), Lensvelt-Mulders, Hox, and van der Heijden (2005a), and Chaudhuri (2011). Furthermore, statistical methods have been developed to analyze multivariate relationships between a response variable generated via the RRT and background covariates (a maximum likelihood approach can be found in Maddala, 1983 and has been implemented by Jann, 2011). Due to the data misclassification induced by the RRT procedure, however, statistical efficiency of estimates gained from RRT data is generally much lower than the efficiency of direct questioning estimates. That is, a much larger sample size is usually required to achieve a desired level of statistical power, which raises questions about cost efficiency and the trade-off between bias and variance. In any case, it is advisable to perform careful power analyses before employing randomized response methods (formulas to calculate the standard errors can be found in the literature cited above).

Given the assumption that respondents have trust in their privacy protection and comply with the RRT rules, more embarrassing answers to sensitive questions are expected in the RRT compared to conventional methods of data collection. A vast number of experimental studies have been conducted to test this hypothesis. Some were validation studies with known true scores (Wolter & Preisendörfer, 2013). Most were, however, comparative studies without known true scores, where the only possibility to "validate" the RRT was to compare its estimates with those of other methods like direct questioning, using the "more-is-better" ("less-is-better") assumption for socially undesirable (desirable) characteristics.[2] In many cases, the RRT yielded more valid estimates for embarrassing or illegal behaviors such as illicit drug use (Goodstadt & Gruson, 1975), abortion (Lara, Strickler, Olavarrieta, & Ellertson, 2004), academic cheating among students (Scheers & Dayton, 1987), or unsocial attitudes such as xenophobia and anti-Semitism (Krumpal, 2012). A meta-analysis conducted by Lensvelt-Mulders, Hox, van der Heijden, and

Maas (2005b) suggests that, overall, more honest answers are elicited with RRT than with alternative methods of data collection. In other empirical studies, however, serious problems regarding the application of the RRT are documented, such as higher item-nonresponse and increased break-off rates (Krumpal, 2010). Even more serious, there is evidence that some respondents refuse to comply with the RRT rules and provide self-protective "no" answers even if the result of the randomizing device instructs them to answer "yes" (Ostapczuk, Musch, & Moshagen, 2009; Coutts & Jann, 2011).[3] Furthermore, in a randomized experiment assigning respondents to either RRT or direct questioning, Weissman, Steer, and Lipton (1986) reported that 55 (47.8%) of the 115 respondents allocated to the RRT mode denied its use and switched to the direct questioning mode. Such self-selection could seriously bias the estimates based on the RRT. A brief overview of RRT failures, that is, of studies reporting no significant differences or even significantly lower estimates of sensitive characteristics for the RRT measures compared to direct self-reports, can be found in Holbrook and Krosnick (2010a).

From a practical point of view it is crucial that respondents understand and trust the procedure. Therefore, it is highly recommended to develop RRT instructions that are easy to understand and are kept as simple as possible. This particularly holds for self-administered survey modes such as CASI or online surveys where RRT instructions must be self-explanatory (an example of RRT instructions for online interviews can be found in Lensvelt-Mulders, van der Heijden, Laudy, & van Gils, 2006, pp. 316–317). Furthermore, in interviewer-administered survey modes (such as CAPI or CATI) special interviewer training is needed to communicate the rules of the RRT comprehensibly and such that respondents trust in their privacy protection (an example of RRT instructions for a CATI survey can be found in Krumpal, 2012). This implies a higher pretesting effort and higher data collection costs (besides the statistical power aspect). On the benefit side, if the RRT design is carefully tailored to the specific population under investigation and if the data generation process is closely monitored, more valid prevalence estimates and better data quality can result, as various successful implementations confirm (Lensvelt-Mulders et al., 2005b).

11.3 THE CROSSWISE MODEL (CM)

Recently, an interesting variant of the RRT, called the crosswise model (CM), has been proposed by Yu, Tian, and Tang (2008; see also Tan, Tian, & Tang, 2009; Tian & Tang, 2013). Although the CM is formally equivalent to Warner's RRT, its unique conceptual approach makes it a promising candidate to overcome one central flaw of RRT designs, namely the problem of self-protective "no" answers. In most RRT schemes at least some of the respondents are instructed to provide an answer to the sensitive question, even if this is obscured from the researcher. Furthermore, in many designs, a clear dominant answer strategy exists to reject any association with the sensitive behavior (for example, answering "no" in the forced-response RRT). The CM circumvents these problems by instructing the respondents to provide an answer based on the combination of a sensitive question and an unrelated nonsensitive question. Let X be the sensitive variable of interest. X is equal to 1 for respondents who carry the sensitive characteristic (e.g. who plagiarized a seminar paper or thesis) and 0 otherwise. In addition, let Y denote a nonsensitive binary variable that is independent of X and for which the population prevalence $p = Pr(Y = 1)$ is known. For example, Y may be equal to 1 for respondents whose father is born between October and December ($p = .25$, assuming a uniform birthday distribution across months) and 0 otherwise. Instead of answering either the sensitive question or the nonsensitive question (e.g. as in the unrelated question RRT), respondents are asked to provide an answer depending on whether X and Y are the same or different, as illustrated in Figure 11.2.

That is, respondents are instructed to choose answer option "A" or "the same" if their answer to both items is the same. Likewise, the response is "B" or "different" if the answers to the two items differ. Hence, option "A" ("the same") contains the members of both the nonsensitive subclass of respondents who did not commit plagiarism and whose father is born between January and September ($X = 0$ and $Y = 0$) as well as the sensitive subclass of respondents who plagiarized and whose father is born between October and December ($X = 1$ and $Y = 1$). Similarly, option "B" ("different") contains the members of both the nonsensitive subclass of respondents who did not commit plagiarism and whose father is born between October and December ($X = 1$ and $Y = 1$) as well as the sensitive subclass of respondents who plagiarized and whose father is born between January and September ($X = 0$ and $Y = 0$).

| | | Sensitive Question | |
		$X = 0$	$X = 1$
Nonsensitive Question	$Y = 0$	A (the same)	B (different)
	$Y = 1$	B (different)	A (the same)

FIGURE 11.2
The crosswise model

As long as the individual answers to the nonsensitive question are unknown to the researchers, the link between a respondent's answer in the CM and his or her true status with respect to the sensitive item is only probabilistic. Therefore, choosing either answer option does not reveal anything definite about the individual respondent. If the distribution of the nonsensitive item is known, the prevalence of the sensitive item can be estimated on the basis of probability theory. Let λ be the expected proportion of answer "A" ("the same"), given the known population prevalence p of the nonsensitive item and the unknown prevalence π of the sensitive item. Since λ can be written as $\lambda = (1 - p)(1 - \pi) + p\pi$ (as is evident from Figure 11.2), a natural estimate for π is given with $\hat{\pi} = \dfrac{\hat{\lambda} + p - 1}{2p - 1}$, where $\hat{\lambda}$ is the observed proportion of answer "A" ("the same") in the sample (note the equivalence to Warner's RRT in Figure 11.1).

The CM appears to be more robust to noncompliance than most other RRT schemes because there is no obvious self-protective answering strategy. Both answer options comprise a mixture of "sensitive" and "nonsensitive" subclasses of respondents, and respondents have hence little incentive to deviate from the instructions. In addition, compared to most other RRT schemes, the CM is relatively simple to implement and communicate to respondents. However, the CM also faces drawbacks with respect to statistical efficiency, requiring a larger sample size to achieve a given level of statistical power than standard direct questioning.

The CM has been applied in an experimental survey measuring plagiarism at different universities in Switzerland and Germany, comparing the CM to direct questioning (Coutts, Jann, Krumpal, & Näher, 2011; Jann, Jerke, & Krumpal, 2012). Subjects were university students who were interviewed via self-administered paper-and-pencil questionnaires in a classroom setting. Accepting the "more-is-better" assumption (see Tourangeau & Yan, 2007), the results of this study confirm the benefits of the CM for reducing social desirability bias. Similar results were found in a recent large-scale online student survey ($N = 6,000$) in Switzerland. In this study, the CM again yielded consistently higher prevalence estimates than direct questioning for a number of items about exam cheating and plagiarism (Höglinger, Jann, & Diekmann, 2014). Furthermore, CM also proved to be highly beneficial in a paper-and-pencil survey on illicit drug use among students in Tehran (Shamsipor et al., 2014).

From a practical viewpoint, recommendations with respect to the implementation of the CM are similar to other RRT schemes. It is crucial to develop and pretest the instruments thoroughly, for example, using cognitive interviews (a practical example of CM instructions for self-administered paper-and-pencil questionnaires including a brief guideline on how to develop and pretest them can be found in Jann et al., 2012). An open research question, however, is how the CM will perform in a survey of a broader (nonstudent) population. In addition, only self-administered survey modes have been used with the CM so far.

11.4 THE ITEM COUNT TECHNIQUE (ICT)

The item count technique (ICT) is an alternative method to ask sensitive questions that allows keeping an individual's true status with respect to some sensitive characteristic secret. The item count technique (Droitcour et al., 1991) is also known as "unmatched count technique" (Dalton, Wimbush, & Daily, 1994), "block total response" (Raghavarao & Federer, 1979), or the "list experiment" (Kuklinski et al., 1997). All these labels refer to the following basic concept. The survey respondents are randomly divided into two subsamples. Subjects in one subsample are instructed to respond to a "short list" (SL), containing a set of j nonsensitive dichotomous items. Subjects in the other subsample are requested to answer to a "long list" (LL), containing the identical set of j nonsensitive items plus one sensitive dichotomous item. To estimate the prevalence of a sensitive characteristic (e.g. whether respondents engage in illicit work), the following list of items could be used (Kirchner, Krumpal, Trappman, & von Hermanni, 2013):

- Do you use public transportation more than five days a week? (SL and LL)
- Do you have liability insurance? (SL and LL)
- Did you carry out any illicit work for a private individual this year? (sensitive item, LL only)
- Did you grow up in the country? (SL and LL)

Respondents are then asked to indicate the number of items that apply to them (i.e. the total number of "yes" answers), without answering each question individually. Therewith it remains unknown whether a specific respondent engaged in illicit work unless he or she reports that none or all items in the list apply. Calculating the mean difference of answers between the two subsamples yields an unbiased estimate of the population prevalence π of illicit work, that is, $\hat{\pi} = \bar{X}_{LL} - \bar{X}_{SL}$, where $\bar{X}_{LL}$ and $\bar{X}_{SL}$ are the means of the answers in the LL- and SL-subsamples, respectively. Variations of the basic ICT design (such as the double-list variant where both subsamples answer to an LL *and* an SL with differing sets of items, therefore enhancing the statistical efficiency), different estimation procedures, and advanced data analysis techniques can be found in Droitcour et al. (1991), Biemer and Brown (2005), Tsuchiya, Hirai, and Ono (2007), Corstange (2009), Imai (2011), Blair and Imai (2012), and Glynn (2013). A generalization of the ICT for quantitative sensitive characteristics was developed by Trappmann, Krumpal, Kirchner, and Jann (2014).

Several experimental studies confirm the expectation that ICT reduces social desirability bias compared to direct self-reports. Under ICT interview conditions, a higher extent of socially undesirable answers have been documented for sensitive behaviors such as employee theft (Wimbush & Dalton, 1997), risky sexual activities (LaBrie & Earleywine, 2000), hate crime victimization (Rayburn, Earleywine, & Davison, 2003), and shoplifting (Tsuchiya et al., 2007). However in some studies employing a self-administered survey mode, the results for the ICT have been mixed, for example, for voter turnout (Holbrook & Krosnick, 2010b) or cocaine use (Biemer, Jordan, Hubbard, & Wright, 2005). An overview on recent empirical research can be found in Holbrook and Krosnick (2010b).

Compared to the RRT, the ICT has several advantages. First, the respondents do not have to apply a randomizing device. Second, the principle of "counting items" appears less complex than the probabilistic concepts behind the RRT. Therefore, the cognitive burden imposed on the respondents seems lower. Third, the implementation is simple and straightforward in interviewer- and self-administered survey modes. Coutts and Jann (2011, p. 179) reported lower response times and lower item nonresponse rates for the ICT than for the RRT, while at the same time self-reported levels of trust and understanding were higher. Furthermore, in the study by Holbrook and Krosnick (2010a, 2010b), the ICT outperformed the RRT in reducing social desirability bias in self-reports about voter turnout. One drawback of the ICT, however, is its low statistical efficiency. Estimates based on the ICT have wider confidence intervals than estimates based on direct questioning for a given sample size, and usually also than estimates based on the RRT.

For the practical implementation of the ICT, a crucial aspect is the selection of the nonsensitive items in the lists (Droitcour et al., 1991; Krumpal, 2010). First, items that are too long or use complicated wording should be avoided (e.g. no double negations). Second, it seems advisable to use nonsensitive items that are coherent with the topic of the survey. Third, the maximum length of the short list should probably be restricted to three to five items. Tsuchiya et al. (2007) conducted a study in which the number of the nonsensitive items was varied at random. They conjectured that a longer short list would conceal a respondent's true status for the sensitive item more effectively and thus increase privacy protection. However, the sampling variance of the ICT estimator increases with the number of nonsensitive items and longer lists impose more cognitive burden on the respondents (Biemer et al., 2005, p. 150). For practical details and qualitative aspects regarding the construction of adequate short lists see also Tsuchiya and Hirai (2010). Fourth, with respect to statistical efficiency, the nonsensitive items should have low variances, that is, one should use items for which the population prevalence is either very low or very high. Furthermore, the statistical efficiency of the procedure can be improved by selecting negatively correlated items (Glynn, 2013). However, note that low variances and strong negative correlations can also reduce the perceived privacy protection.

11.5 CONCLUSIONS

In sensitive surveys, reducing social desirability bias in respondents' self-reports has proved to be a challenging task. There is cumulative evidence that misreporting about sensitive issues is quite common when standard direct questioning techniques are used. Much of the misreporting can be explained by the degree of anonymity in the survey situation. If respondents trust in their privacy protection, they will be more likely to reveal self-discrediting or embarrassing information. In this chapter, we discussed different "indirect methods" for the collection of data on sensitive topics that are geared towards making the interview conditions more anonymous: the randomized response technique (RRT), the crosswise model (CM), and the item count technique (ICT). None of these techniques completely solves the problem of social desirability bias in sensitive surveys. However, the empirical research reviewed in this chapter indicates that, if the design is set up carefully and the implementation is tailored to the specific topic and population under investigation, these techniques can diminish the problem of social desirability bias and improve the validity of survey measures.

When deciding on which method to use, it might be relevant that RRT and ICT variants to measure quantitative variables exist, while the CM so far only has been used to study dichotomous variables. A strength of the CM, however, is to circumvent the problem of self-protective "no" answers. The methods likely differ also in their viability and empirical practicability for different respondent subgroups. While the CM so far was used for university students only, the ICT and RRT were also successfully implemented for respondents known for lower cognitive abilities (respondents with low educational background, low reading skills, and/or low survey experience; see, e.g. van der Heijden, van Gils, Bouts, & Hox, 1998; Lara et al., 2004).

More detailed recommendations rely on further research. Validation studies so far have shown high heterogeneity in results that could only partly be traced back to different survey techniques, modes, or samples (Lensvelt-Mulders et al., 2005b). Hence one still has to better research the conditions under which the methods work (or do not work). Another promising route for future research would be to combine question-and-answer approaches (such as direct self-reports or RRT) with alternative strategies for collecting sensitive data. The latter could include, for example, the analysis of process generated data, record linkage approaches, and nonreactive measurement (e.g. biomarkers). Gaining more valid information by such innovative combinations of data collection methodologies may help to further improve our research on sensitive topics.

NOTES

1. Warner (1965) phrased the scheme in terms of belonging to group A (the "sensitive" group) or the complementary group B.
2. Because of the expected systematic underreporting (overreporting) of socially undesirable (desirable) characteristics, the "more-is-better" ("less-is-better") assumption assumes that, in comparing prevalence estimates of two different questioning techniques, the higher (lower) estimates will be the more valid ones.
3. To detect and correct for such noncompliance, several "cheating detection" procedures have been suggested. In these procedures, "cheaters" are identified as a latent class in repeated measurements (Böckenholt & van der Heijden, 2007), through multiple samples with varying design parameters (Clark & Desharnais, 1998; Moshagen, Musch, & Erdfelder, 2012), or a combination thereof (van den Hout, Böckenholt, & van der Heijden, 2010).

REFERENCES

Biemer, P. P., & Brown, G. (2005). Model-based estimation of drug use prevalence using item count data. *Journal of Official Statistics, 21*(2), 287–308.
Biemer, P. P., Jordan, B. K., Hubbard, M. L., & Wright, D. (2005). A test of the item count methodology for estimating cocaine use prevalence. In J. Kennet & J. Gfroerer (Eds.),

Evaluating and improving methods used in the National Survey on Drug Use and Health (pp. 149–174). Rockville, MD: Department of Health and Human Services, Substance Abuse and Mental Health Services Administration, Office of Applied Studies.

Blair, G., & Imai, K. (2012). Statistical analysis of list experiments. *Political Analysis, 20,* 47–77. doi:10.1093/pan/mpr048

Böckenholt, U., & van der Heijden, P.G.M. (2007). Item randomized-response models for measuring noncompliance: Risk-return perceptions, social influences, and self-protective responses. *Psychometrika, 72*(2), 245–262. doi:10.1007/s11336-005-1495-y

Boruch, R. F. (1971). Assuring confidentiality of responses in social research: A note on strategies. *The American Sociologist, 6*(4), 308–311.

Chaudhuri, A. (2011). *Randomized response and indirect questioning techniques in surveys.* Boca Raton: Chapman & Hall/CRC Press.

Chaudhuri, A., & Mukerjee, R. (1988). *Randomized response. Theory and techniques.* New York: Macel Dekker.

Clark, S. J., & Desharnais, R. A. (1998). Honest answers to embarrassing questions: Detecting cheaters in the randomized response model. *Psychological Methods, 3*(2), 160–168. doi:10.1037/1082-989X.3.2.160

Corstange, D. (2009). Sensitive questions, truthful answers? Modeling the List Experiment with LISTIT. *Political Analysis, 17*(1), 45–63. doi:10.1093/pan/mpn013

Coutts, E., & Jann, B. (2011). Sensitive questions in online surveys. Experimental results for the Randomized Response Technique (RRT) and the Unmatched Count Technique (UCT). *Sociological Methods and Research, 40*(1), 169–193. doi:10.1177/0049124110390768

Coutts, E., Jann, B., Krumpal, I., & Näher, A. F. (2011). Plagiarism in student papers: Prevalence estimates using special techniques for sensitive questions. *Journal of Economics and Statistics, 231*(5+6), 749–760.

Dalton, D. R., Wimbush, J. C., & Daily, C. M. (1994). Using the Unmatched Count Technique (UCT) to estimate base rates for sensitive behavior. *Personnel Psychology, 47*(4), 817–829. doi:10.1111/j.1744-6570.1994.tb01578.x

Droitcour, J., Caspar, R. A., Hubbard, M. L., Parsely, T. L., Visscher, W., & Ezzati, T. M. (1991). The Item Count Technique as a method of indirect questioning: A review of its development and a case study application. In P. P. Biemer, R. M. Groves, L. E. Lyberg, N. A. Mathiowetz, & S. Sudman (Eds.), *Measurement errors in surveys* (pp. 185–210). New York: Wiley. doi:10.1002/9781118150382.ch11

Fox, J. A., & Tracy, P. E. (1986). *Randomized response: A method for sensitive surveys.* Beverly Hills: Sage.

Gjestvang, C. R., & Singh, S. (2007). Forced quantitative Randomized Response Model: A new device. *Metrika, 66*(2), 243–257. doi:10.1007/s00184-006-0108-1

Glynn, A. N. (2013). What can we learn with statistical truth serum? Design and analysis of the List Experiment. *Public Opinion Quarterly, 77*(S1), 159–172.

Goodstadt, M. S., & Gruson, V. (1975). The Randomized Response Technique: A test of drug use. *Journal of the American Statistical Association, 70*(352), 814–818. doi:10.1080/01621459.1975.10480307

Greenberg, B. G., Abul-Ela, A.-L.A., Simmons, W. R., & Horvitz, D. G. (1969). The unrelated question randomized response model: Theoretical framework. *Journal of the American Statistical Association, 64*(326), 520–539. doi:10.1080/01621459.1969.10500991

Greenberg, B. G., Kuebler, R. R. Jr., Abernathy, J. R., & Horvitz, D. G. (1971). Application of the Randomized Response Technique in obtaining quantitative data. *Journal of the American Statistical Association, 66*(334), 243–250. doi:10.1080/01621459.1971. 10482248

Himmelfarb, S., & Edgell, S. E. (1980). Additive constants model: A Randomized Response Technique for eliminating evasiveness to quantitative response questions. *Psychological Bulletin, 87*(3), 525–530. doi:10.1037/0033-2909.87.3.525

Höglinger, M., Jann, B., & Diekmann, A. (2014). Sensitive questions in online surveys: An experimental evaluation of the Randomized Response Technique and the Crosswise Model. University of Bern Social Sciences Working Papers No. 9. Retrieved from http://ideas.repec.org/p/bss/wpaper/9.html

Holbrook, A. L., & Krosnick, J. A. (2010a). Measuring voter turnout by using the Randomized Response Technique: Evidence calling into question the method's validity. *Public Opinion Quarterly, 74*(2), 328–343. doi:10.1093/poq/nfq012

Holbrook, A. L., & Krosnick, J. A. (2010b). Social desirability bias in voter turnout reports: Tests using the item count technique. *Public Opinion Quarterly, 74*(1), 37–67. doi:10.1093/poq/nfp065

Horvitz, D. G., Shah, B. V., & Simmons, W. R. (1967). The unrelated question Randomized Response Model. In *Proceedings of the Social Statistics Section, American Statistical Association* (pp. 65–72).

Imai, K. (2011). Multivariate regression analysis for the Item Count Technique. *Journal of the American Statistical Association, 106*(494), 407–416. doi:10.1198/jasa.2011.ap10415

Jann, B. (2011). *RRLOGIT: Stata module to estimate logistic regression for Randomized Response Data.* Statistical Software Components S456203 (first version: 2005), Boston College Department of Economics.

Jann, B., Jerke, J., & Krumpal, I. (2012). Asking sensitive questions using the crosswise model: An experimental survey measuring plagiarism. *Public Opinion Quarterly, 76*(1), 32–49. doi:10.1093/poq/nfr036

Kirchner, A., Krumpal, I., Trappmann, M., & von Hermanni, H. (2013). Messung und Erklaerung von Schwarzarbeit in Deutschland—Eine empirische Befragungsstudie unter besonderer Beruecksichtigung des Problems der sozialen Erwuenschtheit. *Zeitschrift fuer Soziologie, 42*(4), 291–314.

Krumpal, I. (2010). *Sensitive questions and measurement error: Using the Randomized Response Technique to reduce social desirability bias in CATI surveys.* Dissertation, University of Leipzig.

Krumpal, I. (2012). Estimating the prevalence of xenophobia and anti-semitism in Germany: A comparison of Randomized Response and Direct Questioning. *Social Science Research, 41*(6), 1387–1403. doi:10.1016/j.ssresearch.2012.05.015

Krumpal, I. (2013). Determinants of social desirability bias in sensitive surveys: A literature review. *Quality & Quantity, 47*(4), 2025–2047. doi:10.1007/s11135-011-9640-9

Kuk, A.Y.C. (1990). Asking sensitive questions indirectly. *Biometrika, 77*(2), 436–438. doi:10.1093/biomet/77.2.436

Kuklinski, J. H., Sniderman, P. M., Knight, K., Piazza, T., Tetlock, P. E., Lawrence, G. R., & Mellers, B. (1997). Racial prejudice and attitudes toward affirmative action. *American Journal of Political Science, 41*(2), 402–419. doi:10.2307/2111770

LaBrie, J. W., & Earleywine, M. (2000). Sexual risk behaviors and alcohol: Higher base rates revealed using the unmatched-count technique. *Journal of Sex Research, 37*(4), 321–326. doi:10.1080/00224490009552054

Lara, D., Strickler, J., Olavarrieta, C. D., & Ellertson, C. (2004). Measuring induced abortion in Mexico. A comparison of four methodologies. *Sociological Methods and Research, 32*(4), 529–558. doi:10.1177/0049124103262685

Lee, R. M. (1993). *Doing research on sensitive topics.* London: Sage.

Lensvelt-Mulders, G.J.L.M., Hox, J. J., & van der Heijden, P.G.M. (2005a). How to improve the efficiency of Randomized Response Designs. *Quality & Quantity, 39*(3), 253–265. doi:10.1007/s11135-004-0432-3

Lensvelt-Mulders, G.J.L.M., Hox, J. J., van der Heijden, P.G.M., & Maas, C.J.M. (2005b). Meta-analysis of Randomized Response Research. Thirty-five years of validation. *Sociological Methods & Research, 33*(3), 319–348. doi:10.1177/0049124104268664

Lensvelt-Mulders, G.J.L.M., van der Heijden, P.G.M., Laudy, O., & van Gils, G. (2006). A validation of a computer-assisted randomized response survey to estimate the prevalence of fraud in social security. *Journal of the Royal Statistical Society, Series A, 169*(2), 305–318. doi:10.1111/j.1467-985X.2006.00404.x

Maddala, G. S. (1983). *Limited dependent and qualitative variables in econometrics.* New York: Cambridge University Press.

Mangat, N. S. (1994). An improved randomized response strategy. *Journal of the Royal Statistical Society, Series B, 56*(1), 93–95.

Moors, J.J.A. (1971). Optimization of the unrelated question randomized response model. *Journal of the American Statistical Association, 66*(335), 627–629. doi:10.1080/01621 459.1971.10482320

Moshagen, M., Musch, J., & Erdfelder, E. (2012). A stochastic lie detector. *Behavior Research Methods, 44*(1), 222–231. doi:10.3758/s13428-011-0144-2

Ostapczuk, M., Musch, J., & Moshagen, M. (2009). A randomized-response investigation of the education effect in attitudes towards foreigners. *European Journal of Social Psychology, 39*(6), 920–931. doi:10.1002/ejsp.588

Raghavarao, D., & Federer, W. T. (1979). Block total response as an alternative to the randomized response method in surveys. *Journal of the Royal Statistical Society, Series B, 41*(1), 40–45.

Rayburn, N. R., Earleywine, M., & Davison, G. C. (2003). Base rates of hate crime victimization among college students. *Journal of Interpersonal Violence, 18*(10), 1209–1221. doi:10.1177/0886260503255559

Scheers, N. J., & Dayton, C. M. (1987). Improved estimation of academic cheating behavior using the Randomized-Response Technique. *Research in Higher Education, 26*(1), 61–69. doi:10.1007/BF00991933

Shamsipour, M., Yunesian, M., Fotouhi, A., Jann, B., Rahimi-Movaghar, A., Asghari, F., & Akhlaghi, A. A. (2014). Estimating the prevalence of illicit drug use among students using the crosswise model. *Substance Use & Misuse, 49*(10), 1303–1310. doi:10.3109 /10826084.2014.897730

Tan, M. T., Tian, G.-L., & Tang, M.-L. (2009). Sample surveys with sensitive questions: A Nonrandomized Response Approach. *The American Statistician, 63*(1), 9–16. doi:10.1198/tast.2009.0002

Tian, G.-L., & Tang, M.-L. (2013). *Incomplete categorical data design: Non-randomized response techniques for sensitive questions in surveys.* Boca Raton: Chapman & Hall/ CRC Press.

Tourangeau, R., & Yan, T. (2007). Sensitive questions in surveys. *Psychological Bulletin, 133*(5), 859–883. doi:10.1037/0033-2909.133.5.859

Trappmann, M., Krumpal, I., Kirchner, A., & Jann, B. (2014). Item sum: A new technique for asking quantitative sensitive questions. *Journal of Survey Statistics and Methodology, 2*(1): 58–77. doi:10.1093/jssam/smt019

Tsuchiya, T., & Hirai, Y. (2010). Elaborate item count questioning: Why do people under-report in item count responses? *Survey Research Methods, 4*(3), 139–149.

Tsuchiya, T., Hirai, Y., & Ono, S. (2007). A study of the properties of the item count technique. *Public Opinion Quarterly, 71*(2), 253–272. doi:10.1093/poq/nfm012

van den Hout, A., Böckenholt, U., & van der Heijden, P.G.M. (2010). Estimating the prevalence of sensitive behavior and cheating with a dual design for direct questioning and randomized response. *Journal of the Royal Statistical Society, Series C, 59*(4), 723–736. doi:10.1111/j.1467-9876.2010.00720.x

van der Heijden, P.G.M., van Gils, G., Bouts, J., Hox, J. (1998). A comparison of Randomized Response, CASAQ, and direct questioning; eliciting sensitive information in the context of social security fraud. *Kwantitative Methoden, 19,* 15–34.

Warner, S. L. (1965). Randomized response: A survey technique for eliminating evasive answer bias. *Journal of the American Statistical Association, 60*(309), 63–69. doi:10.1 080/01621459.1965.10480775

Weissman, A. N., Steer, R. A., & Lipton, D. S. (1986). Estimating illicit drug use through telephone interviews and the Randomized Response Technique. *Drug and Alcohol Dependence, 18*(3), 225–233. doi:10.1016/0376-8716(86)90054-2

Wimbush, J. C., & Dalton, D. R. (1997). Base rate for employee theft: Convergence of multiple methods. *Journal of Applied Psychology, 82*(5), 756–763. doi:10.1037/ 0021-9010.82.5.756

Wolter, F., & Preisendörfer, P. (2013). Asking sensitive questions: An evaluation of the Randomized Response Technique versus direct questioning using individual validation data. *Sociological Methods and Research 42*(3), 321–353. doi:10.1177/ 0049124113500474

Yu, J. W., Tian, G. L., & Tang, M. L. (2008). Two new models for survey sampling with sensitive characteristic: design and analysis. *Metrika, 67*(3), 251–263. doi:10.1007/ s00184-007-0131-x

12

The Factorial Survey as a Method for Measuring Sensitive Issues

Katrin Auspurg, Thomas Hinz, Stefan Liebig and Carsten Sauer

Factorial Surveys (FS) are a widely used method to measure normative rules and attitudes or decision criteria in many subdisciplines of the social sciences (for a review: Wallander, 2009; for introductions: Jasso, 2006; Rossi & Anderson, 1982). FSs are often considered to be less prone to social desirability bias (SDB) than conventional surveys (Mutz, 2011). The method links elements of experiments with those of surveys. Survey participants respond to descriptions of hypothetical objects or situations (*vignettes*); within these vignettes, *levels* of attributes (*dimensions*) are varied experimentally. Figure 12.1 shows a vignette used to measure justice principles in regard to fair earnings (for similar studies: Jasso & Rossi, 1977; Jasso & Webster, 1997, 1999). The dimensions highlighted in bold were experimentally varied in their levels across the vignettes. Respondents were asked to rate the fairness of earnings on an 11-point rating scale.

Multivariate methods can be used to estimate how dimensions influence respondents' judgments, and also to reveal how judgment principles vary across respondents. This can be done by subgroup analyses or cross-level interactions between vignettes and respondents' characteristics. Additionally, the method allows conclusions to be drawn on the relative importance and the interactions of single dimensions (like gender-specific returns to education; Auspurg & Jäckle, 2012; Jasso & Webster, 1997, 1999). The multifactorial design in which several dimensions vary at the same time forces respondents to make trade-offs between single dimensions. Furthermore, as sensitive issues and attitudes are assessed indirectly, FSs are considered to be less susceptible to SDB than direct questioning (Alexander & Becker, 1978; Armacost, Hosseini, Morris, & Rehbein, 1991). At the same time, the response task is more complex compared to standard questionnaire modules, which makes methodological research particularly important.

A **50-year-old woman** with **no vocational training** has **two** children. She works as a **clerk** and has gained **a lot of** job experience. She has worked for the company **for a long time**.
Her monthly gross earnings total **1,200 euros** (before tax and extra charges).
Are the monthly gross earnings of this person fair or are they, from your point of view, unfairly high or low?

Unfairly low					Fair					Unfairly high
−5	−4	−3	−2	−1	0	+1	+2	+3	+4	+5
☐	☐	☐	☐	☐	☐	☐	☐	☐	☐	☐

FIGURE 12.1
Example of a vignette

This chapter provides first general recommendations based on recent methodological research (Section 12.1) and then, in the second part, the special capability of FS techniques to reduce SDB is analyzed (Section 12.2). Data from a population survey are used to address the following research questions: Do respondents reveal higher levels of socially undesirable attitudes when an FS design is used instead of direct questioning? Is this particularly true when employing between-subject experimentation? And, are FS methods able to reduce SDB even for highly educated respondents?

12.1 METHODOLOGICAL RECOMMENDATIONS AND STATE OF RESEARCH

The following recommendations mainly focus on issues recently studied, with more than 50 experiments on the design of FSs conducted as part of the research project "The Factorial Survey as a Method for Studying Attitudes in Population Surveys" (Hinz & Liebig, 2006).[1] Within this project, vignettes on the fairness of earnings were used, like the one shown in Figure 12.1. All experiments were carried out in 2008 or 2009 with large samples of university students in Germany. Experiments on possible overburdening of respondents were additionally conducted with large general population samples, always comprising more than 1,000 respondents.

Number of Dimensions and Vignettes

The ability to comprehend complex vignettes depends (1) on the number of vignettes single respondents have to rate and (2) the number of dimensions each vignette consists of. The more vignettes, the more likely respondents are to learn the task. At the same time there is also a higher risk that respondents get tired or use simplifying heuristics. More dimensions could lead to information overload. However, with too few dimensions, respondents might quickly become bored and have to make up more information themselves (for choice experiments: Caussade, Ortuzar, Rizzi, & Hensher, 2004; Deshazo & Fermo, 2002; Hensher, 2006). To reveal the ideal amount of complexity splits with five, eight, and 12 dimensions were crossed with those of ten, 20, and 30 vignettes per respondent.

All in all, the analyses documented in diverse publications (Auspurg, Hinz, & Liebig, 2009; Auspurg, Hinz, Sauer, & Liebig, 2009a, 2009b; Sauer, Auspurg, Hinz, & Liebig, 2011; Sauer et al., 2014) showed the greatest consistency in judgments—measured by the explained variance in multivariate regressions—at a mid-level complexity of eight dimensions. While the responses to five dimensions seemed to be slightly more inconsistent, there was clearly a lower consistency in the split with 12 dimensions. This was especially true for respondents of higher age ($\geq$ 60 years old) or lower educational background. Indicators of cognitive overload seemed to be additionally more pronounced when respondents were less familiar with the topic of the FS. As expected, these symptoms of cognitive overload were more evident when respondents had to evaluate many vignettes (20 or 30). In addition, there were indications for heuristics. After around the tenth vignette, respondents paid less or no more attention to some dimensions. Results indicated in general that a high response consistency is bought at the cost of ignoring some dimensions. Hence, in particular for respondents with lower cognitive abilities, complexity should be limited to a mid-range of around eight dimensions and ten vignettes.

Sampling of Vignettes

The majority of studies so far have used simple random samples to select vignettes from the universe of all possible vignettes (Wallander, 2009), and also randomly allocated the vignettes to different vignette decks. However, with deliberate fractions of vignettes one can gain more statistical efficiency, that is, minimize correlations of dimensions, and at the same time maximize the variance of dimensions as well as the balance of their levels (Kuhfeld, 1997). These are all important target criteria as they allow, in data analysis, estimations of the effects of single dimensions with maximum precision and hence statistical power. In this respect and to avoid the unwanted confounding of dimensions (Atzmüller & Steiner, 2010), so-called 'D-efficient' samples of vignettes are clearly preferable to alternative sampling techniques. A maximization of D-efficiency should also guide researchers who want to split the sample into different decks. Many of these aspects have already been well documented (Kuhfeld, 1997; Louviere, 1998; Atzmüller & Steiner, 2010), but they are still widely ignored in FS research.

Implausible Cases

While some researchers praise implausible, reality-expanding cases as a strength of the FS method (see, for example, Rossi & Anderson, 1982), others fear that these cases encourage artificial response behavior (Faia, 1980). Surprisingly, the question of whether such vignettes should be removed from the sample has been almost completely ignored in methodological research. In one experiment of our methodological project, deliberately implausible vignette combinations were used (for example, unrealistically high salaries for occupations). Both oral pretest feedback as well as multivariate analyses of the data showed implausible cases to have problematic effects in regard to data validity (Auspurg et al. 2009, 2010). After being confronted with those cases the respondents paid less attention to the dimensions causing the implausibility. One could also say they tended towards no longer taking these dimensions quite as seriously. Therefore, it is advisable to exclude implausible vignettes. However, it should be noted that such vignettes should already be excluded before building up fractionalized vignette samples; eliminating them afterwards distorts desirable features like the orthogonality of dimensions.

Response Scales

For FSs, techniques of number matching or other forms of magnitude response scales (Stevens, 1957) are often recommended. This is motivated by the hope to reach an interval scale level, to allow respondents to express their feelings as freely as possible, and to avoid self-censorship. Closed-ended scales might be too restrictive to accommodate the differentiations respondents perceive while processing the FS module (Jasso, 2006; Rossi & Anderson, 1982).

To empirically evaluate these assumptions, a magnitude scale employing a number-matching technique was compared with a closed-ended, 11-point rating scale.[2] The results clearly demonstrate the problems of magnitude scales already known from survey research (Schaeffer & Bradburn, 1989). For instance, the proportion of item nonresponse was much higher for the magnitude scale (14%, or 23% if one takes the necessity of a valid reference judgment into account; for the rating scale, nonresponse was a mere 3%). Respondents tended to skip the magnitude evaluation task by rating the vignettes as 'fair' (32% compared to only 23% for rating scale). In addition, there was frequent use of extremely high values within the magnitude scale. Including those values led to very implausible results for fair earnings (see also Markovsky & Eriksson, 2012). All in all, the magnitude scale showed lower statistical power to discover significant effects. The recommendation is therefore to abandon number-matching techniques, and probably other forms of magnitude scales, in favor of more standardized response scales.

Prior Research on SDB

Many researchers argue that FSs are superior to direct questioning in minimizing SDB (Mutz, 2011; Wallander, 2009). Respondents are asked about hypothetical tasks only (Finch 1987) and do not have to state their opinions explicitly (Lee Badgett & Folbre, 2003). Moreover, with many factors varying at the same time, respondents' attention is probably less attracted to one single dimension, meaning that the experimental treatment is less obtrusive (Alexander & Becker, 1978; Wallander, 2009). There are, however, also contrary opinions. The explicit mentioning of characteristics like race and gender might lead respondents to suspect discrimination research (Mutz, 2011). The prevention of SDB while using an FS could therefore rely on avoiding the variation of a sensitive dimension, i.e. respondents receive only vignettes that hold a sensitive dimension such as race or gender constant. Dimensions of the sensitive variable are varied solely between subjects (Pager & Freese, 2004; Schuman & Bobo, 1988). Differences in the variable's evaluation would be logically restricted to between-subject comparisons, making it impossible to identify any single individual as discriminating (Mutz, 2011, p. 56).

So far there are only a few studies on these issues. Armacost and colleagues (1991) studied the prevalence of sensitive business practices of chief executive officers in the U.S., not varying any dimension within their vignettes. Burstin, Doughtie, and Raphaeli (1980) used a between-subject design to study the influence of race, gender and religion on evaluations of the behavior of parents, mainly using student samples. Both found FSs to perform better compared to direct questioning, provided that higher levels of sensitive issues are an indication of more valid responses. Armacost and colleagues additionally reported the FS to be superior to randomized response techniques (see Chapter 11 for these methods).[3] Other-based FS designs (that is, describing the behavior of others within the vignettes) were found to lead to higher rates of admitting sensitive behavior than individual-based vignettes (describing respondents' own hypothetical behavior).

Both studies, however, were not typical for FS designs, as they varied at maximum two dimensions and used only a few vignettes per respondent. In addition, comparisons of a between- and within-subject variation are lacking and there are no results on FSs' ability to reduce SDB, particularly for highly educated respondents, who have been found to be more likely than lower-educated respondents to conceal their true attitudes if they are not in line with political correctness (Ostapczuk, Musch, & Moshagen, 2009; Schuman & Bobo, 1988, p. 276).

12.2 EXPLORING FSS' CAPACITY TO REDUCE SDB

Experimental Set-Up and Data

To overcome these limitations, a special survey was designed. The respondent sample consisted of the adult population of a small city in southwest Germany (Constance), where in 2008 more than 400 respondents were interviewed using common sampling techniques for population surveys.[4] Within the FS module all respondents had to evaluate ten different vignettes on the fairness of earnings (on an 11-point rating scale). The employees in the vignettes were characterized by eight dimensions. The dimension 'sex of employee' was assumed to trigger SDB, because there is clear evidence for a gender pay gap in many countries, including Germany, which seems at least partly caused by discriminatory attitudes (Auspurg, Hinz, & Sauer, 2013; Blau & Kahn, 2007). At the same time, such discrimination is strictly prohibited by the constitution of Germany.

To test the effect of different FS designs, a split-half design was employed: half of the respondents received vignettes with the sex of the vignette person varying across their vignettes (within-subject design), while the other half rated male or female vignette persons only (between-subject design). All other vignette dimensions were varied in a within-subject design. As the combination of all dimension levels gave rise to more than 50,000 possible vignettes, we used a *D*-efficient fraction of 240 vignettes (excluding illogical cases like medical doctors without a university degree). Twenty-four decks and ten vignettes were then randomly allocated to respondents.[5]

All data were collected by personal assisted paper-and-pencil interviews. The FS module was integrated after some initial questions as a self-administered module. After evaluating the vignettes, respondents were asked to rate directly on a 7-point rating scale how much impact each of the vignette dimensions, including employees' sex, should have for a fair distribution of earnings. The realized dataset was nearly balanced in regard to the experimental split: $n = 234$ respondents (52.2%) evaluated the within-subject design, while $n = 215$ respondents (47.8%) evaluated vignettes on only male ($n = 102$ respondents, 22.7%) or female vignette persons ($n = 113$ respondents, 25.2%). Additional tests showed these splits to be balanced in terms of respondent characteristics, including sex, educational level, household size, and labor market experience. Respondents with a university degree were classified as being 'higher' educated compared to other respondents ($n = 163$ respondents, 36.3%).

Results

When directly questioned, the large majority of respondents (84.2%) stated that the sex of employees should have no impact at all on fair earnings. This was in particular true for highly educated respondents (89.0%). The influence of educational background on ratings was also evident in multivariate logistic regression including several characteristics of the respondents and interview situation (like age, sex, presence of other persons; results not shown here but available on request). Higher-educated respondents had on average an 11 percentage point lower likelihood of directly stating that sex should matter than lower-educated respondents ($p \le .001$).

For the FS module, Table 12.1 displays several OLS regressions estimating the influence of vignette dimensions on the vignette evaluations, using robust standard errors clustered for the single respondents to address the hierarchical data structure. The first two columns display estimations separately for respondents who stated that sex should matter or should not matter. In both groups, the sex of vignette persons revealed a statistically significant impact on evaluations ($\beta = 0.190$; $p = .004$; respectively $\beta = 0.373$; $p = .047$), with the positive sign indicating that female employees should get comparatively lower earnings. The effect was less pronounced but still at a statistically significant level for those respondents who stated—when directly asked—that sex should *not* matter.[6] This finding suggests that the indirect evaluation task given with the FS method is indeed less prone to SDB (alternative explanations are discussed in Section 12.3).

To find out if SDB is even smaller in a between-subject design, the results across the two experimental splits are compared (see the columns in the middle of Table 12.1). Surprisingly, the effect of the vignette person's sex was more pronounced and only reached a significant level when varied in a within- and not in a between-subject design. The difference between both models was, however, statistically insignificant.[7]

TABLE 12.1

OLS regressions of vignette evaluations on vignette dimensions by respondent characteristics and experimental splits

	(1) By response to direct question		(2) By experimental split		(3) By educational background and exp. split			
					Within-subject design		Between-subject design	
	Sex should not matter	Sex should matter	Within-subject design	Between-subject design	Lower educ.	Higher educ.	Lower educ.	Higher educ.
Female vign. person [1 = yes]	0.190**	0.373*	0.327***	0.128	0.292**	0.385**	0.0698	0.302
	(0.0659)	(0.184)	(0.0770)	(0.102)	(0.0986)	(0.124)	(0.119)	(0.182)
Age	-0.00944***	-0.0102+	-0.0121***	-0.00696+	-0.00428	-0.0232***	-0.00573	-0.0107+
	(0.00257)	(0.00582)	(0.00311)	(0.00357)	(0.00367)	(0.00526)	(0.00449)	(0.00581)
Vocational training	-0.362***	-0.456*	-0.350***	-0.385***	-0.415***	-0.257+	-0.378**	-0.423*
	(0.0717)	(0.171)	(0.0855)	(0.0998)	(0.100)	(0.149)	(0.126)	(0.174)
University degree	-0.406***	-0.458*	-0.454***	-0.366***	-0.585***	-0.256	-0.446**	-0.226
	(0.0782)	(0.178)	(0.0941)	(0.109)	(0.106)	(0.165)	(0.132)	(0.193)
Occup. prestige [MPS score]	-0.0147***	-0.0121***	-0.0133***	-0.0155***	-0.0122***	-0.0146***	-0.0153***	-0.0161***
	(0.000766)	(0.00224)	(0.00101)	(0.00102)	(0.00134)	(0.00149)	(0.00122)	(0.00183)
Lot of job experience [1 = yes]	-0.499***	-0.583**	-0.496***	-0.530***	-0.509***	-0.469**	-0.510***	-0.522*
	(0.0847)	(0.199)	(0.104)	(0.115)	(0.126)	(0.176)	(0.136)	(0.221)
Long job tenure [1 = yes]	-0.199**	-0.0342	-0.174+	-0.179+	-0.113	-0.270*	-0.255*	-0.0235
	(0.0738)	(0.193)	(0.0912)	(0.101)	(0.128)	(0.121)	(0.114)	(0.202)
Number of children	-0.153***	-0.129*	-0.178***	-0.117***	-0.191***	-0.166***	-0.116**	-0.123+
	(0.0215)	(0.0508)	(0.0257)	(0.0302)	(0.0308)	(0.0444)	(0.0376)	(0.0485)
Income (log.)	2.532***	2.521***	2.492***	2.566***	2.482***	2.511***	2.546***	2.605***
	(0.0484)	(0.124)	(0.0631)	(0.0634)	(0.0784)	(0.105)	(0.0703)	(0.130)
Constant	-18.05***	-18.22***	-17.63***	-18.33***	-17.85***	-17.39***	-17.83***	-19.25***
	(0.422)	(1.200)	(0.540)	(0.562)	(0.702)	(0.838)	(0.608)	(1.149)
Observations	3692	596	2252	2095	1355	897	1432	663
(Respondents)	(371)	(60)	(226)	(211)	(136)	(90)	(144)	(67)
R-squared	0.629	0.638	0.636	0.623	0.643	0.635	0.628	0.629

Note: Regression coefficients, robust standard errors in parentheses. All models were estimated controlling for the following respondent characteristics: sex, age, educational level, labor market experience, and household size.

*** $p < .001$, ** $p < .01$, * $p < .05$, + $p < .1$

Finally, it was of interest how respondents with different educational backgrounds rated the vignettes. We repeated the estimations, now additionally distinguishing between lower- and higher-educated respondents (columns on the right-hand side of Table 12.1). The effect size found for the higher-educated respondents was more pronounced than the one for the lower-educated respondents, particularly in the between-subject design. Additional analyses, however, showed none of these group differences to be statistically significant.[8] Nonetheless, this provides additional evidence for FSs being able to reduce SDB. Highly educated persons seem to be no less discriminatory than others, but more likely to conceal their true opinions when directly asked.

12.3 CONCLUSIONS AND OUTLOOK

As the review of Wallander (2009) documents, FSs are a widely used research tool in social sciences. The method borrows the advantages of both experimental designs and survey research. Consequently, it enables particular insights into the judgment principles underlying social attitudes, definitions, or decision-making. Relying on our methodological research with more than 50 experiments, we conclude with some precise advice:

1. Reduce the number of vignettes and dimensions: When using no more than eight dimensions and ten vignettes per respondent, different age and educational groups seem able to perform the demanding evaluation task, producing a high level of response consistency without indications of cognitive overload or fatigue effects.
2. Use fractionalized vignette samples: Particularly when drawing small samples of vignettes out of large vignette universes, one gains statistical efficiency and power and at the same time prevents a problematic confounding of dimensions by employing *D*-efficient fractions.
3. Exclude implausible vignettes: These trigger the use of heuristics and hence lead to artificial results. The exclusion of implausible cases should be done before building up the vignette fractions because when eliminating them afterwards desirable design features like the orthogonality of dimensions are distorted.
4. Use standard response scales: Number-matching techniques should be abandoned in favor of more standardized response scales, at least in self-administered surveys, to achieve high data quality and low unit nonresponse.

5. FSs seem to have the capacity to reduce SDB: FSs were found to minimize SDB compared to direct questioning, especially for higher-educated persons. According to our results, no between-subject experimentation is necessary to achieve this.

However, further research on SDB is needed. Direct questioning and the FS method differ in more details, with the former being able to reveal only those attitudes the respondents are fully aware of. It might be that income discrimination is based on latent sentiments not open to conscious reflection. In addition, respondents might assume further differences across male and female employees that were not explicitly stated within the vignettes, which could also cause differences between general justice principles and evaluations of employees (see, however, Auspurg et al., 2013). For all these reasons, one should expand research on FSs' capacity to reduce SDB, including other research areas and testing further design features.

There are more issues that should be considered for improving FS data. Clearly, more research on response heuristics is needed. Many respondents seem to keep producing consistent evaluations by fading out some dimensions. As we do not know if this represents a problematic satisficing or if respondents have good reasons for fading out dimensions they consider unimportant, future research should address this question of the cognitive processes underlying FS responses.

Another aspect that should attract more scholarly attention is the problem of order effects. Effects of vignette order can be neutralized with random ordering of vignettes. Preventing effects from the dimension order is more demanding. Initial analyses found dimension order effects in highly complex vignettes only (with 12 rather than eight dimensions), which supports the recommendation given above to use fewer dimensions (Auspurg & Jäckle, 2012). Additionally, more research on the selection of dimensions' levels should be done. Some work on these issues found weak evidence for a number of level or range effect (e.g. Markovsky & Eriksson, 2012).

All in all, FSs can reveal a considerable amount of information and reduce SDB, and one can advise their further use in survey research if methodological recommendations are considered. This is also true in regard to researching sensitive topics: Researchers must walk a very fine line between making dimensions unobtrusive enough to not trigger SDB while nonetheless making sure that respondents notice the single dimensions (Mutz, 2011).

NOTES

1. The project was funded by the German Research Foundation (DFG) as part of the Priority Programme on Survey Methodology (PPSM).
2. In the magnitude task, respondents were allowed to use any numbers to express their feelings of injustice. They could skip this task if they evaluated the vignette as fair. To aid calibration, all respondents had to evaluate an identical baseline vignette at the beginning of the FS module.
3. Similarly, there is evidence that related experimental survey methods like conjoint analysis preclude higher proportions of discriminatory attitudes (Van Beek, Koopmans, & Van Praag, 1997). Less optimistic are the results of validation studies (Eifler, 2007; Pager & Quillian, 2005) that showed a much higher prevalence of socially sensitive behavior in real situations. However, the discrepancy between FS and audit or observational measurement might be caused by other reasons than SDB, like real decision-making being based on additional factors (Pager & Quillian, 2005, p. 372).
4. About one third of respondents were recruited by a population registry, one third by a random route, and a final third by quota sampling. This was done to evaluate different sampling procedures. We do not report on these results in this chapter. For the registry and random route sample, the response rates were about 25%.
5. First the sample for the within-subject design was built up. After that, this sample was quadrupled and the sex of vignette persons was standardized in half of the decks to male or female vignette persons only. This procedure ensured that exactly the same vignette samples were used within all splits.
6. The difference across both groups did not reach a statistically significant level (estimated in a pooled model, the interaction term of female vignette person and group of respondents was not statistically significant: $\beta = 0.205$; $p = .298$).
7. The interaction effect of sex and experimental split when estimated in a pooled model was: $\beta = -0.186$; $p = .148$.
8. The interaction effect of sex and respondents' education when estimated in a pooled model was: $\beta = 0.076$; $p = .631$ for the within-subject design and $\beta - 0.247$; $p = .282$ for the between-subject design.

REFERENCES

Alexander, C. S., & Becker, H. J. (1978). The use of vignettes in survey research. *Public Opinion Quarterly 42*(1), 93–104. doi:10.1086/268432

Armacost, R. L., Hosseini, J., Morris, S. A., & Rehbein, K. A. (1991). An empirical comparison of direct questioning, scenario, and randomized response methods for obtaining sensitive business information. *Decision Sciences, 22*, 1073–1090. doi:10.1111/j.1540-5915.1991.tb01907.x

Atzmüller, C., & Steiner, P. M. (2010). Experimental vignette studies in survey research. *Methodology: European Journal of Research Methods for the Behavioral and Social Sciences 6*(3), 128–138.

Auspurg, K., Hinz, T., & Liebig, S. (2009). Complexity, learning effects, and plausibility of vignettes in factorial surveys. Paper presented at the 104th Annual Meeting of the American Sociological Association. San Francisco.

Auspurg, K., Hinz, T., Liebig, S., & Sauer, C. (2009b). Auf das Design kommt es an. Experimentelle Befunde zu komplexen Settings in Faktoriellen Surveys. *SoFid Methoden und Instrumente der Sozialwissenschaften 2009/2*, 23–39.

Auspurg, K., Hinz, T., & Sauer, C. (2013). Status construction or statistical discrimination? New insights on fair earnings from a Factorial Survey Study. Paper presented at the 108th Annual Meeting of the American Sociological Association. New York.

Auspurg, K., Hinz, T., Sauer, C., & Liebig, S. (2009). How numbers matter. Experimental results on the effects of complex settings in factorial survey designs. Paper presented at the 3rd Meeting of the PPSM. Bremen.

Auspurg, K., Hinz, T., Sauer, C., & Liebig, S. (2010). Wie unplausibel darf es sein? Der Einfluss von Designmerkmalen auf das Antwortverhalten in Faktoriellen Surveys. In Deutsche Gesellschaft fuer Soziologie (Eds.), *Kongressband des 24. Kongresses der DGS*. Wiesbaden: VS Verlag fuer Sozialwissenschaften.

Auspurg, K., & Jäckle, A. (2012). First equals most important? Order effects in vignette-based measurement. *ISER Working Paper 2012–01*. Essex: Institute for Social & Economic Research.

Blau, F. D., & Kahn, L. M. (2007). The gender pay gap: Have women gone as far as they can? *Academy of Management Perspectives 21*, 7–23.

Burstin, K., Doughtie, E. B., & Raphaeli, A. (1980). Contrastive Vignette Technique: An indirect methodology designed to address reactive social attitude measurement. *Journal of Applied Social Psychology 10*, 147–165. doi:10.1111/j.1559-1816.1980.tb00699.x

Caussade, S., Ortuzar, J., Rizzi, L. I., & Hensher, D. A. (2004). Assessing the influence of design dimensions on stated choice experiments estimates. *Transportation Research, Part B 39*, 621–640.

Deshazo, J. R., & Fermo, G. (2002). Designing choice sets for stated preference methods: The effects of complexity on choice consistency. *Journal of Environmental Economics and Management, 44*, 123–143. doi:10.1006jeem.2001.1199

Eifler, S. (2007). Evaluating the validity of self-reported deviant behavior using Vignette Analyses. *Quality & Quantity, 41*, 303–318. doi:10.1007/s11135-007-9093-3

Faia, M. (1980). The vagaries of the vignette world: A comment on Alves and Rossi. *American Journal of Sociology, 85*, 951–954.

Finch, J. (1987). The Vignette Technique in survey research. *Sociology, 21*, 105–114. doi:10.1177/0038038587021001008

Hensher, D. (2006). Revealing differences in willingness to pay due to the dimensionality of stated choice designs: an initial assessment. *Environmental and Resource Economics, 34*, 7–44. doi:10.1007/s10640-005-3782-y

Hinz, T., & Liebig, S. (2006). Der Faktorielle Survey als Instrument zur Einstellungsmessung in Umfragen. Antrag an die Deutsche Forschungsgemeinschaft (DFG). Konstanz und Duisburg-Essen: Universitaet Konstanz und Universitaet Duisburg-Essen.

Jasso, G. (2006). Factorial survey methods for studying beliefs and judgments. *Sociological Methods & Research, 34*, 334–423. doi:10.1177/0049124105283121

Jasso, G., & Rossi, P. (1977). Distributive justice and earned income. *American Sociological Review, 42*, 639–651.

Jasso, G., & Webster, M. Jr. (1997). Double standards in just earnings for male and female workers. *Social Psychology Quarterly, 60*, 66–78.

Jasso, G., & Webster, M. Jr. (1999). Assessing the gender gap in just earnings and its underlying mechanisms. *Social Psychology Quarterly, 62*, 367–380.

Kuhfeld, W. F. (1997). Efficient experimental designs using computerized searches. Saw-tooth Software Research Paper Series. Sequim. SAS Institute. Retrieved from http://homepage.stat.uiowa.edu/~gwoodwor/AdvancedDesign/KuhfeldTobiasGarratt.pdf

Lee Badgett, M. V., & Folbre, N. (2003). Job gendering: Occupational choice and the marriage market. *Industrial Relations: A Journal of Economy and Society, 42*, 270–298. doi:10.1111/1468-232X.00290

Louviere, J. J. (1998). *Analyzing decision making. Metric Conjoint Analysis*. Newbury Park: Sage.

Markovsky, B., & Eriksson, K. (2012). Comparing direct and indirect measures of just rewards. *Sociological Methods & Research, 41*, 199–216.

Mutz, D. C. (2011). *Population-based survey experiments*. Princeton and Oxford: Princeton University Press.

Ostapczuk, M., Musch, J., & Moshagen, M. (2009). A randomized-response investigation of the education effect in attitudes towards foreigners. *European Journal of Social Psychology, 39*, 920–931.

Pager, D., & Freese, J. (2004). Who deserves a helping hand? Attitudes about government assistance for the unemployed by race, incarceration status, and worker history. Paper presented at the 104th Annual Meeting of the American Sociological Association. San Francisco.

Pager, D., & Quillian, L. (2005). Walking the talk? What employers say versus what they do. *American Sociological Review, 70*, 355–380. doi:10.1177/000312240507000301

Rossi, P. H., & Anderson, A. B. (1982). The factorial survey approach: an introduction. In P. H. Rossi & S. L. Nock (Eds.), *Measuring social judgements: The factorial survey approach* (pp. 15–67). Beverly Hills: Sage.

Sauer, C., Auspurg, K., Hinz, T., & Liebig, S. (2011). The application of factorial surveys in general population samples: The effects of respondent age and education on response times and response consistency. *Survey Research Methods, 5*, 89–102.

Sauer, C., Auspurg, K., Hinz, T., Liebig, S., & Schupp, J. (2014). Method Effects in Factorial Surveys: An Analysis of Respondents' Comments, Interviewers' Assessments, and Response Behavior. *SOEP papers on Multidisciplinary Panel Data Research*. Berlin. German Institute for Economic Research (DIW).

Schaeffer, N. C., & Bradburn, N. M. (1989). Respondent behavior in magnitude estimation. *Journal of the American Statistical Association, 84*, 402–413.

Schuman, H., & Bobo, L. (1988). Survey-based experiments on white racial attitudes toward residential integration. *American Journal of Sociology, 94*, 273–299.

Stevens, S. S. (1957). On the psychophysical law. *Psychological Review, 64*, 153–181. doi:10.1037/h0046162

Van Beek, K.W.H., Koopmans, C. C., & Van Praag, B.M.S. (1997). Shopping at the labour market: A real tale of fiction. *European Economic Review, 41*, 295–317.

Wallander, L. (2009). 25 years of factorial surveys in sociology: A review. *Social Science Research, 38*, 505–520.

Part IV

Conducting Web Surveys

13

Conducting Web Surveys

Overview and Introduction

Lars Kaczmirek

Much has been written about the proliferation of web surveys and about how web surveys have continued to increase their share among available survey modes (e.g., Das, Ester, & Kaczmirek, 2011). While in the early years of research on web surveys differences and particularities of online research were revealed, recent efforts seem to concentrate on reintegrating the methodology of web surveys into the canon of survey methodology. What seems to be a fruitful approach is to discuss web surveys with respect to the total survey error framework (e.g., Tourangeau, Conrad, & Couper, 2013); an approach which can also be found in this volume (e.g., Bethlehem; De Leeuw, & Hox). Following such a general framework should make it easier for researchers to compare web surveys to other survey modes or to assess new developments and their implications for online research. This is especially true in research domains where the focus lies on a methodological problem and the internet is merely the most appropriate or convenient mode to collect the data.

The next three chapters in this volume focus on methodological issues in web surveys. Bethlehem provides an introductory overview of the different sources of errors in surveys and discusses them in the context of web surveys. Vehovar, Petrovčič, and Slavec discuss the benefits and obstacles of information communication technology (ICT) when going through the different stages of developing and conducting a survey. Here, the authors specifically emphasize the process of developing web questionnaires. Braun, Behr, Kaczmirek, and Bandilla explain how probing questions in web surveys can be used to evaluate cross-national item equivalence of questions. In the following, these three chapters are described in more detail.

Bethlehem addresses how web surveys may produce high quality estimates. As this problem is not restricted to official statistics alone, he begins by describing the different sources of error in surveys. Based on the corresponding formulas, he explains the circumstances under which web surveys may lead to biased estimates. The first and foremost problem in web surveys is the technological barrier. Only seemingly trivial, people without access to the internet are unable to participate in this mode. This constitutes under-coverage error. Second, non-probabilistic sampling procedures are described as a serious threat to data quality. Nevertheless, even when participation probabilities are known, estimates might be severely biased under specific circumstances. Third, nonresponse bias is explained. The problem increases with lower response probabilities, greater variation in response probabilities across respondents and a higher correlation between response probabilities and the target variable. An often suggested remedy to these problems is to apply weighting techniques. Bethlehem discusses several approaches to post-stratification, including ways to benefit from auxiliary variables and reference surveys. Finally, the author addresses the question of in what way these problems affect decision-making in official statistics. Several purposes of official statistics are connected with demands that forbid biased estimates and thus would not permit restricting a survey to respondents with internet access. However, not unaffected by financial considerations, web surveys are often discussed as part of mixed-mode approaches. And although this introduces the problem of mode effects, examples of successfully conducted mixed-mode surveys exist.

In the context of e-social science, Vehovar, Petrovčič, and Slavec introduce how the use of information communication technology (ICT) shapes and affects the research process. The authors take a look at the entire research process, extending the use of ICT beyond mere data collection. An illustrative example of the current practices highlights the main struggles in the research process: The authors describe the typical difficulties in the questionnaire development process with its many cycles of commenting, drafting and versioning related to a survey project. Having set the stage, the authors suggest that an integrated software for questionnaire development that considers the entire research process would be highly beneficial for survey researchers in terms of achieved quality, required time and user satisfaction. The software must include features which would allow researchers to abandon their use of word processors and email exchange in the process. Several important features are discussed, among them the minimum requirements which would include direct inline editing, drag-and-drop functionality and cut/paste commands. As the authors have developed a software with said features, they describe an experiment in which two questionnaires had to be developed. The process was either implemented traditionally or used the software. The authors conclude that such an integrated software for questionnaire development is capable of reducing or even eliminating the use of word processors and email exchanges in the development process. In the future, data collection tools will increasingly support and integrate more stages of the survey research process.

The chapter by Braun, Behr, Kaczmirek, and Bandilla describes a methodology which allows researchers to use web surveys in order to evaluate cross-national item equivalence of questions. The authors report on three web surveys across six countries with several thousand respondents which aimed at replicating and assessing questions from the International Social Survey Program (ISSP). The methodology uses probing questions. A probe is a question which is asked after a substantive question and requests more details, for example about either the understanding of the previous question or the reasons for picking a specific answer. The analysis of the respondents' answers shows that online access panels are useful in this approach, and the authors explain which research questions can be addressed by employing such non-probability samples. As there are several methodological questions related to how to implement probes, the results of the experiments are described and suggestions are made concerning the design of optimal probes. Finally, two sets of items are assessed with respect to their cross-national item equivalence. Here, the leading questions are: Does it affect item equivalence if respondents in different countries think of different immigrants? Is the term "civil disobedience" perceived differently in different countries and how does this affect the item scores? The authors conclude with a list of settings in which probing in web surveys could prove useful (e.g., lack of cognitive interviewers in a country, during item development, to assess potential problems after a survey has been conducted).

Other chapters in this volume also use or refer to web surveys. However, the web survey methodology is not their main concern. They address specific methodological challenges or compare web surveys to other modes. The respective chapters cover topics about sensitive questions (Diekmann & Höglinger), access panels (Scherpenzeel), incentives (Göritz), mode effects and mode comparison (De Leeuw & Hox) and paradata (Kreuter). These chapters underline that web surveys have established themselves as a common research tool similar to other modes of data collection.

REFERENCES

Das, M., Ester, P., & Kaczmirek, L. (2010). *Social and behavioral research and the Internet: Advances in applied methods and research strategies.* New York: Taylor & Francis.

Tourangeau, R., Conrad, F., & Couper, M. (2013). *The science of web surveys.* Oxford: Oxford University Press.

14

Web Surveys in Official Statistics

Jelke Bethlehem

14.1 INTRODUCTION

There is an ever-growing demand for statistical information in our societies. National statistical institutes have to satisfy this demand. The way they attempt to accomplish this changes over time. Changes in survey methodology for official statistics may have been caused by new developments, for example, in computer technology, but they may also be due to new challenges like increasing nonresponse rates, decreasing budgets, or demands for reducing the response burden.

National statistical institutes have to produce reliable and accurate statistics. Traditionally, they conduct face-to-face or telephone surveys to collect the data for statistics about the general population. Since interviewers are deployed, this is an expensive way of survey data collection. Experience has shown, however, that such modes of data collection are necessary in order to obtain high-quality data.

National statistical institutes in many countries are nowadays faced with budget constraints. This causes these institutes to look for less expensive ways of data collection. A web survey seems a promising alternative. Web surveys have already become increasingly popular, particularly in the world of market research. This is not surprising as a web survey is a simple, fast, and inexpensive means to collect a lot of data.

At first sight, a web survey is just another mode of data collection. Questions are not asked face-to-face or by telephone, but over the internet. However, there are a number of methodological aspects that may complicate using the web for surveying the general population:

- *Under-coverage.* Since not everyone in the general population has access to the internet, portions of the population are excluded from web surveys. This may lead to biased estimates.

- *Sample selection.* How to select a simple random sample of individuals having access to the internet? Sometimes researchers rely on self-selection of respondents. Unfortunately, this approach is known to produce biased estimates.
- *Nonresponse.* Almost every survey suffers from nonresponse. Nonresponse rates are particularly high for self-administered surveys like mail and web surveys. Unfortunately, low response rates increase the bias of estimators.

These methodological issues are discussed in more detail in this chapter. It will be shown that under-coverage, self-selection, and nonresponse may cause estimators to be biased. The question is if it is possible to correct estimates for such biases. An overview of some correction techniques is given. It is made clear, however, that application of these techniques is no guarantee for success.

14.2 UNDER-COVERAGE

Under-coverage occurs in a survey if the sampling frame does not contain all elements of the target population. Consequently, there will be elements having a zero chance of being selected in the sample. If these elements differ (on average) from those in the sampling frame, there is a risk of estimators being biased.

The obvious sampling frame for a web survey would be a list of email addresses. Sometimes such a sampling frame exists. For example, all employees of a large company may have a company email address. Similarly, all students of a university usually have an email address. The situation is more complicated for a general population survey. In the first place, not everyone in the population has access to the internet, and in the second place, there is no list of email addresses of those with internet.

Figure 14.1 shows the internet coverage for countries in Europe in 2011. Internet access of households varies between 43% (Turkey) and 94% (The Netherlands). Internet access is also high in the Scandinavian countries and Luxemburg. Internet access is low in many Balkan countries.

The problem would be less severe if there were no differences between those with and those without internet access. Then it would still be possible to draw a representative sample. However, there are differences, even in a country like The Netherlands with very high internet coverage (94%). Data on The Netherlands show that of the low-educated people, 90% have access

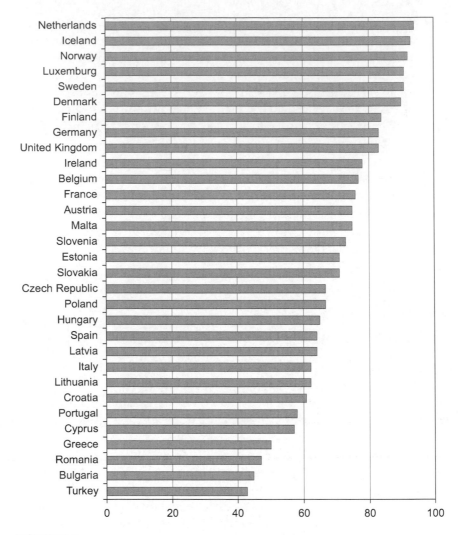

FIGURE 14.1
Percentage of households with Internet access at home in 2011 (Source: Eurostat)

to the internet, whereas the percentage is 99% for the high-educated. Of the employed, 99% have internet and only 88% of the unemployed. In the lowest income group internet coverage is 89%, while in the highest income group it is 99% (CBS, 2012). Looking at age, it turns out that only 34% of people of aged 75 and older use the internet (CBS, 2013).

Scherpenzeel and Bethlehem (2011) describe the LISS panel. This is a Dutch web panel recruited by means of probability sample from a population register. The elderly and ethnic minority groups are underrepresented.

Moreover, internet access among single households is much lower. They also conclude that voters for the general elections are overrepresented.

Similar patterns can be found in other countries. For example, Couper (2000) describes coverage problems in the United States. It turns out that Americans with higher incomes are much more likely to have access to the internet. Black and Hispanic households have much less internet access than White households. People with a college degree have more internet access than those without one. Furthermore, internet coverage in urban areas is better than in rural areas.

Duffy, Smith, Terhanian, and Bremer (2005) conclude that in the United States and the United Kingdom web survey respondents tend to be politically active, are more likely to be early adopters of new technology, tend to travel more, and eat out more.

Bethlehem and Biffignandi (2012) show that the bias due to under-coverage of the sample mean $\bar{y}_I$ as an estimator of the population mean $\bar{Y}$ of a target variable Y is equal to

$$B(\bar{y}_I) = \frac{N_{NI}}{N}(\bar{Y}_I - \bar{Y}_{NI}),\qquad(14.1)$$

where N_{NI} is the number of people in the population without internet access, $\bar{Y}_I$ is the mean of the target variable for people with internet access, and $\bar{Y}_{NI}$ is the mean of Y for those without internet access. The magnitude of this bias is determined by two factors:

- The *relative size* N_{NI}/N of the non-internet population. The more people have access to the internet, the smaller the bias will be.
- The *contrast* $\bar{Y}_I - \bar{Y}_{NI}$ between the internet population and the non-internet population. This is the difference between the population means of the two subpopulations. The more the mean of the target variable differs for these two subpopulations, the larger the bias will be.

Figure 14.1 shows that relative size of the non-internet population cannot be neglected in many countries. Moreover, there are substantial differences between those with and those without internet. Specific groups are underrepresented in the internet population, for example, the elderly, and those with a low level of education. So, the conclusion is that generally a random sample from an internet population will lead to biased estimates for the parameters of the target population.

It is to be expected that internet coverage will increase over time. Hence, the factor N_{NI}/N will be smaller, and this will reduce the bias. It is unclear, however, whether the contrast will also decrease over time. It is even possible that it increases, as the remaining group of people without internet access may differ more and more from the internet users. So the combined effect of a smaller non-internet population and a larger contrast need not necessarily lead to a smaller bias.

It is important to realize that the value of expression (14.1) does not depend on sample size. Consequently, increasing the sample size will have no effect on the bias. So the problem of under-coverage in web surveys cannot be solved by increasing the sample size.

The fundamental problem of web surveys is that persons without internet are excluded from the survey. A first approach to reduce this problem is that of the LISS panel. This is a Dutch web panel consisting of approximately of 5,000 households. The panel is based on a true probability sample of households drawn from the population register of The Netherlands. Households without access to internet, or who were worried that an internet survey might be too complicated for them, were offered a simple-to-operate computer with internet access that could be installed in their homes for free for the duration of the panel. More details about the LISS panel can be found in Scherpenzeel (2009).

A second approach is to turn the single-mode web survey into a mixed-mode survey. One simple way to do this is to send an invitation letter to the persons in the sample, and give them a choice to either complete the questionnaire on the internet or on paper. So, there are two modes here: web and mail.

Another mixed-mode approach is to do it sequentially. The fieldwork starts with the cheapest approach and that is the web. People are invited to fill in the questionnaire on the internet. Nonrespondents are re-approached by CATI, if a registered telephone number is available. If not, these nonrespondents are re-approached by CAPI.

It will be clear that a mixed-mode approach increases the costs of the survey, and it also may increase the length of the fieldwork period. However, this may be the price to be pay in order to get precise and reliable statistics.

14.3 SAMPLE SELECTION

Application of the principles of probability sampling is fundamental to conducting surveys in official statistics. The first ideas about sampling go back to 1895, see e.g. Bethlehem (2009). Horvitz and Thompson (1952) showed in their seminal paper that unbiased estimates of population characteristics can be computed if a real probability sample has been selected, every element in the population has a nonzero probability of selection, and all these probabilities are known to the researcher. Furthermore, under these conditions, the precision of estimates can be computed.

Web surveys should also be based on probability sampling. Unfortunately, many web surveys, particularly those conducted by market research organizations, do not apply probability sampling. The survey questionnaire is simply put on the web. Respondents are those people who happen to have internet, visit the website, and decide to participate in the survey. As a result, the survey researcher is not in control of the selection process. Selection probabilities are unknown. Therefore, no unbiased estimates can be computed nor can the precision of estimates be determined. These surveys are called here *self-selection surveys*. Sometimes they are also called *opt-in surveys*.

Self-selection surveys have a high risk of being not representative. It is even possible that certain groups in the population attempt to manipulate the outcomes of the survey. This may typically play a role in opinion polls. There are examples where organizations press their members to participate in a survey in order to influence the outcome. For some of these polls, people outside the target population can also participate, and sometimes it is even possible to complete the questionnaire more than once.

As an example, the flaws of self-selection web surveys became clear during the parliamentary elections in The Netherlands in September 2012. There were four major pollsters: Maurice de Hond, Ipsos, TNS NIPO, and Intomart GfK. They all used web panels for their polls. All four came with a final predication one day before the election and these predictions were all significantly wrong (see Bethlehem, 2012b). There was also a group of 2,500 people attempting to manipulate the results of one of the polls. Their plan was to first express a preference for the seniors' party 50PLUS and then gradually to change to the Christian-Democrats (see Bronzwaer, 2012). This manipulation attempt was detected accidently when many people applied for panel membership at the same time.

Selecting a probability sample provides a safeguard against these manipulations. It guarantees that sampled persons are always from the target population, and they can participate only once in the survey. The researcher is in control of the selection process.

To show the effects of self-selection on estimators, it is assumed that each element k in the internet population has unknown probability π_k of participating in the survey. A naive researcher assuming that every element in the internet population has the same probability of being selected in the sample will use the sample mean $\bar{y}_S$. Bethlehem and Biffignandi (2012) show that the bias of this estimator can be written as

$$B(\bar{y}_S) = \frac{R_{\pi,Y} S_\pi S_Y}{\bar{\pi}}, \qquad (14.2)$$

in which $R_{\pi,Y}$ is the correlation coefficient between the participation probabilities and the values of the target variable. Furthermore, S_π is the standard deviation of the participation probabilities, S_Y is the standard deviation of the target variable, and $\bar{\pi}$ is the mean of all participation probabilities. The bias of the sample mean (as an estimator of the mean of the internet population) is determined by three factors:

- The average participation probability. If people are more likely to participate in the survey, the average response probability will be higher, and thus the bias will be smaller.
- The variation in participation probabilities. The more these probabilities vary, the larger the bias will be.
- The relationship between the target variable and participation behavior. A strong correlation between the values of the target variable and the participation probabilities will lead to a large bias.

Due to these selection problems, it is difficult to draw scientifically sound conclusions from a self-selection web survey. Because the selection probabilities are unknown, it is not possible to apply the theory of Horvitz and Thompson (1952), and therefore unbiased estimates cannot be computed. Such problems can be avoided if a probability sample is drawn from a proper sampling frame.

In considering using the web for general population surveys, the ideal sampling frame would be a list of email addresses of every member of the target population. Unfortunately such sampling frames do not exist. A way out is to do recruitment in a different mode. One way of accomplishing this is sending sample persons a letter with an invitation to complete the survey questionnaire in the internet. To that end, the letter must contain a link to the survey website, and also the unique identification code. This way of recruitment by mail is more cumbersome than by email. In the case of email recruitment, the questionnaire can simply be started by clicking on the link in the email. In the case of mail recruitment, more actions are required: going to the computer (e.g. upstairs in the study), starting the computer, connecting to the internet, and typing in the proper internet address (with the risk of making typing errors).

Beukenhorst and Wetzels (2009) describe a test with a mixed-mode survey in which the web was one of the modes. The survey was an experiment with the Safety Monitor of Statistics Netherlands. This survey measures how the Dutch feel with respect to safety, quality of life, and level of crime experienced. For the traditional Safety Monitor, data was collected with CATI (if a registered telephone number was available) or CAPI. The new Safety Monitor was a mix of mail, web, CATI, and CAPI. The sample was selected from the Dutch population register. All sample persons received a letter in which they were invited to complete the questionnaire on the internet. The letter also contained a postcard that could be used to request a paper version of the questionnaire. Two reminders were sent to persons who did not respond (by web or mail). If there still was no response, CATI was attempted (if a registered telephone number was available) or else CAPI was attempted. The new survey design did not have an impact on the response rate, but the costs were much lower as interviewers were involved in only 42% of the cases.

14.4 NONRESPONSE

Like any other type of survey, web surveys also suffer from nonresponse. Nonresponse occurs when individuals in the selected sample, who are also eligible for the survey, do not provide the requested information. The problem of nonresponse is that the availability of data is determined both by the (known) sample selection mechanism and the (unknown) response mechanism. Therefore, selection probabilities are unknown. Consequently, it is impossible to compute unbiased estimates. Moreover, use of naïve estimators will lead to biased estimates.

It is usually assumed that every person k in the population has an unknown response probability ρ_k. Suppose a simple random sample is selected. Just concentrating on nonresponse, and assuming there are no coverage problems, Bethlehem, Cobben, and Schouten (2011) show that the bias of the response mean $\bar{y}_R$ is equal to

$$B(\bar{y}_R) \approx \frac{R_{\rho,Y} S_\rho S_Y}{\bar{\rho}} \qquad (14.3)$$

in which $R_{\rho,Y}$ is the correlation coefficient of the response probabilities and the values of the target variable. Furthermore, S_ρ is the standard deviation of the response probabilities, S_Y is the standard deviation of the target variable, and $\bar{p}$ is the mean of all response probabilities. This expression is similar to expression (14.2) for bias in a self-selection web survey. Note, however, that the participation probabilities of a self-selection survey are usually much smaller than the response probabilities. Therefore, the bias of an estimator in a self-selection survey is potentially much larger.

The bias of the response mean (as an estimator of the population mean of the internet population) is determined by three factors:

- The average response probability. The higher the response rate, the smaller the bias.
- The variation in response probabilities. The more these probabilities vary, the larger the bias will be.
- The relationship between the target variable and response behavior. A strong correlation between the values of the target variable and the response probabilities will lead to a large bias.

The bias vanishes if all response probabilities are equal, in which case the response can be seen as a simple random sample. The bias also vanishes if response probability is unrelated to the target variable.

The response rate depends on the mode of data collection. Typically, interviewer-assisted surveys have higher response rates than self-administered surveys. Since a web survey is a self-administered survey, one can expect the response rate to be lower than, for example, CAPI and CATI surveys. Indeed, the literature seems to show that this is the case. Already in the early days of the internet, Cook, Heath, and Thompson (2000) explored response rates of 68 web surveys. The average response rate was approximately 40%. Kaplowitz, Hadlock, and Levine (2004) compared response rates of web surveys and mail surveys. They concluded that these rates are comparable, between 20% and 30%. Shih and Fan (2008), however, concluded from their meta-analysis that mail surveys have higher response rates than web surveys. And Lozar Manfreda, Bosnjak, Berzelak, Haas, and Vehovar (2008) found that, on average, the response rate of web surveys was 11% lower than that of other surveys.

Beukenhorst and Wetzels (2009) describe an experiment with the Safety Monitor of Statistics Netherlands. The traditional Safety Monitor was done with CATI (if a registered telephone number was available) or CAPI. The response rate was 63.5%. A sequential mixed-mode survey was conducted as part of the experiment. All sample persons were first asked to complete the survey questionnaire on the internet. After two reminders, remaining nonrespondents were approached by CATI (if a listed telephone number was available) or CAPI. The response rate of this mixed-mode survey was 59.7%. The response rate of the first mode (web) was only 25%. The conclusion was that a single-mode web survey leads to a lower response rate. If the web was used as the first mode in a mixed-mode survey, almost the same response rate could be obtained, but at much lower costs (as a web mode case is less expensive than a CAPI or CATI case).

14.5 WEIGHTING ADJUSTMENT

The phenomena of under-coverage, self-selection, and nonresponse can all affect the representativity of survey response. Consequently, estimators may be biased. To reduce the impact of these phenomena usually some kind of correction procedure is carried out. This comes down to applying a weighting adjustment technique.

The fundamental idea of weighting adjustment is to restore the representativity of the survey. To that end, weights are assigned to responding persons. Persons in underrepresented groups are assigned weights larger than 1, and those in overrepresented groups get a weight smaller than 1. Weights can only be computed if *auxiliary variables* are available. Such variables must have been measured in the survey, and also their population distribution (or complete sample distribution) must be available. By comparing the population distribution of an auxiliary variable with its response distribution, it can be assessed whether the response is representative with respect to this variable. If these distributions differ considerably, one must conclude that the response is selective.

Weighting adjustment is only effective if two conditions are satisfied: first, auxiliary variables must have a strong relationship with the selection mechanism of the survey, and second, auxiliary variables must be correlated with the target variables of the survey. If these conditions are not fulfilled, the bias of estimators will not be reduced. The availability of effective auxiliary variables is often a problem. Usually, there are not many variables that have a known population distribution and that satisfy the two conditions.

A well-known and frequently used weighting adjustment technique is *post-stratification*. Strata (sub-populations) are constructed by crossing qualitative auxiliary variables. All respondents within a stratum are assigned the same weight. Post-stratification is effective if the strata are homogeneous, i.e. persons within a stratum resemble each other in terms of response behavior and target variables.

If there are many auxiliary variables, it may not be possible to apply post-stratification. There could be strata without observations preventing computations of weights. Also the population distribution of the crossing of the variables may be missing. Other, more general, weighting techniques can be applied in these situations, such as *generalized regression estimation* (*linear weighting*) or *raking ratio estimation* (*multiplicative weighting*). See Bethlehem and Biffignandi (2012) for more information.

A different approach to weighting is called *propensity weighting*. Participation in the survey is modeled by means of a logistic regression model. This comes down to predicting the probability of participation in a survey from a set of auxiliary variables. The estimated participation probabilities are called *response propensities*. A next step could be to carry out post-stratification, where strata are constructed by grouping respondents with (approximately) the same response propensity. A drawback of propensity weighting is that the individual values of the auxiliary variables for the nonparticipating persons are required. Such information is often not available. Note that response propensities can also be used in other ways to reduce bias, see e.g. Bethlehem et al. (2011) and Bethlehem (2012a).

If proper auxiliary variables are not available, one might consider conducting a *reference survey*. The objective of this survey is an unbiased estimation of the population distribution of relevant auxiliary variables. Such a reference survey could be based on a small probability sample, where data collection takes place with a mode different from the web, e.g. CAPI or CATI. Under the assumption of no nonresponse, or ignorable nonresponse, this reference survey will produce unbiased estimates of the population distribution of auxiliary variables.

The reference survey approach also has disadvantages. In the first place, it is expensive to conduct an extra survey. However, it should be noted that this survey need not be very large, as it is just used for estimating the population distribution of auxiliary variables. And the information can be used for more than one web survey. In the second place, Bethlehem (2010) shows that the variance of the post-stratification estimator is, for a substantial part, determined by the size of the (small) reference survey. So, the large number of observations in the web survey does not guarantee precise estimates. The reference survey approach reduces the bias of estimates at the cost of a higher variance.

The conclusion can be that some form of weighting adjustment must certainly be applied in order to reduce the bias of estimator. However, success is not guaranteed. The ingredients for effective bias reduction may not always be available.

14.6 CAN WEB SURVEYS BE USED IN OFFICIAL STATISTICS?

Can web surveys be used in official statistics, where the focus is on obtaining precise and unbiased estimates of general population characteristics? The previous sections described a number of potential issues. This section explores whether these problems can be solved.

Web surveys suffer from under-coverage, because there are people without access to internet. Since there are differences between those with and those without internet access, under-coverage will often cause estimates to be biased. Fortunately, internet coverage will increase over time. This helps to reduce the bias. However, it is not impossible that those without internet will diverge (on average) more and more from those with internet. Hence, there is no guarantee that problems will vanish in the near future. One solution is to conduct a mixed-mode survey, where a mode other than a web survey is used for those without internet. Another solution is to provide potential respondents without internet with free internet access.

Many web surveys rely on self-selection of respondents. It has been shown that this can cause estimators to be substantially biased. This makes self-selection surveys useless for official statistics. Application of the principles of probability sampling is of crucial importance. Without it, computation of unbiased estimators is very difficult, if not impossible.

It is possible to conduct a web survey that is based on probability sampling. This requires a sampling frame. Unfortunately, there are no sampling frames containing email addresses of everyone in the population. A solution can be to do recruitment in a different mode. One option is to send a letter with the request to go to a specific website, where the online questionnaire can be completed. Such a letter should also contain a unique identification code that has to be entered. Use of such identifying codes guarantees that only sampled persons respond, and that they respond only once. Another option is to approach sampled persons face-to-face or by phone and to ask them for their email address. If they give one, they are sent a link to the online questionnaire.

Even if a survey is based on probability sampling, one may encounter problems. One of the most important ones is probably nonresponse. In fact, this also introduces a form of self-selection.

If the representativity of a web survey is affected by nonresponse, under-coverage, or self-selection, a weighting adjustment procedure can be applied to repair this. These correction techniques are only effective if proper auxiliary variables are available. They must have been measured in the survey, their population distribution must be known, and they must be correlated with response behavior and the target variables of the survey.

Weighting adjustment, however, is no guarantee for success. Often the required conditions are not satisfied. The proper auxiliary variables are simply not available. One way out is to estimate the population distribution of the auxiliary variables in a different survey. This reference survey should not be a web survey: It should preferably be a CAPI or CATI survey that does not suffer from the problems of the web survey, and the nonresponse rate should be negligible. The question is whether or not this is feasible in practice. Moreover, use of a web survey may reduce bias, but also dramatically decrease the precision of estimates.

One may wonder if it is possible at all to conduct a web survey that is not affected by under-coverage and self-selection. The Dutch LISS panel is the result of such an attempt (see Scherpenzeel, 2008). This online panel has been constructed by selecting a random sample of households from the population register of The Netherlands. Selected households were recruited for this panel by means of CAPI or CATI, so sample selection was based on true probability sampling. Moreover, cooperative households without internet access were provided with equipment giving them access to internet. An analysis by Scherpenzeel and Bethlehem (2011) shows that the results of this panel are much closer to those of surveys based on probability sampling than to those of surveys using self-selection web surveys.

Response rates are an important issue. Response rates for traditional CAPI and CATI surveys vary between 60% and 70% at Statistics Netherlands. First experiences with web surveys (based on probability sampling) resulted in response rates of around 30% (see, for example, Beukenhorst & Wetzels, 2009). An experiment with a housing demand survey showed that for large and complex questionnaires response rates may even drop to 20%. One can conclude from these experiences that a change from CAPI or CATI to the web will reduce survey costs, but the price to be paid is a much lower response rate.

There is growing interest in mixed-mode surveys in the world of official statistics. The idea is to conduct a sequential mixed-mode survey, where the first mode is the web (the cheapest mode). Nonrespondents are followed up by the next cheapest mode, and this is CATI. Finally, any remaining nonresponse can be followed up by means of CAPI. This approach may keep response rates at a reasonable level, at the same time reducing the survey costs.

Mixed-mode surveys introduce a new problem: *mode effects*. The same question is answered differently when asked in a different mode of data collection. Removing mode effects is not a simple problem (see, for example, Dillman, Smith, & Christian, 2009; Buelens et al. 2012).

REFERENCES

Bethlehem, J. G. (2009). *The rise of survey sampling.* Discussion Paper 09015. The Hague/ Heerlen, The Netherlands: Statistics Netherlands.

Bethlehem, J. G. (2010). Selection bias in web surveys. *International Statistical Review, 78,* 161–188.

Bethlehem, J. G. (2012a). *Using response probabilities for assessing representativity.* Discussion Paper 201212. The Hague/Heerlen, The Netherlands: Statistics Netherlands.

Bethlehem, J. G. (2012b, December). *Ruis in de steekproef, of is er echt iets aan de hand?* Retrieved from www.survey-onderzoek.nl

Bethlehem, J. G., & Biffignandi, S. (2012). *Handbook of web surveys.* Hoboken, NJ: Wiley.

Bethlehem, J. G., Cobben, F., & Schouten, B. (2011). *Handbook of nonresponse in household surveys.* Hoboken, NJ: Wiley.

Beukenhorst, D., & Wetzels, W. (2009). *A comparison of two mixed-mode designs of the Dutch Safety Monitor: Mode effects, costs, logistics.* Technical paper DMH 206546. Heerlen, The Netherlands: Statistics Netherlands.

Bronzwaer, S. (2012, September). Infiltranten probeerden de peilingen van Maurice de Hond te manipuleren. *NRC.* Retrieved from www.nrc.nl

Buelens, B., Van Der Laan, J., Schouten, B., Van Den Brakel, J., Burger, J., & Klausch, T. (2012). *Disentangling mode-specific selection and measurement bias in social surveys.* Discussion Paper 201211. The Hague/Heerlen, The Netherlands: Statistics Netherlands.

CBS (2012, October), *ICT-gebruik van personen naar persoonskenmerken.* Retrieved from www.cbs.nl

CBS (2013, May), *Een derde van de 75-plussers gebruikt internet.* Retrieved from www.cbs.nl

Cook, C., Heath, F., & Thompson, R. L. (2000). A meta-analysis of response rates in web- or internet-based surveys. *Educational and Psychological Measurement, 60,* 821–836.

Couper, M. P. (2000). Web surveys: A review of issues and approaches. *Public Opinion Quarterly, 64,* 464–494.

Dillman, D. A., Smith, J. D., & Christian, L. M. (2009). *Internet, mail and mixed-mode surveys. The Tailored Design Method.* Hoboken, NJ: Wiley.

Duffy, B., Smith, K., Terhanian, G., & Bremer, J. (2005). Comparing data from online and face-to-face surveys. *International Journal of Market Research, 47,* 615–639.

Horvitz, D. G., & Thompson, D. J. (1952). A generalization of sampling without replacement from a finite universe. *Journal of the American Statistical Association, 47,* 663–685.

Kaplowitz, M. D., Hadlock, T. D., & Levine, R. (2004). A comparison of web and mail response rates. *Public Opinion Quarterly, 68,* 94–101.

Lozar Manfreda, K., Bosnjak, M., Berzelak, J., Haas, I., & Vehovar, V. (2008). Web surveys versus other survey modes, meta-analysis comparing response rates. *International Journal of Market Research, 50,* 79–104.

Scherpenzeel, A. (2008). An online panel as a platform for multi-disciplinary research. In I. Stoop & M. Wittenberg (Eds.), *Access panels and online research, panacea or pitfall?* (pp. 101–106). Amsterdam, The Netherlands: Aksant.

Scherpenzeel, A. C. (2009). *Start of the LISS Panel: Sample and recruitment of a probability-based internet panel.* Tilburg, The Netherlands: CentERdata.

Scherpenzeel, A. C., & Bethlehem, J. G. (2011). How representative are online panels? Problems of coverage and selection and possible solutions. In M. Das, P. Ester, & L. Kaczmirek (Eds.), *Social and behavioral research and the internet* (pp. 105–132). New York and London: Routledge.

Shih, T. H., & Fan, X. (2008). Comparing response rates from web and mail surveys: A meta-analysis. *Field Methods, 20* (3), 249–271.

15

e-Social Science Perspective on Survey Process

Towards an Integrated Web Questionnaire Development Platform

Vasja Vehovar, Andraž Petrovčič and Ana Slavec

15.1 INTRODUCTION: SURVEYS WITHIN THE CONTEXT OF E-SOCIAL SCIENCES

Survey research literature predominantly focuses on methodological issues (such as survey errors and survey modes) which are related to the fielding activities of the survey data collection process. Much less attention is given to the broader administrative, managerial, infrastructural and process-integration aspects of pre-fielding (i.e., planning, conceptualization, questionnaire development, testing) and post-fielding (i.e., data preparation, automated analysis, archiving, dissemination, publication). There is also a serious lack of attention to the integrative potential of information-communication technology (ICT) for the survey process, at least in the mainstream (or in vast majority) of ICT tools that support the survey data collection process. This issue is only dealt with in some large survey data collection organizations (see, for example, the special issue of Journal of Official Statistics, e.g., Biemer, Eltinge, & Holmberg, 2013), which however are not the focus of this chapter.

With the rise of the internet, the interaction between modern society and ICT has in general moved to a new level, being addressed in various contexts, from social informatics (Kling, Rosenbaum, & Sawyer, 2005) to Science, Technology and Society (STS) studies (Hackett, Amsterdamska, Lynch, & Wajcman, 2007). The notion of *e-social science* also appears here, referring to digital communication, collaboration and computational tools in the social science research process. Within this context ICT increasingly integrates the research stages, providing potential gains in resources, time and quality (Dutton & Jeffreys, 2010; Jankowski, 2007, 2009a; Schroeder & Fry, 2007; Searight, Mauldin, Ratwik, Conboy, & Searight, 2011).

However, some initial applications of the e-social science concept (Jankowski, 2009b; Dutton & Jeffreys, 2010; Schroeder & Fry, 2007) also suggest that a broader framework is needed to accommodate the increasingly complex transformation of empirical social science research supported by online research tools and methods (Jankowski, 2009a). Hence, the study of the technological affordances of ICTs that support social scientists needs to be accompanied by a conceptual and empirical reflection on how researchers react and actively participate in the undergoing technological transformation of their work environment (Meyer & Dutton, 2009). Within this context, relatively little systematic knowledge is available about internet-based tools that would support online collaboration and data collection phases of a research project within an integrated platform (Jankowski, 2009a). In fact, the existing e-social sciences literature observes that the tools, which are designed for online collaboration and communication among social scientists, are generally not fully integrated into ICT-based solutions that support other phases of the (empirical) social science research process. On the one hand, this condition might stem from the heterogeneity of scientific communities and disciplines in social sciences (Dutton & Meyer, 2009). On the other hand, the technical design of existing (non-integrated) software solutions further stimulates the separation of the research process (Macer & Wilson, 2011).

We argue in this chapter that conceptual barriers often keep research processes (unnecessarily) disintegrated, despite the fact that the technical potential of ICT is already developed enough for much more integration. With reference to web survey software tools, this issue can be observed as very late integration with various Web 2.0 solutions, so platforms conceived in the late 1990s with relatively limited (as of 2014) support for Web 2.0 features still dominate the market.

Another typical example for such a lack of integration is the situation of initial versions of survey questionnaires which are still predominantly designed using word processors (e.g., MS Word, Google Docs) and communicated with simple email exchange. Only when a draft becomes mature or even final it is converted into a computerized form. As suggested by Macer and Wilson (2011) such fragmented ICT-based support also neglects the needs of researchers, who strongly prefer more integration.

This chapter deals with a specific case of (web) questionnaire development, which illuminates the above mentioned barriers. First, we illustrate current practice (Section 15.2). Next, we show gains of a conceptually integrative approach in a case study (Section 15.3). With such an approach many barriers can be removed even with relatively primitive technical solutions. Finally, in the conclusion (Section 15.4), we discuss the findings and identify potential directions for future research.

15.2 WEB QUESTIONNAIRE DEVELOPMENT: AN ILLUSTRATION OF CURRENT PRACTICE

The core of the ICT integrative support for the survey research process has been related to Computer Assisted Survey Information Collection (CASIC), which links the corresponding data collection stages (Vehovar & Lozar Manfreda, 2008). The notion of CASIC emerged in the 1980s with computer assisted telephone interviewing (CATI), then it took momentum in the 1990s with the emergence of the internet and now it blossoms in numerous directions, from web and mobile research to virtual interviewers. However, despite these advancements, CASIC preserved the focus on the fielding stage, with a certain shift towards *CASIC-specific* survey modes, while the integrative role of ICT still remained outside of corresponding ICT (i.e., CASIC) platforms. The modern web survey tools thus predominantly still support only the core data collection process (i.e., fielding stage), while other stages are generally not integrated (Kaczmirek, 2008; Macer & Wilson, 2012; Vehovar, Čehovin, Kavčič, & Lenar, 2012). As mentioned above, the exceptions are tailored in-house and case-specific projects in some large survey data collection organizations, but also some attempts among some more complex tools.

The development of a survey questionnaire is a very suitable object to illustrate the above assertions. Namely, many researchers and corresponding clients may have already experienced how non-integrated, sometimes cumbersome and even painful (e.g., lost comments, wrong versions) it can be to comment questionnaire versions in word processors (e.g., MS Word, Google Docs) and exchange them via email or web.

Here, we first present a typical situation of the questionnaire development process related to the 7EU-VET project (2010–2012)[1] with a survey in seven EU countries, using a 30-minute self-administered questionnaire (both paper-and-pencil and web) among students in the vocational education system.

The initial conceptualization of the topics was done from March to June 2010 at a partner meeting and via email correspondence, followed by initial word processor[2] versions of the questionnaire:

- 1st, 2nd and 3rd internal outlines, July, August 2010,
- 4th, 5th and 6th internal drafts, September, 2010
- 7th, 8th and 9th draft versions for partners' feedbacks, September 2010.

The word processor also served as a communication platform since comments were better written there with the track-changes function enabled (shown as the colored input, directly into the text). This way they were also further discussed using the corresponding commenting functions (Figure 15.1).[3] The commented version was then distributed via email to project partners. After the ninth version the questionnaire was turned into an online form in October 2010 as the first online version, followed—after online commenting—by the second online version. The latter was then exported again into a word processor, where the tenth, eleventh and twelfth versions were further commented (due to complexity, some contributors

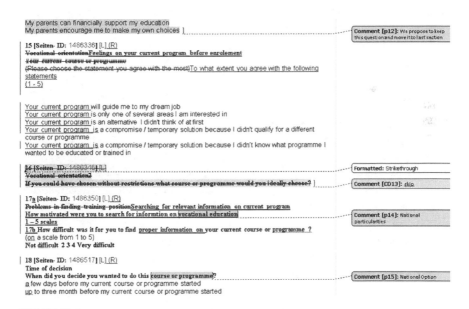

FIGURE 15.1
A screen from a word processor version of the draft 7EU-VET questionnaire

believed that the issues would be better dealt with by commenting offline rather than online). However, this time the corrections were imputed into the online version,[4] which was exported again into a word processor for further comments. After the twelfth offline (word processor) version—exported from corresponding online versions (not explicitly numbered here)—the third, fourth, fifth, sixth, seventh and eighth online versions were exposed only to the online commenting system. The ninth computerized version was then accepted as the final draft ready for English proofreading in November 2010.

This was then further followed by translations and back-translations, resulting in additional comments and versions. The same was true for the final activities of proofreading, field testing and laying out the design, which resulted in several more versions until January 2011, when the final versions in all languages were concluded.

In a comparative research framework and with given complexity, this questionnaire development process was perhaps neither excessively lengthy nor very complex. However, we suggest it would still benefit from a more integrated ICT support, which would, at the very least, avoid switches between word processor and computerized versions.

As a matter of fact, in reality very often even many more changes and comments could be found than in Figure 15.1, all resulting in cumbersome and colorful screens where it was increasingly difficult for researchers to provide further comments and to trace the current status of a certain comment (i.e., whether it is solved, rejected or still in process).

15.3 INTEGRATED SUPPORT FOR QUESTIONNAIRE DEVELOPMENT: AN EXPERIMENT

We argue that the above-illustrated fragmentation of ICT integration, which apparently seems to be a technical problem, is rather a conceptual one. The implementation of e-social sciences would conceptually mean that ICT integrates—as much as possible—all sub-stages of the questionnaire development process within one single tool. Of course, questionnaire development is only one specific aspect of the survey process, while the ICT integration of the entire survey research process (i.e., pre-fielding, fielding and post-fielding) is much more complex. However, conceptually there is not much difference, so we will continue with this example, showing that technical obstacles can be overcome relatively easily (even with a relatively primitive pilot tool) once a conceptual breakthrough occurs. With conceptual breakthrough we mean here starting to think about the survey process (and corresponding ICT support) as one entity and not as a composite of separated steps. The latter is often reinforced in practice because the ICT tools were frequently conceptualized and designed by computer personnel and not by survey methodologists.

The ICT integration of questionnaire development into the process of producing the computerized (i.e., CASIC) questionnaire would basically require abandoning the word processor and email exchanges of the questionnaire. To achieve this, the integrated alternative tool must include two essential functionalities, whose absence are nowadays (still) forcing researchers to rely on word processors when developing (early) drafts of questionnaires. First, *direct inline editing* is needed to replace the usual practice in web survey software tools, which is to first open the question, followed by the editing itself and then concluded with another (third) step of saving the changes. Instead, users should have an user-friendly option allowing them to move the cursor to a desired location, click there and edit the question immediately (without any opening/saving the question), the same as in any word processor. Second, a drag/drop or cut/paste command for questions must enable moving questions with a mouse or other pointing device (which is a standard Web 2.0 feature for web tools). Even though these seem trivial solutions in terms of technical implementation, a study showed that out of the 15 most popular software tools only one enabled inline editing, while only four had drag/drop functions (Vehovar, Slavec, & Berzelak, 2011). In recent years more tools actually incorporate these two features, however, these are still far from being a mainstream functionalities.

Of course, in addition to these two essential components, the integrated tool should also provide all standard features of modern software for creating CASIC questionnaires. A very important functionality is the collapsed view (i.e., seeing one line per question), which simplifies editing the questionnaire structure (e.g., question orders, conditions, blocks). Moreover, an internal (for editors) and external (for respondents) commenting system needs to be incorporated, as well as functionalities of copying, versioning and archiving of the questionnaire. A recent overview of web survey software tools (Vehovar & Čehovin, 2013) showed relatively little progress with respect to these issues. At most, the tools may (increasingly) support these features, but we could not find the corresponding integration.

In order to carry out the experiment presented here, we have developed and used a prototype of an academic research tool for producing a CASIC (in this specific case we limit to web) questionnaire, with all standard industry functionalities.[5] We further extended it with the above-mentioned inline editing and drag/drop options, so that the entire process of questionnaire development could run without a word processor and email exchange.

Our hypothesis is that the integrated online tool will outperform the standard procedure (relying on word processor and email exchange before computerization of the questionnaire into the CASIC tool) in time, quality and user satisfaction.

Methodology

A small experiment was performed with 16 graduate students in the *Research Methods* course at the Faculty of Social Sciences of the University Ljubljana in 2011. Half of them were foreign students and the other half were local ones. They all had some previous experience with survey methodology and statistics. Four groups were formed randomly (each with two international students) and each group worked in both modes. One option was developing a questionnaire in the integrated mode, using the prototype tool (experimental group); for simplicity we will call this *online mode*. The other option was a standard approach using a word processor and email communication (control group), where computerization of the questionnaire was performed only when the questionnaire was developed—we call this option the *offline mode*.

All groups had to work on two topics defined in advance—one was related to attitudes towards wild animals kept as domestic pets, while the other dealt with sports activities of foreign students at the university. Groups 1 and 3 worked on the animal topic as the experimental group (online mode), while Groups 2 and 4 were assigned to this topic as control groups (offline mode). It was vice versa for the sports topic: Groups 1 and 3 were the control group (offline) and 2 and 4 the experimental (online). Each group thus worked on two projects, but—due to experimental design—each also worked with both topics and both modes, so eight distinctive questionnaires were developed, two by each group.

Students were assigned four roles: online editor, offline editor, tester and evaluator. The editors were responsible for questionnaire development, handling comments, moderating discussions, archiving versions, spell checking, etc. One editor in the group was assigned to the offline development, the other to the online one. The third role was the tester, responsible for all testing issues. The fourth member was evaluator, whose task was to write evaluations of all activities, detecting problems, monitoring timing, etc. In addition, the evaluator helped testing the questionnaire (live test with participants). All four members were required to contribute ideas and comments to both questionnaires. Other duties also existed (e.g., data collection, analysis, report writing), but were not relevant for this study.

In the offline mode of questionnaire preparation only email exchange was allowed outside the classroom, while for the online mode only communication through the prototype tool (i.e., commenting system) was allowed. Everybody was obliged to respond to requests promptly and to accomplish tasks in due time. All time spent on various tasks was meticulously recorded on time sheets.

Procedure

The experiment lasted six weeks. During the first week each student reviewed relevant substantive sources for both topics and prepared a brief with ideas. Then students met, discussed the briefs and editors started with the questionnaires.

In the second week, online editors prepared their questionnaire outlines (Version 0) in the online prototype tool, while offline editors prepared them as MS Word documents. In total, as mentioned, there were eight versions, two for each group, four for each topic and four for each mode (Table 15.1). The feedback for the online version was submitted through a special commenting functionality of the prototype tool, while for the offline version it was made in the word processor and exchanged by email. The editors reviewed the comments and then prepared the first draft version of the questionnaire (Version 1).

In the third week the evaluators systematically checked questionnaires according to formal design guidelines in the course literature and prepared a report for the respective editors. In parallel, the two other members of the group made the second wave of internal comments. The next draft of the questionnaire (Version 2) was then created and testers prepared a proposal for the testing procedure.

TABLE 15.1

Quantitative evaluation results

Topic	Offline			Online		
	Group	**Time**	**Evaluation**	**Group**	**Time**	**Evaluation**
Animals	G2	42h 30 min	3.0	G1	38h 30 min	4.3
	G4	38h 30 min	3.3	G3	36h 00 min	4.5
Sports	G1	28h 30 min	3.7	G2	32h 00 min	3.3
	G3	41h 00 min	4.0	G4	32h 00 min	4.0

In the fourth week the testers performed quantitative testing on a small sample of respondents, while the evaluators performed qualitative interviews (one for each topic) using the think-aloud method. In the online mode, quantitative testing was done via the prototype tool using online comments, while in the offline mode the word processor version was sent to respondents asking them to provide written comments and email them back as soon as possible. Respective editors then prepared another draft (Version 3).

In the fifth week, Version 3 of each offline questionnaires was entered in the online tool[6] (Version 3b) and after this point—in this mode too—the questionnaire was developed exclusively online, except for the comments which were still being exchanged via email. Next, another wave of internal feedback exchange was conducted in both modes. As a result, editors had to prepare the new draft questionnaire (Version 4).

In the sixth week, Version 4 was evaluated by three external experts. In addition, the evaluators also reviewed the questionnaires according to the Statistics Sweden Checklist.[7] The questionnaire (Version 5) was finalized by the end of the sixth week. The four animal questionnaires were 36 to 66 response items long (depending on how ambitious and motivated the group members were), while the sports questionnaires had 22 to 32 response items. All eight questionnaires were complex and included lots of conditioning and many stages of branching.

Results

We used time sheets and the final evaluation survey to summarize key findings (Table 15.1).

Three out of four groups needed more time (i.e., the number of hours recorded in time sheets) to finalize the questionnaire (Version 5) in the offline mode. Overall, the means were 34 h 36 minutes (online) and 37 h 30 min (offline). However, with only four groups and with two measurements the ANOVA test did not show statistical significance. Nevertheless, a tendency was shown towards this difference.

Similarly, the overall quality—measured by the self-evaluation question *"How would you rate the quality of your groups' animal/sports questionnaire? 1 – Poor, 2 – Fair, 3 – Average, 4 – Good, 5 – Excellent"*—was lower for the online mode only in one group, with the largest difference of averages between the experimental (online) and control (offline) group being for Group 4 (3.3 offline and 4.0 online). Nevertheless, despite showing the same tendency, the repeated measures ANOVA showed no statistical significance. Of course, the existing differences could be partly due to the interaction with questionnaire topic. Controlling for this shows that the difference between the offline and online group are quite obvious within the animal questionnaires (3.0–3.3 offline, 4.3–4.5 online) and also within sports questionnaires (3.7–4.0 offline; 3.3–4.0 online). Here, on the other hand, it is important to note that, of course, the questionnaires varied among groups due to characteristics of groups that we were not able to control. Higher satisfaction of Group 1 with the offline sports question-naire than Group 2 with the corresponding online version (Table 15.1) can be thus explained by group characteristics (i.e., Group 1 was generally very satisfied, while Group 2 had lower general satisfaction).

While the above results may only indicate some tendencies and are not fully convincing, more explicit confirmation in favor of the integrated online version arises from the comparisons of individual student evalu-ations. There, all but one student rated the online questionnaire (with the evaluation question above) at least as good as the offline or (much) bet-ter. A corresponding paired samples t-test indicates significant differences ($p < .05$). However, here we still may have some disturbing interaction between the groups and the questionnaire.

Furthermore, user satisfaction was measured by posing the following question: *"If you were to develop a questionnaire with a group of colleagues, which method would you choose? Online definitely, online preferably, offline preferably, offline definitely?"* Half responded with *online definitely* and the other half with *online preferably*. No student chose *offline preferably* or *offline definitely*, despite some technical difficulties and shortcomings of the online prototype tool. This result strongly reconfirms the above tendencies and most clearly demonstrates the advantage of the online version, which was—due to small sample sizes—only weakly shown in previous results.

In addition, students provided extensive open comments, additionally confirming the above findings with uniformly favoring the online version. They also provided many specific comments on methodological and tech-nical details. On the one hand, the most frequently mentioned advantages of the online questionnaire were its speed, instant availability of all ver-sions and easiness to edit, preview, test and comment. The main disadvan-tages here were some technical difficulties (bugs) and time needed to learn the tool. On the other hand, the disadvantages of the offline development were the time taken and difficulty to merge comments, slow communica-tion and confusion with versioning. Rare comments related to advantages of the offline mode were mentioning the ease of distinguishing between versions and clearer previews, which basically indicated room for improvement of the online prototype tool.

15.4 DISCUSSION AND CONCLUSIONS

Contemporary social sciences are increasingly supported with ICT (Jankowski, 2007, 2009a, 2009b). However, when talking about social science research, only parts of this process—spanning from conceptualization to analysis and dissemination—have been fully integrated with ICT. Even when a certain shift occurred, it usually remained isolated from some other parts of the process. If we talk more specifically about the survey research process, integrated ICT support is provided predominantly for the fielding stage (i.e., computerization of questionnaire and data collection covered, both with standard CASIC), while other stages (e.g., questionnaire development) are either not supported or they are typically supported by separated ICT-based tools and services, which are not integrated into one platform.

In this chapter we first addressed this problem by illustrating current deficiencies with an example from the 7EU-VET project, where a complex multi-language questionnaire was developed for seven countries. There, a word processor and email communication were substantially used for the development of the questionnaire. This was in large part a separate process from creating a computerized version of the questionnaire. Such non-integrated—although ICT supported—administration resulted in cumbersome procedures and many unnecessary complexities.

Further, we claimed that this deficiency does not derive so much from technical limitations, because we presented an example of a pilot study using a relatively simple academic prototype web survey software tool, which already resolved corresponding technical problems. Instead, we argue that conceptual limitations were preventing an earlier and more effective integrative support of ICT for survey research process.

In the empirical part we showed that word processors and email exchanges can be entirely eliminated from the questionnaire development process. The experiment revealed that participants who were designing an online questionnaire preferred doing that in one single platform, rather than switching between multiple tools. The results also indicated that even a relatively primitive prototype (online) solution was better, or at least equivalent, to the standard process of questionnaire development, where initial sub-stages are performed in a word processor (offline) and exchanged via email (or via web).

The differences in perceived performance of online and offline mode showed some tendencies in favor of the integrative (online) mode, however, they were non-significant. This was somehow expected owing to a relatively small sample size, being a potential limitation of the study. However, when asked about future preferences, the users would clearly select the integrated (online) version, which was additional reconfirmed with qualitative assertions.

Of course, students as researchers may present an obvious limitation of the study; however this does not change the internal consistency of these results. One may also raise the issue of the web survey software tools used in the *control group*. Namely, by using some other (i.e., better) software the differences may shrink and led to some other conclusions. However, extensive comparisons of this prototype with mainstream research tools showed no lagging in performance, at least for the purpose of academic survey questionnaire development.

In future, of course, inevitable progress of the ICT integration is foreseen. The computer assisted questionnaire development and data collection tools will increasingly support and integrate more and more stages of the survey research. Specifically, the continuously evolving technological affordances such as increased speed, expanded implementation of Web 2.0 features and advanced SaaS (software as a service) platforms will undoubtedly enable more effective ICT support. We already observe that more and more popular tools now enable the option of inline editing and inclusion of an elaborated commenting system. Nevertheless, this does not change our initial thesis that the lack of integrated conceptual thinking (i.e., e-social science) contributes to slower ICT integration of the survey research process and social science research in general.

We should also repeat that we address here the mainstream CASIC tools and we do not include in our discussion the few very elaborate and expensive ICT tools and/or tailored ICT systems which support survey processes in some large data collection organizations.

If we limit ourselves only to the questionnaire development stage, the ultimate solution would perhaps be an online word editor with full functionalities of the existing offline word processors together with an integrated full-scale commenting management system, which would support online collaboration between researchers. However, it seems that we are still far from this overreaching goal, as currently even the online word processors themselves seriously underperform compared to corresponding offline software.

Nevertheless, viewed from a broader perspective, beyond the stage of questionnaire development, the future will pave the way also to the increased integrated ICT support for the entire survey research process, including management, communication and other stages of pre-fielding and post-fielding. Of course, artificial intelligence, data mining and decision support will be increasingly used to incorporate human knowledge into this process (e.g., Grobelnik & Mladenić, 2005; Mladenić, Lavrač, Bohanec, & Moyle, 2004). It is in this particular sense that we suggest that throughout these future developments, the implementation of the e-social sciences concept might serve as a sound conceptual basis for fostering a dynamical and theoretically grounded process of ICT integration into survey methodology. Needless to say, this can also contribute to the speed, quality and cost-efficiency of the survey process.

NOTES

1. Detailed Methodological Approach to Understanding the VET Education, www.7 eu-vet.org.
2. MS WORD was used for word processing.
3. Comments were placed on right of the body of text (MS WORD command: Review→New comment).
4. One of the most comprehensive tools was used, one that also provided an advanced online commenting system: GlobalPark EFS, acquired later by QuestBack.
5. 1KA (http://1ka.si).
6. The same web survey software tool (1KA), however, without the usage of the commenting system.
7. www.scb.se/statistik/_publikationer/OV9999_2004A01_BR_X97OP0402.pdf.

REFERENCES

Biemer, P. P., Eltinge J. L., & Holmberg, A. (2013). Prelude to the special issue on systems and architectures for high-quality statistics production. *Journal of Official Statistics, 29*(1), 1–4.

Dutton, W. H., & Jeffreys, P. W. (2010). World Wide Research: An introduction. In W. H. Dutton & P. W. Jeffreys (Eds.), *World Wide Research: Reshaping the sciences and humanities* (pp. 1–19). London: MIT Press.

Dutton, W. H., & Meyer, E. T. (2009). Experience with new tools and infrastructures of research: An exploratory study of distance from, and attitudes toward, e-Research. *Prometheus, 27*(3), 223–338. doi:10.1080/08109020903127802

Grobelnik, M., & Mladenić, D. (2005). Automated knowledge discovery in advanced knowledge management. *Journal of Knowledge Management, 9*(5), 132–149.

Hackett, E. J., Amsterdamska, O., Lynch, M., & Wajcman, J. (Eds.). (2007). *The handbook of science and technology studies* (3rd ed.). Cambridge, MA: MIT Press.

Jankowski, N. W. (2007). Exploring e-science: An introduction. *Journal of Computer-Mediated Communication, 12*(2), 549–562.

Jankowski, N. W. (Ed.). (2009a). *e-Research: Transformation in scholarly practice.* New York: Routledge.

Jankowski, N. W. (2009b). The context and challenges of e-Research. In N. W. Jankowski (Ed.), *e-Research: Transformation in scholarly practice* (pp. 3–33). New York: Routledge.

Kaczmirek, L. (2008). Internet survey software tools. In N. G. Fielding & R. M. Lee (Eds.), *Sage handbook of online research methods* (pp. 236–254). London: Sage.

Kling, R., Rosenbaum, H., & Sawyer, S. (2005). *Understanding and communicating social informatics: A framework for studying and teaching the human contexts of information and communication technologies.* Medford, NY: Information Today.

Macer, T., & Wilson, S. (2011). *Globalpark annual market research software survey 2010: Results and report.* Retrieved from www.meaning.uk.com/resources/reports/2010-Globalpark-MR-software-survey.pdf

Macer, T., & Wilson, S. (2012). *The confirmit annual market research software survey 2011.* Retrieved from www.meaning.uk.com/your-resources/2011-mr-software-survey/#

Meyer, E. T., & Dutton, W. H. (2009). Top-down e-Infrastructure meets bottom-up research innovation: The social shaping of e-research. *Prometheus, 27*(3), 239–250. doi:10.1080/08109020903127810

Mladenić, D., Lavrač, N., Bohanec, M., & Moyle, S. (Eds.). (2004). *Data mining and decision support: Integration and collaboration.* Amsterdam: Springer.

Schroeder, R., & Fry, J. (2007). Social science approaches to e-Science: Framing agendas. *Journal of Computer-Mediated Communication, 12*(2), 563–582. Retrieved from: http://jcmc.indiana.edu/vol12/issue2/schroeder.html

Searight, H. R., Mauldin, R. K., Ratwik, S., Conboy, R., & Searight, B. K. (2011). e-Research in the social sciences: The possibilities and the reality (A review article). *Current Research Journal of Social Sciences, 3*(2), 71–80. Retrieved from http://maxwellsci.com/print/crjss/v3-71-80.pdf

Vehovar, V., & Čehovin, G. (2013). *Survey software overview: A WebSM study update.* Internal material.

Vehovar, V., Čehovin, G., Kavčič, L., & Lenar. J. (2012). *Survey software features overview: A WebSM study.* Retrieved from www.websm.org/uploadi/editor/1362408700WebSM_WSS_report_b_v04.pdf

Vehovar, V., & Lozar Manfreda, K. (2008). Overview: Online surveys. In N. G. Fielding & R. M. Lee (Eds.), *Sage handbook of online research methods* (pp. 177–194). London: Sage.

Vehovar, V., Slavec, A., & Berzelak, J. (2011, August). *Web survey software.* Paper presented at the 5th Internet Survey Methodology Workshop, Den Haag, Netherlands. Retrieved from http://workshop.websm.org/uploadi/editor/1314653351Websurveys oftware_final.pdf

16

Evaluating Cross-National Item Equivalence with Probing Questions in Web Surveys

Michael Braun, Dorothée Behr, Lars Kaczmirek and Wolfgang Bandilla

16.1 INTRODUCTION

Comparability in Cross-National Survey Research

Large-scale cross-national survey projects, such as the World Value Surveys (WVS), the European Values Study (EVS), the International Social Survey Program (ISSP), the European Social Survey (ESS), and the Eurobarometer have established long time series, partly beginning in the 1970s and 1980s. A major goal of these studies is the continued and equivalent measurement of constructs. However, equivalent measurement is threatened due to the intercultural character of the projects. Countries can differ in the way the majority interprets a question. In addition, social change over time may also lead to different interpretations of items. These two aspects are a threat to the long-term validity of cross-national surveys because some of the changes over time and differences between countries can be attributed to methodological artifacts. If this is the case, they must not be interpreted as substantive results.

The traditional method to establish equivalence of measurement is applying one or more data-analytic approaches (Vandenberg & Lance, 2000). However, most of these approaches are only helpful in deciding whether measurement equivalence is given or not (e.g., multi-group structural equation modeling), but not at getting at the causes of non-equivalence. One exception is multilevel structural equation modeling where variables which might explain the lack of equivalence can be explicitly included in the model. Unfortunately, even this method is unable to detect what respondents in different countries have in mind when answering survey questions. For example, it remains unclear which group of immigrants (e.g., in terms of nationality) respondents think of when answering questions about attitudes towards immigration.

Much can be gained from getting at the causes of non-equivalence and from understanding the interpretations of respondents from different countries. This is especially true when there is a chance to redesign problematic items, as it is usually not enough to know that these items do not work properly. To improve problem-ridden items, the question designers need detailed information on where precisely the problems are located. In addition, information on different item interpretation across countries can be integrated into substantive analyses with existing data, thus safeguarding against invalid conclusions. The mismatches themselves could even become the main focus of intercultural research.

Cognitive Interviewing as a Device to Uncover Equivalence Problems

When answering survey items, respondents have several tasks to perform: comprehending the item, retrieving relevant information, using that information to make the required judgment, and selecting and reporting an answer (Tourangeau, Rips, & Rasinski, 2000). The completion of these tasks may be hampered, however. For example, surveys are likely to contain at least some questions which do not reflect or match social reality and issues of public debate. Information retrieval and judgment in these cases may become difficult. Items may also include terms that are so vague that a consistent understanding is unlikely. This then results in different interpretations among respondents. In cross-national surveys, different cultural contexts impact on the completion of the four response tasks and thus provide the ground for potentially different item interpretation across countries and non-equivalence of items.

A possible solution for assessing equivalence of measurement—taking the limitations of statistical procedures into account—is cognitive interviewing (CI). CI helps to uncover the processes respondents use in answering survey items as well as differences in item interpretation. There are two major cognitive interviewing techniques used in survey research, namely *think-aloud*, where respondents verbalize their thoughts as they answer survey questions, and *probing*, where interviewers ask follow-up questions to obtain additional information on responses (Beatty & Willis, 2007; Willis, 2005). Suitable probing questions for the cross-national context are comprehension probing ("What does the term 'public services' mean to you?"), category-selection probing ("Why did you choose 'agree'?"), or specific probing ("What type of immigrant did you think of when you answered the previous item?"; e.g., Prüfer & Rexroth, 2005; Willis, 2005). These probes help reveal invalid item interpretations across countries. Results of CI can be fed back into the development process of new items or, alternatively, inform substantive analyses with existing items.

The present use of CI in survey research has its limitations (Behr, Braun, Kaczmirek, & Bandilla, 2012; Behr, Braun, Kaczmirek, & Bandilla, 2013). First, CI is mainly used at the pretesting stage and rarely in post-survey evaluation, although the latter can be of benefit as well. Second, CI can both be implemented in a highly standardized form with pre-scripted and planned probes, or in a more non-standardized fashion allowing the interviewer to intervene whenever needed. However, the more interviewers are supposed to play an active or non-standardized role, the lower the comparability of the results obtained by different interviewers might be (Conrad & Blair, 2004, 2009). Third, CI is traditionally based on small quota samples (often not more than 20 interviews are conducted), a fact that is challenged, for example, by Blair and Conrad (2011). Already a few interviews can help detect major problems with items (Beatty & Willis, 2007), but they do not allow for quantifying the findings in a meaningful way, evaluating the prevalence of problems, or revealing interpretation patterns of special subpopulations characterized by their response behavior. The small sample size is probably the major limitation of traditional CI.

Cross-national CI studies add a layer of complexity to the usual type of CI. The great challenge is to set up a truly comparative cross-national CI study. Experienced cognitive interviewers may not be available in all countries, and even if they were, it would be necessary to standardize procedures across countries for reasons of comparability. For instance, different house styles in recruiting respondents or different guidelines specifying the conduct of interviews will need to be harmonized, at least to some extent (Lee, 2012; Miller et al., 2011; Thrasher et al., 2011). Furthermore, the typically low case numbers also in cross-national studies (maximum 20, in Fitzgerald, Widdop, Gray, & Collins, 2011) prevent generalizable conclusions on the differences between country-specific answer patterns.

Against this backdrop, we propose to implement cognitive probes in cross-national web surveys, in the following called *cross-national web probing*. Web probing can be implemented relatively easily prior to, alongside, or after a survey. Web probing can do without interviewers and, thus, tackle both the issues of interviewer availability and standardization of procedures. Finally, it paves the way for larger case numbers and, thus, for a meaningful analysis of diverging answer patterns across countries. Cross-national web probing is in line with recent calls for mixing qualitative and quantitative methods in cross-national research (van de Vijver & Chasiotis, 2010). It also matches the latest developments within the cross-cultural CI community itself to validate findings, assess the prevalence of results, and combine quantitative and qualitative methods (e.g., Reeve et al., 2011). Last but not least, cross-national web probing can be seen as following in the footsteps of Schuman (1966), who already in 1966 suggested random probing in a foreign cultural setting.

The Implementation of Web Probing in Web Surveys

Web probing can draw on previous work on open-ended questions in web surveys, which shows that narrative open-ended questions on the web fare as well or even better than their counterparts in self-administered paper surveys (Denscombe, 2008; Holland & Christian, 2009; Smyth, Dillman, Christian, & McBride, 2009). When compared to traditional CI, web probing has the advantage of offering anonymity of answers. This might allow for more honest answers, particularly with regard to sensitive topics. Despite these positive aspects of web probing, the drawbacks common to asking open-ended questions should not be ignored. These are item nonresponse, dropout, and answer quality hinging on interest in a topic or on certain background characteristics (Denscombe, 2008; Galesic, 2006; Holland & Christian, 2009; Oudejans & Christian, 2010).

The remainder of the chapter gives an overview of recent research into the use of cross-national web probing. This research has been undertaken as part of the project "Enhancing the Validity of Intercultural Comparative Surveys: The Use of Supplemental Probing Techniques in Internet Surveys".[1] The first part is dedicated to methodological issues; the second part presents selected substantive findings.

16.2 DATA AND METHODS

As part of the web probing project, three web studies were conducted in total: (1) a pretest in Germany in June/July 2010 with 1,023 completed interviews; (2) a cross-national study conducted in January 2011 with

3,695 completed interviews from Canada (English-speaking), Denmark, Germany (eastern/western), Hungary, Spain, and the U.S.; and (3) a second cross-national study conducted in the same countries in October 2011 with 3,718 completed interviews. The selection of the countries was based on theoretical expectations about different item functioning of the questions included in the survey. For both cross-national studies, approximately 500 respondents per country/region were recruited. Quota samples based on sex, age, and education were used in order to have a balanced number of respondents in the major demographic groups. The questionnaires were set up with an average response time of 15 minutes. They contained screening questions, substantive items (mainly on gender roles and politics), and a demographic section. The number of probing questions was set to a maximum of eight to keep the response burden to an acceptable level.[2] Different experimental splits were implemented in each questionnaire, including rotation of thematic blocks to prevent sequence effects.

Based on the data, three research goals were pursued: (1) testing whether the use of online access panels is appropriate for web probing, (2) identifying ways of how best to implement probing questions online, and (3) assessing equivalence in cross-national surveys. Addressing goals (1) and (2) was seen as the cornerstone upon which to build (3).

Adequacy of Using Online Access Panels for Probing Purposes

Respondents for all web surveys were drawn from online access panels, i.e., pools of registered persons who have consented to regularly participate in web surveys (e.g., Baker et al., 2010). The commissioned online access panels were all non-probability panels, predominantly active in the market research sector. They were selected based on their answers to the ESOMAR questions and their panel book, and, if applicable, the ISO 26362 certification. The ESOMAR questions are a standard set of questions answered by panel providers that are meant to help buyers of online panels in making their judgment and decision.[3] A panel book typically provides information on the general sociodemographic distributions in a panel. The ISO 26362 is a standard, particularly for access panels in market, opinion, and social research. The lack of probability-based panels in the countries of this study (with the exception of the U.S.) prevented the deployment of representative panels. The major research questions pertained to (1) whether the panel respondents would be willing to answer open-ended cognitive probes, which demand a higher level of motivation and commitment than closed-ended items, and (2) whether some panels would be a better option for web probing than others.

Are Respondents Willing to Answer Probing Questions?

Drop-out rates similar to the average drop-out rates of the panel providers indicated a general acceptance among respondents: Between 9% and 13% (depending on country) dropped out in the first cross-national study, and similar rates occurred in the second cross-national study. The probe nonresponse rate was a more important quality indicator, however. We regarded the following answers as probe nonresponse: don't knows, refusals, meaningless entries such as "?", ". . .", or "gfd", non-substantive answers such as "it is like that", or non-intelligible answers. Two examples shall be given in the following: In the first cross-national study, the nonresponse rate for a specific probe to an immigrant item ("Which type of immigrants were you thinking of when you answered the question?") ranged from 10% to 15%, depending on the country. The category-selection probe following an item on civil disobedience ("Please explain why you selected "[answer category inserted]"") received between 22% and 35% of nonresponse answers. Clearly, these nonresponse rates only cover the basic level of nonresponse. The usefulness of the answers to a substantive probe depends on the research question. We regarded the nonresponse rates as acceptable since the analyses for a number of dependent variables revealed that the correlation between probe nonresponse and attitudes was not problematic.

Is there a Panel Best Suited to Web Probing?

The pretest in Germany gave us the opportunity to test different panels. We commissioned both a "community panel", in which panelists can create their own polls or write opinions in addition to answering the usual surveys, and a conventional panel, in which panelists answer surveys but are not involved in other panel activities. We expected that community panelists would be more willing to answer open-ended probe questions and would also produce longer answers than conventional panelists. Contrary to these assumptions, however, the panel character *per se*—whether community or non-community—did not seem to play a major role. Rather, panel-specific distributions of attitudes related to the topic of the probes (that can be taken as an indicator for interest) had an impact on both the likelihood to respond and on word count. According to these findings, the formal difference between a community and a conventional panel seems negligible in terms of web probing (Behr, Kaczmirek, Bandilla, & Braun, 2012).

Adaptation of Cognitive Interviewing Techniques to Web Surveys

Web survey methodologists have recently discovered the value of narrative open-ended questions on the web and have looked into factors impacting this form of data collection (Holland & Christian, 2009; Smyth et al., 2009; Oudejans & Christian, 2010). This field of research triggered several design experiments on how best to implement cognitively demanding probing questions. Research questions pertained to (1) the optimal design of a category-selection probe, (2) the impact of different text box sizes on the answer quality, and (3) the monitoring of answer processes.

What Would Be an Optimal Design for a Category-Selection Probe?

Within the pretest in Germany, three versions of a category-selection probe ("Please explain why you selected [answer value from previous question inserted].") were tested in terms of their impact on answer quality. The three versions differed with regard to the context provided on the probe screen (e.g., previous closed item and chosen answer presented or not) as well as probe wording.[4] Summing up the major finding, a category-selection probe without any context on the probe screen (i.e., only the probe, without reference to the item and the respondent's answer choice) resulted in the highest nonresponse rate. The respondent burden linked to actively recalling the answer, and possibly even the item, or to going back to the previous screen to help recall, was obviously too great for some of the respondents. A category-selection probe design that had the closed reference item, the respondent's answer to it, and the probe on a screen turned out to be the superior design choice (Behr, Kaczmirek et al., 2012). When designing category-selection probes in our cross-national studies, we took these findings into account and particularly took care to provide the relevant context for category-selection probes, that is, the item and the chosen answer value. Figure 16.1 presents a slightly redesigned and optimized category-selection probe from our first cross-national study.

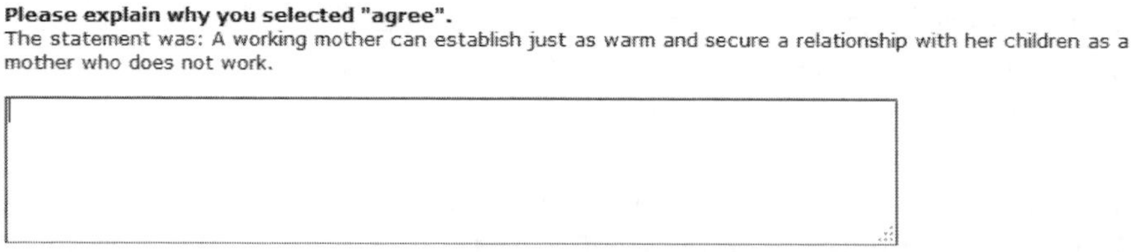

Please explain why you selected "agree".
The statement was: A working mother can establish just as warm and secure a relationship with her children as a mother who does not work.

FIGURE 16.1
Category-selection probe with respondent's answer and closed item on one screen

How Would Text Box Size Impact on Answer Quality?

Previous experiments from web and paper-and-pencil surveys have shown that the text box hints at the kind of answer that is expected (Couper, Kennedy, Conrad, & Tourangeau, 2011; Christian & Dillman, 2004; Christian, Dillman, & Smyth, 2007; Fuchs, 2009; Smyth et al., 2009). As part of our first cross-national study, we took up this research theme and tested the impact of different text box sizes on answer quality: We experimented with two text box sizes, that is, *standard* (= oversized for the response task) and *small* (= fitting for the response task) for a specific immigrant probe ("Which type of immigrants were you thinking of when you answered the question?"). Respondents also received the standard text box size for the other probes in the survey, which were mainly category-selection probes asking for the reasoning behind choosing the answer value. Due to rotation, respondents received different numbers of category-selection probes prior to the immigrant probe, resulting in high and low habituation, respectively, to category-selection probing. We found that respondents who received the standard text box for the immigrant probe and who had had a high habituation to category-selection probing were more likely to provide mismatching answers to the immigrant probe. The mismatch consisted of not answering the specific immigrant probe but rather providing a reasoning answer as typically expected for a category-selection probe (e.g., "This is too broad a statement to agree. I feel some immigrants do increase crime rates because they bring their own 'feuds' with them, but I do not feel this applies to all immigrants.") Thus, previous experience within the questionnaire was able to override the actual probe wording. The visual presentation of individual open-ended questions thus always needs to be considered, not only regarding the question itself, but also in the context of the overall questionnaire (Behr et al., 2013).

How Do Respondents Go about Answering the Probes?

Further methodological work included the integration of a script which logs key strokes or takes the time for each webpage. Respondents were informed about the recording of these technical data at the beginning of the survey. The advantage of logging key strokes consists of identifying respondents who use the key combination CTRL + V to copy and paste text from the web as an answer to a comprehension probe, for instance. This occurred when asking about the meaning of "civil disobedience", but only in 24 cases out of more than 1,500 respondents. A more recent version of the script includes the possibility to analyze whether respondents actually stay on the website or take breaks and leave the website. Leaving can be regarded as a weak indicator for respondents surfing the web to find an answer to a probe.

Substantive Results

The substantive goal of our web probing project was to learn about item interpretation in different countries in order to assess equivalence of items. For implementation in our studies, we mainly selected items that had already been fielded in the International Social Survey Program (ISSP) and whose interpretation across countries remained unclear or that had produced suspicious statistical results. Research questions pertained, for instance, (a) to the type of immigrants respondents have in mind when faced with immigrant items or (b) to respondents' thought processes when asked about citizens' rights to engage in acts of civil disobedience.

What Type of Immigrants Do Respondents Have in Mind in Different Countries?

In the ISSP 2003 questionnaire on "National Identity" (ISSP Research Group, 2003), four items on immigrants were asked: They relate to (a) whether immigrants increase crime rates, (b) whether they are generally good for the economy, (c) whether they take jobs away from native people, and (d) whether they improve society by bringing in new ideas and cultures. Interested in the comparability of immigrant groups that respondents think of, we implemented these items in our web surveys. Four splits were employed and each of the four items figured as the first item in one of the split versions. Only the first item in each split was followed by the probe "Which type of immigrants were you thinking of when you answered the question?" The results for the closed items replicated (with the exception of eastern Germany and particularly Hungary) quite neatly ISSP results in terms of frequency distributions. We considered a neat replication as a precondition for using the web survey data to shed light on the ISSP data. The probe answers revealed that the reasoning in the six countries was roughly similar on an abstract level. For instance, one-fifth to one-third of respondents indicated to have thought of immigrants in general. While the concrete groups of immigrants mentioned differed, there was a strong correspondence between respondents' reports and recent immigration patterns. However, there was some distortion in favor of visible immigrant groups (e.g., EU-15 migrants played hardly any role, even in Spain where they are a large immigrant group). On the basis of the web data it can be excluded that respondents think of entirely incomparable groups. Broadly speaking, respondents consistently reflect immigration reality in their countries and, in this sense, have "comparable" images in mind. The results demonstrate that xenophobia, as measured in cross-cultural surveys, cannot be treated like a personality characteristic measured by a psychological test. Attitudes towards immigrants are much more context-dependent than personality characteristics. Changes in the migration context can dramatically change attitudes. In sum, our results are comforting as differences across countries could have been much bigger, making any comparisons impossible (Braun, Behr, & Kaczmirek, 2012).

What Is Respondents' Stance on Civil Disobedience?

In the ISSP 2004 questionnaire on "Citizenship" (ISSP Research Group, 2004), a six-item battery on the rights of people in a democracy was included. The sixth item regarding the importance of civil disobedience behaved suspiciously across countries ("How important is it that citizens may engage in acts of civil disobedience when they oppose government actions?"). The battery was implemented in our first cross-national study and the civil disobedience item was probed with either a comprehension or a category-selection probe (random split). Looking at the frequency distributions for the closed-ended items first, a strikingly similar pattern across countries to that revealed by the ISSP data could be reproduced. This was once again the precondition for using the web data to shed light on what may have happened in the ISSP. The comprehension probe answers on the meaning of "civil disobedience" showed that respondents mainly in Canada and the U.S. to some extent associated violent and destructive activities with civil disobedience. These countries were also lowest in the rating regarding the importance of civil disobedience. In Spain, Germany, and Hungary, category-selection probe answers revealed that politicians were more often seen to get decoupled from the mandate they got from their voters than in the other countries. When the two variables "violence/destruction" and "decoupling of politicians from voters", as derived from the open answers, were entered into regression models for the two split versions, country differences were markedly reduced, though they remained significant. Unfortunately, both variables could not be entered into one single regression, as they were collected in different splits. While the decoupling from the mandate is substantive in nature and, therefore, does not endanger the equivalence of the data, the different meanings attached to the key term "civil disobedience" cause concern about comparability. We thus suggest that the wording of the civil disobedience item should be revised (Behr, Braun et al., 2012).

16.3 CONCLUSIONS AND FURTHER RESEARCH GAPS

The pretest and the two cross-national studies have shown that web probing is feasible and that it provides a valuable source of information to the cross-national research community. Certainly, one has to accept that web probing can result in nonresponse or incomprehensible or other types of mismatching answers, but the advantage of gaining insights into what is considered in various countries when answering survey items is still considerable. Items that are still in the drafting stage could be improved by taking on board the information from the probes. Already fielded and suspicious items could be subjected to thorough web testing. Non-equivalence could then lead to the rejection of countries from analyses, or be the focus of research itself.

Web probing studies lend themselves in particular when there are no cognitive interviewers available in a country. The relative ease of implementation makes it an attractive tool in the toolbox of a comparative researcher. The design examples given above, however, demonstrate that every effort should be directed towards designing a thorough and motivating questionnaire. This includes careful consideration of text box design and probe wording, as well as number and sequence of probes. In addition, translation of probe answers may be required so that the answers are accessible to all researchers working on a project. This calls, once again, for efforts and care so that no errors are introduced through the translation step. Establishing a coding scheme, coding, and inter-coder reliability are further steps taking up time and resources. Depending on the goal of cross-national web probing and its function as a pretest or a post-survey evaluation tool, a quantitative count of interpretation patterns and problems may not always be needed, though.

We cannot call our web probing data *representative*, given that these data come from non-representative online panels, but we ensured that the data is appropriate for our purposes by comparing item frequency distributions between the web surveys and our benchmark study, the ISSP. We regarded a similar pattern as a precondition for relating our probing data to "real" survey data.

There are, of course, limitations to web probing: The way we implemented our studies presupposes the availability of well-controlled online access panels and adequate coverage of the target group in these panels. This may not be given in all countries of a study or the target group may simply be too specific for an online panel. In addition, "professional" paid online respondents may be particularly suitable for our approach whereas self-recruited web respondents may be more difficult to convince to provide narrative text. This needs to be investigated.

Comparing typical cognitive interviewing and web probing, it can be stated that items that are difficult to probe and potentially require back-and-forth communication between interviewer and respondent should exclusively be reserved for cognitive interviewing. If one is interested in distributions of response patterns, web probing with its large(r) sample size seems the method of choice. If one is only interested—on a very abstract level—in the dimensions respondents think of, web probing might serve the same purpose as cognitive interviewing. However, taking into account nonresponse and insufficient answers, the number of web probing respondents should at least be double the number of traditional cognitive interviewing respondents. Similarities and differences between the two methods should in any case be further explored.

To conclude, there is potential in (cross-national) web probing. A follow-up project will therefore tackle existing challenges and address the following issues: (1) following up with respondents who provided nonresponse or insufficient answers, (2) testing methods to prevent mismatching probe answers, such as combing different probe types on one screen, and (3) testing a chat function to gain in-depth information in a follow-up chat to a survey.

NOTES

1. This project was funded by the German Research Foundation (DFG) in the Priority Programme on Survey Methodology (SPP 1292/2) from March 1, 2010 through August 31, 2012 (BR 908/3–1).
2. Rather than having all respondents answer all probes, one could also imagine random probes, where every tenth respondent or so receives a probe for a given item. At the same time, such random probing could be implemented on more items (see also Schuman, 1966).
3. The latest versions are the ESOMAR-28-questions. www.esomar.org/knowledge-and-standards/research-resources/28-questions-on-online-sampling.php
4. The survey was based on a one item per screen design, so a probe was always implemented on a separate probe screen.

REFERENCES

Baker, R., Blumberg, S. J., Brick, J. M., Couper, M. P., Courtright, M., Dennis, J. M., & Zahs, D. (2010). AAPOR report on online panels. *Public Opinion Quarterly, 74,* 711–781. doi:10.1093/poq/nfq048

Beatty, P. C., & Willis, G. B. (2007). Research synthesis: The practice of cognitive interviewing. *Public Opinion Quarterly, 71*, 287–311. doi:10.1093/poq/nfm006

Behr, D., Bandilla, W., Kaczmirek, L., & Braun, M. (2013). Cognitive probes in web surveys: On the effect of different text box size and probing exposure on response quality. *Social Science Computer Review.* Advance access. doi:10.1177/0894439313485203

Behr, D., Braun, M., Kaczmirek, L., & Bandilla, W. (2012). Item comparability in cross-national surveys: Results from asking probing questions in cross-national web surveys about attitudes towards civil disobedience. *Quality & Quantity.* Advance access. doi:10.1007/s11135-012-9754-8

Behr, D., Braun, M., Kaczmirek, L., & Bandilla, W. (2013). Testing the validity of gender ideology items by implementing probing questions in web surveys. *Field Methods, 25*, 124–141. doi:10.1177/1525822X12462525

Behr, D., Kaczmirek, L., Bandilla, W., & Braun, M. (2012). Asking probing questions in web surveys: Which factors have an impact on the quality of responses? *Social Science Computer Review, 30*, 487–498. doi:10.1177/0894439311435305

Blair, J., & Conrad, F. G. (2011). Sample size for cognitive interview pretesting. *Public Opinion Quarterly, 75*, 636–658. doi:10.1093/poq/nfr035

Braun, M., Behr, D., & Kaczmirek, L. (2012). Assessing cross-national equivalence of measures of xenophobia: Evidence from probing in web surveys. *International Journal of Public Opinion Research.* Advance access. doi:10.1093/ijpor/eds034

Christian, L. M., & Dillman, D. A. (2004). The influence of graphical and symbolic language manipulations on responses to self-administered questions. *Public Opinion Quarterly, 68*, 57–80. doi:10.1093/ijpor/eds034

Christian, L. M., Dillman, D. A., & Smyth, J. D. (2007). Helping respondents get it right the first time: The influence of words, symbols, and graphics in web surveys. *Public Opinion Quarterly, 71*, 113–125. doi:10.1093/poq/nfl039

Conrad, F., & Blair, J. (2004). Data quality in cognitive interviews: The case of verbal reports. In S. Presser, J. M. Rothgeb, M. P. Couper, J. T. Lessler, E. Martin, J. Martin, & E. Singer (Eds.), *Methods for testing and evaluating survey questionnaires* (pp.67–87). New York, NY: Wiley.

Conrad, F. G., & Blair, J. (2009). Sources of error in cognitive interviews. *Public Opinion Quarterly, 73*, 32–55. doi:10.1093/poq/nfp013

Couper, M. P., Kennedy, C., Conrad, F. G., & Tourangeau, R. (2011). Designing input fields for non-narrative open-ended responses in web surveys. *Journal of Official Statistics, 27*, 65–85. Retrieved from www.jos.nu/Articles/abstract.asp?article = 271065

Denscombe, M. (2008). The length of responses to open-ended questions: A comparison of online and paper questionnaires in terms of a mode effect. *Social Science Computer Review, 26*, 359–368. doi:10.1177/0894439307309671

Fitzgerald, R., Widdop, S., Gray, M., & Collins, D. (2011). Identifying sources of error in cross-national questionnaires: Application of an error source typology to cognitive interview data. *Journal of Official Statistics, 27*, 569–599. Retrieved from www.jos.nu/Articles/abstract.asp?article=274569

Fuchs, M. (2009). Differences in the visual design language of paper-and-pencil surveys versus web surveys: A field experimental study on the length of response fields in open-ended frequency questions. *Social Science Computer Review, 27*, 213–227. doi:10.1177/0894439308325201

Galesic, M. (2006). Dropouts on the web: Effects of interest and burden experienced during an online survey. *Journal of Official Statistics, 22*, 313–328. Retrieved from www.jos.nu/Articles/abstract.asp?article=222313

Holland, J. L., & Christian, L. M. (2009). The influence of topic interest and interactive probing on responses to open-ended questions in web surveys. *Social Science Computer Review, 27*, 196–212. doi:10.1177/0894439308327481

ISSP Research Group (2003). International Social Survey Program 2003: National Identity II. GESIS Data Archive, Cologne, Germany. ZA3910 Data file Vers. 2.0.0. doi:10.4232/1.10077

ISSP Research Group (2004). International Social Survey Program 2004: Citizenship. GESIS Data Archive, Cologne, Germany. Data file Vers. 1.2.0. doi:10.4232/1.10078

Lee, J. (2012). Conducting cognitive interviews in cross-national settings. *Assessment.* Advance access. doi:10.1177/1073191112436671

Miller, K., Fitzgerald, R., Padilla, J.-L., Willson, S., Widdop, S., Caspar, R., & Schoua-Glusberg, A. (2011). Design and analysis of cognitive interviews for comparative multinational testing. *Field Methods, 23*, 379–396. doi:10.1177/1525822X11414802

Oudejans, M., & Christian, L. M. (2010). Using interactive features to motivate and probe responses to open-ended questions. In M. Das, P. Ester, & L. Kaczmirek (Eds.), *Social and behavioral research and the Internet: Advances in applied methods and research strategies* (pp. 304–332). London, New York: Routledge.

Prüfer, P., & Rexroth, M. (2005). Kognitive Interviews. *ZUMA How-to-Reihe, 15.* Retrieved from www.gesis.org/fileadmin/upload/forschung/publikationen/gesis_reihen/howto/How_to15PP_MR.pdf?download=true

Reeve, B. B., Willis, G., Shariff-Marco, S. N., Breen, N., Williams, D. R., Gee, G. C., & Levin, K. Y. (2011). Comparing cognitive interviewing and psychometric methods to evaluate a racial/ethnic discrimination scale. *Field Methods, 23*, 397–419. doi:10.1177/1525822X11416564

Schuman, H. (1966). The random probe: A technique for evaluating the validity of closed questions. *American Sociological Review, 31*, 218–222.

Smyth, J. D., Dillman, D. A., Christian, L. M., & McBride, M. (2009). Open-ended questions in web surveys: Can increasing the size of answer boxes and providing extra verbal instructions improve response quality? *Public Opinion Quarterly, 73*, 325–337. doi:10.1093/poq/nfp029

Thrasher, J. F., Quah, A.C.K., Dominick, G., Borland, R., Driezen, P., Awang, R., & Boado, M. (2011). Using cognitive interviewing and behavioral coding to determine measurement equivalence across linguistic and cultural groups: An example from the International Tobacco Control Policy evaluation project. *Field Methods, 23*, 439–460. doi:10.1177/1525822X11418176

Tourangeau, R., Rips, L. J., & Rasinski, K. A. (2000). *The psychology of survey response.* Cambridge: Cambridge University Press.

Vandenberg, R. J., & Lance, C. E. (2000). A review and synthesis of the measurement invariance literature: Suggestions, practices and recommendations for organizational research. *Organizational Research Methods, 3*, 4–70. doi:10.1177/109442810031002

Van de Vijver, F.J.R., & Chasiotis, A. (2010). Making methods meet: Mixed designs in cross-cultural research. In J. A. Harkness, M. Braun, B. Edwards, T. P. Johnson, L. Lyberg, P. P. Mohler, B.-E. Pennell, & T. Smith (Eds.), *Survey methods in multinational, multiregional, and multicultural contexts* (pp. 455–473). Hoboken, NJ: Wiley.

Willis, G. B. (2005). *Cognitive interviewing: A tool for improving questionnaire design.* Thousand Oaks, CA: Sage.

Part V

Conducting Access Panels

17

Conducting Access Panels

Overview and Introduction

Uwe Engel and Annette Scherpenzeel

17.1 TWO RESEARCH PANELS AND A PANEL OF OFFICIAL STATISTICS

In the present section we are dealing with three panels: two research panels and a panel for Germany's official statistics. We will call these panels "access panels" or simply "panels". Access panels are basically pools of addresses of people who have agreed to receive invitations to surveys. First of all, access panels are frames for the sampling of surveys, which may be cross-sectional surveys or panel surveys. Since we can draw samples from an access panel frame that do not lead to any repeated-measurement design like a "true" panel study, it might be arguable to distinguish linguistically between "access panels" and "panels". However, as especially for English-speakers there seems to be a clear preference for dismissing this distinction, particularly in the case of probability-based online panels, we follow that line.

The first research panel is located in the Netherlands, the LISS (Longitudinal Internet studies for the Social Sciences) panel. It is a large, probability-based online panel of 5,000 households which was constructed in 2007 and since then refreshed several times. The setup of this panel and the participation of panel members over time is described in detail in Chapter 19.

The second research panel is located in Germany, the Priority Programme on Survey Methodology (PPSM) panel. This is a large probability-based mixed-mode (telephone and internet) panel. The main recruitment of panel members took place during 2009. Since then the panel has been refreshed three times. The researchers recruited 7,021 persons in the first recruitment period in 2009, an additional 1,542 persons in the second recruitment period in 2010 and 289 in a third such period in 2012. The setup of this panel is described in detail in Engel, Bartsch, Schnabel, and Vehre (2012). Furthermore, relevant information about the initial recruitment process in 2009 is published in Engel (2013), and Chapters 4 and 18 of the present volume.

The third panel is the household access panel of German official statistics. Panel members are recruited from the German Microcensus (MC). We call it therefore the "MC panel". It is a probability-based panel because the Microcensus itself is a probability sample. While participation in the MC is mandatory, participation in the access panel is voluntary. The setup and recruitment processes are described in detail in Chapter 20. This access panel works, for instance, as a sampling frame for the German subsample of EU-SILC, the prominent European Statistics on Income and Living Conditions study. This study uses a self-administered mail questionnaire as survey mode. This too is described in Chapter 20.

In the present section the three panels are used to study the recruitment process into a panel or the participation behavior after a respondent has entered a panel.

17.2 PANELS AS SAMPLING FRAMES

There exists a key issue: If access panels represent sampling frames of addresses of basically survey-friendly people, can such panels be used for statistical inference to the general population? One could object with the fact that the general population also consists of people who refuse survey requests, which precludes any generalization. Contrary to this view, one could argue that we need only suitable probability sampling for this purpose. However, is probability sampling alone sufficient to guarantee unbiased sample estimates? The answer is certainly "no", since selective forces can easily impair the randomness of a recruitment sample. In particular Chapters 18 and 20 deal with such systematic factors in recruitment processes that should actually be random processes. Only if such systematic factors are understood well is it possible to adjust for their impact in attempts at making otherwise biased sampling frames more appropriate. In case no corrective action is undertaken, even strict random sampling from such frames would in turn lead to biased samples as well. This holds true for any access-panel mode, be it web, phone or postal.

A study of selective forces in the recruitment of access panel members has to consider a sequence of selection stages. The first stage always refers to participation vs. non-participation in the random sample used to recruit panel members. In the LISS panel, this is a simple random sample of households drawn from the nationwide address frame of Statistics Netherlands. In the PPSM panel, using the RLD (randomized last digits) method these are telephone samples drawn at random from the universes of landline and cell phone frames. Since participation is of course *voluntary* in both panels, selective forces can impair the randomness of such samples from the outset. We are accordingly in need of a thorough nonresponse analysis of this first selection stage in order to find out which systematic factors (if any) determine the initial response propensity of target persons. This is different to the third panel to be considered here. In the MC panel, the random recruitment sample is the Microcensus (MC) itself, i.e. a one percent sample of the entire German population. Since participation is *mandatory* in this sample for official statistics, selective forces should ideally have no chance to exert an influence on the probability of taking part in the survey. However, the MC panel and the PPSM panel have a comparable second selection stage in common. This stage consists of asking respondents at the end of their interviews if they were willing to join the respective panel afterwards.

17.3 PARTICIPATION IN THE RECRUITMENT SAMPLE

In the PPSM panel, considerable effort went into the analyses of the first selection stage. Chapter 18 reports corresponding findings in greater detail. Using response propensity modeling, systematic factors are identified that affect either the contact probability or the cooperation probability of households and persons. Different aspects of the contact course as well as interviewers' attempts at responding to queries and concerns of contact/target persons prove influential. The authors present a detailed analysis of the effectiveness of arguments by which interviewers try to convince reluctant persons to take part in the survey. The chapter highlights the limits of refusal conversion attempts, sheds light on the influence of prior survey experience and discusses the question of whether people should be contacted in single- or mixed-mode. Furthermore, the chapter addresses the role of adaptive survey designs, shows how refusal conversion attempts affect nonresponse bias in sample estimates and discusses the role of auxiliary variables in response propensity modeling.

In the LISS panel, extensive efforts were also undertaken to attain high initial recruitment rates and to include the most difficult groups such as non-internet households. Chapter 19 briefly describes the recruitment procedures, the incentive strategy and the resulting response rates in the different stages of recruitment.

17.4 WILLINGNESS TO JOIN A PANEL

The setup of the PPSM panel permits the analysis of an important intermediate step. In the concluding part of the recruitment interview every respondent was asked about his/her willingness to join an access panel. The term "survey community" ("Befragungsgemeinschaft" in German) was used to translate the idea of an "access panel" into a precise survey question. The whole questioning program preceding this question can now be used to detect systematic factors that shape the propensity to join the panel at this stage. A detailed exposition of this set of factors is available in Engel (2013, pp. 16–18, 53–76).

Another possible bias, specific for online probability-based panels, is in the underrepresentation of people who are slow in adopting new technology. Leenheer and Scherpenzeel (2013) showed that in the LISS panel, which offers households with no internet a computer and a cost-free internet connection, the willingness of these non-internet households to join an online panel is much lower than for households with internet.

If access panels are used as sampling frames, then these frames will be biased by exactly such systematic factors if no corrective action is undertaken. Of course the same holds true for factors at the preceding initial selection stage.

17.5 PANEL PARTICIPATION

In the PPSM panel, factual panel participation depends substantially on the survey mode "web" vs. "telephone", the survey mode preferences of respondents and their response propensities at the two preceding selection stages (Engel, 2013, pp. 18–19, 78). Regarding the MC panel, Chapter 20 analyzes if participation in this panel depends on a set of available profile variables. This set comprises age, gender, marital status, citizenship, employment status, education and income. The chapter reports substantial variation of recruitment success across federal states and different household structures. Furthermore, the analysis reveals that e.g. the lowest income group, the group with missing income data and self-employed persons are underrepresented in the panel. In addition, the effects of education level, citizenship and recruitment quarter are explored in detail. Furthermore, Chapter 20 analyzes in which way participation in the German subsample of the EU-SILC study depends on the list of profile variables. It also makes clear in which way legal restrictions complicated the analysis of recruitment and survey response.

The focus of Chapter 19 is on the long-term participation rates in the LISS panel during its first five years of existence. Amongst other topics it describes in more detail the participation in the monthly surveys, the attrition rates, the difficult-to-keep groups and the efforts to keep panel members motivated. In this context the chapter reports an incentive experiment on reactivating panel members who have not participated for some time, and experiments on the effect of providing feedback about study results to panel members. The incentive experiment on inactive panel members showed that it is important to prevent long-term inactivity and contact panel members within three months after they become inactive. The most effective way to reactivate such panel members is a brief personal telephone call in combination with the offer of a conditional €10 additional incentive. The feedback about study results had no significant effects on the long-term participation or dropout in the LISS panel.

17.6 ESTIMATION

The final chapter of the present section on (access) panels deals with estimation. Thus Chapter 21 is intertwined with Chapter 20. It also focuses on the MC panel as a source for the German subsample of the EU-SILC study. In its first part, the chapter introduces some classical well-known concepts of estimation using survey weights, while the second part focuses on an evaluation using a simulation study in a close-to-reality framework. As described in detail in Chapter 21, this evaluation makes clear "how essential it may become to consider the correct response propensities in different estimation methods" or "how regression estimation methods may fail in inference even if the correct response propensities and survey weights have been considered". As the authors note in their summary of findings, a proper weighting including survey design and response propensities is essential to foster unbiased estimates in statistical modeling. They point to the fact that one has to be especially careful in drawing correct inferences for regression coefficients in the design context, and continue: "A boot-strap variance estimator for population totals helped to correctly include the additional sources from randomness in access panels using complex survey designs".

REFERENCES

Engel, U. (2013). *Access panel and mixed-mode internet survey. PPSM Panel Report.* Retrieved from www.sozialforschung.uni-bremen.de/html/downloads.html

Engel, U., Bartsch, S., Schnabel, C., & Vehre, H. (2012). *Wissenschaftliche Umfragen. Methoden und Fehlerquellen.* Frankfurt am Main: Campus.

Leenheer, J., & Scherpenzeel, A. (2013). Does it pay off to include non-internet households in an internet panel? *International Journal of Internet Science, 8,* 17–29.

18

Response Behavior in an Adaptive Survey Design for the Setting-Up Stage of a Probability-Based Access Panel in Germany

Uwe Engel

18.1 INTRODUCTION

Access panels have spread remarkably in recent years. These consist of persons who agree to receive invitations to participate in surveys. Thus access panels are basically used as sampling frames. Many such panels are "opt-in" panels: Potential respondents become aware of a panel and decide to join. A scientifically controlled selection of units does not take place, which makes statistical inference difficult. One way to cope with this complication is the use of probability sampling. Probability samples are drawn from e.g. the general population to recruit panel members on this basis. This strategy is certainly superior to any uncontrolled self-selection, though it is likely to remain a still insufficient way of ensuring unbiased access-panel sampling frames. In survey practice, probability samples may suffer seriously from selective (non-random) unit nonresponse. The change from an opt-in to a probability-based way of panel recruitment alone may thus help little. Rather, it is essential to understand who joins a probability-based access panel if asked to participate and who does not.[1]

An answer to this question may be obtained by modeling the propensity to take part in a survey which requires auxiliary information. The first question addressed in the present chapter is therefore which information should be used when external information is of only limited usefulness and the survey design allows for interviewer tailoring and the pursuit of a basic question approach. Related to this is the question of how attempts at convincing reluctant persons affect response probabilities and in turn possibly bias sample estimates. A third question concerns the contact and survey mode: Is it reasonable to use telephone samples using the RLD (randomized last digits) method for the recruitment of web panels?

18.2 AUXILIARY INFORMATION IN RESPONSE PROPENSITY MODELING

Response propensity modeling requires relevant information not only about respondents: For the estimation of response probabilities information about nonrespondents is needed as well. One principal solution to bridging this gap is the use of external sources of information like population registers. For instance, in Germany common practice is the use of registration office samples and area data linked to the places of residence. Preceding the present study, Engel, Schnabel, and Simonson (2006) explored the utility of this approach on the basis of three administrative district surveys and found that the probability of survey participation depends only to a small to negligible degree on such registered demographic variables (gender, age) and characteristics of the neighborhoods and districts in which the persons live (logistic regression analyses explained variances of 1.1 to 3.2 percent).

These figures are quite low and accordingly of only limited usefulness in attempts at adjusting for differential response propensities. This applies, *a fortiori*, for another reason as well. Survey variables and variables taken from e.g. population registers may be totally uncorrelated. As Lynn (2003, p. 239) aptly notes: "Frame data or external population data (...) are at best modestly correlated with the survey variables". Then any attempt at adjusting for such external sources of variation will leave potential bias in sample estimates unaffected for just those survey variables that are of actual interest to the researcher.

It appears reasonable therefore to consider other external sources of variation as well. Much information can be obtained from the initial contact process itself. Adopting current terminology, this refers to the analysis of "paradata" in one way or another (Bethlehem, Cobben, & Schouten, 2011, p. 454). Some data of this sort arise in any conventional survey design (e.g. the number of contact attempts needed or if appointments could be made or not), others require a decision to draw on interviewer assessments as an additional source of information and a correspondingly styled contact protocol. A rating of response propensities is a case in point.

18.3 ADAPTIVE SURVEY DESIGNS

Paradata can enlarge the basis for understanding survey responses significantly. They are useful because they add relevant information to the actual survey data. A typical example is the data obtained when interviewers try to convince reluctant persons to give the requested interview and these attempts are recorded in a standardized fashion. Closely related to this is an approach which pursues another aim. Instead of adding information to the body of survey data, one can try to enlarge this body itself. To obtain such extra information on frequency distributions of relevant survey variables, however, special survey design features need to be implemented. These concern the flexibility of survey designs in at least two respects. On the one hand, this flexibility is discussed in the perspective of "interviewer tailoring" (Groves, Singer, & Corning, 2000). The question is if and how the survey design enables interviewers to cope with the queries and concerns of potential respondents when they ask these persons for an interview. On the other hand, the notion of flexibility relates to the question of if a survey design offers the respondent a choice as to the accepted interview length. A reluctant person might not be ready for a telephone interview with a length of 15 minutes, though perhaps such a person would participate in an interview of half this duration. Other people might be unwilling to participate in even such a short interview, though they would agree to answer one to three key questions of a study. The "basic question approach" is a current term for this kind of approach (Bethlehem, 2009, pp. 239; Bethlehem et al., 2011, p. 295; see also Lynn's (2003) Pre-Emptive Doorstep Administration of Key Survey Items [PEDAKSI] methodology). In the present analysis, we distinguish between the "full" version of an interview and its "core" version of about half the length of the full version. If just one or two key questions could be asked, this is termed the "exit" version of an interview, as an allusion to the corresponding contact situation where the contact or target person is already going to hang up the phone.

Designs which introduce elements of flexibility are called "adaptive survey designs". Bethlehem et al. (2011, p. 395) present a detailed exposition of this approach. It seems promising to check systematically if the introduction of elements of flexibility can improve survey response in a double sense. To win over more sample members to the survey is certainly one way to think of improved response, another is to think of improved possibilities of modeling the response process. To adjust for possible bias one needs to discern the factors which determine individual response propensities and thereby sample composition. Adaptive survey designs are certainly helpful to the extent to which they provide information about people who would otherwise be nonrespondent.

18.4 DATA

The data come from the recruitment stage of the PPSM Access Panel. This panel is part of the German Priority Programme on Survey Methodology (PPSM) to assist research on survey methods. Three fixed-line probability samples and one cell-phone probability sample of the adult population of Germany (aged 18+ and entitled to vote for the German Federal Parliament) were selected[2] to set up the access panel in 2009. The sampling method is the RLD (randomized last digits) method for telephone surveys as usually applied in Germany. The sample and its realization are described in more detail elsewhere (Engel, Bartsch, Schnabel, & Vehre, 2012; Engel, 2013). While the initial response rate amounted to just 13.6 percent (full interviews) plus 0.9 percent (core and exit interviews), all downstream conditional response probabilities range around 0.70 and higher. Note that "core" and "exit" interviews were offered to the target persons in just one of the four recruitment samples as part of a field experiment. Gross sample size is 170,349 telephone numbers, of which 102,138 prove relevant according to AAPOR response rate definition 4. In 56,848 of these cases it was possible to achieve contact with the household. The analysis of prior survey experience refers to the subset of cases to which it was possible to offer core and exit versions of the interview.

18.5 MODELS

The response propensity models were estimated using two-level random-intercept logistic regression equations, with respondent data (level 1) nested within interviewers (level 2). Three equations were set up. The first one studies the response propensity of person i nested within interviewer j as a function of a set of variables which record different aspects of the contact procedure ($N = 102,138$):

$$p_{ij} = \frac{1}{1+e^{-(b_{0j}+\sum_q b_q x_{ijq}+u_{0j})}}$$ (18.1)

This set of q variables is described below in the section of the same name. All estimates of effect are available online in Engel (2013, pp. 34–37, Tables 2.1 to 2.4 for samples 1 to 4). Then a second equation was set up to study how refusal conversion attempts affect the propensity to respond to the survey request. This equation refers to the subset of cases where contact with the household was achieved (N = 56,848). It is this equation that controls for the impact of a set of level-2 interviewer data collected by a web survey a few days prior to the main telephone survey:

$$p_{ij} = \frac{1}{1 + e^{-(b_{0j} + \sum_k b_k x_{ijk} + \sum_l b_l x_{ji} + \sum_m b_m x_{jm} + u_{0j})}} \qquad (18.2)$$

The equation comprises k individual-level dummy terms which refer to concerns and refusal conversion attempts, l interviewer characteristics and m indicator variables to control for missing level-2 information. The complete set of effect estimates is available online in Engel (2013, pp. 39–40, Table 2.6 and 2.7) along with the underlying coding scheme, of which a relevant subset is transformed to e^b-factors presented in the "interviewer tailoring" section below. In order to compute an overall score for the propensity to take part in the full version of the recruitment interview, we take advantage of the possibility to decompose an overall probability into components. Using observed probabilities, the target probability of obtaining a full interview p_F may be decomposed into the probability of achieving contact with the household times the conditional probability of a full interview, given that contact with the household has been achieved:

$$p_F = \frac{13{,}910}{102{,}138} = \frac{56{,}848}{102{,}138} \times \frac{13{,}910}{56{,}848} = 0.136 \qquad (18.3)$$

Using this structure of decomposition, an overall propensity score is obtained if we replace the two observed probabilities with their estimated counterparts, using for estimation the respective sets of auxiliary variables of equations (18.1) and (18.2) respectively. It is the score obtained in this way that underlies the estimates of effect presented in Table 18.2.

18.6 CONTACT COURSE

As outlined elsewhere in detail (Engel, 2013, pp. 12–13, 26–37) there is one set of auxiliary variables which affects the probability of survey participation via shaping the immanent contact probability. Some households are easily reached by phone, while others need more contact attempts and accordingly more time needs to be spent to yield a final outcome. The "number of contact attempts" preceding the final outcome is thereby shaped by one modifying condition: whether there is an answering machine/voice mail involved in the contact process or not. If yes, this weakens both the initial increase and the subsequent decrease in the estimated target probability. Answering machines/voice mail make the curvature smoother. The related "time span between the first and last contact attempt" is also modified by an influential condition: namely whether it is possible to make appointments with contact or target persons or both. In addition to this modifying effect, the main effects of making appointments with contact or target persons prove extraordinarily strong in increasing the probability of obtaining a requested interview. If no interview is possible at the first contact with the household, being able to make an appointment for an interview at a later date is of great advantage.

18.7 INTERVIEWER TAILORING: RESPONDING TO QUERIES AND CONCERNS

Given that contact has been established, another list of variables reflects factors which affect the probability of survey participation by shaping the probability of obtaining survey cooperation.

Two considerations have led us to the assumption that the image of a one-dimensional space ranging from easily reached and interviewed sample persons to those who—despite all design arrangements and fieldwork efforts—remain nonrespondents, may be too simplistic (see Stoop, 2005 for an insightful discussion). First, there are likely to be wholly different sets of conditions which affect the contact probability on the one hand and the cooperation probability on the other hand. Second, the pilot studies conducted prior to the main PPSM survey for the development of a detailed contact protocol revealed the pretty diverse nature of queries and concerns that were raised in initial contact situations. We concluded that the development of a typological approach might be more promising if based upon a suitable probabilistic classification device. In line with another recent work on the analysis of survey errors (Biemer, 2011), latent class analysis (LCA) appeared to be most suitable for identifying individual concern/persuasion argument patterns.

An LCA of seventeen individual concerns revealed five latent concerns groups, while another LCA of seventeen single refusal conversion attempts uncovered four basic persuasion arguments. The analysis is described in detail in a panel report available online (Engel, 2013, pp. 41–44, Tables 2.8 to 2.11). The $5 \times 4 = 20$ concern/persuasion argument patterns revealed a

TABLE 18.1

Effect of "concerns/refusal conversion" patterns on the odds of obtaining a full interview

	e^b	b/s.e
Having no concerns (Ref.cat.: despite concerns no RC attempt)	5.0	31.51
Refusal conversion attempts (Ref.cat.: despite concerns no RC attempts)	1.7	9.49
Concerns/Refusal conversion attempts patterns (Ref.cat: if concerns & RC-attempts):		
Trustworthiness/Trustworthiness	19.3	33.26
Trustworthiness/Trustworthiness + respondent plays a decisive role	26.2	22.38
Trustworthiness/Not much time needed	22.9	16.67
No interest + trustworthiness/Trustworthiness + respondent plays a decisive role	18.8	16.48
Lack of time (weak concern)/Not much time needed	4.3	15.61
No interest + trustworthiness/Trustworthiness + respondent plays a decisive role	3.1	9.88
No interest + trustworthiness/Trustworthiness	8.3	9.08
Lack of time (weak concern)/Trustworthiness	2.6	8.48
Trustworthiness/Later interview possible	6.5	7.76
Too old/Trustworthiness + respondent plays a decisive role	3.6	6.73
Lack of time (weak concern)/Trustworthiness + respondent plays a decisive role	3.2	5.61
Too old/Not much time needed	2.0	4.74
No interest/Trustworthiness	1.6	4.45
No interest + trustworthiness/Not much time needed	1.5	4.07
Too old/Trustworthiness	2.3	2.98
Too old/Later interview possible	1.5	0.85
No interest + trustworthiness/Later interview possible	0.4	−4.55
McFadden's Pseudo-R^2 = 0.060		

N = 56,848 cases; i = 203 interviewers. The table displays the estimates of effect of a random-intercept logistic regression equation which controls for interviewer characteristics. The complete analysis is online available in Engel (2013: 39f., Tables 2.6 and 2.7).

clear ranking in that some patterns were stronger than others in contributing to an increased survey-participation probability. Table 18.1 reports on the major results.

If concerns are raised, it is easier to cope with concerns about trustworthiness than to cope with concerns about being too old for an interview or about not being interested in it. This is especially true if these latter concerns come alone and not in combination with concerns about trustworthiness. It proves to be most effective if the interviewer responds to a given type of concern with the same type of argument and not another one. This applies primarily to the trustworthiness topic, but also to the lack-of-time topic. It is advantageous if the interviewer's response to a concern involves a respondent-centered argument while the most disadvantageous combination is if a "no interest" concern comes alone and the interviewer tries to meet it by the weak argument that it is possible to conduct the interview at a later date. The model explains 6 percent of variation. While this is far from explaining a great deal, it is, however, too much to neglect the influence of concern/conversion-attempt patterns on the resulting sample composition. It changes this composition by winning persons over to the sample who would otherwise remain nonrespondents.

18.8 LIMITS OF INTERVIEWER TAILORING

Compared to the constellation that despite concerns no refusal conversion attempts were made, the target probability is significantly higher in the case where no concerns were raised or weak conversion attempts were made to respond to weak concerns. Although already strong, the effect of having raised no concerns is likely to underestimate the true "concern effect" for a simple reason: One can decide not to raise concerns despite the fact that one has concerns. In the PPSM panel 27.8 percent of the cases in which the target households were reached ($N = 56,848$) raised concerns. By definition, these are "reluctant persons". In addition, another 43.9 percent were refusals who raised no concerns. The distinction is that the former group is open to reason, while the latter is not. These "instantaneous refusals" consist of the following refusal types: 10.8 percent hung up the phone instantly before any conversation came about. In addition to this type of refusal, another consists of the immediate and definite statement that one is not willing to take part in the survey: 20.3 percent of the households, 1.0 percent of the contact persons and 11.8 percent of the target persons fall into this category. In Germany, data protection regulations prohibit refusal conversion attempts in cases where a person clearly states his or her unwillingness to take part in the survey. The result is as trivial as it is influential: It narrows the applicability of refusal conversion attempts via interviewer-tailoring techniques considerably.

18.9 PRIOR SURVEY EXPERIENCE

Prior survey experience proves to be an important selective force. Compared to the case that despite invitations someone had not previously participated in surveys, the probability of obtaining an interview is significantly higher when someone has never previously been invited to take part in surveys and increases even more strongly when someone has previously been invited to participate in surveys and has done so. Prior survey experience alone explains 3.5 percent of variation in the probability of initial survey participation (as indicated by McFadden's pseudo-R^2 value) and sheds light on an important source of hidden selectivity in probability samples: If invited, one takes part in surveys because one has already taken part in surveys in the past, thereby supporting an endogenous explanation of survey participation. Without an adaptive survey design that employs a basic question approach it would not have been possible to obtain this information and the related estimates to adjust for this otherwise hidden selective force. The offer of core and exit versions of an interview does not necessarily result in enhanced response rates. However, it provides a useful basis to adjust statistically for sample selectivity if it is used in conjunction with questions about prior survey experience.

18.10 INTERVIEWER EFFECTS

The initial contact situation is likely to be influenced by background characteristics on both sides. While concerns, or their absence, may be viewed as reflecting the impact of respondents' background characteristics at least to some degree, interviewers' background characteristics are likely to work through interview experience, expectations and images of how to proceed in the contact situation to win a person over to an interview (Hox & De Leeuw, 2002). The effect estimates reported in Table 18.1 are part of a larger equation that also comprises such interviewer characteristics. These estimates are reported in detail in Engel (2013, p. 39, Table 2.6, and related findings on pp. 45–50, Tables 2.12 to 2.16).

18.11 NONRESPONSE BIAS IN SAMPLE ESTIMATES

Based on the "random response model" (Bethlehem et al., 2011, pp. 43–45) it is possible to assess the amount of bias in mean estimates by a formula (Bethlehem, 2009, p. 222):

$$B\left(\overline{y}_R\right) = \tilde{Y} - \overline{Y} = \frac{Cov_{\rho Y}}{\overline{\rho}} \tag{18.4}$$

which relates the covariance of a target variable Y and a response probability p to the mean response probability. $\tilde{Y}$ symbolizes the expected value of the response mean $\left(E\left(\bar{y}_R\right) \approx \tilde{Y}\right)$ and $\bar{Y}$ the population mean. A positive value of B indicates that the expected value of the response mean is larger than the population mean, and a negative value indicates that it is smaller.

Since response probabilities are unknown, they have to be estimated (Bethlehem et al., 2011, pp. 330–331; Bethlehem & Biffignandi, 2012, p. 401). This, however, is only possible with respect to auxiliary variables. Since different sets of such variables are likely to result in different response propensities, the selection of proper auxiliary variables is of great importance. Though it is clear in theory which ones would be particularly effective (Bethlehem et al., 2011, p. 249), in survey practice one may choose only variables that are available according to circumstances (Bethlehem & Biffignani, 2012, p. 399). If, for instance, a telephone sample is based on RLD sampling, no data from population registers can be used as auxiliary variables. In this case, only possible paradata and perhaps area data are potentially available. This is exemplified in Table 18.2 with respect to three survey attitude items and two different propensity scores.

The first score is based on information about the contact course and "concern/refusal conversion" patterns. It is the overall propensity score referred to above in the context of equation (18.3). The second score estimates the

TABLE 18.2

Bias in sample estimates of mean values of three survey attitudes

$$B\left(\bar{y}_R\right) = \frac{Cov_{\rho Y}}{\bar{\rho}}$$

	Propensity estimate based on …			
	…the contact process†		…community-level data††	
	B	N	B	N
Surveys are interesting in themselves	−0.0505*	13,840	−0.0001	9,831
Surveys are important for society	−0.0404*	13,789	−0.0014	9,793
Opinion polls are an invasion of privacy	0.0707*	13,785	0.0048*	9,790

Sig.: $^*p \leq 0.05$

7pt scales (respectively): 1 = doesn't agree at all, … , 7 = agree totally. † Overall estimate according to equations (18.1) and (18.2) combined as described above; ††Mean social status, voter turnout, mean age (random samples 1, 2 and 3 only). Correlation between the two propensity scores: 0.037* ($N = 10,228$). Source (formula): Bethlehem 2009: 222.

response propensity on the basis of district-level data, namely the mean social status, voter turnout and the mean age of administrative districts. Both propensity scores are correlated only weakly ($r = 0.037$). Table 18.2 displays the results. It becomes evident that the amount of bias varies considerably across the two ways of estimating the response propensity. Though the direction of bias is the same, the bias turns out to be much larger in the case where the propensity score reflects information about the contact process.

In the analysis reported above, the response propensities were estimated on a basis which includes the impact of possible refusal conversion attempts. This raises the question of how results would change if no such efforts were possible. A field experiment conducted on one of the four random recruitment samples of the PPSM panel may help to assess this point. Figure 18.1 displays the structure of this experiment and reports on the correlations obtained between four corresponding response propensity scores.

Condition a. estimates the response probabilities on the basis of contact course information only. Condition b. adds information about refusal conversion attempts to this set of variables. Condition c. enlarges the variables of condition a by a set of variables that were also collected in the core and exit version of the interview, while d. comprises all the previously stated variables. A detailed description is given in Table A18.1 in the online appendix to this chapter.

It becomes evident that the four field-experimental conditions are associated with clearly different response propensities. It obviously makes a difference if conversion attempts are allowed or not and if interviewers are

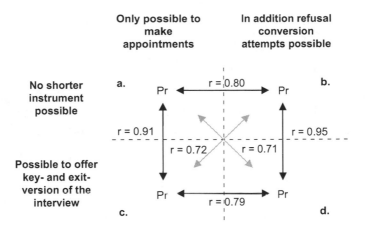

FIGURE 18.1
Correlations between measures of response propensity across four field-experimental conditions

allowed to offer a core and exit version of the interview in addition to the full version. If these four propensity scores are used to assess possible bias in two sets of survey variables using formula (18.4), a clear trend emerges. The relevant tables are part of the online appendix to this chapter. There Table A18.2 reports on possible bias with reference to a set of sociodemographic variables and Table A18.3 with reference to a set of items on survey attitudes. If we compare condition a with b and c with d, the entries in these tables suggest by and large two patterns: (a) If the propensity score reflects possible refusal conversion attempts, this shifts the estimated bias to an algebraically smaller figure. We observe the variants that an otherwise positive bias is reduced, that an otherwise non-existing bias becomes a negative bias and that an otherwise negative bias becomes a stronger negative bias. This indicates that the expected response mean overestimates the population mean less than before, or that it underestimates it more if the sample composition is altered by means of refusal conversion attempts. This applies to education and income and respondent ratings of items, where giving consent indicates more survey-friendly attitudes. In contrast, the opposite pattern (b) applies to age and ratings of items, where giving consent indicates more survey-critical attitudes: If the propensity score reflects possible refusal conversion attempts on that condition, this shifts the estimated bias to a larger figure. We observe particularly the variant that a non-existing bias becomes a positive bias. Considered all in all, this suggests that refusal conversion attempts are likely to affect nonresponse bias by winning over persons to the survey whose attitudes toward surveys are more critical.

18.12 CONTACTING PEOPLE IN SINGLE- OR MIXED-MODE?

The contact mode of the PPSM panel is the "telephone" mode. Accordingly, RLD sampling is used. This section discusses sampling from population registers (i.e. registration office samples) as a possible alternative to this mode, if e.g. a web panel is to be set up.

First of all, the realization of telephone sampling requires less administrative effort than the realization of registration office samples, since population registers are held at the district level in Germany. There is no nationwide population register available that could be used for sampling. Furthermore, interviewer mediated surveys allow for refusal conversion attempts. This speaks in favor of RLD sampling. On the other hand, the use of RLD sampling is coupled with some serious disadvantages. As indicated above, despite all efforts only low response rates were achieved: 13.6 percent[3] is certainly a disappointing figure, though in line with response rates of other current telephone surveys (cf. Häder, Häder, & Kühne, 2012, p. 124; Engel et al., 2012, p 66f.). Particularly disadvantageous is that the use of randomly generated telephone numbers precludes the use of personalized advance letters and accompanying prepaid incentives (for large, nationwide surveys like the present one that are financed by public funds the use of incentives may of course also be too expensive). Evidence shows, however, that both are really efficient tools in increasing survey cooperation (Engel & Schnabel, 2004; Engel et al., 2012, p. 128f.; Schnell, 2012, p. 182). In addition, a survey-taking climate in Germany that leads people to spontaneously refuse if contacted by phone is really disadvantageous. This limits any attempt at refusal conversion considerably and is likely to be one major source of nonresponse bias. A slight disadvantage emerges from the fact that possible nonresponse adjustments can rely on neighborhood data only to a comparably limited extent. Although in Germany an official district-level identifier is available for landline telephone surveys to link area data to the survey, this identifier does not differentiate between e.g. subdistricts within cities. That limits its usefulness in larger cities. In addition, no area data can be added to cell-phone samples. This all speaks in favor of registration office samples.

A third possible way may consist of a combination of both strategies (De Leeuw, Dillman, & Hox, 2008, p. 303ff.). Recently, a field experiment was set up to compare a mixed-mode contact strategy with a single-mode one in an attempt at recruiting members for a web panel (Engel & Schmidt, 2013). The experiment is restricted to one district. Table A18.4 in the online appendix to this chapter describes the design and the relevant figures. First of all, a random sample of persons aged 18+ was drawn from the district's population register to compare two ways of contacting target persons: by including in a personalized advance letter the announcement of a telephone call or by excluding such an announcement. The apparent weakness of this approach is its restriction to target persons who allow their numbers to be listed in the telephone directory. In an attempt at balancing the exclusion of persons with unlisted numbers, the overall sample was split into three (instead of only two) groups, namely into two random subgroups of persons with listed telephone numbers, of which one received the announcement while the other received the same advance letter as the third group of persons, which was comprised of those with an unlisted telephone number. This resulted in remarkably different response rates: 36.4 percent (if call announced) vs. 9.5 percent (despite known number no call announced) vs. 6.1 percent (no call announced, because number unknown). One might have expected the slightly higher response propensity in the case of people who permit publication of their telephone numbers (9.5 percent vs. 6.1 percent). It should be noted however that we observed only a small difference in the main recruitment study of the PPSM panel. There the probability of obtaining a full interview depends only to a small, though approximately significant, extent on a listed (vs. not listed) telephone number (e^b = 1.04; b/s.e = 1.64, N = 48,899; pseudo-R^2 = 0.0003; see Engel, 2013, p. 51, Table 2.18[4]). Comparing the 9.5 and 6.1 percent response rates with the 13.6 percent reported above for the RLD sampling, the rates are even lower in the present case. Even if we consider the fact that no reminders were employed in the present experiment, it may be not so promising just to turn from RLD to registration office sampling alone when attempting to recruit members for a web panel.

More promising may be the combination of a personalized advance letter with an announcement of a telephone call, if possible. If, in addition to this combination, prepaid incentives were also offered, this raised the response rate additionally from 36.4 to 49.5 percent. This is the result of an incentive experiment carried out within the "call announced" subsample (see Table A18.4 in the online appendix). This confirms the finding of a previous experiment where a response rate of 50.8 percent was achieved under the condition of a prepaid monetary incentive of €5 (see Table A18.6 in the online appendix). As this previous incentive experiment also showed, such incentives not only help to raise response rates, they may also help to reduce bias in sample composition. Table A18.6 indicates this fact with respect to the education bias of a sample when an external reference distribution (Microcensus) is taken as a benchmark.

The level of the response rate is just one possible criterion when registration office and RLD samples are to be compared. Another one is the sample composition. One of the four PPSM-Panel pilot studies was used to explore this aspect. The study was carried out early in 2008. Table A18.7 reports on the design of this study and relevant response rates. It becomes evident that at that time a comparably higher response rate was achieved when selecting the subset of cases with listed telephone numbers in a registration office sample (24.2 percent vs. 18.8 percent in the case of RLD sampling). Small subsample sizes certainly limit the information value of the findings of the covariance analysis reported in Tables A18.8 and A18.9 in the online appendix to this chapter. Small subsamples are likely to be capable of just providing the tentative impression that at least in that sample no significant mean differences have been found across the subsamples and the variables compared (political and survey attitude items). In contrast, we observe a couple of significant response propensity effects on those mean values. The same pattern emerges with respect to the "basic question" implemented in that study, i.e. the intention to vote. Table A18.10 indicates an approximately significant propensity effect, although there is no significant variation across the compared subsamples.

Considered all in all, it seems to be less promising to pursue a single-mode approach in attempts at recruiting web panels or mixed-mode panels on a probabilistic basis. Both approaches yield lower response rates if adopted alone than in cases where they were mixed in the way described above. RLD samples suffer particularly from the missing opportunity to employ advance letters and thus prepaid incentives and the limited possibilities to avoid spontaneous refusals. In contrast, they offer at least limited ways of converting reluctant persons. Registration office samples are advantageous in that they allow for the implementation of advance letters and prepaid monetary incentives in a relatively straightforward way. They also offer a reasonable opportunity to link area data to the survey body. One complication, however, remains: target persons receive an invitation to a web survey by mail to their postal addresses. Thus the contact mode differs from the requested data collection mode. This alone may contribute to the low observed response rates. Then the announcement of a telephone call may help to bridge this "mode gap" if it is combined with the offer to let the target person choose his or her preferred data collection mode (as in the field experiment described above; see Table A18.4 for these preferences). This mixed-mode approach depends on listed telephone numbers, though, and it does not appear possible to control effectively for differences between persons who allow their numbers to appear in directories and persons who do not. In that regard further research is certainly needed.

NOTES

1. This is the major research question underlying the research project "Access Panel and Mixed-Mode Internet Survey". The financial support for this project received from the DFG, the German Research Council (EN 318/9-1) and the University of Bremen is gratefully acknowledged. The project is part of the German Priority Programme on Survey Methodology (PPSM).

2. The fieldwork for sample 1 was realized by the project group at the University of Bremen, while the fieldwork for samples 2, 3 and 4 were realized by a survey institute at the University of Duisburg called "Sozialwissenschaftliches Umfragezentrum" (SUZ).

3. In addition to the factors considered in the text one should add that due to cost considerations only a maximum number of ten to fifteen contact attempts were possible in the recruitment samples 2, 3 and 4.

4. We analyzed the influence of sociodemographic characteristics on the odds of having a number that is listed in the telephone directory. Table A18.5 in the online appendix to this chapter reports the relevant figures. The odds are significantly reduced if persons are divorced or have a higher level of schooling or are in higher income classes. In contrast, the odds are significantly raised in larger households.

BIBLIOGRAPHY

Bethlehem, J. (2009). *Applied survey methods: Statistical perspective*. Hoboken: Wiley.
Bethlehem, J., & Biffignandi, S. (2012). *Handbook of web surveys*. Hoboken: Wiley.
Bethlehem, J., Cobben, F., & Schouten, B. (2011). *Handbook of nonresponse in household surveys*. Hoboken: Wiley.
Biemer, P. P. (2011). *Latent Class Analysis of survey error*. Hoboken: Wiley.
De Leeuw, E. D., Dillman, D. A., & Hox, J. J. (2008). Mixed mode surveys: When and why. In E. D. De Leeuw, J. J. Hox, & D. A. Dillman (Eds.), *International handbook of survey methodology* (pp. 299–316). New York: Lawrence Erlbaum.
Engel, U. (2013). Access panel and mixed-mode internet survey. PPSM panel report. Retrieved from www.sozialforschung.uni-bremen.de/html/downloads.html
Engel, U., Bartsch, S., Schnabel, C., & Vehre, H. (2012). *Wissenschaftliche Umfragen. Methoden und Fehlerquellen*. Frankfurt/New York: Campus.
Engel, U., & Schmidt, B.-O. (2013). Ein Feldexperiment zur Wirkung von Befragungsanreizen innerhalb eines Mixed-Mode Designs. Retrieved from www.sozialforschung. uni-bremen.de/html/downloads.html
Engel, U., & Schnabel, C. (2004). Markt- und Sozialforschung. Metaanalyse zum Ausschoepfungsgrad. Retrieved from www.adm-ev.de/index.php?id=forschungsprojekte
Engel, U., Schnabel, C., & Simonson, J. (2006). Register data and the explanation of response propensity in surveys and access panels. Retrieved from www.sozialforschung. uni-bremen.de/Explaining_response_propensity.pdf
Groves, R. M., Singer, E., & Corning, A. (2000). Leverage–saliency theory of survey participation. Description and an illustration. *Public Opinion Quarterly, 64*(3), 299–308. doi:10.1086/317990
Häder, S., Häder, M., & Kühne, M. (Eds.). (2012). *Telephone surveys in Europe. Research and practice*. Heidelberg: Springer.
Hox, J., & De Leeuw, E. (2002). The influence of interviewers' attitude and behavior on household survey nonresponse: An international comparison. In R. M. Groves, D. A. Dillman, J. L. Eltinge, & R.J.A. Little (Eds.), *Survey nonresponse* (pp. 103–120). New York: Wiley.
Lynn, P. (2003). PEDAKSI: Methodology for collecting data about survey non-respondents. *Quality & Quantity, 37*, 239–261.
Schnell, R. (2012). *Survey-Interviews. Methoden standardisierter Befragungen*. Wiesbaden: VS Verlag fuer Sozialwissenschaften.
Stoop, I.A.L. (2005). *The hunt for the last respondent*. The Hague: Social and Cultural Planning Office.
Vehre, H., Bartsch, S., & Engel, U. (2013). The education bias in a telephone survey with incentives. Retrieved from www.sozialforschung.uni-bremen.de/html/downloads.html

19

Survey Participation in a Probability-Based Internet Panel in the Netherlands

Annette Scherpenzeel

19.1 INTRODUCTION

This chapter describes the set-up of an online panel based on a probability sample, called the LISS panel, and the participation rates in this panel over time. The main objective of all investments in sampling, initial response rates, and long-term participation rates was to meet the standards for a scientific longitudinal study with an online panel.

Many internet panels and internet surveys are based on some form of non-probability sampling. A study across 19 internet panels of Dutch market research organizations showed that most of them use self-selection, links and banners on websites, or snowballing (NOPVO Research, see Van Ossenbruggen, Vonk, & Willems, 2006). This means that most internet research has two fundamental methodological flaws: under-coverage and self-selection. However, internet interviewing can be seen as just another mode of data collection that could also be applied to a proper probability sample. Questions are not asked face-to-face or by telephone, but over the internet.

With support of the Netherlands Organization for Scientific Research, the research institute CentERdata has built up the LISS (Longitudinal Internet Studies for the Social sciences) panel. It is part of a broader effort, entitled Measurement and Experimentation in the Social Sciences (MESS). An important characteristic of the panel is that it is based on a probability sample. In addition, the LISS panel is a "true" longitudinal panel in the scientific sense. In a "true" panel, a set of repeated measures is collected at regular intervals (for example: every year) from the same group of people. In the LISS panel, a yearly recurring core questionnaire is combined with an assembly of research projects of varying duration. To enable longitudinal analyses with a large enough number of cases over all waves, it is essential to keep up the participation rate of the original sample members over years. Therefore, several studies were conducted in the past years to develop the optimal strategy to stimulate long-term participation in the LISS panel.

The focus of this chapter is on the long-term participation rates in the LISS panel during its first five years of existence. We first summarize the sample, the recruitment process, and the initial response rates of the LISS panel. Next, we describe in more detail the participation in the monthly surveys, the attrition rates, the difficult-to-keep groups, and the efforts to keep panel members motivated.

19.2 GENERAL SET-UP OF THE LISS PANEL

The LISS panel is a probability-based online panel of 5,000 households. All individual members of these households aged 16 years or older are asked to participate. Every month, members complete online questionnaires of about 30 minutes in total. They receive a monetary incentive for each completed questionnaire. One member of the household provides the household data and updates this information at regular time intervals.

Half of the interview time available in the LISS panel is reserved for the LISS Core Study. This longitudinal study is repeated yearly and is designed to follow changes in the life course and living conditions of the panel members. The other half of the available interview time is offered as free data collection to the academic world. New studies can be linked to core modules or with other studies and thus can benefit from the rich amount of data that is already available.

In addition to the online questionnaires, new forms of data collection are used from different fields of research. For example, studies are carried out using self-administered measurement devices for the collection of biomarkers. The project also offers possibilities to exploit graphical tools, to register response times, and to analyze mouse movements. Furthermore, with the permission of the panel members, survey data can be linked to administrative data of Statistics Netherlands on, for example, income, pension entitlements, and health.

All LISS data are published on the website www.lissdata.nl and are freely available for academic researchers.

19.3 SAMPLE AND RECRUITMENT

The reference population for the LISS panel is the Dutch-speaking population permanently residing in the Netherlands. The sampling and survey units of the LISS panel are the independent, private households, thereby excluding institutions and other forms of collective households. The reference population does not include households in which no adult is capable of understanding the Dutch language. The sample frame is the nationwide address frame of Statistics Netherlands. From this address frame a simple random sample of 10,150 addresses was drawn.

The sample from the population registers naturally includes individuals and households who do not (yet) have internet access. These participants are loaned equipment to provide access to the internet. The computer provided, called the "simPC", is especially developed for elderly people having no experience with computers. It is a small and simple device using centralized support and maintenance. It can be operated by large "buttons" for the most frequently used functions, and has screens that are designed to be readable by elderly people.

Recruitment of the sampled households was done from May until December 2007. Households were contacted in a traditional way: first, an announcement letter was sent in combination with a brochure explaining the nature of the panel study. A €10 note was included with the letter, because a pilot study had shown that a prepaid, €10 incentive effectively increased the willingness to participate in the panel (Scherpenzeel & Toepoel, 2012). Next, respondents were contacted by an interviewer in a mixed-mode design. Those households for which a telephone number was known were contacted by telephone. The remaining households were visited by an interviewer and thus contacted face-to-face. The interviewers who recruited the panel members were instructed to focus on obtaining the cooperation of the selected households, rather than on maximizing the response/interview time ratio. For a detailed description of the recruitment and refusal conversion procedure, see Scherpenzeel and Das (2011) and Scherpenzeel (2009).

The intensive efforts to re-contact and motivate respondents to participate resulted in satisfactory initial response rates. Table 19.1 shows that the final household recruitment rate was 48% of the total gross sample of usable addresses. All household members aged 16 and older were asked to participate, but they were not obliged to. Households in which at least one person participated were included in the panel. The second row of Table 19.1 shows the total number of persons aged 16 years and older living

TABLE 19.1

Initial response rates, estimated in April 2008

	N[1]	Proportion of total gross sample of usable addresses[2]
Total gross sample of addresses	10,150	
Total 16+ persons in gross sample[2]	18,630	
Household registered as panel member	4,722	0.48
Participating persons in panel households	7,556	0.41

[1] Numbers given by Statistics Netherlands, based on the population register at the moment the sample was drawn.

[2] Not usable includes, among other things, non-existing or non-inhabited addresses, companies, long-term infirm or disabled respondents, language problems. The total number of usable addresses was 9,844.

at the sampled addresses at the time the sample was drawn. The last line of the table shows that 43% of these persons had started to answer panel questionnaires in February 2008. This percentage represents the Recruitment Rate (RECR) at the person level for probability-based web panels, as defined by Callegaro and DiSogra (2008).

Each month, between 66% and 87% of the invited persons complete one or more LISS panel questionnaires, with an average of 76% (*sd* = 5%) per month between January 2008 and January 2013. In the definition of Callegaro and DiSogra (2008), this is the study-specific Completion Rate (COMR). Multiplied by the initial person-level response rate of 43%, the result is 33% (43% × 76%) average cumulative response (CUMRR1) at the person level,[1] in the definition of the same authors.

Every two years, a refreshment sample is drawn for the LISS panel, to compensate for attrition and keep the number of panel households at the target of 5,000 households. The first refreshment sample, drawn in 2009, was a stratified sample drawn to correct the initial nonresponse bias in the panel. In cooperation with Statistics Netherlands, we oversampled the groups which had a below-average response in the main recruitment: elderly, single-person households, and people with a non-Western ethnic background (for a detailed description of the initial bias in the LISS panel, see Knoef & De Vos, 2008). Because these are the most difficult groups to recruit for an online panel, the final household panel membership rate for this sample was only 26%.

The second refreshment sample, drawn in 2011, was drawn randomly from the population register by Statistics Netherlands, in the same way as the original sample of 2007. The final household panel membership rate for this sample was 45%, close to the 48% of the original sample.

19.4 PARTICIPATION AND ATTRITION

The LISS panel aims to be a longitudinal panel in the scientific sense, by means of its yearly recurring core questionnaire. In addition to a high initial response rate, it is hence essential to ensure the continued participation of original panel members from year to year.

Table 19.2 shows the number of households registered as LISS panel households and the number of persons in these households who participate in the panel, at the start of the panel in January 2008 and four years later, in January 2012. The LISS panel households originate from different samples: the pilot sample, the main household sample of 2007, and the two refreshment samples of 2009 and 2011. The retention of individual panel members from each of these samples is shown in Table 19.2. More detailed figures depicting the year-by-year development of the samples can be found in the online appendix to this chapter (online appendix, Figure A19.1 and Figure A19.2). In addition, these figures show the increase over time in the number of panel members due to split-offs of sampled households (divorce, children moving into independent households, etc.). As described in the LISS panel-following rules (see www.lissdata.nl/followrules), the panel follows new households after the split of an original household under the condition that the new household contains at least one original panel member. An additional category are the children who were younger than 16 years when their household entered the panel and started to participate after their 16th birthday.

In January 2012, 61% of the panel households originating from the main 2007 sample were still participating in the panel (Figure A19.1 in the

TABLE 19.2

Participating households and panel members, LISS panel, from 2008 to 2012

	January 2008	January 2013
	N	N
Registered households, total	5416	5067
Participating persons, total	8884	6968
From main sample 2007	7785	3787
From refreshment sample 2009		886
From refreshment sample 2011/2012		1139
Other (pilot sample, splitoff households, became 16 years)	1099	1156

online appendix). In January 2012, 49% of the individual panel members originating from the households of the main sample were still participating in the panel (Table 19.2).

In conclusion, the attrition rate of the LISS panel is about 10% per year for households (39% over four years, Figure A19.1 in the online appendix) and about 12% per year for persons (51% over four years, Figure A19.2 in the online appendix).

De Vos (2009) examined whether specific groups showed especially high or low attrition rates in the first year of the panel. The probability of attrition was significantly affected by age, the provision of a computer and broadband internet connection, and the employment status of the persons in the household (i.e., regarding age: elderly are more likely to drop out; regarding provision of computer and internet: households are less likely to drop out; and regarding employment status: two-earner households are least likely to drop out). However, attrition was much more related to respondents' past response behavior than to household characteristics. Skipping a questionnaire or completing questionnaires irregularly turn out to be the best predictors for future drop-out. This was confirmed by Lugtig, Scherpenzeel, and Das (2014). Using a latent class framework, Lugtig, Scherpenzeel, and Das identify two groups of panel members, the sleepers and the irregular participants, that are characterized by incomplete response patterns across all questionnaires. Both studies (De Vos, 2009; Lugtig et al., 2014) showed that attrition from the panel is often preceded by periods of inactivity of panel members. This makes it possible to identify the at-risk panel members in an early stage, after a few consecutive months of nonparticipation, and implement strategies to motivate and reactivate them again. In the next section, we describe a study conducted with the aim of developing the best strategy for the reactivation.

19.5 HOUSEHOLDS WITHOUT INTERNET ACCESS

The LISS panel provides households with no internet access at the time of the sampling with cost-free equipment and an internet connection. Leenheer and Scherpenzeel (2013) showed that the recruitment rate for households without internet in the sample frame is much lower (35.1%) than for households with internet (84.2%): Of all households that answered in the recruitment interview that they did not have internet access, only 35.1% registered in the panel, whereas 84.2% of the households that answered they had internet access registered.[2]

The approach by the LISS panel resulted in a substantial group of non-internet households in the panel. In 2008, 7.9% of the entire panel consisted of non-internet households, in 2012 this was 8.9%.[3] The non-internet households show a high degree of loyalty after they join the panel: Leenheer and Scherpenzeel (2013) showed that attrition between April 2008 and January 2010 was 9.9% for households without internet and 13.8% for households with internet.

19.6 REACTIVATING PANEL MEMBERS AND PREVENTING ATTRITION

As described above, panel members who start to participate irregularly and skip questionnaires are at risk of dropping out. This suggests a need for a general strategy to keep panel members "awake" by regularly attracting their attention and encouraging their participation. To develop such a strategy, in the first half of 2010 the so-called "sleeper study" was carried out: The inactive panel members were contacted by telephone for a brief questionnaire. This sleeper study focused on the question of what strategies could be used to keep the panel members "awake" and motivated.

In the LISS panel we call respondents "sleepers" when they are still registered as panel members but have not completed any questionnaires for three consecutive months or longer. In January 2010 the percentage of sleepers was around 30% of the total number of panel members recruited in 2007.

All sleepers received a letter in February 2010 announcing that they would be contacted by an interviewer to ask them a few questions. Soon afterwards they received a phone call or a visit[4] from an interviewer. The interviewer asked them some questions about the reasons for their non-participation, about the number, length, and difficulty of the LISS questionnaires, and some general survey questions about voting and interests. At the end of the interview, the interviewer tried to persuade sleepers to participate again, offering them different extra incentives of €10, €20, or €30. A part of the respondents were told they would get this incentive just because we hoped they would participate again, without any demand. A second group was told they would receive the incentive only after they had actually participated again the next month. The third group was promised the incentive only after they had participated again for the next three months.

TABLE 19.3

The effect of incentive and type of sleeper on sleeper reactivation. Observed percentage of sleepers that became active again, and logistic regression coefficients

	N	Re-activated between February and June 2010	
		Observed Percentage re-activated sleepers	Logit coefficient: effect on re-activation
	N	%	B
Incentive			
No additional incentive	357	32%	
Conditional €10 additional incentive	224	43%	.493*
Conditional €20 additional incentive	241	35%	.157
Conditional €30 additional incentive	261	40%	.385*
Prepaid €10 additional incentive	121	31%	.011
Prepaid €20 additional incentive	118	40%	.264
Prepaid €30 additional incentive	123	44%	.620**
Type of sleeper			
Participated before, now inactive for 3–6 months	289	65%	
Participated before, now inactive > 6 months	978	32%	−1.423**
Never participated, but did register	178	21%	−1.970**

* $p < .05$, ** $p < .01$

A total of 2,454 sleepers in the LISS panel were approached, 63% of them (1,536) were contacted, and 59% (1,447) answered the entire interview or at least one of the core questions of the interview. Table 19.3 shows how many sleepers were reactivated in the months after the telephone interview. Without any additional incentive, 32% of the sleepers were reactivated in the following months, where reactivated is defined as completing at least one questionnaire between February and June 2010. The most efficient method to reactivate sleepers was to promise them €10 conditional on participation: 43% (observed percentage) did then participate again. Thirty euros additional incentive (both conditional and unconditional) gave about the same result, but at much higher cost. Offering sleepers €10 or €20 unconditionally as an incentive to start participating again was less effective: the (observed) percentage of members who resume participation is between 31% and 40%.

Another factor that appeared important, in addition to the promised incentive, was how long a person had already been a sleeper. Those who had not participated for three to six months were much easier to reactivate than those who had not participated for longer than six months or those who registered as panel members but never actually started completing questionnaires (Table 19.3). Hence, it is important to prevent long-term sleeping and contact panel members within three months after they become inactive.

19.7 KEEPING PANEL MEMBERS INTERESTED

The most important encouragement for long-term participation in the LISS panel is the €15 per hour incentive which panel members earn for participating in the monthly questionnaires. However, in addition to that payment, we have experimented with other encouragements, appealing more to feelings of closeness, interest, and helping science than to reciprocity alone.

Between 2009 and 2011, we conducted a series of experiments with traditional methods to provide feedback about study results, such as newsletters, free postcards, and booklets, but also innovative feedback methods that make use of the specific possibilities of an online panel, for example, short "You Tube-like" videos in which a researcher informs viewers about the results or graphs at the end of a questionnaire, representing the real-time answer distribution on one of the questionnaires the respondent has just answered. In these experiments, we selected control groups of panel members who did not get the extra encouragement, and a baseline "zero-condition" group of panel members who did not get any feedback of this type. Scherpenzeel and Toepoel (2013) describes these experiments in more detail.

In general, the feedback did not have significant effects on long-term participation in the LISS panel, neither the traditional information materials, nor the innovative feedback. We evaluated the effects of each material on the probability of staying a "perfect" panel member, that is, completing questionnaires each month without exception, and the probability of becoming a "sleeping" panel member at the end of the period of experimentation. When controlling for the effects of demographic variables, for example, age, education, and occupation, these two output variables were not affected by the presentation of the new materials (Scherpenzeel & Toepoel, 2013). Furthermore, we also found no substantive, clear effects of the different materials within specific subgroups of panel members having a higher than average probability of becoming a sleeper over time (young people; people in paid work; lower-educated people) or a lower than average probability (the elderly).

The results of these experiments raise the question of whether it is worthwhile to keep giving different forms of feedback to panel members, as it does not have a positive effect on participation rates and does require budget. Furthermore, our results are in line with the findings of Göritz (this volume), who examined the effects of offering study results and found that it decreased the response or had no effect at all. The new interactive materials offered by the LISS panel were appreciated rather positively by the panel members, more so than the old materials, but for the aim of stimulating long-term participation, the feedback of study results to LISS panel member seems useless.

19.8 CONCLUSIONS

The LISS panel is a typical example of an internet panel survey based on a probability sample of the full population, which, as stated in Couper (2000), is the only approach that allows generalization beyond the current population of internet users. Other institutes that have built this type of internet panel are Knowledge Networks, RAND in the United States, and more recently, the University of Mannheim in Germany and the institute Sciences Po Paris in France.

For this probability-based type of internet panels, true response rates can be calculated since the total number of eligible respondents is known and the population is defined. However, nonresponse in such panels can occur at various stages in the survey process: first, in the recruitment stage of the internet panel; second, when panel members do not participate in a particular wave of the survey; and finally, when respondents drop out of the panel after some time (Hoogendoorn & Daalmans, 2009). Callegaro and DiSogra (2008) describe a similar, more extended sequence of response stages in their computation guidelines for online panels. The product of each of the response rates in this multistage process can lead to a dramatically low cumulative response rate as low as 16%, as Callegaro and DiSogra (2008) show.

Couper (2000) states that the initial response is often relatively low because the common techniques to stimulate response, such as advance letters, personalized signatures, letterhead, and incentives, cannot be implemented in internet surveys. However, the recruitment strategy of the LISS panel did implement such techniques. A lot of attention and testing was devoted, for example, to the design and content of the advance letter, and prepaid incentives were included with the letter (Scherpenzeel & Toepoel, 2012). Together with extensive nonresponse follow-up procedures, described by Scherpenzeel (2009), this resulted in an initial response rate of 48% of the gross sample of households. At the person level, the Recruitment Rate (RECR) was 43% of the total number of eligible persons living in the sampled households at the time of the sample drawing.

With an average monthly Completion Rate (COMR) of 76%, the average cumulative response (CUMRR1) at the person level, for the main sample of the LISS panel, is 33% (43% × 76%). Furthermore, we saw that the dropout rate of the LISS panel, the stage 3 response in terms of Hoogendoorn and Daalmans (2009), is about 10% per year for households and about 12% per year for persons. Many efforts are taken to motivate panel members to participate each month and to prevent sleeping and attrition. We have shown that effective measures include a follow-up call in the event of nonresponse (inactivity) for longer than two months. Contact could be resumed after three months with an offer of a (€10) conditional incentive. This type of procedure has been implemented since 2010 by the LISS panel management. Panel members who do not participate for two months are immediately contacted by means of a brief personal telephone call. If a person still remains inactive, a flow of steps is initiated, starting in the third month including the conditional €10 additional incentive.

Whereas the follow-up calls combined with extra incentives are an effective way to motivate panel members for future participation, the provision of feedback about study results is not. We showed that for the LISS panel, an online panel in which members are contacted at high frequency rates, sending or presenting feedback does not increase long-term participation rates. This might be different in panels for which respondents are contacted less often, for example, once a year. Traditional household panels often have a common strategy of sending newsletters or brochures with study results to their panel members, as a way of keeping in contact between panel waves, for example, the British Household Panel Survey (Laurie, Smith, & Scott, 1999) and the Swiss Household Panel (Budowski & Scherpenzeel, 2005). Many panel members appreciate receiving feedback, as we saw in the LISS panel experiments, and which was also noted by Laurie et al. (1999). We therefore still provide electronic newsletters and videos to the LISS panel members, which are relatively low-cost materials that respondents can choose either to read/watch or not.

In the LISS panel, we continue to experiment to develop more strategies. Future experiments are planned on the effect of higher monetary payment for completing questionnaires; the effect of more interesting panel questionnaires that include questions tailored to the interests of the respondents; the possibilities of tracking and tracing changed email addresses and "lost" panel members; and offering smartphone and tablet questionnaires to the difficult-to-reach groups such as adolescents or working singles. By investing in the development of optimal strategies to stimulate long-term participation, we aim to establish the online LISS panel as a truly longitudinal survey that meets the high standards for scientific research.

NOTES

1. In the definition of Callegaro and Disogra (2008), CUMRR1 is the product of the recruitment rate, the profile rate, and the survey-specific completion rate. In the LISS panel, the person-level recruitment rate includes the profile rate, since person-level recruitment is defined as the number of eligible persons in the total sample that answered at least one LISS panel questionnaire.
2. This is a different average registration rate than given in Table 19.1, because this rate is not calculated on the gross sample but is conditional on willingness to respond in the recruitment interview and answer the question about internet access.
3. The percentage of households without internet access at home as given by Statistics Netherlands decreased from 14% in 2008 to 6% in 2012.
4. The majority of the LISS panel sleepers were approached and interviewed by telephone. A small group of 112 sleepers for whom no phone number was available were visited at home by an interviewer.

REFERENCES

Budowski, M., & Scherpenzeel, A. (2005). Encouraging and maintaining participation in household surveys: the case of the Swiss Household Panel. *ZUMA Nachrichten* 29(56), 10–36.

Callegaro, M., & DiSogra, C. (2008). Computing response metrics for online panels. *Public Opinion Quarterly, 72*(5), 1008–1032. doi:10.1093/poq/nfn065

Couper, M. P. (2000). Web surveys. A review of issues and approaches. *Public Opinion Quarterly, 64*(4), 464–494. doi:10.1086/318641

De Vos, K. (2009). Panel attrition in LISS. Working paper, CentERdata, Tilburg University, The Netherlands. Retrieved from www.lissdata.nl/assets/uploaded/Attrition%20in%20the%20LISS%20panel.pdf

Hoogendoorn, A., & Daalmans, J. (2009). Nonresponse in the recruitment of an internet panel based on probability sampling. *Survey Research Methods, 3*, 59–72.

Knoef, M., & de Vos, K. (2008). The representativeness of LISS, an online probability panel. Working paper, CentERdata, Tilburg University, the Netherlands. Retrieved from www.lisspanel.nl/assets/uploaded/representativeness_LISS_panel.pdf

Laurie, H., Smith, R., & Scott, L. (1999). Strategies for reducing nonresponse in a longitudinal panel survey. *Journal of Official Statistics, 15*, 269–282.

Leenheer, J., & Scherpenzeel, A. C. (2013). Does it pay off to include non-internet households in an internet panel? *International Journal of Internet Science, 8*, 17–29.

Lugtig, P., Scherpenzeel, A., & Das, M. (2014). Nonresponse and attrition in a probability based Internet panel for the general population. In M. Callegaro, R. Baker, J. Bethlehem, A. S. Göritz, J. A. Krosnick, & P. J. Lavrakas (Eds.), *Online panel surveys: An interdisciplinary approach.* Chichester, UK: Wiley.

Scherpenzeel, A. (2009). Start of the LISS panel: Sample and recruitment of a probability-based Internet panel. Retrieved from www.lissdata.nl/assets/uploaded/Sample_and_Recruitment.pdf

Scherpenzeel, A., & Das, M. (2011). True longitudinal and probability-based internet panels: evidence from the Netherlands. In M. Das, P. Ester, & L. Kaczmirek (Eds.), *Social and behavioral research and the internet: Advances in applied methods and research strategies.* Boca Raton, FL: Taylor & Francis.

Scherpenzeel, A., & Toepoel, V. (2012). Recruiting a probability sample for an online panel: Effects of contact mode, incentives and information. *Public Opinion Quarterly, 76*(3): 470–490. doi:10.1093/poq/nfs037

Scherpenzeel, A., & Toepoel, V. (2014). Informing panel members about study results: Effects of traditional and innovative forms of feedback on participation. In M. Callegaro, R. Baker, J. Bethlehem, A. S. Göritz, J. A. Krosnick, & P. J. Lavrakas (Eds.), *Online panel surveys: An interdisciplinary approach.* Chichester: Wiley.

Van Ossenbruggen, R., Vonk, T., & Willems, P. (2006). *Results Dutch Online Panel Comparison Study (NOVPO).* Retrieved from www.nopvo.nl

20

The Access Panel of German Official Statistics as a Selection Frame

Ulrich Rendtel and Boyko Amarov

20.1 INTRODUCTION

In 2004 the German Federal Statistical Office (Destatis) initiated the recruitment of a household access panel (AP) from a master sample, the annual German Microcensus (MC). The MC is a 1-percent sample from the entire German population with a broad questionnaire and mandatory participation. This AP, a pool of persons who have declared their willingness to participate in further statistical surveys by Destatis, serves as a sampling frame for a cost-efficient selection of samples from the general population. The most prominent survey sampled from the AP is the German subsample (DE-SILC) of the European Statistics on Income and Living Conditions (EU-SILC).

An indispensable quality requirement for EU-SILC is that its national subsamples have to be selected according to a probability sampling design to ensure that the population estimates from EU-SILC have reliable statistical properties, for example asymptotic unbiasedness and known precision. Therefore, uncontrolled volunteer opt-in access panels, commonly found in market research, fail to meet this standard.

The final respondent sample of DE-SILC can be regarded as the result of a multistage sampling procedure with two self-selection stages. The first self-selection occurs when persons are recruited from the master sample, because the decision to join the AP is voluntary. The recruitment probabilities are thus unknown and need to be estimated in order to evaluate the statistical properties of population estimators.

The MC contains a rich set of characteristics known for both the participants and the nonparticipants of the AP that could be used for the estimation of the recruitment probabilities and the assessment of selective recruitment. The MC itself is an area sample with a four-year rotation cycle. Each sampling point (a group of residential units) remains in the survey for four consecutive years and all households living in it are interviewed. At the end of their last interview, the MC participants are asked whether they would be willing to take part in future voluntary surveys from Destatis. The households where all adult members sign a written consent form are selected into the AP. The latter requirement contributes to a low overall recruitment rate of about 9 percent.

Because of privacy protection concerns, however, the MC does not contain a participation indicator and the AP database itself is separate from the MC (see Section 20.2). The variables that are available for the analysis of recruitment are a small set of characteristics (so-called profile variables) from the last interview of the household. These variables are stored directly in the AP and cover age, gender, marital status, citizenship, employment status, education and income. A further limitation is that the AP does not contain variables directly related to the fieldwork of the MC (paradata), although they can be expected to have a substantial impact on recruitment success. Our empirical results in Section 20.3 suggest a strong variation in recruitment rates between the field institutes conducting the interviews that may reflect differences in fieldwork organization.

Furthermore, the database management of the AP itself puts another limitation on recruitment analysis. The profile variables were primarily intended to serve as auxiliary variables for sampling purposes (e.g. stratification) and were therefore regularly updated from ongoing surveys and update questionnaires. Unfortunately, the original values from the MC interviews were overwritten for some of the AP participants and were no longer available at the time of analysis.

The AP's recruitment stage is followed by further sampling stages. A stratified sample is taken from the AP using the profile variables generating the strata (Amarov & Rendtel, 2013; Horneffer & Kuchler, 2008). Furthermore, not all persons in the AP fulfill their promise to participate when they are asked to fill-in the DE-SILC questionnaire which results in a second self-selection stage. The overall response rate of about 70 percent is much higher than in the standard voluntary surveys of official statistics where it is below 50 percent, though a nonresponse rate of 30 percent appears high given that the AP participants have signed a written consent form to cooperate. A possible cause may be the switch between interview modes from face-to-face in the MC to a self-administered mail questionnaire in DE-SILC. As in the case of recruitment to the AP, the response probabilities are unknown and need to be estimated. The profile variables in the AP are available for both responders and nonresponders and are used to fit a Logit model for the response probability (see Section 20.3).

The empirical results for the recruitment stage and the response rate in Section 20.3 follow a discussion of some methodological problems in Section 20.2. Finally, in Section 20.4 we will draw some conclusions and give recommendations for the use of the AP.

20.2 LEGAL AND OTHER RESTRICTIONS FOR THE RECRUITMENT ANALYSIS

As a mandatory survey the content of the MC questionnaire is regulated by a special law. The question as to whether persons are willing to participate in other voluntary surveys was not a regular MC question, which implied that the answers to this question had to be recorded separately from the main MC files. This creates a difficulty for the analysis of recruitment success, because it prevented a direct analysis of the outcome based on all available information in the MC.

Instead we had to use an approach that does not require direct knowledge of the individual participation indicators in the MC. We compared frequency counts for fixed covariate values using the profile variables of the AP to estimate the recruitment probabilities. Consider p discrete profile variables with L different combinations (cells). Let $N_{AP,l}$ be the number of AP members with covariate combination $l = 1, \ldots, L$ and let $N_{MC,l}$ denote the number of MC participants with the same covariate combination. The ratio of these two counts is the ML estimator for the probability of recruitment in cell l that corresponds to a Logit model for the probability of recruitment involving all possible interaction effects between the covariates. For a fixed number of MC participants and an increasing number of profile variables the variance of these estimators becomes very large. Furthermore, some covariate combinations are expected to be empty.[1] In order to obtain more stable estimators we used a simpler main effects Logit model to smoothen these cell proportions. Note that a Logit model can be estimated on the basis of the two frequency tables $(N_{AP,l})_{l=1,\ldots,L}$ and $(N_{MC,l})_{l=1,\ldots,L}$.

Though this approach allows the estimation of Logit models it limits the set of explanatory variables to the profile variables of the AP. Most importantly, the AP file lacks important information about the fieldwork organization of the MC. The AP does contain indicators for the federal state and the administrative district (Gemeinde) of the households and the quarter year in which the MC interview was conducted. The first two variables are related to the fieldwork of the MC which is carried out in a decentralized fashion: The statistical agencies of the federal states (Statistische Landesaemter) are responsible for the recruitment and training of the interviewers, as well as data collection and processing. A survey of interviewers (Destatis, 2009) shows a large variation in interviewer characteristics between federal states. Furthermore, the fieldwork procedures and data management are not fully standardized between the state agencies. Thus, the state of residence may reflect field institute effects on recruitment. The households living in an MC sampling point are usually interviewed by the same interviewer in order to keep travel costs low. The AP contains only an indicator for the households' administrative district (Gemeinde), which generally encompasses several sampling points. Other fieldwork-related variables, such as the mode of the MC interview (CAPI, CATI or self-administered), are not available in the AP, although they can be expected to have a strong effect on the recruitment success.

Furthermore, apart from year of birth and gender, the profile variables change over time. Because they are intended to provide auxiliary information for sampling designs, they are updated regularly. However, some of the past values were overwritten in this process. In some cases this resulted in covariate combinations with $N_{AP} > N_{MC}$ implying that there were more persons in the AP than there were in the MC with the same covariate combination which is logically impossible. In these cases we assumed that $N_{AP} = N_{MC}$.

All these problems occurred as a consequence of the absence of participation indicators in the MC. We should mention that we were also not allowed to match the AP and the resulting DE-SILC files. However, in this case the DE-SILC participation indicators were part of the AP, so a nonresponse analysis could be conducted with the design indicators (selection for DE-SILC from AP) and the response indicators (response in DE-SILC given design selection). The same comments on the stability of the profile variables apply here.

This separation of the AP and the resulting surveys makes it impossible to use weight corrections in DE-SILC that are based on AP information. For example, if the duration of participation in the AP were a good predictor of response in DE-SILC then it should be included in the response model. The separation of the data sources prevents this, however, as we do not know the duration in the AP for the DE-SILC participants. Enderle and Münnich (Chapter 21) describe the consequences of the use of survey weights that do not reflect important features of the selection process.

20.3 EMPIRICAL RESULTS

Table 20.1 summarizes the AP recruitment and DE-SILC response rates as well as their sample sizes. There is a steady decline in the recruitment rate from 10.7 percent in 2005 to 8.7 percent in 2009. The response rates in DE-SILC also drop from over 70 percent in 2008 to 65–67 percent in 2009. Although the recruitment rate for the AP appears low, its level alone is not a reliable quality indicator (Groves, 2006; Schneekloth & Leven, 2003). It merely determines the maximal bias that can arise by selective recruitment (Bethlehem, 1988).

In this section we model the probabilities of recruitment and survey response by means of logistic regression models using the profile variables of the AP. We try to evaluate stable patterns of participation that have a causal interpretation. Very often participation analysis is done by screening long lists of estimated coefficients for significance. An extreme case is the attrition analysis of the Socio-Economic Panel, where 73 dummy variables enter a Logit model (Kroh, 2011). Although the strategy of 'picking significances' is frequently met in practice, the statistical reasoning of the procedure is biased. Because of this we repeat the analysis for the years 2005 until 2009. We argue that a substantial effect on participation should show up in each cohort. An important caveat with this strategy is that we cannot account for unmeasured changes in fieldwork procedures or other unobserved events with an impact on the participation propensity.

The MC is a stratified sample of clusters of geographically close residential units (sampling points). All households living in a sampling point are interviewed, usually by the same interviewer in order to keep field costs low. Interviewer information is not available in the MC at all and the sampling point indicators could not be used in this analysis due to privacy

TABLE 20.1

AP recruitment and DE-SILC sample sizes and response rates 2005–2009. N: total number of sampled households, R: number of responding households

	AP recruitment			DE-SILC response		
Year	N	R	Rate	N	R	Rate
2005	165,407	17,677	10.7	5,303	3,865	73
2006	172,455	17,772	10.3	5,749	4,107	71
2007	168,256	15,957	9.48	5,679	4,082	72
2008	165,089	15,274	9.25	5,376	3,486	65
2009	164,707	14,384	8.73	6,318	4,240	67

restrictions. As a rough proxy for the sampling point indicators we used the next largest area available, the administrative districts (Gemeinden), which generally contain several sampling points. To account for the regional homogeneity of households and for interviewer effects at the recruitment stage, the probability of success is modeled by a mixed logistic regression model with normally distributed random intercepts varying over districts.

The model is estimated at household level in a Bayesian framework using non-informative priors for both the fixed effects and the variance of the random effect. The estimated posterior means and 95 percent credible intervals for the parameters are presented in Table A20.1 available from the Internet appendix.

The probability of successful response for DE-SILC was also modeled at the household level. A household was classified as responding if the person with the highest income in the household returned the questionnaire. The model was estimated by means of Firth's penalized likelihood method (Firth, 1993) in order to obtain finite estimates for the coefficients of several federal states[2] which did not register any nonresponse in some of the years. The estimated coefficients and confidence intervals are presented in Table A20.2 in the Internet appendix.

For the sake of comparability we present similar Logit model specifications for the recruitment and the survey response stages. We fitted both models as a main effects model using the household's federal state of residence, the number of adults in the household, net household income, the presence of household members with non-German citizenship, the employment status of the highest income person in the household (HIP), the type of school and vocational training degree as well as the persons' weekly working hours.

Federal State

The model estimates reveal large differences in the recruitment success between federal states (Figure 20.1) that are not explained by variation in the other covariates in the model. While these differences appear to be largely stable for the recruitment stage, the DE-SILC nonresponse rate does not show such a pattern. A possible reason for the variability of the recruitment success is the impact of the interviewers whose recruitment and training is the responsibility of the statistical agencies of the states. A recent survey of interviewers (Destatis, 2009) displayed large differences in interviewer characteristics between the states. The mode of the MC interview may also partially explain the variation of recruitment propensities. Though the majority

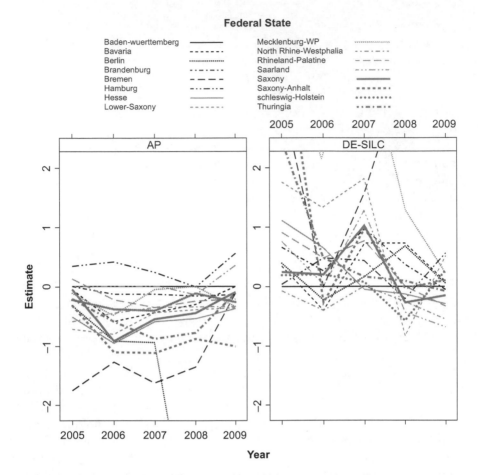

FIGURE 20.1

The recruitment success of the AP (left) and the response in DE-SILC (right): Estimated coefficients of the effect of federal state in a Logit model (positive coefficients indicate recruitment success or response with respect to the reference category State = Baden Wuerttemberg).

of the interviews are conducted face-to-face, about 20 percent of the households fill in a self-administered questionnaire, mainly in cases where the interviewers failed to contact the household personally. The share of self-administered interviews varies between federal states, but its impact on the recruitment propensities has not been investigated yet. The response propensity for DE-SILC also appears to vary strongly between the states but without a clear pattern over time.

Household Structure

A household is accepted in the AP only with the consent of all its adult members, which causes underrepresentation of larger households in the panel. Persons living in households with three or more adults entered the panel with a lower probability (1.7 times less likely) than those in single-person households, a pattern that appears to be stable over time. The negative effect of household size is, however, largely absent in households of married couples where the odds for successful recruitment are close to the odds of single-person households.

The odds for recruitment success also appear to be higher in households with children. The difference remained largely stable over the years at about 1.2 times higher odds for recruitment of households with children under 18 compared to households without children.

The models indicate significantly lower odds for successful recruitment of households with a widowed Highest Income Person (HIP; 1.2 times less likely than a never married HIP). In the DE-SILC response models, the household size and the marital status of the HIP appear to be less important. The number of adults is not significant.

Households with a widowed HIP showed lower propensity to respond to DE-SILC in 2005 and 2006 but the difference to households with a single HIP is not significant after 2007. Unlike the recruitment stage, the response propensity for DE-SILC does not appear to differ between households with or without children.

Income and Employment

Since DE-SILC is used to estimate poverty indicators, the analysis of selectivity with respect to income is especially important. The model estimates indicate underrepresentation of the lowest income group (€0 – €900 per month) both at the recruitment and survey nonresponse stages, while the differences between the other income groups are negligible (Figure 20.2). Persons in households with missing income data due to item nonresponse in the MC ('No answer' group) were also reluctant to join the AP, in line with earlier results indicating that item nonresponse is a strong predictor of unit nonresponse in later waves of a panel (Rendtel, 1995). A steady pattern that is visible in both recruitment and survey stages is the reluctance of self-employed persons to participate in the AP and in surveys drawn from it. Furthermore, households with a retired or otherwise non-employed HIP showed a higher propensity to participate than those with an employed HIP.

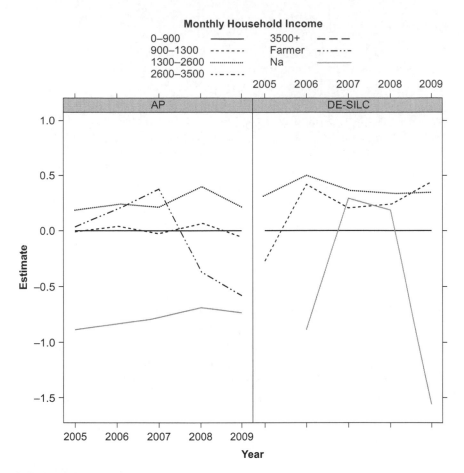

FIGURE 20.2

The recruitment success of the AP (left) and the response in DE-SILC (right): Estimated coefficients of the effect of net monthly household income groups in Euros in a Logit model (positive coefficients indicate recruitment success or response with respect to the reference category income = €0 – €900).

Age

The only stable effect of age on recruitment propensity is the lower partici-pation rate of persons over 75 years of age (Figure 20.3). The propensity to participate in DE-SILC appears to increase with age, reaching a maximum in the group of 56–65-year-olds. However, the coefficient estimates do not appear to follow a stable pattern. Only persons aged 76 and older show a significantly lower propensity to join the AP. The pattern of DE-SILC nonre-sponse, however, is less clear. While the differences between most age groups remain stable over time, the level of the estimated coefficients vary strongly

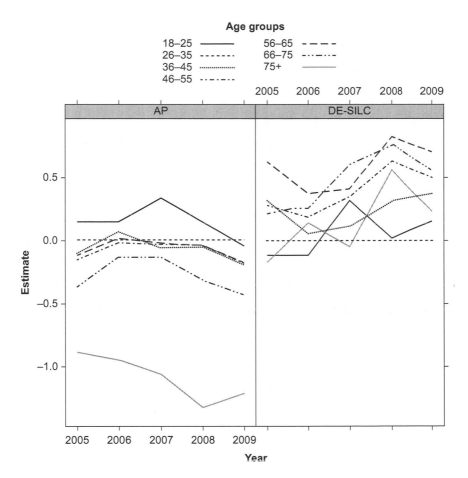

FIGURE 20.3

The recruitment success of the AP (left) and the response in DE-SILC (right): Estimated coefficients of the effect of age groups in a Logit model (positive coefficients indicate recruitment success or response with respect to the reference category age = 26 – 35).

over time and the highest age group does not appear to be less inclined to cooperate with DE-SILC than the others (with the exception of 2005).

Gender

At the recruitment stage male HIPs were slightly less likely to be recruited than female HIPs, the difference remaining constant over time. There is less evidence of differential response rates for males and females at DE-SILC recruitment, however (only significant in 2006).

Education Level

The MC measures the education level by the highest school leaving certificate and vocational qualification. With regard to the school leaving certificate, the estimated coefficients do not indicate substantial differences in the participation propensity between persons with different certificates. The lack of a school leaving certificate, however, had a negative effect on the propensity with coefficients' estimates remaining under approximately −0.5 in every year between 2005 and 2009. In contrast to the recruitment stage, the estimates for lack of a school leaving certificate in the access panel do not reveal a stable pattern. The estimates for vocational qualification indicate reluctance to enter the AP on the part of persons with an apprenticeship, a vocational qualification or no qualification at all. The coefficients for apprenticeship and vocational qualification vary strongly over the years, showing two shifts in 2005 and 2009, at least partly due to the larger standard errors of the coefficients' estimators. As in the case of school leaving certificates, the coefficients for the DE-SILC nonresponse do not show any clear pattern over time.

Citizenship

An important factor in both recruitment success and DE-SILC nonresponse appears to be a person's migration history. Non-German citizens are more reluctant to participate at both stages. A possible explanation may be that language problems make participation in surveys more difficult for persons with a migrant background.

Recruitment Quarter

The model for recruitment success included a recruitment-specific term not present in the DE-SILC response model: the quarter year of the MC interview. This term refers to the field organization of the MC (Afentakis & Bihler, 2005). As the fieldwork of the MC is organized in a rolling annual scheme, each household is allocated to a fieldwork quarter. Here households recruited in the first quarter of the year were more likely to participate in the AP than later in the year and the last quarter appears to have the lowest success rate (1.5 times less likely). Such behavior would be compatible with an incentive for each agency to recruit a fixed number of AP members. Once the limit is reached, there would no longer be a gain for the interviewer for investing in recruitment effort. However, the federal statistical agency denied the existence of such rules.

Duration of Stay in AP

Households with longer duration in the AP are expected to be more responsive to survey requests, not least because unwilling households would have dropped out of the panel. The duration in the AP is indeed highly significant and indicates a higher response propensity for 'older' households. However, further analysis indicates that the higher propensity can be attributed to the experimental cohort of the AP, recruited in 2001, that has been in the AP for four years before the first recruitment. As the share of those households in the DE-SILC sample declined and disappeared completely in 2009, the coefficient for length of stay was no longer significant.

20.4 SUMMARY

The use of an AP recruited from a mandatory general purpose survey can effectively reduce the costs due to nonresponse, especially when the survey is based on face-to-face interviews. On the other hand, the maintenance of the AP has to be counted against this cost reduction. In the case of DE-SILC, with an entirely postal mode, the gains from lower nonresponse will be moderate.

For a probability sample resulting from the AP, sufficient control of the selection process is needed. It is not enough to control the resulting sample, here the German subsample of EU-SILC, by stratification with respect to the profile variables. There are some indications that fieldwork related variables, the so-called paradata, play a crucial part in the recruitment process and to a lesser extent in the response rate to the voluntary survey after the recruitment. This information was partly not available for our analysis. Most of our analytical difficulties were due to the fact that legal restrictions prevented us from linking the master sample, the AP and the resulting surveys. As the German MC law is updated every four years, the AP screening question could be included in the list of MC questions.

The inclusion of a participation indicator in the MC would not only allow the analysis of the full set of MC cross-sectional variables: the longitudinal structure of the MC would also allow the linkage of four panel waves; see, for example, Basic and Rendtel (2007) or Schimpl-Neimanns (2008). Apart from a better understanding of the recruitment and nonresponse processes, this would enrich the AP by allowing specialized surveys that can use stratification defined by changes of characteristics over time, e.g. income increases or decreases.

Finally, we found evidence for the fact that low-income households and households with older persons (75+) or immigrants are more difficult to recruit. Further, missing income is a strong indicator for reduced cooperation. Other classical survey variables, like marital status, level of education and gender, seem to be of less importance, with the exception of the lack of a vocational training degree.

In the next chapter, Enderle and Münnich simulate the effect on population estimates of a recruitment process that is not well understood. They also investigate whether a standard calibration can be taken as a surrogate of missing control of the recruitment process. They regard the relative bias of population estimates, the precision of these estimates and the coverage rates of confidence intervals (see also Enderle, Münnich, & Bruch, 2013).

ACKNOWLEDGEMENTS

We were supported by a DFG RE 1445/6–2 research grant as a part of the Priority Programme 1292 'Survey Methodology'. We thank the Research Data Centre of the Federal Statistical Office (Statistisches Bundesamt) for providing access to the data.

NOTES

1. An additional problem was that Destatis regarded cells with frequency counts below three as too sensitive for publication. However, in this case the table is only an intermediate step, while the final output is the estimated coefficients.
2. Bremen, Mecklenburg-Vorpommern and Saxony-Anhalt.

BIBLIOGRAPHY

Afentakis, A., & Bihler, W. (2005). Das Hochrechnungsverfahren beim unterjaehrigen Mikrozensus ab 2005. *Wirtschaft und Statistik, 10/2005*, 1039–1048.

Amarov, B., & Rendtel, U. (2013). The recruitment of the access panel of German Official Statistics from a large survey. *Survey Research Methods, 7*, 103–114.

Basic, E., & Rendtel, U. (2007). Assessing the bias due to non-coverage of residential movers in the German Microcensus Panel: An evaluation using data from the Socio-Economic Panel. *Advances in Statistical Analysis, 91*, 311–334.

Bethlehem, J. G. (1988). Reduction of the nonresponse bias through regression estimation. *Journal of Official Statistics, 4*, 251–260.

Destatis. (2009). *Ergebnisse der Interviewerbefragung im Mikrozensus.* Wiesbaden: Statistisches Bundesamt.

Enderle, T., Münnich, R., & Bruch, C. (2013). On the impact of response patterns on survey estimates from access panels. *Survey Research Methods, 7,* 91–101.

Firth, D. (1993). Bias reduction of Maximum Likelihood Estimates. *Biometrika, 80,* 27–38.

Groves, R. M. (2006). Nonresponse rates and nonresponse bias in household surveys. *Public Opinion Quarterly, 70*(5), 646–675.

Horneffer, B., & Kuchler, B. (2008). Drei Jahre Panelerhebung EU-SILC. Erfahrungen und methodische Weiterentwicklungen. *Wirtschaft und Statistik, 8/2008,* 650–661.

Körner, T., & Nimmergut, A. (2004). Using an access panel as a sampling frame for voluntary household surveys. *Statistical Journal of the United Nations Economic Commission for Europe, 21,* 33–52.

Körner, T., Nimmergut, A., Nökel, J., & Rohloff, S. (2006). Die Dauerstichprobe befragungsbereiter Haushalte. *Wirtschaft und Statistik, 5/2006,* 451–467.

Kroh, M. (2011). *Documentation of sample sites and panel attrition in the German Socio Economic Panel (SOEP) (1984 until 2010).* Data Documentation, 59, DIW Berlin, German Institute for Economic Research.

Rendtel, U. (1995). *Lebenslagen im Wandel: Panelausfaelle und Panelrepraesentativitaet.* Frankfurt am Main: Campus Verlag.

Schimpl-Neimanns, B. (2008). Bildungsverlaufe und Stichprobenselektivitaet. Analysen zur Stichprobenselektivitaet des Mikrozensuspanels 1996–1999 am Beispiel bildungsstatistischer Fragestellungen. *GESIS-Forschungsberichte, Reihe Sozialwissenschaftliche Daten, Bd. 1.*

Schneekloth, U., & Leven, I. (2003). Woran bemisst sich eine "gute" allgemeine Bevoelkerungsumfrage? Analysen zu Ausmass, Bedeutung und zu den Hintergruenden von Nonresponse in zufallsbasierten Stichprobenerhebungen am Beispiel des ALLBUS. *ZUMA-Nachrichten, 53,* 16–57.

21

Accuracy of Estimates in Access Panel Based Surveys

Tobias Enderle and Ralf Münnich

21.1 INTRODUCTION

In empirical applications, researchers and data analysts often use standard statistical models which are implemented in software packages. In practice, however, data generally come from complex surveys which increases the need to incorporate weights in the estimation. This becomes essentially difficult when access panels are used for estimation, since several sources and stages of weighting have to be considered. The major problem is that classical estimation methods using survey weights may though consider an appropriate bias correction but the inference, in general, is still not met correctly due to the complexity of the sampling design and the response behavior. This is especially the case when standard software routines are used.

In the present chapter, we focus on the German access panel as a source for the German Statistics on Income and Living Conditions (DE-SILC). In the first part, we introduce some classical well-known concepts of estimation using survey weights. The focus will be laid on the special type of estimation for the access panel. The second part focuses on the evaluation of the methodology including inferences using a simulation study in a close-to-reality framework. This evaluation is two-fold. First, we present how essential it may become to consider the correct response propensities in different estimation methods. Second, we show how regression estimation methods may fail in inference even if the correct response propensities and survey weights have been considered. To our knowledge, this failing is present in almost all software packages. In order to overcome this problem, we use a design-based regression approach on the given access panel design. Further, we introduce a specialized design-based Monte Carlo bootstrap in order to derive correct inferences for survey estimates.

21.2 ESTIMATION USING ACCESS PANELS

Totals and Indicators

Point Estimates

Survey estimates become important when estimating population totals such as total income, counts or indicator values. The total estimate $\hat{\tau}$ of y, the variable of interest, is the weighted sum of all individual values over the sample S with design weights w_i:

$$\hat{\tau}_{y,\mathrm{HT}} = \sum_{i \in S} w_i \cdot y_i. \qquad (21.1)$$

This unbiased estimator of the general population value is called the Horvitz-Thompson (HT) estimator, named after the authors Horvitz and Thompson (1952). A more efficient estimator is the generalized regression estimator (GREG estimator), that is the HT augmented by some g-weights (Deville & Särndal, 1992)

$$\hat{\tau}_{y,\mathrm{GREG}} = \sum_{i \in S} w_i \cdot g_i \cdot y_i. \qquad (21.2)$$

The GREG estimator additionally calibrates the sample to the marginal totals of some auxiliary variables in a linear regression model. Typical auxiliary variables are demographics that are available for the general population. Särndal, Swensson, and Wretman (1992) provide a formal derivation of these g-weights.

The estimates of interest will be simple total estimates and Laeken indicators $\hat{I}$ such as inequality measures (like the GINI coefficient) and poverty measures (like the At-Risk-of-Poverty-Rate, ARPR).

Accuracy Estimation Using Resampling

Complex sample designs suffer from the fact that direct variance estimation methods must incorporate every source of randomness. Enderle, Münnich, and Bruch (2013) conclude that in such situations it is recommendable to use resampling methods. Further, direct or approximative estimators that do not account for complex survey weights which cover different kinds of survey features perform poorly (Lee & Valliant, 2009). Within the present chapter we use a simple Monte Carlo Bootstrap (MCB) routine which had the best performance in an earlier simulation (Enderle et al., 2013). The MCB draws subsamples from a given (survey) sample of the original sample size n with replacement. At each replication the MCB computes an estimate $\hat{\theta}^*$ (e.g., a total estimate, an indicator or regression coefficient). The variation of these estimates provides the basis for the MCB which is finally computed as

$$\hat{V}_{\text{MCB}}(\hat{\theta}) = \frac{1}{B-1} \sum_{i=1}^{B} (\hat{\theta}_{n,i}^* - \frac{1}{B} \sum_{j=1}^{B} \hat{\theta}_{n,i}^*)^2 \qquad (21.3)$$

where we have chosen $B = 499$ replications (Münnich, 2008; Bruch, Münnich, & Zins, 2011). An introduction to variance estimation is given by Wolter (1985) and Shao and Tu (1995).

Regression Using Weights

A well-known regression equation, used in many econometrical, socio-logical and statistical introductory text books (e.g., in Wooldridge, 2008), is regressing a monetary variable y on a set of k demographic variables $(x_1, \ldots, x_k)$

$$\log(\text{wage}) = \beta_0 + \beta_1 \text{ female} + \cdots + \beta_k \text{ age} + u \qquad u \sim N(0,1) \qquad (21.4)$$

where β_0 is the intercept and $\beta_1, \ldots, \beta_k$ are the regression slopes of the independent variables. Taking the natural logarithm of the dependent variable leads to a log-level model. Thus, the coefficients will have a multiplicative interpretation.

Significance of estimates of regression coefficients is a desired result. Most standard routines like ordinary least squares or logistic regression in R, SAS, Stata or SPSS yield p-values for the regression parameters. It is the smallest α-level where the null hypothesis, that the parameter is zero and has no effect (i.e., H_0: $\beta = 0$) can still be rejected. Hence, the smaller the p-value, the higher the level of significance of the parameter estimate. An analyst typically chooses significance levels α of 0.1, 1 or 5%.

Survey regression estimates will also benefit from using weights. Researchers tend to use already implemented weighting options in statistical software packages for convenience. However, Lumley (2010) points out that these packages often assume precision (i.e., used for heteroscedasticity reasons) or frequency weights rather than sampling weights. Since point estimates normally will not be affected by such applications, biased standard errors are the consequence. Thus, the whole inference can be incorrect. Therefore, we will run regressions using such an approach and compare it with a more appropriate weighting technique that computes design-based standard errors. However, both methods compute point estimates in the same way.

Weighted Least Squares (WLS)

A method for ordinary least squares (OLS) that incorporates precision weights is the WLS approach. Whereas OLS makes the sum of squared residuals $\sum_{i \in S} (y_i - \hat{y}_i)^2$ as small as possible by varying the coefficients $\beta_1, \ldots, \beta_k$ the weighted least squares estimator minimizes

$$\sum_{i \in S} (y_i - \hat{y}_i)^2 / h_i = \sum_{i \in S} (y_i^* - \hat{y}_i^*)^2, \tag{21.5}$$

where $\hat{y}_i$ are the fitted values of y_i, h_i a transformation function and y_i^* the transformed variables. Since both estimators have the same functional form, the interpretation of the estimates, standard errors and tests can be done in the same way. Typically, WLS is used to correct for homoscedasticity violations in the errors. More weight is given to observations with less error variance (i.e., $h_i = \sigma_i^2$ the variance of observation y_i). OLS is a special case if all observations have the same weight.

A possible approach in empirical work is to replace the precision weights by survey weights $h_i = w_i^{-1}$. That means, more weight will be given to underrepresented observations and vice versa.

Design-Based Approach

The design-based approach of Lumley (2010) fits a general linear model to the sample data with inverse-probability weighting. The method is available in the package 'survey' for the statistical software R. The function *svyglm()* estimates identical point estimates of regression slopes but differs in the computation of standard errors which are design-based. Since model-based standard errors force the need for a correct specification of the random part of the model, the design-based approach is valid regardless of the model. However, the design must be configured according to the survey (e.g., clustered or stratified) and can be passed to the function via the argument list.

Survey Estimation and Weights

The idea behind sampling weights is to reduce biases due to e.g., design or response propensities of the survey estimates. Each drawn unit will be weighted with its inverse inclusion probability π_i. The weight for unit i is

$$w_i = \frac{1}{\pi_i}. \tag{21.6}$$

Complex surveys need multiple weights which must be considered when computing design-based inference. In the case of DE-SILC there are several sampling stages that must be covered using the following probabilities:

- $\pi_{i,\text{MC}}$ Microcensus sample probability (1%),
- $\pi_{i,\text{AP}}$ participation in the Access Panel (AP),
- $\pi_{i,\text{PA}}$ continuation in the AP (i.e., panel attrition),
- $\pi_{i,\text{RS}}$ DE-SILC sample probability (i.e., stratified random sample) and
- ϕ_i participation in DE-SILC.

First, participating households must be selected for the 1%, probabilistic-based sample of the German population. This sample is called the Microcensus (MC). At the recruitment stage, they are asked to participate in the AP. The resulting self-selection can be modeled using logistic regression resulting in response propensities. In the AP, households are able to exit the AP for several reasons (e.g., leaving of own accord, no contact after residential mobility or are unreachable). Staying in the panel enables being sampled for the survey (e.g., resulting in DE-SILC sample probabilities). Finally, there is the probability of responding. Thus, the individual weight for household i in DE-SILC is

$$w_{i,\text{D-SILC}} = \frac{1}{\pi_{i,\text{MC}} \cdot \pi_{i,\text{AP}} \cdot \pi_{i,\text{PA}} \cdot \pi_{i,\text{RS}} \cdot \phi_i}. \tag{21.7}$$

21.3 SIMULATION

Motivation and Setup

Theoretical results, in general, help to set up estimators correctly. A comparative evaluation of these estimators, however, may be performed for very specific cases which may considerably lack in practical interest. Hence, we aim at comparing the estimators and strategies in a close-to-reality framework applying a large-scale Monte Carlo simulation study that allows us to give advice on possible drawbacks in applications. With the help of a proper simulation study, we can derive proxies of small sample size properties. The simulation study in the present chapter tries to generate distributions of estimates in moderate sample sizes which allow us to understand how to apply a method and which methods yield better performances.

These sample sizes were chosen in accordance with the settings in the AP. Since the real population values in real (survey) data are unknown, we run a simulation study using synthetic data. This enables a wide range of applicable sample designs and accuracy measurement methods with known population values and distributions. The main emphasis is on the importance of using weights in general and, in particular, response propensities. We compare different methods using appropriate and inadequate weighting techniques with methods that ignore survey weights. Then we evaluate their performance by using a response propensity model that most realistically covers the self-selection process.

The master sample of the simulation study is a synthetic dataset on household level. It is generated close to the procedure outlined in Münnich, Gabler, Ganninger, Burgard, and Kolb (2012) but with several modifications in order to define the $N_{\text{population}} \approx 40$ million households. The set of variables is limited to the key variables listed in the access panel database (such as demographic variables) augmented by some income variables (e.g., equivalent disposable income, EDI). At the first sampling stage we draw the MC sample as described in Meyer (1994). The computation of the design and calibration weights is done close to the procedure described by Afentakis and Bihler (2005). The second sampling stage is the recruitment of volunteer access panel members. The implementation of the dropout using Logit models is based on the empirical findings in Amarov and Rendtel (2013). Finally, the last sampling stage is conducted nearly as proposed in the original design of DE-SILC described in Körner, Nimmergut, Nökel, and Rohloff (2006) and Horneffer and Kuchler (2008). The size of the cross-sectional sample is $n = 14{,}000$ households.

To make the simulation study more feasible we abstract from an implementation of unit nonresponse at DE-SILC; i.e., ($\phi = 1$). Since the evaluation is cross-sectional, there is no panel attrition (i.e., $\pi_{i,PA} = 1$). Hence, equation (21.7) reduces to

$$w_{i,\text{D-SILC}} = \frac{1}{\pi_{i,\text{MC}} \cdot \pi_{i,\text{AP}} \cdot \pi_{i,\text{RS}}}. \tag{21.8}$$

Total and Indicator Estimates

Enderle et al. (2013) compares different classes of estimation strategies to compute point estimates of totals or Laeken indicators within DE-SILC. A first strategy intends to directly gross up the sample to the population of interest using design and calibration weights. Another strategy additionally estimates response propensities in order to model the self-selection process and include them as sampling weights. In the present simulation study, we make the inference for the German population. Hence, we establish adjusted versions of the two strategies which performed best.

- Strategy A is a standard approach that uses calibration and design weights as follows

$$\hat{w}_{i,\text{D-SILC}}^{(A)} = \frac{1}{\hat{\pi}_{i,\text{MC}} \times \hat{\pi}_{i,\text{RS}}}, \tag{21.9}$$

where the stratification weights $\hat{\pi}_{i,\text{RS}} = n_h/N_{h,\text{MC}}$ refer to the stratum $h = 1, \ldots, H$ and, hence, are constant within each stratum.

- Alternatively, in Strategy B the response propensity scores can be estimated and included as weights, $\hat{\pi}_{i,\text{AP}}$, to correct for the self-selection bias. The weights read as follows

$$\hat{w}_{i,\text{D-SILC}}^{(B)} = \frac{1}{\hat{\pi}_{i,\text{MC}} \times \hat{\pi}_{i,\text{AP}} \times \hat{\pi}_{i,\text{RS}}} \tag{21.10}$$

Hence, the stratification weights refer this time to the strata cells of the access panel (i.e., $N_{i,AP}$).

Further, both strategies, A and B, will be augmented by a composite calibration weight $\hat{g}_{i,\text{D-SILC}} = g_{i,\text{Pop}} \times g_{i,\text{MC}}$. The calibration weight $g_{i,\text{Pop}}$ adjusts the MC to the population and $g_{i,\text{MC}}$ calibrates the sample DE-SILC to the Microcensus.

Point Estimates

The estimation of response propensities and their use as an additional weight factor to correct for a selection bias is an important task. For the evaluation we estimated point estimates using the equivalized disposable income variable: the total (TOT) and the three Laeken indicators GINI coefficient, quintile-share-ratio (QSR) and at-risk-of-poverty-rate (ARPR). Whereas strategy A produces a bias in each case, strategy B performs pretty well. Strategy A has an average relative underestimation (negative bias) of about 3% for the GINI and 12% for the QSR and an overestimation (positive bias) of about 1% for the TOT and 2% for the ARPR. On average, strategy B produces only a negative bias for the GINI of about 1% and for the QSR of about 2%. The TOT and ARPR appear unbiased. Strategy B relies on an estimation of propensity weights and, hence, has a larger variance (Enderle et al., 2013).[1]

A comparison of the mean squared errors (MSE) justifies the general preference for strategy B which has a smaller value for two out of four statistics. In detail,

$$\overline{MSE}(\hat{\theta}_{TOT,A}) = 2.30 \times 10^{18} < 4.54 \times 10^{18} = \overline{MSE}(\hat{\theta}_{TOT,B})$$
$$\overline{MSE}(\hat{\theta}_{GINI,A}) = 1.85 > 1.34 = \overline{MSE}(\hat{\theta}_{GINI,B}) \quad\quad (21.11)$$
$$\overline{MSE}(\hat{\theta}_{QSR,A}) = 2.01 > 0.60 = \overline{MSE}(\hat{\theta}_{QSR,B})$$
$$\overline{MSE}(\hat{\theta}_{ARPR,A}) = 0.34 < 0.55 = \overline{MSE}(\hat{\theta}_{ARPR,B}).$$

These simulation results imply that $\overline{MSE}(\hat{\theta}_A) > \overline{MSE}(\hat{\theta}_B)$ does not hold in general. However, strategy B is preferable even for the TOT and ARPR estimators due to its unbiasedness even at the expense of a higher variance.

Variance Estimates

The MCB routine can be applied at different stages of the sampling process of DE-SILC. A first approach (BootDSILC) is a stratified bootstrap that resamples already sampled households in DE-SILC. Figure 21.1 (upper) shows the estimated variances of total income in box-plots. The benchmarks (vertical lines) are the Monte Carlo variances estimated out of 10,000 replicated point estimates. A reference case is given in the upper cell, TOT.BootDSILC (MCAR), where recruitment is conducted completely at random (i.e., no self-selection). The bootstrap routine yields unbiased variances as it does in Enderle et al. (2013). However, within the present simulation study (see TOT.BootDSILC), the approach yields an inherent (negative) bias in the case of strategy B.

Variance estimation should cover each random process of a multistage sampling procedure. Since this procedure may not cover the whole variation of the self-selection process, due to an informative selection (Pfeffermann & Sverchkov, 2007) caused by an interaction of the recruitment

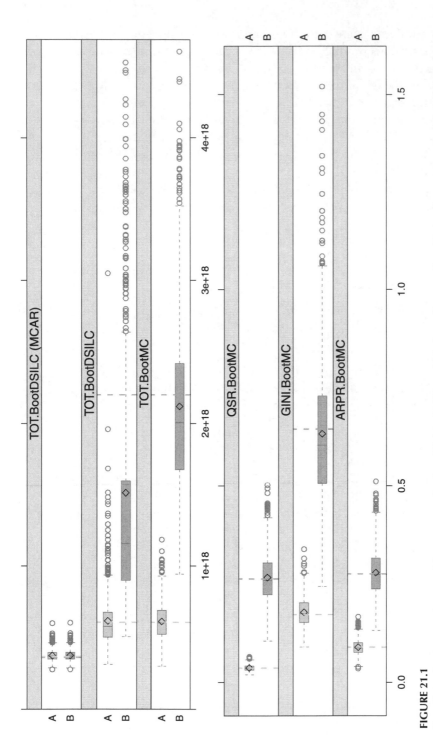

FIGURE 21.1

Box-plots of variance estimates of the two strategies A and B (vertical line within box-plot = median, diamond = mean, vertical dotted line = benchmark). Upper: Variance estimates of the totals using both bootstrap approaches: application at D-SILC (BootDSILC) and at the MC (BootMC). In the upper graph we illustrate the BootDSILC approach in case of a self-selection process that is completely at random. Lower: Variance estimates of the three Laeken indicators using the BootMC approach that yields better estimates.

stage and the stratification, we implement a further approach. This second approach (BootMC) additionally accounts for the variation when bootstrapping on the sampled households in the MC (i.e., the approach resamples units from the MC that will not be in the final sample). The lower cell, TOT.Boot.MC, shows that we can correct for the bias. This also holds for the variances of the Laeken indicators in Figure 21.1 (lower).

Regression Estimates

The regression model on a log-level relationship in our simulation is

$$\log(income) = \beta_0 + \beta_1 \, female + \beta_2 \, foreign + \beta_3 \, age$$
$$+ \beta_4 \, ilo2 + \beta_5 \, ilo3 + \beta_6 \, ilo4$$
$$+ \beta_7 \, edu2 + \beta_8 \, edu3 + \beta_9 \, edu4 + \beta_{10} \, edu5$$
$$+ \beta_{11} \, edu50 + \beta_{12} \, edu90 + u \qquad (21.12)$$

where income is the monthly income, female and foreign are binary variables and age a rescaled (i.e., age minus 16) continuous variable. Furthermore, there are two variables that are included using dummies for their multiple categories. Ilo is the employment status defined by the International Labour Office (ILO) and edu is education. The categories of these variables read as follows:

ilo (employment status)

1 employed
2 unemployed
3 inactive
4 inactive + retirement pension or other support

edu (education)

1 secondary
2 secondary (in former East Germany)
3 secondary (general certificate; completion of 10th grade)
4 secondary (granting access to advanced technical college)
5 higher
50 unknown
90 not available

When estimating the income model in equation (21.12) using the synthetic data as general population, we obtain

$$\widehat{\log(income)} = \frac{6.3052}{(0.0006)} - \frac{0.4368}{(0.0004)} female - \frac{0.2334}{(0.0012)} foreign + \frac{0.0298}{(0.0000)} age$$

$$- \frac{1.1519}{(0.0010)} ilo2 - \frac{0.7896}{(0.0017)} ilo3 - \frac{1.5604}{(0.0006)} ilo4$$

$$+ \frac{0.0312}{(0.0008)} edu2 + \frac{0.2322}{(0.0006)} edu3 + \frac{0.3353}{(0.0009)} edu4 \quad (21.13)$$

$$+ \frac{0.4863}{(0.0006)} edu5 - \frac{1.0281}{(0.0021)} edu50 - \frac{0.8436}{(0.0010)} edu90$$

$$n = N \approx 40,000,000, \ R^2 = 0.4836, \ \overline{R}^2 = 0.4836,$$

where the standard errors of the coefficients are shown in parentheses. Henceforth, the coefficient estimates in equation (21.13) will be defined as true population parameters and serve as benchmarks for the simulation study. Then, the regression model is also applied to DE-SILC using different estimation techniques (i.e., WLS and the design-based approach) as well as both strategies, A and B. Table 21.1 shows the averaged results over

TABLE 21.1

Averaged regression estimates using different estimation techniques (WLS and design-based approach) as well as both strategies (A and B)

| | | | OLS | | Grossing up (A) | | | Propensity weighting (B) | | |
| | | | | | | WLS | des.-b. | | WLS | des.-b. |
		$\overline{\hat{\beta}}$	$\widehat{s.e.}$	$\overline{\hat{\beta}}$	$\widehat{s.e.}$	$\widehat{s.e.}$	$\overline{\hat{\beta}}$	$\widehat{s.e.}$	$\widehat{s.e.}$
intercept		6.5802	0.0176	6.5580	0.0181	0.0274	6.3342	0.0228	0.0896
female		−0.3303	0.0114	−0.3140	0.0118	0.0153	−0.4278	0.0151	0.0527
foreign		−0.2669	0.0639	−0.2311	0.0344	0.0907	−0.4429	0.0444	0.1758
age		0.0184	0.0005	0.0186	0.0005	0.0009	0.0284	0.0006	0.0032
employment	2	−1.2082	0.0493	−1.2478	0.0463	0.1175	−1.1534	0.0403	0.1951
	3	−0.8017	0.0847	−0.8190	0.0778	0.1555	−0.7898	0.0687	0.2330
	4	−1.1144	0.0203	−1.1471	0.0203	0.0475	−1.4869	0.0212	0.1253
education	2	0.0378	0.0197	0.0295	0.0216	0.0250	0.0297	0.0301	0.0689
	3	0.2267	0.0144	0.2299	0.0151	0.0188	0.2312	0.0204	0.0621
	4	0.3444	0.0261	0.3381	0.0280	0.0366	0.3448	0.0318	0.0830
	5	0.5138	0.0150	0.5204	0.0159	0.0197	0.4944	0.0207	0.0625
	50	−1.0172	0.1699	−1.0413	0.1723	0.5133	−1.0323	0.1038	0.5495
	90	−0.8743	0.0526	−0.8760	0.0494	0.1212	−0.8297	0.0419	0.2248

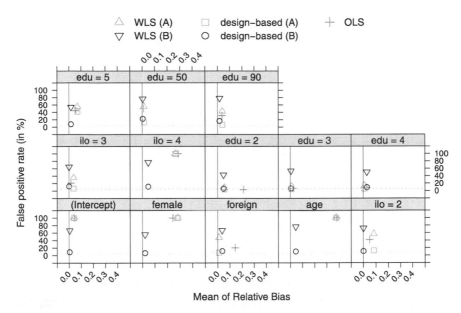

FIGURE 21.2

Comparison of the regression coefficients when running R = 1,000 simulations using different weighting and estimation methods. The abscissa depicts the mean of the relative bias and the ordinate the type I error rate (in %). The rate displays how often true null hypothesis H_0 in equation (21.18) is rejected using a significance level of $\alpha = 0.05$.

$R = 1000$ simulation runs. As mentioned above, both techniques yield the same coefficient estimates but differ in the computation of their estimated standard errors.

Whereas, once again, grossing up to the population of interest without propensity weighting (strategy A) results in biased point estimates, the propensity approach (strategy B) yields good beta estimates. The abscissa of Figure 21.2 shows the mean of the relative bias of point estimates for the regression parameters. On average, strategy B has the smallest biases and, hence, is superior for the vast majority of the coefficients.[2]

For log-level models, the change in income for a one unit increase of continuous independent variable (e.g., age) is

$$\%\Delta\text{income} \approx (100 \times \hat{\beta}_3)\,\Delta\text{age}. \tag{21.14}$$

From using equation (21.13),

$$\%\Delta\text{income} \approx (100 \times 0.0298)\,\Delta\text{age} = 2.98\,\Delta\text{age} \tag{21.15}$$

follows that getting one year older increases income by about 2.98%. In case of qualitative or binary information (i.e., dummy variables), the exact difference in percentage in income between, for example, females versus males, holding other factors fixed, is

$$100 \times [exp(\hat{\beta}_1) - 1] \tag{21.16}$$

Once again, using equation (21.13), the proportionate difference is

$$100 \times [exp(-0.4368) - 1] = -35.39. \tag{21.17}$$

The estimate implies that a woman's income is, on average, 35% below a comparable man's income.[3] This explains the popularity of log-level models in empirical research.

Researchers tend to confirm such findings using hypothesis tests. Since $H_0 : \beta = 0$ is not feasible in the evaluation and the general population parameters are known, we are able to state the null hypothesis that the estimated regression parameter equals the true coefficient versus a two-tailed alternative. This is,

$$H_0 : \hat{\beta} = \beta \text{ versus } H_a : \hat{\beta} \neq \beta \tag{21.18}$$

where $\hat{\beta}$ is the estimate of the true regression parameter β. The latter is also an estimate when running the regression on the synthetically generated general population as described above.

The null hypothesis (two-tailed) has to be rejected if

$$c = t_{\frac{\alpha}{2}, n-(k+1)} < |T| = \left| \frac{\hat{\beta} - \beta}{\hat{\sigma}_\beta} \right| \tag{21.19}$$

where T is the test statistic and the critical values are t-distributed with $n - (k + 1)$ degrees of freedom. Typically we choose the alternative hypothesis H_α only if the chance of making the wrong choice is small, say below 5%. Thus, p-values of .05 or smaller lead us to conclude H_α.

The ordinate of Figure 21.2 depicts the type I error, resulting when the test rejects the true null hypothesis. The significance level α of the tests is 5%. Since α equals the probability of an error of the first kind, the horizontal dotted line in Figure 21.2 is chosen as benchmark.

Weighted Least Squares

The tests using the standard errors of the weighted least squares (WLS) approach generally cause too high type I error rates. Even the unweighted approach (OLS) reduces the rate and is preferable to the weighting method for some coefficients (in the case of strategy A as well as B).

Design-Based Approach

In general, the design-based standard errors perform much better. Using propensity weighting (i.e., the preferred and more appropriate strategy B) often has a smaller rate than the alternative strategy A. It is important to mention that we run the regression applying solely a stratified sampling design. To estimate more precisely, we should incorporate the entire design of DE-SILC. Strictly speaking, the procedure can be more sophisticated in order to improve performance. However, even assuming a simple stratified design yields good standard errors and good type I error rates.

21.4 SUMMARY

The present research on estimation from surveys in the context of the German Access Panel has produced two different findings. First, a proper weighting including survey design and response propensities is essential to foster (approximately) unbiased estimates for classical total estimates and complex indicator estimates, as well as regression coefficient estimates in statistical modeling. Drawing inferences from classical survey estimates is well known to be appropriate in the design context. However, one has to be especially careful in drawing correct inferences for regression coefficients in this context. A bootstrap variance estimator for population totals helped to correctly include the additional sources from randomness in access panels using complex survey designs. The bootstrap could be a further design-based approach that provides correct inference in regression analysis.

ACKNOWLEDGEMENTS

An earlier draft of the recent paper was presented at the second International Conference on 'Advancing Survey Methods' in Bremen in 2011.

The research of the present paper was done within the Priority Programme 1292 on Survey Methodology (cf. www.survey-methodology.de) of the German Research Foundation (DFG). Special thanks go to our colleagues from the Economic and Social Statistics department for lively discussions which furnished improvements of the evaluation.

NOTES

1. For further reading, we added density plots to the internet appendix.
2. A further overview of the relative bias is given in the internet appendix.
3. The huge difference in income can be explained by the underlying synthetic universe and definition of the head of the household. The dataset we used is on a household level where the head is the member with the highest income. Hence, the representativeness of the estimate is not valid on the personal level.

REFERENCES

Afentakis, A., & Bihler, W. (2005). Das Hochrechnungsverfahren beim unterjaehrigen Mikrozensus ab 2005. *Wirtschaft und Statistik, 10,* 1039–1048. Retrieved from www.destatis.de/

Amarov, B., & Rendtel U. (2013). The recruitment of the access panel of German Official Statistics from a large survey in 2006: Empirical results and methodological aspects. *Survey Research Methods, 7*(2), 103–114.

Bruch, C., Münnich, R., & Zins, S. (2011). *Variance estimation for complex surveys* (Research Project Report No. WP3—D3.1). FP7-SSH-2007-217322 AMELI. Retrieved from http://ameli.surveystatistics.net

Deville, J. C., & Särndal, C.-E. (1992). Calibration estimators in survey sampling. *Journal of the American Statistical Association, 87,* 376–382.

Enderle, T., Münnich, R., & Bruch, C. (2013). On the impact of response propensities on access panel based estimates. *Survey Research Methods, 7*(2), 91–101.

Horneffer, B., & Kuchler, B. (2008). Drei Jahre Panelerhebung EU-SILC: Erfahrungen und methodische Weiterentwicklungen. *Wirtschaft und Statistik, 8,* 650–661. Retrieved from www.destatis.de/

Horvitz, D. G., & Thompson, D. J. (1952). A generalization of sampling without replacement from a finite universe. *Journal of the American Statistical Association, 47*(260), 663–685.

Körner, T., Nimmergut, A., Nökel, J., & Rohloff, A. (2006). Die Dauerstichprobe befragungsfreiwilliger Haushalte—Die neue Auswahlgrundlage fuer freiwillige Haushaltsbefragungen. *Wirtschaft und Statistik, 5,* 451–467. Retrieved from www.destatis.de/

Lee, S., & Valliant, R. (2009). Estimation for volunteer panel web surveys using propensity score adjustment and calibration adjustment. *Social Methods & Research, 37,* 319–343.

Lumley, T. (2010). *Complex surveys: A guide to analysis using R.* Hobeken, NJ: Wiley Series in Survey Methodology.

Meyer, K. (1994). Zum Auswahlplan des Mikrozensus ab 1990. In S. Gabler, J. P. Hoffmeyer-Zlotnik, & D. Krebs (Eds.), *Gewichtung in der Umfragepraxis* (pp. 106–111). Opladen, Germany: Westdeutscher Verlag.

Münnich, R. (2008). Varianzschaetzung in komplexen Erhebungen. *Austrian Journal of Statistics, 37*(3&4), 319–334.

Münnich, R., Gabler, S., Ganninger, S., Burgard, J. P., & Kolb, J.-P. (2012). *Stichprobenoptimierung und Schaetzung im Zensus 2011* (Vol. 21). Statistisches Bundesamt, Statistik und Wissenschaft.

Pfeffermann, D., & Sverchkov, M. (2007). Small-area estimation under informative probability sampling of areas and within the selected areas. *Journal of the American Statistical Association, 102*, 1427–1439.

Särndal, C.-E., Swensson, B., & Wretman, J. (1992). *Model assisted survey sampling*. New York, NY: Springer.

Shao, J., & Tu, D. (1995). *The Jackknife and Bootstrap*. New York, NY: Springer Series in Statistics.

Wolter, K. M. (1985). *Introduction to variance estimation*. New York, NY: Springer.

Wooldridge, J. M. (2008). *Introductory econometrics* (4th ed.). Mason, OH: Cengage Learning Emea.

Part VI

Surveys—Expanding the Horizon

22

Combining Surveys with Non-Questionnaire Data

Overview and Introduction

Rainer Schnell

Historically, survey research is quite a recent invention. If random sampling and using the units of statistical interest as the source of information are considered to be the two main ideas of survey research, then this field is more or less only 100 years old.[1] Nowadays the extent of survey research in social sciences has reached a point where data collection without asking the respondent seems to be a rare event, sometimes even considered unethical.

On the other hand, the growing number of surveys seem to have led to uninterested respondents and a widespread public perception of surveys as inconsequential polls. These unintended consequences of the huge success of survey research as a data collection method now produce nonresponse rates that need statistical arguments beyond public understanding to justify the high costs of random sampling. The increasing use of web surveys, not only for market research but also for political polling and even for medical research, shows the erosion in the understanding of the need for random sampling even in academic circles. In the long run, survey sampling for public opinion research based on random samples will be difficult to defend against the fast and cheap alternative of web surveys if no external validation criteria exist. However, this is not true for factual data. If external validation criteria do exist, random sampling and the reduction of measurement error can be defended easily: Nothing else works. At least not repeatedly.

In fields not dedicated to opinion research, we observe an increase in the use of technology to reduce measurement error. Since measurement relies on questions in traditional surveys, an obvious way to reduce measurement error is the reduction of information relying on questions. Chapter 24 in this volume ("Enhancing Surveys with Objective Measurements and Observer Ratings") gives a selective overview of measurement techniques used in survey research which do not rely on questions. The catalogue of these techniques is impressive: From paper-and-pencil diaries to satellite technology, survey researchers have used nearly every technical gadget available for collecting data within surveys. The boom in biological, especially genetic, research has given additional thrust to innovative data collection methods in surveys. By using hard measurement techniques combined with sampling, biosocial surveys may reduce measurement error and misspecification of causal models in the social sciences. For biomedical research, the opportunity to validate observational results from volunteers or patients with subjects from random samples may increase the generalizability of medical research results. Another major impact on survey research is due to ubiquitous computing. Some of the current and future options of these technologies are also discussed in this chapter. However, these data collection options will change the social conditions of fieldwork for surveys in general.

Since data collection in surveys is nowadays nearly always done partially (CATI, CAPI) or completely using computers (web surveys), recording the behavior of interviewers and respondents has become easier. This kind of data is now commonly referred to as "paradata". Frauke Kreuter ("The Use of Paradata," Chapter 25 this volume) gives an overview of the history and recent extension of the word to all data that arise (or can be gathered) during the survey data collection process. She describes three uses of paradata in detail: improving data quality through monitoring and interventions, improving data collection efficiency and improving survey estimates. Kreuter also lists the problems associated with paradata, for example, different units of analysis to the survey data and measurement error. Although paradata seem to come free of charge, in practice, transforming paradata into useful information requires a lot of data processing and analytical knowledge. Using this information in research practice of large organizations might be the true challenge of paradata, since real-time case management in large scale data collection organizations is far from trivial.

Since information on individuals is available in many administrative databases, using this already collected information instead of asking respondents is an attractive alternative to standard survey research. Chapter 23, this volume ("Linking Surveys and Administrative Data"), describes the many options available for this kind of research. The most interesting technological developments here are techniques of privacy pre-serving record linkage: Surveys and administrative data can now be linked without a Personal Identification Number revealing the identity of respon-dents. Using recent developments in computer science, this can even be done using encrypted identifiers, even if these identifiers contain errors. In some countries and some legal systems, this will allow linking survey data with administrative data without the need of consent. Of course, interna-tional review boards and legal constraints will limit this kind of research to special circumstances, but at least the technological problems have been solved. Record linkage centers for social research have started to be estab-lished in Europe (for example, in the UK and Germany) but the routine use of these options will take at least another decade.

All chapters in this section focus on linking survey data with other data sources at the level of individuals. Although the boundaries are blurred, this excludes sources of aggregated data. Some of these data collections are available in the public domain (for example, area pollution data) or can be bought from commercial enterprises (for example, tenancy rates). Most of these databases are aggregated within geographical units, so they can be subsumed under data within Geographic Information Systems (GIS). Depending on the level of aggregation or resolution, GIS data are, unlike the record linkage of social security data, the collection of genetic material within a survey or the recording of key stroke timings without consent, usually not subject to privacy objections. However, since GIS data are usu-ally highly aggregated, the information on individuals is limited.[2]

The common theme of all chapters is the necessary and technologi-cally possible extension of surveys with additional data not collected by asking the respondent. Relying on this data source alone, progress in the social sciences so far has been slower than could have been expected after 100 years of survey research. Using surveys for random sampling and ask-ing for informed consent for linking administrative data, collecting objec-tive measures (including paradata) and ratings might be a better way to collect social science data than continuing with the methods used today for another 100 years.

NOTES

1. Using the two criteria mentioned, the publication of "Livelihood and Poverty" in 1915 by Arthur L. Bowley and Alexander Robert Burnett-Hurst, can be considered as the starting point. For details, see Dale and Kotz (2011).
2. The use of GIS data with surveys has been reviewed recently by Howell and Porter (2010).

REFERENCES

Howell, F. M., & Porter, J. R. (2010). Surveys and Geographic Information Systems. In P. V. Marsden & J. D. Wright (Eds.), *Handbook of survey research* (pp. 681–705). Bingley, UK: Emerald.

Dale, A. I., & Kotz, S. (2011). *Arthur L. Bowley: A pioneer in modern statistics and economics*. New Jersey: World Scientific Publishing.

23

Linking Surveys and Administrative Data

Rainer Schnell

23.1 INTRODUCTION

Surveys can be linked to other surveys and to administrative data. For most social scientists, data referring to individual persons or organizations are of primary importance. Linking such datasets of individual units is called record linkage. Record linkage seeks to identify the same objects in two different databases using a set of common identifiers or unique combinations of variables. Record linkage is sometimes confused with data fusion, in which data of different units are merged to generate synthetic datasets. Furthermore, record linkage is not to be mistaken for augmenting surveys with aggregate data. Record linkage of surveys and administrative data aims to link records of the same unit of analysis (usually persons, sometimes organizations, commercial enterprises or patent applications).

23.2 ADVANTAGES AND DISADVANTAGES OF ADMINISTRATIVE DATA

Linking microlevel data of the same unit across datasets offers many opportunities for research, especially if administrative data can be linked to survey data. Administrative data has unique advantages (Brackstone, 1987; Judson, 2005, 2007; Lane, 2010). For example, administrative data usually covers nearly the complete population, providing a large number of cases even for rare populations. The same feature also allows the computation of small area statistics, which can be used to stabilize estimates from surveys (Lehtonen & Veijanen, 2009). Depending on the kind of administrative data, the data quality may be higher (or lower) than that of survey data. If access to administrative data is granted, the linkage is inexpensive and fast. Given preprocessed data and established procedures, linkage can be done even for census operations within days. Administrative data does not generate an additional respondent burden, it is not derogated by memory errors and rarely suffers from unit nonresponse. However, the use of administrative data has disadvantages (Judson & Popoff, 2005). The most serious disadvantage is the limitation of the number of available variables. Administrative databases usually do not contain subjective variables like attitudes. Furthermore, administrative data is based on administrative concepts, which may differ from research concepts (household definitions are an example). Administrative databases have a time lag of months, sometimes years. Finally, even administrative personal identification numbers may have errors, so linkage might be far from perfect. For example, Judson (2005, p. 440) reports error rates in social security numbers between 5 and 10%. So, linking records, in practice, is far from trivial.

23.3 EXAMPLES FOR LINKING SURVEYS AND ADMINISTRATIVE DATA

The amount of existing information for record linkage is often surprising. However, to become useful for research purposes, it is not unusual that data from many different databases must be extracted, transformed and very often linked across different data holders. Since the use of different databases is not common in social science research, some examples of the use of record linkage with surveys may be helpful.

Generating Sampling Frames

In modern societies, most members of the population are listed in many different administrative databases. Using the databases for the determination of common subsets, record linkage can be used to construct sampling frames for special populations. For example, the research institute of the German Social Security Administration planned a panel study of the low-income population. To study the mechanisms of entering and leaving the welfare population, a sampling frame of people with a high risk of entering the welfare population was needed. The persons had to be sampled before they entered the welfare population. Schnell (2007) suggested a series of record linkage operations, using municipal registries, welfare benefit registries and commercial credit risk databases for sampling frame construction. A simplified version of this design has been used for the resulting panel study PASS, now one of the largest German population surveys.

Under-coverage Estimation for Census Operations

Harper and Mayhew (2012) tried to estimate the census under-coverage for a densely populated inner London borough. By using locally available administrative data (GP register, school census, electoral register, council tax register, council tax and housing benefits, births, deaths, housing waiting list, local land and property gazetteer) they estimated a census under-coverage of 1.7%, with the under-coverage rate varying between age groups.

Deduplication of Samples and Sampling Frames

The Los Angeles Women's Health Risk Study was a survey among street prostitutes in Los Angeles in the early 1990s. One of the goals of the survey was the estimation of the prevalence of HIV infections in this population. The survey used an area-time-sample. The respondents received $25 for their participation. The 998 respondents were asked for self-generated identification codes based on names. Using elaborate record linkage techniques, Belin, Ishwaran, Duan, Berry, and Kanouse (2004) estimated about 14.9% duplicates in the sample. However, they concluded that the main results of the study were not undermined by the presence of duplicates.

Constructing Panels Retrospectively

Linking subjects between independently collected datasets allows the construction of longitudinal datasets long after data collection. A simple example is given by Jacobs, Boulis, and Messikomer (2001). All physicians working in the U.S. are represented in the American Medical Association Physician Masterfile. Every year, one-third of the records are updated with a survey. By using record linkage, Jacobs et al. (2001) built a longitudinal data file of the 1994 and 1998 cohorts with more than 500,000 physicians. This huge file permits the study of a rare event in a rare population: the probability of the change between different specialties within the medical profession.[1] Surprisingly, the probability of a professional change seems to be nearly independent of age.

Linking Panels Over Time with Respondent Generated Codes

In many panel studies on sensitive topics, respondent-generated identification codes are used to link records across surveys because the use of identifiers like social security numbers or names is considered a privacy violation. Therefore, respondent-generated codes are based on stable but not obvious personal characteristics like respondents' mothers' maiden names, the initials of close friends or the names of pets. Since these codes are error prone, usually a substantial number of cases are lost due to the codes. These losses may cause biased estimates. Schnell, Bachteler, and Reiher (2010) suggested the use of record linkage for these kinds of data: By using more components and linking the codes by the Levenshtein string distance function the losses could be reduced. The linking can be done with standard record linkage software. In two field experiments, the proposed procedure outperformed the methods that had previously been applied.

Imputing Missing Survey Responses

Zanutto and Zaslavsky (2002) discussed the use of administrative data as a replacement for missing survey responses. Missing data can be replaced by data or the mean of multiple records from administrative records of the same case. Sometimes, the replacement may be useful only for a subset of cases. Finally, a statistical model based on administrative data might be used for the imputation of missing survey responses.

Validating Responses

An obvious application of record linkage is the validation of responses. Due to the large number of possible sources of response error (Weisberg, 2005), the validity of survey responses is often doubtful. For example, in the practice of survey research, responses to questions on socially undesirable traits or behaviors are often considered more valid when the results show a higher prevalence of undesirable behaviors. This assumption is rarely tested. One exception is the record linkage study of Maxfield, Weiler, and Widom (2000). They compared the responses of 1,196 young adults (mean age 28.7 years) with administrative records on imprisonments. They concluded that 21% of all subjects with no history of arrest reported at least one arrest to the interviewers.

In a recent study Averdijk and Elffers (2012) linked a victimization survey of the city of Amsterdam to the police registry of crimes ($n = 8,887$).

Despite the widespread use of victimization surveys, such validation studies in criminology have been rarely reported during the last 25 years. 48% of the victimizations recorded by the police were not reported in the survey, and 65% of the reported victimizations in the survey could not be found in the police records. For 18% of all respondents, survey and administrative records do not agree.

Checking Anonymity for Scientific Use Files

The demand for social research microdata has increased the number of available Scientific Use Files (SUF). The release of such files depends largely on the degree of anonymity which can be guaranteed to the respondents, therefore methods for an empirical disclosure risk assessment are needed. An obvious candidate for such a method is record linkage. Using the percentage of correctly linked record pairs between an SUF and a publicly available dataset as a measure for disclosure risk, Domingo-Ferrer and Torra (2003) demonstrated that record linkage for re-identification by cluster analysis of highly correlated variables does not require necessarily shared variables between the publicly available dataset and an SUF. A similar approach was published slightly earlier by Bacher, Brand, and Bender (2002) for a German survey.

23.4 TECHNICAL PROBLEMS AND SOLUTIONS

From a technical point of view, linking with a universally available unique personal identification number (PID) is ideal. In countries with universal and available national PIDs (for example, in Europe: Belgium, Denmark, Finland, Norway, Sweden) they cover the whole population. Under such conditions, linking different databases is technically trivial. But these conditions exist in only very few countries. In practice, in most countries and for most linkage operations other identifiers have to be used. Most commonly, these are personal identifiers like name, date of birth or address. These identifiers have many disadvantages. They are not unique, therefore they must be used in combination. They are not stable, since persons change their names, place of residence and sometimes even their sex. Finally, many identifiers are recorded with errors. If the linkage is done on identical identifiers only, many actual matches will be missed. For example, Winkler (2009, p. 362) reports that 25% of true matches in a census operation would have been missed by exact matching. In one region, 25% of the first names and 15% of the last names did not match perfectly.

Linkage with Imperfect Identifiers

If linkage has to be done with imperfect identifiers like names, things get a bit more complicated. In a first step, the identifiers have to be standardized. This step includes the conversion to the same code table used for representing characters, removing titles and punctuation, transforming to uppercase, removing umlauts, replacing nicknames and so on. This preprocessing step cannot be done automatically and is therefore always more tedious and lasts longer than expected by beginners.

Then a measure of similarity between names (strings) is needed. There are many different string similarity measures, but in many record linkage studies, the Jaro-Winkler (Winkler, 1995) string similarity measure has shown superior performance. For example, Schnell, Bachteler, and Bender (2003) reported an increase of correctly linked pairs from 3.0% with exact matching to 32.1% with Jaro-Winkler.

Then the measures of similarity of different identifiers have to be combined to make the decision if a potential pair should be considered a match. Even today social scientists sometimes simply sum up the similarity scores and decide ad hoc on a similarity threshold. This is a suboptimal procedure since different identifiers should have different weights in deciding the match status. There are formal methods for determining the optimal weights of identifiers in this decision. These methods are based on a statistical decision theory for matching, described by Fellegi and Sunter (1969). The techniques for estimating the weights are now quite elaborate and beyond the scope of this paper. The application of these optimal weights for a decision on potential matching records is called "probabilistic record linkage" (see Herzog, Scheuren, & Winkler, 2007 for a textbook). There are many programs available for estimating the optimal parameters and performing probabilistic record linkage (details can be found at the end of the paper). However, probabilistic record linkage is far from being an automatic procedure, since preprocessing is usually laborious, estimating optimal parameters needs a lot of experimentation and after the linkage a clerical processing of unresolved pairs is needed. In practice, probabilistic record linkage is usually an iterative process. Depending on the quality of the identifiers, the size of datasets and the costs of producing false positive links (linking records that do not belong together) and false negatives (missing true links), the process may take many months of labor.

Privacy Preserving Record Linkage

If record linkage needs to be done with personal identifiers, privacy concerns increase. Therefore, record linkage with encrypted identifiers is widely used, for example in medical research contexts like cancer registries. If record linkage is performed without revealing any information which can be used to identify the persons whose data are linked, it is called privacy preserving record linkage (PPRL) or private record linkage. The simplest variants of PPRL encrypt the identifiers, and then linkage is done with the encrypted identifiers. This technique is highly secure, but even one different character in a name will result in two very different encrypted identifiers. Therefore, linking encrypted identifiers with exact matching will miss many true links between two files. Since the probability of slight changes in identifiers might depend on variables of interest, the missed true links might be different from detected links. For example, names in migrant populations often require transliteration; rules for transliteration might vary between database systems. Furthermore, slight changes in names can be used intentionally by persons not wishing to be linked across databases. Under such conditions, the successfully linked pairs are not a random sample of all pairs.

Because of these problems, it is common practice to replace string identifiers by an algorithmic substitution with special pseudonyms before encryption. These special pseudonyms are called phonetic codes. The most widely used phonetic code in English-speaking countries is the nearly 95-year-old "Soundex" (see for example Christen, 2012, p. 74). A phonetic code maps similarly pronounced strings to the same key. For example, the names Engel, Engall, Engehl, Elingel, Elingehl, Eiingeel, Ehnkiehl and Ehenckichl all produce the same code (in this example: E524). For privacy preserving record linkage, these codes are then encrypted with a cryptographic function (Borst, Allaert, & Quantin, 2001). There are many variants of this simple technique, resulting from different choices of preprocessing of strings, phonetic codes and cryptographic functions. However, the main problems of this approach are the same for all variants: These codes do not allow a similarity computation of the string identifiers of a potential pair: Either the code matches or it does not. Therefore, this approach suffers from missing many potential matches. Finally, within a group of potential pairs with the same code such as the example code E524 mentioned above, cases with identical other identifiers (birthday etc.) cannot be separated. Under such conditions, this approach will produce false positive links. Many procedures for privacy preserving record linkages have been suggested (for an overview: Christen, 2012, pp. 199–207). In real-world settings only a few of these procedures can be used. A procedure which has been used successfully in different practical settings will be described below.

Privacy Preserving Record Linkage with Cryptographic Bloom Filters

Schnell, Bachteler, and Reiher (2009) suggested a new method for the calculation of similarity between two encrypted strings for use in record linkage procedures (Safelink). This method is based on the idea of splitting an identifier into substrings and mapping the set of substrings to a binary vector. Only these vectors are used for linkage. Since a one-way mapping is used, persons cannot be identified by the vectors. In the rest of this subsection, some technical details are given.

In general, the substrings of a string consisting of subsequent letters are called "n-grams". Usually, a string is extended at both ends with blanks before splitting into n-grams ("padding"). Padding is useful to distinguish n-grams in the middle of a name from n-grams at the beginning and end of a name.

For example, the set of 2-grams (called bigrams) of the name SMITH is the set _S,SM,MI,IT,TH,H_. This set of bigrams is mapped with a function to a vector (see Figure 23.1). In this procedure, the functions are so-called cryptographic hash functions (HMACs). One HMAC named MD5 is known to many computer users today, since it is also used as a checksum algorithm for CD-ROMs. HMACs are one of the building blocks in modern cryptography; a description can be found in any modern textbook on cryptography (for example, Stallings, 2011). For record linkage, a variant of HMACs with a password is used ("keyed HMACs").

HMACs are one-way functions, so that two different inputs will be mapped to two different outcomes, but there is no way of finding the input given only the outcome. Schnell et al. (2009) proposed mapping each n-gram with several different HMACs. The result of the function is mapped to a long vector of bits, initially all set to zero. The combination of a bit vector with hash functions is called a Bloom filter in computer science (Bloom [1970] invented this combination for an entirely different purpose).

Encoding the n-grams of a string with many HMACs to a Bloom filter has many advantages. The most important advantage is the fact that given the Bloom filters alone, the initial string cannot be reconstructed. Since only the Bloom filters are used for linkage, the identifiers are encrypted. But this mapping allows the computation of the similarity of two strings by only using Bloom filters.

The procedure is best explained using an example. If we want to compare the similarity of the names "Smyth" and "Smith", we can use a standard string similarity measure like the Dice coefficient. The Dice similarity of two unencrypted strings can be determined as

$$D_{a,b} = \frac{2h}{(|a|+|b|)},$$ (23.1)

where h is the number of shared bigrams and $|a|$ + $|b|$ is the number of n-grams in the strings a, b. For example, the bigram similarity of "Smith" and "Smyth" can be computed by splitting the names into two sets of six bigrams each ({_s,sm,mi,it,th,h_} and {_s,sm,my,yt,th,h_}), counting the shared bigrams {_s,sm,th,h_} and computing the Dice coefficient as $\frac{2 \times 4}{6 + 6} \approx 0.67$.

If we want to compare the two strings with a Bloom filter encoding, we could, for example, use bigrams and Bloom filters with 30 bits and two HMACs only (in practice, Bloom filters with 500 or 1,000 bits and 15 to 50 hash functions are used). Figure 23.1 shows the encoding for this example. In both Bloom filters 8 identical bits are set to 1. Overall, 11+10 bits are set to 1. Using the Dice coefficient, the similarity of the two Bloom filters is computed as 2 × 8/(11 + 10) ≈ 0.76. The similarity of two Bloom filters for two totally different names like SMITH and BLACK is much closer to zero. In general, the similarity between two names can be approximated by only

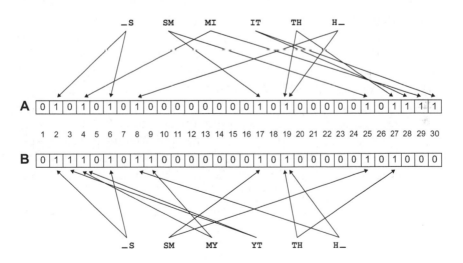

FIGURE 23.1
Example of the encoding of SMITH and SMYTH with two different cryptographic functions into 30-bit Bloom filters A and B (Schnell et al., 2009)

using the Bloom filters. Therefore, the encoding of strings to Bloom filters as proposed by Schnell et al. (2009) allows the computation of string similarity with encrypted identifiers. A privacy preserving record linkage can be done by using the Bloom filters for standard identifiers like names and addresses. By also encrypting numerical identifiers like the date of birth as strings, a privacy preserving record linkage allowing errors is possible.

Privacy Preserving Record Linkage with a Cryptographic Long-Term Key

In some legal environments, record linkage has to be done with exactly one identifier, for example, a PID may be required by law. For such environments, Schnell, Bachteler, and Reiher (2011) suggested the use of the encoding described above, but with one common Bloom filter (called a cryptographic long-term key or CLK) for all identifiers. So first name, last name, address, sex, date of birth etc. are all mapped to the same Bloom filter. For the mapping of each identifier, a different password is applied. Furthermore, the number of hash functions can be varied between identifiers, for example, to reflect the assumed discriminating power of identifiers for possible pairs. Simulations and real-world applications show a remarkable performance of the CLK. For example, in an application to a German cancer registry (Richter, 2013), a CLK based on first name, last name, date of birth, zip code and place of residence was used to link two files with 138,142 and 198,475 records. Considering only exact matches on the CLK, 18 pairs were found which had been not previously matched.

In general, record linkage based on separately encoded Bloom filters should perform slightly better than a linkage based on CLKs of the same identifiers. However, CLKs have an obvious advantage over separate identifiers: An attack on CLKs is much more difficult than an attack on Bloom filters. One successful attack on cryptographic Bloom filters has been reported in the literature (Kuzu, Kantarcioglu, Durham, & Malin, 2011; Kuzu, Kantarcioglu, Durham, Toth, & Malin, 2013). They reported the correct assignment of a few names to separate Bloom filters, given a correct random sample of identifiers. Even this partially successful attack is much harder with CLKs. Currently, CLKs seem to be the only modern privacy-preserving record linkage technique which has been used in applied research settings.

Respondents' Permission for Linkage

The legal framework for record linkage varies from country to country. However, it seems that in most countries privacy considerations could be avoided if respondents' permission to link their survey data to administrative records could be obtained. However, depending on the survey conditions (topic, population, interviewers, kind of request, phrasing of the request), large differences in the proportion consenting to linking have been observed. For example, Sakshaug and Kreuter (2012) reported between 24% and 89% consent to linkage for different surveys. Since consenting to linkage requests can be seen as a special kind of nonresponse, this additional step in a survey response process has generated a recent deluge of studies on linkage consent (for examples, see Sala, Burton, & Knies, 2012; Sakshaug, Tutz, & Kreuter, 2013). Currently, the bias generated by nonconsenting seems to be small, at least in Germany (Sakshaug & Kreuter, 2012). However, it can be expected that consent rates will decrease with an increasing number of requests; furthermore, differences in effects due to populations, research topics and sponsors on consent rates and consent bias must be taken into account. So the effects of non-consenting persons on estimates must be evaluated for each project anew.

Legal Permissions for Linkage

If bias reduction is of primary importance, the use of privacy preserving record linkage techniques might be useful. In some countries, the legal framework allows data protection officers to grant linkage without consent if the public interest outweighs privacy concerns. Arguing with privacy preserving linkage techniques can facilitate the negotiations with data protection officers. Demonstrating the factual anonymity with simulated data for subgroups with record linkage (see the paragraph above on checking anonymity) before the actual linkage has been done will also help. However, these discussions can take a long time. Informal inquiries with international research teams suggest that two years for discussions with data protection agencies and other stakeholders is a reasonable estimate for national surveys.

23.5 SOFTWARE

For serious work with large data files, standalone programs for record linkage should be used. During the last few years, many commercial and open source solutions have become available. Since the requirements vary between research problems, a general recommendation cannot be given. For evaluating record linkage software, Herzog et al. (2007, Chapter 19) provide a checklist. A recent review of current software has been given by Christen (2012, Chapter 10). Only one of these programs can currently handle identifiers encrypted with Bloom filters: The so-called "Merge Toolbox" (MTB). This program (Schnell, Bachteler, & Bender, 2004) is available for free at the German Record Linkage Center (www.german-RLC.de).

23.6 RESEARCH INFRASTRUCTURE FOR RECORD LINKAGE WITH ADMINISTRATIVE DATA

Recently, at least two European countries have established national research centers for linking administrative databases. In the UK, the Administrative Data Liaison Service (ADLS) has been funded by the Economic and Social Research Council (ESRC) to support administrative data based research in the UK (see www.adls.ac.uk/about). The ADLS provides services and data access for the use of administrative data in the UK. In addition to these activities, the report by the Administrative Data Taskforce (2012) gave recommendations for fostering the use of administrative data for research. A very similar development in Germany was the establishment of Research Data Centers, initiated by the German Data Forum (www.ratswd.de). In addition, the German Research Foundation (DFG) funded the startup of an infrastructure for record linkage applications, the German Record Linkage Center (GRLC, for details see the homepage: www.german-rlc. de). The GRLC was established in 2011 to promote research on record linkage and to facilitate practical applications in Germany. The Center provides several services related to record linkage applications, for example, acting as a data trustee for linkages. Within two years, more than 12 record linkage projects (including the large scale surveys SAVE, PASS, GSOEP and PAIRFAM) used the services of the GRLC.

23.7 CONCLUSION

Linking surveys and administrative data offers many unique advantages. Therefore, the linking of records of the same person or institution across different databases will increase. The technical problems of linking even with imperfect identifiers have been solved and suitable software is widely available. The remaining problems are mainly caused by privacy objections. Very recent technical developments make record linkage with encrypted identifiers on microdata possible. The certification of these procedures by data protection agencies and their implementation in administrative contexts may take years. At least the same amount of time will be needed to include the linkage of administrative data to surveys into the standard toolbox of working social scientists. The establishment of national record linkage centers in the UK and in Germany are the first steps on this path.

NOTE

1. Less than 0.4% of employed Americans (about 129.7 million) are physicians; less than 1.1% of them reported a change. Finding them by sampling would have been a challenge.

REFERENCES

Administrative Data Taskforce. (2012, December). Improving access for research and policy. ESRC Report. Swindon.

Averdijk, M., & Elffers, H. (2012). The discrepancy between survey-based victim accounts and police reports revisited. *International Review of Victimology, 18*(2), 91–107. doi:10.1177/0269758011432955

Bacher, J., Brand, R., & Bender, S. (2002). Re-identifying register data by survey data using cluster analysis: An empirical study. *International Journal of Uncertainty, Fuzziness and Knowledge Based Systems, 10*(5), 589–607. doi:10.1142/S0218488502001661

Belin, T. R., Ishwaran, H., Duan, N., Berry, S. H., & Kanouse, D. E. (2004). Identifying likely duplicates by record linkage in a survey of prostitutes. In A. Gelman & X.-L. Meng (Eds.), *Applied Bayesian modeling and causal inference from incomplete-data perspectives* (pp. 319–328). Hoboken: Wiley.

Bloom, B. H. (1970). Space/time trade-offs in hash coding with allowable errors. *Communications of the ACM, 13*(7), 422–426.

Borst, F., Allaert, F.-A., & Quantin, C. (2001). The Swiss solution for anonymous chaining patient files. In V. Patel, R. Rogers, & R. Haux (Eds.), *Proceedings of the 10th World Congress on Medical Informatics* (pp. 1239–1241). Amsterdam: IOS Press.

Brackstone, G. J. (1987). Issues in the use of administrative records for statistical purposes. *Survey Methodology, 13*(1), 29–43.

Christen, P. (2012). *Data matching: Concepts and techniques for record linkage, entity resolution, and duplicate detection.* Berlin: Springer.

Domingo-Ferrer, J., & Torra, V. (2003). Disclosure risk assessment in statistical microdata protection via advanced record linkage. *Statistics and Computing, 13*, 343–354. doi:10.1023/A:1025666923033

Fellegi, I. P., & Sunter, A. B. (1969). A theory for record linkage. *Journal of the American Statistical Association, 64*(328), 1183–1210.

Harper, G., & Mayhew, L. (2012). Using administrative data to count local populations. *Applied Spatial Analysis and Policy, 5*(2), 97–122. doi:10.1007/s12061-011-9063-y

Herzog, T. N., Scheuren, F. J., & Winkler, W. E. (2007). *Data quality and record linkage techniques.* New York: Springer.

Jacobs, J. A., Boulis, A., & Messikomer, C. (2001). The movement of physicians between specialties. *Research in Social Stratification and Mobility, 18*, 2001, 63–95.

Judson, D. H. (2005). Computerized record linkage and statistical matching. In K. Kempf-Leonard (Ed.), *Encyclopedia of social measurement* (Vol. 1, pp. 439–447). New York: Elsevier.

Judson, D. H. (2007). Information integration for constructing social statistics: History, theory and ideas towards a research programme. *Journal of the Royal Statistical Society: Series A, 170*(2), 483–501.

Judson, D. H., & Popoff, C. L. (2005). Administrative records research. In K. Kempf-Leonard (Ed.), *Encyclopedia of social measurement* (Vol. 1, pp. 17–27). New York: Elsevier.

Kuzu, M., Kantarcioglu, M., Durham, E., & Malin, B. (2011). A constraint satisfaction cryptanalysis of Bloom filters in private record linkage. In S. Fischer-Huebner & N. Hopper (Eds.), *The 11th Privacy Enhancing Technologies Symposium* (pp. 226–245). Berlin: Springer.

Kuzu, M., Kantarcioglu, M., Durham, E. A., Toth, C., & Malin, B. (2013). A practical approach to achieve private medical record linkage in light of public resources. *Journal of the American Medical Informatics Association, 20*(2), 285–292. doi:10.1136/amiajnl-2012-000917

Lane, J. (2010). Linking administrative and survey data. In P. V. Marsden & J. D. Wright (Eds.), *Handbook of survey research* (pp. 659–680). Bingley: Emerald.

Lehtonen, R., & Veijanen, A. (2009). Design-based methods of estimation for domains and small areas. In C. Rao (Ed.), *Handbook of statistics* (Vol. 29, Part B, pp. 219–249). Amsterdam: Elsevier.

Maxfield, M. G., Weiler, B. L., & Widom, C. S. (2000). Comparing self-reports and official records of arrests. *Journal of Quantitative Criminology, 16*(1), 87–110. doi:10.1023/A:1007577512038

Richter, A. (2013, January). Ergebnis des Abgleichs Nr. 2, Memo, Cancer Registry Luebeck.

Sakshaug, J. W., & Kreuter, F. (2012). Assessing the magnitude of non-consent biases in linked survey and administrative data. *Survey Research Methods, 6*(2), 113–122.

Sakshaug, J. W., Tutz, V., & Kreuter, F. (2013). Placement, wording, and interviewers: identifying correlates of consent to link survey and administrative data. *Survey Research Methods, 7*(2), 133–144.

Sala, E., Burton, J., & Knies, G. (2012). Correlates of obtaining informed consent to data linkage: Respondent, interview, and interviewer characteristics. *Sociological Methods & Research, 41*(3), 414–439. doi:10.1177/0049124112457330

Schnell, R. (2007). Alternative Verfahren zur Stichprobengewinnung fuer ein Haushaltspanelsurvey mit Schwerpunkt im Niedrigeinkommens- und Transferleistungsbezug. In M. Promberger (Ed.), *Neue Daten fuer die Sozialstaatsforschung* (pp. 33–59). Nuernberg: Bundesagentur fuer Arbeit.

Schnell, R., Bachteler, T., & Bender, S. (2003). Record linkage using error-prone strings. In *Proceedings of the Section on Survey Research Methods*, American Statistical Association (pp. 3713–3717).

Schnell, R., Bachteler, T., & Bender, S. (2004). A toolbox for record linkage. *Austrian Journal of Statistics, 33*(1–2), 125–133.

Schnell, R., Bachteler, T., & Reiher, J. (2009). Privacy-preserving record linkage using Bloom filters. *BMC Medical Informatics and Decision Making, 9*(41), 1–11. doi:10.1186/1472-6947-9-41

Schnell, R., Bachteler, T., & Reiher, J. (2010). Improving the use of self-generated identification codes. *Evaluation Review, 34*(5), 391–418. doi:10.1177/0193841X10387576

Schnell, R., Bachteler, T., & Reiher, J. (2011). A novel error-tolerant anonymous linking code (Working Paper No. WP-GRLC-2011-02). Nuremberg: German Record Linkage Center.

Stallings, W. (2011). *Cryptography and network security: Principles and practice* (5th ed.). Boston: Prentice Hall.

Weisberg, H. F. (2005). *The total survey error approach: A guide to the new science of survey research.* Chicago: The University of Chicago Press.

Winkler, W. E. (1995). Matching and record linkage. In B. G. Cox, D. A. Binder, B. N. Chinnappa, A. Christianson, M. J. Colledge, & P. S. Kott (Eds.), *Business survey methods* (pp. 355–384). New York: Wiley.

Winkler, W. E. (2009). Record linkage. In D. Pfeffermann & C. Rao (Eds.), *Handbook of statistics vol. 29a, sample surveys: Design, methods and applications* (pp. 351–380). Amsterdam: Elsevier.

Zanutto, E., & Zaslavsky, A. (2002). Using administrative records to impute for nonresponse. In R. M. Groves, D. A. Dillman, J. L. Eltinge, & R.J.A. Little (Eds.), *Survey nonresponse* (pp. 403–415). New York: Wiley.

24

Enhancing Surveys with Objective Measurements and Observer Ratings

Rainer Schnell

24.1 INTRODUCTION

Survey responses suffer from many different sources of measurement error (Weisberg, 2005). Respondents may have never noticed some information they are asked for (for example, their vaccination status). They forget information like hospitalization dates and prefer to misreport some other information (for example, infections). Finally, they may simply not be interested enough to work hard in order to give an exact answer. So reliability and validity of survey responses are usually far from perfect. Replacing the responses with objective measurements is an obvious strategy to reduce the impact of non-sampling errors on survey results. Despite the neglect of such measurements in most textbooks of survey methodology, an impressive list of objective measurements and ratings has been used to reduce measurement error. Two recent technological developments have further increased the use of non-questionnaire data within surveys: the universal presence of computing devices such as smartphones, intelligent sensors and smart cards (known as ubiquitous computing) and the increasing awareness of biological constraints and genetic factors for human behavior. This chapter will describe some of the techniques available for enhancing surveys with non-questionnaire data; there are still more not mentioned here and even more will be invented. Finally, some methodological problems regarding respondent burden, nonresponse and sample selection will be discussed.

Interviewers as Observers

It is common practice to include questions directed at the interviewer in a questionnaire. Most often, these questions refer to the interview situation, for example, respondent cooperation as perceived by the interviewer or presence of third parties during the interview. This can be seen as data produced by the data collection process itself. This kind of data is usually referred to as paradata (see Chapter 25 by Kreuter in this volume). Interviewers have rarely been used to rate respondents' attitudes or traits, most probably due to the doubtful validity of such ratings. However, there are studies which have used interviewers as observers for environmental conditions. For example, Hoffmeyer-Zlotnik (2001) developed a set of questions for interviewers to classify the residential areas of respondents. Interviewers classify the distance to the city center, the type of residential building and commercial or private usage of the building. These classifications form a residential index, which is included in many German surveys.

Eifler, Thume, and Schnell (2009) studied the level of agreement between respondent and interviewer in the reported "signs of incivility" of neighborhoods in a national victimization study. Harth and Scheller (2012) replicated the national population studies on the way people live at home of Alphons Silbermann (1963) with a survey of 1,504 respondents. These studies included questions on features of the respondent's living room (design, color scheme, spaciousness) for the interviewer.

Hamermesh and Biddle (1994) report on three labor market surveys. The interviewers in each study were asked to categorize the respondent's physical appearance on a five-point scale. The result was that plain-looking people earn less than average-looking people. The overall effect is about 5–10%, and was for men at least as large as the effect for women. However, in an unpublished paper Doran and Hersch (2009) could not reproduce the results of Hamermesh and Biddle (1994). Recently, Pfeifer (2011) reported strong effects of attractiveness (rated by interviewers) on income and employment status for a German survey.

Collecting additional data by interviewer observation is cheap. If the interviewers are trained and paid for this task, there is no technical obstacle to the use of interviewer observations. However, systematic analyses of the validity of the interviewer data are rare.

24.2 ENVIRONMENTAL DATA

Some health surveys collect samples of environmental material to determine environmental pollution. These include samples of soil, tap water and air. For example, the German Environmental Survey 1998 analyzed the respondent's tap water for industrial toxins. With the consent of the respondents, some studies collect items of daily use, like toothbrushes, combs and vacuum cleaner bags.[1] The content of the vacuum cleaner bags was analyzed for chlorinated disphenyls (PCBs) and other contaminants. Switzerland has a nationwide noise map, showing the objective magnitude of noise exposure (Ingold & Koepfli, 2009). Such maps exist in other countries as well, but usually cover only certain regions.[2]

24.3 REMOTE SENSING AND STREET VIEW

Satellite remote sensing data is becoming more and more available even for very small areas. This can, for example, be used to characterize land use. Remote sensing data can be merged with survey data as contextual information. This can be done even for individual households (Fox, Rindfuss, Walsh, & Mishra, 2004). A recent example is the percentage of green space determined by remote sensing and merged to some of the respondents of the SOEP by Goebel, Wurm, and Wagner (2010).

Google Street View currently covers a few countries like the U.S. and the Netherlands nearly completely and a few others, such as Germany, at least for some urban areas. For the covered areas, the information in Street View can be used for different survey purposes.

Odgers, Caspi, Bates, Sampson, and Moffitt (2012) reported the double coding of 120 PSUs in England and Wales by four raters on signs of physical disorder, physical decay, neighborhood dangerousness, street safety and the percentage of green space. All ratings were based on Google Street View pictures. Finally, Street View might be used for sampling. For example, in Germany one popular sampling method for face-to-face surveys is the so-called random walk. Starting at some randomly selected location the interviewers are instructed to follow a specific path across the settlement. Usually, the path is described by simple rules ("go on the left side of the road; turn right at junctions"). Every nth household on the path is selected for the survey. In practice, this sampling method allows arbitrary decisions of interviewers. Street View is much better suited than maps or aerial photographs to do the sampling of buildings for a random walk selection in advance, thereby reducing the impact of interviewers on sampling.

24.4 CONTINUOUS BEHAVIOR MEASUREMENTS

If data on actual behavior is needed, asking the respondents is not the method of choice. Less reactive measurement methods are more desirable than verbal reports. This is even more true if continuous measurements are needed. The prime example has been audience measurement. Commercial measuring methods use special hardware in panel households, like the GfK meter in Germany (Günther, Vossebein, & Wildner, 2006). In a panel of about 5,500 households a special device recorded which TV channel was being watched. A technically interesting development is the Swiss "Radio Control" system (www.radiocontrol.ch). A random sample of 800 people in Switzerland were asked to wear a special digital clock for one week. This clock recorded environmental noise for four seconds of each minute. A compressed fingerprint of these digital recordings was later compared with the corresponding digital broadcasts of all Swiss radio stations. Similar systems are in use in other countries.

Using the Bluetooth sensors in smartphones, there have been attempts to map social networks by recording the proximity of devices (Eagle, 2011). Other sensors of a smartphone like GPS can also be used (Raento, Oulasvirta, & Eagle, 2009). Aside from the obvious use of GPS for mobility studies, there are some interesting applications. For example, in 2011 German market research companies used a sample of about 3,000 persons in 31 randomly sampled towns to estimate the probability of seeing street advertising (Media-Micro-Census, 2012). The respondents were asked to wear a GPS device, which recorded continuously for a week. Recently, Kelly, Smyth, and Caulfield (2013) reported high accuracy of prediction for characteristics like gender, age or regular visits of parents with a prediction model based on smartphone GPS data.

However, currently the high power consumption of these sensors limits their applications for research in real world settings (Eagle, 2011). Special purpose sensors like GPS loggers can extend the measuring period, but they have to be actively worn and are therefore much more intrusive than smartphones. If only the presence of an object or a person at a given time is of interest, simple RFID (radio frequency identification) chips may be more useful, since the detection of an RFID chip is completely nonreactive. Since only the sensor, but not the chip, requires energy, the chip can be placed in personal equipment like laptops or clothes and used over a long period of time.

It should be mentioned that these sensors can be used not only for the continuous measurement of behavior, but for sampling purposes also. To the best knowledge of the author, this has not yet been suggested before. Techniques for sampling elusive or clandestine populations like center sampling (Baio, Blangiardo, & Blangiardo, 2011) require the estimation of visiting probabilities for selected locations. These estimations are based on respondents' reports after selection and successful interviews. Data from nonrespondents is not available, and data from respondents might be of doubtful validity. Both problems can be avoided by the use of electronic indicators of the presence of persons. Some of the options available are Bluetooth sensors, RFID chips, hardware identification codes transmitted by WLAN chips (MAC addresses) or similar techniques such as NFC (near field communication). Given an increasing (and hopefully, not selective) use of such devices in electronic equipment or even "intelligent clothing", the presence of persons at given locations can be recorded. Since this data is available even for nonrespondents, inclusion probabilities might be estimated with less errors.

24.5 USE OF DOCUMENTS

In different types of surveys, respondents are asked to use different personal documents to clarify dates or numerical details of interest. For example, many districts in Germany conduct a residential rent index biannually. These studies are based on population surveys. Since the written rental agreement is needed as a reference, these surveys are usually done face-to-face. In the German SOEP, mothers are asked for data from their maternity records such as birth weight and body size of the newborn.

Beyond written records, other documents can also be used. One example is the use of photos. Based on ratings of yearbook photos at the age of 18, Jokela (2009) reported the relationship between facial attractiveness and the number of biological children at age 53–56 for 2,241 respondents. Attractive women had 16% more children than the less attractive women. The least attractive men had 13% fewer children than the others.

For many years, respondents have been encouraged to keep diaries on certain behavior.[3] Such diaries include mobility diaries, fuel diaries, shopping diaries, food diaries, pain diaries and time-use diaries.[4] However, diaries have three main problems: The respondent burden generated by the diaries causes selective recordings and panel attrition. The remaining sample is rarely a random sample of the original population. Finally, the writing of diaries may lead to changes in behavior. For example, even the requirement to document nutritional habits can cause changes in eating behavior.

Diaries have been used extensively in commercial consumer panels. Another major application is household budget studies for official statistics. Some of these studies impose an unbearable burden on respondents (see the section on respondent burden below). Methodologists increasingly urge the data collecting agencies to reduce the workload for respondents in diary studies.[5] The respondent burden in diary studies could be reduced by technology, for example by using smartphones or tablet computers for manual data entry (Dillman & House, 2013), the use of RFID chips for logging or simply by using the camera of a smartphone for documenting consumption, behavior or states of objects. A similarly obvious application of these technologies is experience sampling (Kellock et al., 2011). Simple logging devices or diaries can be used with SMS, email systems or web surveys. If the reporting task is reduced by automated recoding systems, the amount of activity required by respondents is low and the attrition rate will probably be smaller.

24.6 BIOSOCIAL SURVEYS

Medical surveys like NHANES or NSHAP have collected data on biological and medical variables for a long time. However, the use of such variables in social surveys for sociological purposes has been rare. This is especially true for social surveys which cannot rely on already established social relations to respondents as in panel or web-based access panel studies. However, even social surveys have started collecting increasing amounts of data on biological variables that might influence social behavior. These include measures of anthropometric variables, tests of body functions for measuring health, biomarkers and genetic information. Biomarkers require the collection of biomaterial (e.g., blood, saliva, hair). With the exception of twin studies, sampling genetic information also depends on biomaterial. The combination of questionnaire data and biological variables measured in a random sample of a population is increasingly denoted as a "biosocial survey" (Finch, Vaupel, & Kinsella, 2001; Weinstein, Vaupel, & Wachter, 2008).

Measuring Anthropometric Variables and Health in Population Surveys

Health is a dependent and an independent variable of interest for many social scientists. Some health and anthropometric measurements can be conducted by medically untrained interviewers in respondent households. These include respondent weight and height, waist-to-hip ratio and blood pressure. Also of interest are measurements like grip strength or pulmonary function with a peak flow meter. A simple but useful test of limited mobility that is occasionally used in surveys of the elderly is how long it takes the respondent to pick up a pencil from the floor. Schumm et al. (2009) describe the use of measures for vision, olfactory function, gustatory function and touch within a population survey. Similar tests of body functions are included in more and more health surveys and social surveys, for example in NHANES, NSHAP and SHARE, PSID or SOEP (Kalton, 2012).

Continuous Measurement of Medical Parameters

Small-sized sensors like SmartPatch allow wireless measurements of heart rate, breathing rate, oxygen saturation of the blood and temperature for 24 hours. Although such instruments are becoming much smaller, more portable and less annoying, they still affect daily routine. Technical developments open up new perspectives every day, for example, the use of mobile phones as accelerometers, since subjects carry mobile phones anyway. Another example is "intelligent clothing" where sensors in the clothes provide information on temperature, pulse rate, skin resistance and transpiration (Solaz et al., 2006).

Collecting Perinatal Data

Different perinatal variables have been associated with human behavior in later life. There are studies on long-term effects of birth weight on cognitive development (Goosby & Cheadle, 2009). Furthermore, effects of birth order have been studied, for example, with regard to school achievements (Booth & Kee, 2009) and homosexuality (Blanchard, 2008). Perinatal data can be retrieved from documents during interviews or linked from administrative databases.

Collecting Biomaterials

Perhaps the most versatile biomaterial usable in surveys is blood. However, the collection of blood samples faces many practical restrictions. Taking blood using the "finger prick" method, where a drop of blood from a fingertip is dried on a small piece of paper (dried blood spot, DBS) is much easier (McDade, Williams, & Snodgrass, 2007). The analytical options are restricted compared to those of venous blood, but sampling, transport and storage of the samples is considerably simpler.

Collecting saliva is the easiest way to obtain material for DNA analysis. Saliva may be used for other tests such as the level of cortisol (as a stress indicator or in the context of aggressive behavior; see Yu & Shi, 2009). Saliva is usually collected from the mouth using a cotton swab. Today, a number of analyses are even possible on material collected by chewing gum. This method is non-invasive and has the potential to become widely accepted for collecting such data in random samples of the population.

Hair and fingernails can be collected without any problems even under survey conditions. These materials can be used for the analysis of absorbed contaminants and consumed drugs (Tobin, 2005).

McCadden et al. (2005) report on a random sample of 5,105 men and women (aged 16 to 44), who were asked for a urine sample after a CAPI interview. Of these, 3,608 samples were collected successfully. The samples are used to screen for a sexually transmittable bacteria. Another noteworthy study collected urine in a mail survey of a random sample of 21,000 Dutch men and women (age 15–29), for whom van Bergen et al. (2006) report a response rate of almost 41%. A number of similar studies are available; Low et al. (2007) give an overview.

Use of Genetic Data

Currently, numerous articles on supposedly genetic causes of social behavior are being published (for examples in political science, see Hatemi & McDermott, 2012). Some of these papers do not refer to any known biological mechanism (for example, genetic causes of nonresponse or mobile phone use). The combination of a small number of cases with strong effects makes the alternative statistical explanation plausible: Among thousands of significance tests, at least 5% of them will be significant. In their review of approaches and pitfalls of genetic research in the social sciences, Benjamin et al. (2012) suspect that the most promising outcomes will be those that are most closely related to the underlying biological mechanisms. In the case of social sciences, these outcomes may be in the fields of social epidemiology, deviant behavior and the sociology of the family.

Examples on the Use of Biological Variables for Sociological Research

Despite the increasing interest in biosocial surveys, the number of studies concerned with biological variables in the social sciences is currently still very small (Schnell, 2009; D'Onofrio & Lahey, 2010: 770). For example, even the consideration of trivial biological relevant variables, such as body mass index

(Klein, 2011) or physical illness (Rapp, 2012) for marital stability is quite recent. Other variables associated with mating behavior, such as interpersonal and intrapersonal hormonal differences are harder to measure within surveys. Nevertheless examples do exist in the sociological literature. Using data from the National Social Life, Health and Aging Project (NSHAP), Pollet, van der Meij, Cobey, and Buunk (2011) reported a significant correlation between testosterone and the number of opposite sex partners in men.

Methodological Problems of Collecting Biosocial Variables

Currently, very little is known on collecting biosocial data and especially of biomaterials by medically untrained interviewers. There are some initial reports (Jaszczak, Lundeen, & Smith, 2009; Hank, Jürges, & Schaan, 2009; Schonlau et al., 2010), but systematic research on measurement errors of different kinds of biosocial information under fieldwork conditions of social surveys is still missing. Furthermore, interviewer, sponsorship and long-term effects on respondent cooperation are unknown for biosocial surveys.

24.7 GENERAL METHODOLOGICAL PROBLEMS

Enhancing surveys with additional measurements will enrich data sets and might reduce measurement errors. Given the well-documented measurement errors in respondents' reports on their past and present behavior,[6] replacing respondents' reports by measurements not based on verbal reports of respondents might increase reliability and validity of these variables. Many applications reported here are just demonstrations of technical options. The resulting data quality will depend on the specific measurement details. If the use of these techniques under the conditions of fieldwork in standard surveys will yield higher data quality is an open question which will require years of research. But relying entirely on verbal reports as most social surveys have done so far is no more acceptable from a methodological point of view. However, depending on the type of measurement, additional methodological problems arise. Two of the main problems will be discussed briefly.

Respondent Burden, Sample Selection and Nonresponse

Some measurement techniques are impossible to use without additional respondent burden. However, a few measurement techniques, like some types of diaries, are simply unbearable for the general population.[7]

Respondent cooperation cannot be taken for granted. If a technique causes high respondent burden, recruitment will be difficult and selective. Many examples of the initial use of new measurement techniques are based on existing panel studies, in which long standing cooperation routines existed. Applying these techniques in initial samples will be much more difficult. Therefore, reducing respondent burden by using non-invasive technology is of vital importance if unbiased population estimates are required. Nonresponse is already one of the main problems in survey methodology. Enhancing surveys with additional measurements will only increase nonresponse problems if the additional measures do not reduce respondent burden.

Therefore, in many applications of new measurement techniques in survey research, we observe the use of special samples, which should not be used for population estimates. For example, the GPS logging study by German market research companies mentioned above is based on a quota sample. Quota samples are popular for studies with high respondent burden, because interviewers can select cooperative people they already know. This may explain the continuous use of quota samples even in official statistics. Of course, studies of self-selected volunteers or local studies on patients are common if a new technique is tested. But after the technical problems have been solved, there is no way other than random sampling at every stage in a population sample, if unbiased estimates are needed.

In practice, such considerations are often ignored. The largest project of the medical research community in Germany is the National Cohort (National Cohort Working Group, 2011). The study attempts to sample 200,000 people in just 18 regional clusters. From a methodological point of view, the sample design is weak. The impressive sample size will be reduced heavily by design effects due to clustering. Although the sample within a cluster is selected at random, the clusters themselves are not sampled randomly. The clusters are chosen according to the proximity to the institutes of the principal investigators. This will make population estimates a nontrivial exercise.

Re-Identification Risks

Enhancing a survey with additional variables always makes re-identification easier. If an attacker knows the sampling unit (for example, a PSU-like an administrative unit) and some simple demographics, re-identification is usually possible for some of the respondents. Additional objective measures or even ratings offer more options for an attack since this information may be available in other databases. Therefore, enhanced surveys are more vulnerable for attacks.[8] The release of scientific use files of enhanced surveys will cause more concerns than the release of a standard survey. Techniques to guarantee statistical confidentiality are therefore indispensable for these surveys (Duncan, Elliot, & Salazar-Gonzalez, 2011). Solving these problems for genetic samples are current research fields (Greely, 2009; McEwen, Boyer, & Sun, 2013).

24.8 CONCLUSION

In the general population and in some academic circles surveys are perceived mostly as more or less unimportant opinion polls. Since this is true to a certain extent, increasing nonresponse rates could be expected of rational respondents. However, surveys have a potential far beyond reporting opinions. In general, the technically interesting applications of surveys concentrate on factual data, like travel and housing demand, welfare, labor force participation or medical problems. In these fields of research, the demand for valid and reliable data is increasing. Furthermore, since gold standards for the evaluation of measurements are available in these fields, the survey measurements can be validated.

For such applications, the technological advances in sensors, smart cards, diagnostic procedures and ubiquitous computing will force survey methodologists to include more and more objective measurement procedures into surveys. This will influence the relationship between research teams and respondents. The standard sociological model of a survey interview relies on the absence of any social consequences of the interview situation: a short, friendly encounter of two strangers. In a biosocial survey with informed consent, this model does not apply. The research group will have knowledge of the respondent, which might not be known to the respondent. Furthermore, the respondent might be re-identified even long after their death. So the respondents in such surveys will need a lot of trust in the data-holding institution. Trust between strangers relies on reputation or repeated successful interaction. Therefore, enhanced surveys will be more successful if the data collection is done by an institute with a high reputation (for example, a nationally known medical research school) or in panel studies, in which respondents have repeated contact over years to the same institute or even the same interviewer. The ad hoc sampling with cold contacts as is often used in opinion polls today will perform badly by comparison. However, the required trust by the respondents will change the interaction between respondents and interviewers, since these can be seen as social agents of the research institution. This will have consequences for the answering process, for example for answers according to social desirability. To sum up: enhancing surveys with objective measurements will improve data quality and the amount of information available, but it will also change the social conditions of survey interviewing with impacts on nonresponse, measurement error, social desirability and data sharing.

NOTES

1. In at least one older American study, household garbage was collected for response validation without the consent of the respondents (Rathje, 1984).
2. EU directive 2002/49/EG (June 25th 2002) states that districts with a population over 250,000 people are committed to publish regional noise maps.
3. For an overview, see Bolger, Davis, and Rafaeli (2003).
4. A recent overview on time-use surveys is given by Gershuny (2011).
5. The "Panel on Redesigning the BLS Consumer Expenditure Surveys" (Dillman & House, 2013) reminded the data collectors that the survey processes have to be workable across the entire population, that respondents have to be relieved from the current burden level of the expenditure survey and that respondents need sufficient motivation to participate.
6. For a short review on measurement errors due to autobiographical memory see Schwarz (2007).
7. An extreme example are the diaries requested by the European Household Budget Survey (European Commission, 2003), which ask for expense diaries: for example, in the case of Belgium, all expenditures in detail and income, including receipts, savings and debts, for the household over a period of one month.
8. Gymrek, McGuire, Golan, Halperin, and Erlich (2013) demonstrated a technique for the re-identification of surnames given a de-identified personal genome data set using only public available genetic genealogy databases.

REFERENCES

Baio, G., Blangiardo, G. C., & Blangiardo, M. (2011). Centre sampling technique in foreign migration surveys: A methodological note. *Journal of Official Statistics*, *27*(3), 451–465.

Benjamin, D. J., Cesarini, D., Chabris, C. F., Glaeser, E. L., Laibson, D. I., Gudnason, V., . . . Lichtenstein, P. (2012). The promises and pitfalls of genoeconomics. *Annual Review of Economics, 4*(1), 627–662.

Blanchard, R. (2008). Review and theory of handedness, birth order, and homosexuality in men. *Laterality, 13*(1), 51–70.

Bolger, N., Davis, A., & Rafaeli, E. (2003). Diary methods: Capturing life as it is lived. *Annual Review of Psychology, 54*, 579–616.

Booth, A. L., & Kee, H. J. (2009). Birth order matters: the effect of family size and birth order on educational attainment. *Journal of Population Economics, 22*(2), 367–397.

Dillman, D. A., & House, C. C. (Eds.). (2013). *Measuring what we spend: Toward a new consumer expenditure survey*. Washington, DC: National Academy.

D'Onofrio, B. M., & Lahey, B. B. (2010). Biosocial influences on the family: A decade review. *Journal of Marriage and Family, 72*(3), 762–782.

Doran, K., & Hersch, J. (2009). *The beauty premium is not robust*. Unpublished preliminary work, University of Notre Dame.

Duncan, G. T., Elliot, M., & Salazar-Gonzalez, J.-J. (2011). *Statistical confidentiality: Principles and practice*. New York: Springer.

Eagle, N. (2011). Mobile phones as sensors for social research. In S. N. Hesse-Biber (Ed.), *The handbook of emergent technologies in social research* (pp. 492–521). Oxford: Oxford University Press.

Eifler, S., Thume, D., & Schnell, R. (2009). Unterschiede zwischen subjektiven und objektiven Messungen von Zeichen oeffentlicher Unordnung. In M. Weichbold (Ed.), *Umfrageforschung: Herausforderungen und Grenzen* (pp. 415–441). Wiesbaden, Germany: Verlag fuer Sozialwissenschaften.

European Commission (Ed.). (2003). *Household budget surveys in the EU*. Luxembourg.

Finch, C. E., Vaupel, J. W., & Kinsella, K. (Eds.). (2001). *Cells and surveys: should biological measures be included in social science research?* Washington, DC: National Academy Press.

Fox, J., Rindfuss, R. R., Walsh, S. J., & Mishra, V. (Eds.). (2004). *People and the environment*. New York, NY: Kluwer.

Gershuny, J. (2011). *Time-use surveys and the measurement of national well-being*. Oxford: Department of Sociology, Oxford University.

Goebel, J., Wurm, M., & Wagner, G. G. (2010). *Exploring the linkage of spatial indicators from remote sensing data with survey data* (Report No. 283). Berlin: DIW.

Goosby, B. J., & Cheadle, J. E. (2009). Birth weight, math and reading achievement growth: A multilevel between-sibling, between-families approach. *Social Forces, 87*(3), 1291–1320.

Greely, H. T. (2009). Collecting biomeasures in the panel study of income dynamics: Ethical and legal concerns. *Biodemography and Social Biology, 55*(2), 270–288.

Günther, M., Vossebein, U., & Wildner, R. (2006). *Marktforschung mit Panels* (2nd ed.). Wiesbaden: Gabler.

Gymrek, M., McGuire, A. L., Golan, D., Halperin, E., & Erlich, Y. (2013). Identifying personal genomes by surname inference. *Science, 339*(6117), 321–324.

Hamermesh, D. S., & Biddle, J. E. (1994). Beauty and the labor market. *The American Economic Review, 84*(5), 1174–1194.

Hank, K., Jürges, H., & Schaan, B. (2009). Die Erhebung biometrischer Daten im Survey of Health, Ageing and Retirement in Europe. *Methoden-Daten-Analysen, 3*(1), 97–108.

Harth, A., & Scheller, G. (2012). *Das Wohnerlebnis in Deutschland: Eine Wiederholungsstudie nach 20 Jahren*. Wiesbaden: Verlag fuer Sozialwissenschaften.

Hatemi, P. K., & McDermott, R. (2012). The genetics of politics: discovery, challenges, and progress. *Trends in Genetics, 28*(10), 525–533.

Hoffmeyer-Zlotnik, J. H. (2001). *Wohnquartiersbeschreibung: Ein Instrument zur Regionalisierung von Nachbarschaften* (How-to-series No. 7). Mannheim: ZUMA.

Ingold, K., & Koepfli, M. (2009). *Laermbelastung in der Schweiz. Ergebnisse des nationalen Laermmonitorings SonBase*. Bern: Bundesamt fuer Umwelt (BAFU).

Jaszczak, A., Lundeen, K., & Smith, S. (2009). Using nonmedically trained interviewers to collect biomeasures in a national in-home survey. *Field Methods, 21*(1), 26–48.

Jokela, M. (2009). Physical attractiveness and reproductive success in humans: evidence from the late 20th century United States. *Evolution and Human Behavior, 30*(5), 342–350.

Kalton, G. (2012). Measuring health in population surveys. *Statistical Journal of the IAOS,* *28*(1), 13–24.

Kellock, A., Lawthom, R., Sixsmith, J., Duggan, K., Mountian, I., Haworth, J. T., . . . Siddiquee, A. (2011). Using technology and the experience sampling method to understand real life. In S. N. Hesse-Biber (Ed.), *The handbook of emergent technologies in social research* (pp. 542–562). Oxford: Oxford University Press.

Kelly, D., Smyth, B., & Caulfield, B. (2013). Uncovering measurements of social and demographic behavior from smartphone location data. *IEEE Transactions on Human-Machine Systems, 43*(2), 188–198.

Klein, T. (2011). Durch Dick und Duenn. Ergebnisse des Partnermarktsurvey 2009. *Koelner Zeitschrift fuer Soziologie und Sozialpsychologie, 63*(3), 459–479.

Low, N., McCarthy, A., Macleod, J., Salisbury, C., Campbell, R., Roberts, T. E., . . . Egger, M. (2007). Epidemiological, social, diagnostic and economic evaluation of population screening for genital chlamydial infection. *Health Technology Assessment, 11*(8), iii–iv, ix–xii, 1–165.

McCadden, A., Fenton, K. A., McManus, S., Mercer, C. H., Erens, B., Carder, C., . . . Johnson, A. M. (2005). Chlamydia trachomatis testing in the second British national survey of sexual attitudes and lifestyles: Respondent uptake and treatment outcomes. *Sexually Transmitted Diseases, 32*(6), 387–394.

McDade, T. W., Williams, S., & Snodgrass, J. J. (2007). What a drop can do: dried blood spots as a minimally invasive method for integrating biomarkers into population-based research. *Demography, 44*(4), 899–925.

McEwen, J. E., Boyer, J. T., & Sun, K. Y. (2013). Evolving approaches to the ethical management of genomic data. *Trends in Genetics, 29*(6), 375–382.

Media-Micro-Census GmbH. (2012, August). *Ma 2012 Plakat. Methoden-Steckbrief zur Berichterstattung.* Frankfurt: AGMA.

National Cohort Working Group. (2011). *The National Cohort. A prospective epidemiologic study resource for health and disease research in Germany.* Heidelberg: German Cancer Research Center.

Odgers, C. L., Caspi, A., Bates, C. J., Sampson, R. J., & Moffitt, T. E. (2012). Systematic social observation of children's neighborhoods using Google Street View: a reliable and cost-effective method. *Journal of Child Psychology and Psychiatry, 53*(10), 1009–1017.

Pfeifer, C. (2011). *Physical attractiveness, employment, and earnings* (Report No. 5664). Bonn: IZA.

Pollet, T. V., van der Meij, L., Cobey, K. D., & Buunk, A. P. (2011). Testosterone levels and their associations with lifetime number of opposite sex partners and remarriage in a large sample of American elderly men and women. *Hormones and Behavior, 60*(1), 72–77.

Raento, M., Oulasvirta, A., & Eagle, N. (2009). Smartphones: An emerging tool for social scientists. *Sociological Methods and Research, 37*, 426–454.

Rapp, I. (2012). In Gesundheit und Krankheit? Der Zusammenhang zwischen dem Gesundheitszustand und der Ehestabilitaet. *Koelner Zeitschrift fuer Soziologie und Sozialpsychologie, 64*(4), 783–803.

Rathje, W. L. (1984). "Where's the beef?": Red meat and reactivity. *American Behavioral Scientist, 28*, 71–91.

Schnell, R. (2009). *Biological variables in social surveys* (Working Paper No. 138). Berlin: German Council for Social and Economic Data (RatSWD).

Schonlau, M., Reuter, M., Schupp, J., Montag, C., Weber, B., Dohmen, T., Siegel, N. A., Sunde, U., Wagner, G. G., & Falk, A. (2010). Collecting genetic samples in population-wide (panel) surveys: Feasibility, nonresponse and selectivity. *Survey Research Methods,* 4(2), 121–126.

Schumm, L. P., McClintock, M., Williams, S., Leitsch, S., Lundstrom, J., Hummel, T., & Lindau, S. T. (2009). Assessment of sensory function in the National Social Life, Health, and Aging Project. *Journal of Gerontology, 64B*(Suppl 1), i76-i85.

Schwarz, N. (2007). Retrospective and concurrent self-reports: The rationale for real-time data capture, In A. A. Stone, S. S. Shiffman, A. Atienza, & L. Nebeling (Eds.), *The science of real-time data capture* (pp. 11–26). Oxford: Oxford University Press.

Silbermann, A. (1963). *Vom Wohnen der Deutschen.* Koeln: Westdeutscher Verlag.

Solaz, J., Belda-Lois, J., Garcia, A., Barbera, R., Dura, J. V., Gomez, J. A., Soler, C., & Prat, J. M. (2006). Intelligent textiles for medical and monitoring applications. In H. R. Mattila (Ed.), *Intelligent textiles and clothing* (pp. 369–398). Cambridge: Woodhead.

Tobin, D. J. (Ed.). (2005). *Hair in toxicology. An important bio-monitor.* Cambridge: RSC.

van Bergen, J., Götz, H., Richardus, J. H., Hoebe, C., Broer, J., & Coenen, T. (2006). Prevalence of urogenital chlamydia trachomatis infections in the Netherlands suggests selective screening approaches. Results from the PILOT CT Population Study. *Drugs Today (Barc), 42*(Suppl A), 25–33.

Weinstein, M., Vaupel, J., & Wachter, K. (Eds.). (2008). *Biosocial surveys.* Washington, DC: National Academy.

Weisberg, H. F. (2005). *The total survey error approach.* Chicago: The University of Chicago Press.

Yu, Y.-Z., & Shi, J.-X. (2009). Relationship between levels of testosterone and cortisol in saliva and aggressive behaviors of adolescents. *Biomedical and Environmental Sciences, 22*(1), 44–49.

25

The Use of Paradata

Frauke Kreuter

25.1 INTRODUCTION

As this edited volume shows, there are many ways to improve survey data collection and survey data analysis. Paradata are one of the tools used in this endeavor. Across the world, data collection agencies use paradata to monitor or manage their data collection, or if they are not currently using paradata, they are engaged in finding out how such data can be used.[1] But before going into detail on why and how paradata can be used, a quick definition might be in order for those readers unfamiliar with the term.

The definition of paradata has been evolving since the term was originally coined by Mick Couper during a talk given at the Joint Statistical Meeting in Dallas, Texas. Couper's use of the term referred to data that are by-products of computer-assisted data collection. Common examples of automated by-products are key-stroke data, time stamps, and the use of "help" functions by interviewers or respondents (Caspar & Couper, 1997; Couper, Hansen, & Sadosky, 1997; Couper, Horm, & Schlegel, 1997; Couper, 1998). While the use of key-stroke data and time-stamps long predates the term paradata (e.g. Fazio, 1990), their use has increased with the rapid growth of computerized data collection, and web surveys in particular (Conrad, Tourangeau, Couper, & Zhang, 2012; Scheuren, 2005).

In the last decade the term paradata has been expanded to cover all data that arise (or can be gathered) during the survey data collection process (Kreuter & Casas-Cordero, 2010). For example, when creating a sampling frame through housing unit listing, interviewer movements can be recorded through GPS devices and electronic recordings can inform about interviewers' attempts to contact housing units (Wagner & Olson, 2011; see Eckman, 2013 for a review). In the process of recruiting respondents, interviewers are often charged with taking notes on when recruitment attempts were made and what their outcomes were. Increasingly, interviewers are also asked to make observations of both responding and nonresponding cases (Kreuter et al., 2010). In telephone surveys the interaction between interviewers and respondents is now often recorded, providing data both about the recruitment process (Conrad et al., 2013) as well as about the measurement process (see Olson & Parkhurst, 2013 for a review). These examples give some of the flavor of the diversity of paradata and the very different nature that these data can have. Since technology is changing rapidly, new paradata are becoming available. Already eye-tracking studies are becoming more common during questionnaire development (Galesic, Tourangeau, Couper, & Conrad, 2008), and increased cell-phone usage to respond to web surveys will allow a variety of new measures while respondents are filling out a questionnaire (Callegaro, 2013).

Paradata and metadata are often discussed jointly, and it might help to differentiate between these two types of data. Paradata are usually defined as data about the process, whereas metadata are described as data about data. The same source can result in paradata as well as metadata. For example, contact history records are paradata about the recruitment process, with time and day of each contact attempt being recorded as well as the result code of each of these attempts. In the aggregate these data are used to form response rates for the entire survey, a typical piece of metadata in data documentation standards.[2] Metadata are macrolevel information about survey data and can also include other information outside the data collection process, such as information about variable labels or value labels used in the final data set. Quality survey documentation should include such metadata.

Even though some paradata are automatic by-products of computerized data collection systems, researchers often have to make an explicit decision to collect and retain such information. Not every CATI or web survey system will store key-stroke data and response times without having been told to do so. Paradata such as interviewer observations about selected cases need to be explicitly designed: Interviewers must be trained in collecting them (West & Kreuter, 2013) and, if they are not entered electronically, additional effort to convert hand-written notes into data is needed. Thus a reasonable question is, why bother collecting such paradata? Three main arguments are usually put forward in favor of collecting paradata. One is their use in *improving data quality* through monitoring and interventions, another is their use in *improving data collection efficiency*, and finally their use in *improving survey estimates*.

25.2 IMPROVING DATA QUALITY

Paradata can contribute towards quality improvement if they are used to detect problems with data collection prior to implementing the actual instrument or through monitoring the fieldwork and issuing interventions. To give a few examples: cognitive interviews and expert reviews are common tools aimed at detecting problems with specific questions (Willis, 2005). However, both show large variability in their results (Conrad & Blair, 2009) and guidelines for the optimal use of such techniques are not yet available. Paradata have the potential to supplement these techniques. For example, paradata can provide a trace of respondents' difficulty with particular questions or question visualizations. Reviewing several experimental studies that used response times, Olson and Parkhurst (2013) reported longer response times to be indicative of complex visual layouts, inconsistent response options, and lack of respondent engagement. Measuring response times while testing several question administration forms against each other during a pretest can therefore provide valuable information about questions in need of repair, and point to questions that are in need of extensive qualitative assessments (e.g. cognitive interviews).

In a much simpler way, response times are also used to evaluate the administration speed for certain sections of a questionnaire before final decisions about the overall questionnaire layout are made. Here response times are merely compared to a set target (overall time). The location of break-offs (in particular in web surveys) are often assessed relative to other questions in the questionnaire and have been found to be particularly high for transitional screens (Horwitz, Tancreto, Zelenak, & Davis, 2013; Peytchev, 2009).

Response times, break-offs, and even mouse clicks can be collected and assessed not only prior to the fielding of a survey, but they can also be monitored during the fieldwork process. Conrad et al. (2012) monitored response times and prompted survey respondents to give the question sufficient thought when the time fell below a given threshold (e.g. 350 milliseconds per word, which is a typical reading time). Such prompts resulted in improved accuracy among respondents with intermediate levels of education. The authors suggest that respondents with higher education may be accurate while "speeding" through the questionnaire and respondents with less education might be unable to improve accuracy on the type of numeracy questions asked in this study.

Also using a web survey, Horwitz (2013) identified a set of movements in which respondents engage with their mouse cursor that suggest they are experiencing difficulty answering a question. These movements can be used to identify problematic questions in real time on a larger scale than pretests allow.

On the interviewer side, the U.S. Census Bureau has for years used its Performance and Data Analysis (PANDA) system[3] to monitor the rate of "don't knows" and "refusals" per interviewer (Rowe, 2009). Supervisors use this information to issue retraining or other forms of interventions.

25.3 IMPROVING DATA COLLECTION EFFICIENCY

Paradata are also used to improve data collection efficiency. CATI surveys have for years made extensive use of paradata to improve call scheduling. Call records, which include the time and day of a contact attempt as well as the specific outcome at the contact attempt, are fundamental to most automated calling systems. Such systems ensure that cases are called across different day parts (morning, afternoon, evening) and on weekdays as well as weekends (Weeks, Jones, Folsom & Benrud, 1980; Greenberg & Stokes, 1990). Outcome codes are used to determine the interval length between calls, with busy cases often being called again right away and cases with ring-no-answer being moved to a different window or day all together. Such call scheduling algorithms are in place in most CATI studios (though it pays off to double check if they are), but are much less common in face-to-face data collections. Here interviewers are often advised to follow such rules, but enforcing such guidelines is much harder, if not impossible (Wagner, 2013). Panel studies provide particularly rich sets of data from prior waves that can be used to improve call scheduling in the subsequent wave. Lipps (2012) showed in a post-hoc analysis of Swiss Household Panel data that the probability of contact and more importantly cooperation at first contact increases if respondents are contacted during the call window that had been successful in the prior wave, though Kreuter and Müller (2013) found only very small efficiency gains when experimentally using prior wave call record information in a panel study in Germany.

Paradata also play a fundamental role in the realization of responsive designs, as suggested by Groves and Heeringa (2006), with the goal of implementing the best possible design while maximizing data collection yield and minimizing costs. The U.S. National Survey of Family Growth (NSFG) is a face-to-face survey that used responsive design for its 2006–2010 data collection, and continues to do so in the current round (Kirgis & Lepkowski, 2013). Through extensive use of paradata, web-based centralized management systems and management tools that attempt to capture what is going on in the field in real time, NSFG was able to almost double the number of interviews conducted without increasing data collection costs (Groves, Mosher, Lepkowski, & Kirgis, 2009). Inspired by this success, Robert Groves restructured data collection at the U.S. Census Bureau to allow for similar centralized management and paradata driven decisions on when and how sampled units should be approached (Thieme & Miller, 2012).

In the 2006–2010 NSFG data collection, paradata and other auxiliary data were used to model response propensity after ten weeks of data collection (Wagner et al., 2012). The model results were used to decide on a recruitment strategy for the next phase. Response propensity models were also estimated continuously during the first ten weeks, informing intervention decisions such as increased screening efforts. Such continuous monitoring and decision-making guided by response propensity models is also the goal of efforts currently being implemented at the U.S. Census Bureau. While one could argue that with this approach to data collection is model dependent (and thus suffers from weak models), the current practice can already be seen as model dependent, only that survey researchers do not know which "working model" any given interviewer has in his or her head when deciding to approach a case or not.

In telephone surveys, fewer covariates are available that can be used to build response propensity models. Peytchev, Riley, Rosen, Murphy, and Lindblad (2010) used paradata (whether the respondent had said they were not interested in the prior wave, and whether the respondent had ever hung up during the introduction in the prior wave) in conjunction with demographic variables from prior survey waves to predict propensities and subsequently assign difficult cases to highly experienced interviewers. Eckman, Sinibaldi, and Möntmann-Hertz (2013) showed that telephone interviewers can distinguish between high and low propensity cases and can assign likelihood ratings: such ratings may supplement or replace response propensity models when there are few variables available, and may either through models or by themselves suggest interventions during data collection efforts.

Sakshaug (2013) suggests the use of paradata to predict responses to within-survey requests. He showed that call record data (in particular number of call attempts) are predictive of data linkage and biomeasure consent in a survey on health and retirement, and paradata reflecting respondents' answer behaviour are predictive of mode switch nonresponse and data quality in a survey of University of Maryland alumni. Knowing about these relationships offers the possibility to alter requests on the fly, or intervene when paradata would raise flags of concern. Along these lines, paradata can not only be used to increase efficiency but also to alter data collection during the fieldwork process to increase the probability of bringing different cases into the respondent pool and with that reduce bias in resulting estimates.

25.4 IMPROVING SURVEY ESTIMATES

Using paradata to make estimates that have smaller standard errors is another way paradata contribute to efficiency, and similarly can be used to estimate or reduce bias in survey estimates. Variables (or combinations of variables) that are used for nonresponse adjustment should ideally reduce nonresponse bias without increasing variance. To accomplish these goals, the variables need to be related to the response mechanism (i.e. successfully predict contact or cooperation) and need to be related to the key variables of interest in the survey. For this reason, surveys like the 2006–2010 National Survey of Family Growth and the current round of the National Health Interview Survey (NHIS) collect paradata in the form of interviewer observations that are direct proxies of key variables of interest. In NSFG the interviewers are charged to judge whether or not children are present in the household and whether or not the sampled person is currently in an active sexual relationship with an opposite sex partner (Groves et al., 2009; West, 2013a). This said, paradata that contribute to successful nonresponse adjustment will likely differ across surveys because the participation decision is sometimes dependent on the survey topic or sponsor (Groves, Singer, & Corning, 2000), and proxy measures of key survey variables will thus naturally vary across surveys and survey topics (Kreuter et al., 2010). Even within the same survey, some paradata will be strong predictors of survey participation, but vary in their association with the important survey variables (Kreuter & Olson, 2011); consequently theoretical support is needed to determine which paradata should be collected.

Very few studies have used paradata to remove measurement error in model estimates. One example is a study by Freedman, Stafford, Conrad, and Schwarz (2012) that used factor analysis to form a scale of observed quality based on interviewer observations, though adding this scale to their regression models predicting time use had no impact on the model coefficients. The idea of using interviewer observations to model respondents' interest in the survey is not new (Fisk, 1950), and additional research in this area is still needed. There certainly has been encouraging empirical evidence for the relationship between interviewer observations of response quality and responses to the survey. For example, Andrews (1989) found respondents rated high in "interest," "intelligence," and "sincerity" provided responses of higher validity compared to the others. Tarnai and Paxson (2005) found that respondents given an "excellent" rating produced less missing data than those given a rating of "fair" or "poor" in 12 telephone studies. Higher likelihoods for missing data among respondents rated unfavorable by interviewers (with respect to intelligence, accuracy of responses, and ability to understand the survey questions) were also found by Barrett, MacLean, and Bell (2006). Likewise Peytchev and Peytcheva (2007) found that respondents rated by interviewers as having very good question understanding produced less measurement error than those rated as not having very good question understanding.

25.5 SPECIAL CHALLENGES IN THE COLLECTION AND USE OF PARADATA

Despite the promise and hope of paradata to improve the quality of data collected, to increase cost efficiency, and to decrease bias as well as variance in resulting estimates, this new data source does present several challenges. First, paradata often have a challenging data structure, and the nature of the paradata will vary across data collection modes. Paradata are also often not collected on the same unit of analysis as the survey data. For example, call record data are usually collected at each call, which could easily generate up twenty or more records for cases fielded in a telephone survey. Response times are collected at an item level and sometimes twice within one item (if the time to administer the item is measured separately from the time the respondent took to answer the question). Vocal properties of an interviewer are recorded on a finer level and could generate several records even within the administration of a single item.

Second, some paradata are difficult to interpret directly. For example, respondents naturally vary in how quickly they answer questions, and interviewers also vary in the speed with which they administer questions (Mayerl & Urban, 2008; Couper & Kreuter, 2013). To interpret time-stamps under such conditions, speed benchmarks are needed in one form or another, if not within the questionnaire, then through comparisons to prior administrations of the same question in a different survey or at a different time point, provided that other covariates that influence response times can be controlled for. In such analyses, it is important that the models take the hierarchical (and, in the case of CATI surveys, often complex cross-classified) nature of the data into account (Yan & Olson, 2013; Durrant, D'Arrigo, & Müller, 2013).

Third, recent research has shown that the quality of paradata can vary considerably across respondents, interviewers, and surveys (West & Sinibaldi, 2013). Interviewers may erroneously record certain housing unit characteristics, can misjudge features about the respondents, or can fail to record a contact attempt altogether (Sinibaldi, Durrant, & Kreuter, 2013; Biemer, Chen, & Wang, 2013; West & Kreuter, 2013). Such errors can harm the use of paradata in nonresponse adjustments (West, 2013b). Differences in the quality and the usability of paradata across countries are discussed in Stoop, Billiet, Koch, and Fitzgerald (2010).

Fourth, while collecting automatically generated paradata is fairly easy and cheap, preparing and analyzing the data can take substantial effort. Given that many CAPI or CATI data collections use the same software products, researchers planning to extract paradata can benefit from pre-existing code examples (Mai, Myers, Ganapathi, & Wickelgren, 2008) to save costs. For analytical purposes it can help to work with software that allows convenient transformation of time data to minimize hand coding efforts (and associated errors). Working with mouse click data can be particularly complex: mouse click data usually include recordings of each action the respondent or interviewer takes when using the computer's mouse, and as such have for each position of the mouse information on the presence or absence of a mouse click. Here survey methodologists can borrow code and analytic approaches from other fields because such click data are commonly used to assess usability of websites and placement of commercial advertisements (Callegaro, 2013). Chapter 10 has more information on the use of such data in web surveys. Readers interested in paradata from web surveys are also advised to familiarize themselves with the Universal Client Side Paradata project (Kaczmirek, 2009).

Fifth, in order to monitor incoming data and to make useful design decisions, the field needs tools that display and summarize the large amount of incoming information. Some survey organizations, including the U.S. Census Bureau, have applied theories and methods from the quality control literature to their survey processes (Jans, Sirkis, & Morgan, 2013). The monitoring of paradata about fieldwork progress (number of cases contacted, number of cases screened, number of cases interviewed) relative to a planned budget is an endeavor that most survey organizations have in place already, though often in specific ways for each survey product. Large organizations are currently working on unifying such tracking systems (for response to invitation see Thalji et al., 2013; for Statistics New Zealand see

Struijs, Camstra, Renssen, & Braaksma, 2013; for Statistics Netherlands see Seyb, McKenzie, & Skerrett, 2013).

Finally, monitoring during the ongoing data collection process requires that survey data as well as paradata are captured and fed back into the central office in real time or with short delays, which is still a challenge for many face-to-face data collection operations. When issuing interventions, in particular in reaction to interviewer behavior, it is important to have well-justified evaluation metrics. For example, evaluating interviewers purely based on their response rates can be inferior to creating performance scores that take the predicted difficulty of a case into account (West & Groves, 2013).

25.6 CONCLUSION

We have seen successful uses of paradata to gain efficiency, to alert for errors, and to help with post-survey adjustments of estimates. Currently under development, but certainly needed given the changes in the field, are methods to expand the concurrent analytic use of paradata, the tailored collection of paradata, and the transfer across modes, surveys, and survey organizations. In addition, survey methodologists will likely benefit from linkages with cost data and other auxiliary data, and from the use of paradata in modeling. Very few researchers have taken a closer look at respondents' consent in the collection of paradata (Couper & Singer, 2013). As the use of paradata increases, such issues will need to be addressed.

NOTES

1. See, for example, the presentations from the FedCASIC plenary panel in 2012. https://fedcasic.dsd.census.gov/fc2012/index.php#1_2.
2. www.ddialliance.org/.
3. www.ifdtc.org/PC2009/presentation_2009_files/11A-Christina%20Rowe.pdf.

REFERENCES

Andrews, F. M. (1989). Some observations on meta-analysis of MTMM studies. In W. E. Saris & A. van Meurs. (Eds.), *Evaluation of measurement instruments by meta-analysis of multi-trait multi-method studies: Proceedings of the International Colloquium* (pp. 172–184). Amsterdam: North Holland.

Barrett, R.D.H., MacLean, R. C., & Bell, G. (2006). Mutations of intermediate effect are responsible for adaptation in evolving Pseudomonas fluorescens populations. *Biology Letters, 2*(2), 236–238. doi:10.1098/rsbl.2006.0439

Biemer, P., Chen, P., & Wang, K. (2013). Using level-of-effort paradata in non-response adjustments with applications to the field surveys. *Journal of the Royal Statistical Society, Series A, Statistics in Society, 176*(1), 147–168. doi:10.1111/j.1467–985X.2012.01058.x

Callegaro, M. (2013). Paradata in web surveys. In F. Kreuter (Ed.), *Improving surveys with paradata. Making use of process information* (pp. 261–276). New York: Wiley.

Caspar, R. A., & Couper, M. P. (1997). Using keystroke files to assess respondent difficulties with an ACASI instrument. *Proceedings of the American Statistical Association, Section on Survey Research Methods*, 239–244. Alexandria, VA: American Statistical Association.

Conrad, F., & Blair, J. (2009). Sources of error in cognitive interviews. *Public Opinion Quarterly, 73*(1), 32–55. doi:10.1093/poq/nfp013

Conrad, F., Broome, J. S., Benkí, J., Groves, R. M., Kreuter, F., Vannette, D., & McClain, C. (2013). Interviewer speech and the success of survey invitations. *Journal of the Royal Statistical Society, Series A, 176*(1), 191–210. doi:10.1111/j.1467-985X.2012.01064.x

Conrad, F., Tourangeau, R., Couper, M. P. & Zhang, C. (2012). Interactive intervention to reduce satisficing in web surveys. Presentation. Westat, Rockville, MD, January 24, 2012.

Couper, M. P. (1998, August). Measuring survey quality in a CASIC environment. Proceedings of the surveys research methods section, 41–49. American Statistical Association, Dallas, TX.

Couper, M. P., Hansen, S. E., & Sadosky, S. A. (1997). Evaluating interviewer performance in a CAPI survey. In L. Lyberg, P. Biemer, M. Collins, E. De Leeuw, C. Dippo, N. Schwarz, & D. Trewin (Eds.), *Survey measurement and process quality* (pp. 267–285). New York, NY: Wiley.

Couper, M. P., Horm, J., & Schlegel, J. (1997). Using trace files to evaluate the national health interview survey CAPI instrument. *American Statistical Association 1997 Proceedings of the Section on Survey Research Methods*. Washington, DC: American Statistical Association.

Couper, M. P., & Kreuter, F. (2013). Using paradata to explore item level response times in surveys. *Journal of the Royal Statistical Society, Series A, Statistics in Society, 176*(1), 271–286. doi:10.1111/j.1467-985X.2012.01041.x

Couper, M. P., & Singer, E. (2013). Informed consent for web paradata use. *Survey Research Methods, 7*(1), 57–67. Retrieved from www.surveymethods.org

Durrant, G., D'Arrigo, J., & Müller, G. (2013). Modeling call record data: examples from cross-sectional and longitudinal surveys. In F. Kreuter (Ed.), *Improving surveys with paradata. Making use of process information* (pp. 281–304). New York: Wiley.

Eckman, S. (2013). Paradata for coverage research. In F. Kreuter (Ed.), *Improving surveys with paradata. Making use of process information* (pp. 97–116). New York: Wiley.

Eckman, S., Sinibaldi, J., & Möntmann-Hertz, A. (2013). Can interviewers effectively rate the likelihood of cases to cooperate? *Public Opinion Quarterly*. doi:10.1093/poq/nft012

Fazio, R. H. (1990). A practical guide to the use of response latency in social psychological research. In C. Hendrick & M.S. Clark (Eds.), *Review of Personality and Social Psychology* (pp. 74–97). Vol. 11. Research Methods in Personality and Social Psychology. Newbury Park, CA: Sage.

Fisk, G. (1950). Interviewer ratings of respondent interests of sample surveys. *Journal of Marketing, 14*(5), 725–730. Retrieved from www.jstor.org/stable/1246950

Freedman, V. A., Stafford, F., Conrad, F., & Schwarz, N. (2012). Assessing time diary quality of older couples: an analysis of the Panel Study of Income Dynamics' Disability and Use of Time (DUST) supplement. *Annals of Economics and Statistics, 105/106*, 1–19. Retrieved from www.ncbi.nlm.nih.gov/pmc/articles/PMC3613756/

Galesic, M., Tourangeau, R., Couper, M. P., & Conrad, F. G. (2008). Eye-tracking data: New insights on response order effects and other cognitive shortcuts in survey responding, *Public Opinion Quarterly, 72*(5), 892–913. doi:10.1093/poq/nfn059

Greenberg, B. S., & Stokes, S. L. (1990). Developing an optimal call scheduling strategy for a telephone survey. *Journal of Official Statistics, 6*, 421–435.

Groves, R. M., & Heeringa, S. (2006). Responsive design for household surveys: tools for actively controlling survey errors and costs. *Journal of the Royal Statistical Society, Series A: Statistics in Society, 169*, Part 3, 439–457. doi:10.1111/j.1467-985X.2006.00423.x

Groves, R. M., Mosher, W. D., Lepkowski, J., & Kirgis, N. G. (2009). Planning and development of the continuous National Survey of Family Growth. *National Center for Health Care Statistics. Vital Health Statistics, 1*, 48.

Groves, R. M., Singer, E., & Corning, A. (2000). Leverage-salience theory of survey participation: description and an illustration, *Public Opinion Quarterly, 64*(3), 299–308. doi:10.1086/317990

Horwitz, R. (2013). *Classifying Mouse Movements and Providing Help in Web Surveys.* (Doctoral Dissertation.) University of Maryland.

Horwitz, R., Tancreto, J. G., Zelenak, M. F., & Davis, M. C. (2013). Use of paradata to assess the quality and functionality of the American community survey internet instrument. *United States Census Bureau.* Washington, DC. Retrieved from www.census.gov/acs/www/Downloads/library/2013/2013_Horwitz_01.pdf

Jans, M., Sirkis, R., & Morgan, D. (2013). Managing data quality indicators with paradata-based statistical quality control tools. In F. Kreuter (Ed.), *Improving surveys with paradata: Analytic use of process information* (pp.191–230). New York: Wiley.

Kaczmirek, L. (2009). *Human-survey interaction: Usability and nonresponse in online surveys.* Cologne: Halem Verlag.

Kirgis, N., & Lepkowski, J. M. (2013). Design and management strategies for paradata-driven responsive design. In F. Kreuter (Ed.), *Improving surveys with paradata. Making use of process information* (pp. 123–143). New York: Wiley.

Kreuter, F., & Casas-Cordero, C. (2010). Paradata. Working paper series of the German Council for Social and Economic Data 136, German Council for Social and Economic Data (RatSWD).

Kreuter, F., & Müller, G. (2013). A note on improving process efficiency in panel surveys with paradata. *Field Methods.* Conditionally accepted for publication.

Kreuter, F., & Olson, K. (2011). Multiple auxiliary variables in nonresponse adjustment, *Sociological Methods and Research, 40*(2), 311–332. doi:10.1177/0049124111400042

Kreuter, F., Olson, K., Wagner, J., Yan, T., Ezzati-Rice, T. M., Casas-Cordero, C., Lemay, M., Peytchev, A., Groves, R. M., Raghunathan, T. E. (2010). Using proxy measures and other correlates of survey outcomes to adjust for nonresponse: Examples from multiple surveys. *Journal of the Royal Statistical Society, Series A, 173*, Part 3, 1–21. doi:10.1111/j.1467-10.1111/j.1467-985X.2009.00621.x

Lipps, O. (2012). A note on improving contact times in panel surveys. *Field Methods, 24*(1), 95–111. doi:10.1177/1525822X11417966

314 • *Frauke Kreuter*

Mai, Y., Myers, S., Ganapathi, N., & Wickelgren, V. (2008). Order from chaos: Using the power of SAS® to Transform Audit Trail Data. *SESUG Proceedings*. Retrieved from http://analytics.ncsu.edu/sesug/2008/CC-027.pdf

Mayerl, J., & Urban, D. (2008). *Antwortreaktionszeiten in Survey-Analysen*. Wiesbaden: Verlag für Sozialwissenschaften.

Olson, K., & Parkhurst, B. (2013). Collecting paradata for measurement error evaluations. In F. Kreuter (Ed.), *Improving surveys with paradata. Making use of process information* (pp. 43–65). New York: Wiley.

Peytchev, A. (2009). Survey breakoff. *Public Opinion Quarterly, 73*(1), 74–97. doi:10.1093/poq/nfp014

Peytchev, A., & Peytcheva, E. (2007). Relationship between measurement error and unit nonresponse in household surveys: An approach in the absence of validation data. In *JSM Proceedings, Survey Research Methods Section*, 3864–3871. Alexandria, VA: American Statistical Association.

Peytchev, A., Riley, S., Rosen, J., Murphy, J., & Lindblad, M. (2010). Reduction of nonresponse bias in surveys through case prioritization, *Survey Research Methods, 4*(1), 21–29.

Rowe, C. (2009). Using paradata to monitor quality. Paper presented at the International Field Director's & Technology Conference (IFD&TC), May 20, 2009.

Sakshaug, J. W. (2013). Using paradata to study response to within-survey requests. In F. Kreuter (Ed.), *Improving surveys with paradata: Analytic use of process information* (pp. 171–190). New York: Wiley.

Scheuren, F. (2005). Paradata from Concept to Completion. Proceedings of Statistics Canada Symposium 2005. Methodological Challenges for Future Information Needs.

Seyb, A., McKenzie, R., & Skerrett, A. (2013). Innovative production systems at Statistics New Zealand. Overcoming the design and build bottleneck. *Journal of Official Statistics*, pp. 73–97.

Sinibaldi, J., Durrant, G., & Kreuter, F. (2013). Evaluating the measurement error of interviewer observed paradata. *Public Opinion Quarterly*, 77, S1, 173–193. doi:10.1093/poq/nfs062

Stoop, I., Billiet, J., Koch, A., & Fitzgerald, R. (2010). *Improving survey response. Lessons learned from the European Social Survey*. Chichester: Wiley.

Struijs, P., Camstra, A., Renssen, R., & Braaksma, B. (2013). Redesign of statistics production within an architectural framework: the Dutch experience. *Journal of Official Statistics, 29*(1), 49–71.

Tarnai, J., & Paxson, M. C. (2005). Interviewer judgments about the quality of telephone interviews. *2005 proceedings of the American Statistical Association, Survey Methods Research Section* [CD-ROM]. Alexandria, VA: American Statistical Association.

Thalji, L., Hill, C. A., Mitchell, S., Suresh, R., Speizer, H., & Pratt, D. (2013). The general survey system initiative at RTI international: an integrated system for the collection and management of survey data. *Journal of Official Statistics, 29*(1), 29–48.

Thieme, M., & Miller, P. (2012). The center for adaptive design. Presentation to the National Advisory Committee on Racial, Ethnic, and Other Populations. October 25, 2012, Washington, D.C.

Wagner, J. (2013). Using paradata-driven models to improve contact rates. In F. Kreuter (Ed.), *Improving surveys with paradata. Making use of process information* (pp. 145–169). New York: Wiley.

Wagner, J., & Olson, K. (2011). Where do interviewers go when they do what they do? An analysis of interviewer travel in two field surveys. *Proceedings of the American Statistical Association, Section on Survey Research Methods*, Miami, FL.

Wagner, J., West, B. T., Kirgis, N., Lepkowski, J. M., Axinn, W. G., & Kruger-Ndiaye, S. (2012). Use of paradata in a responsive design framework to manage a field data collection. *Journal of Official Statistics*, *28*(4), 477–499.

Weeks, M. F., Jones, B. L., Folsom, R. E., & Benrud, C. H. (1980). Optimal times to contact sample households. *Public Opinion Quarterly*, *44*(1), 101–114. doi:10.1086/26856

West, B. T. (2013a). An examination of the quality and utility of interviewer observations in the National Survey of Family Growth. *Journal of the Royal Statistical Society, Series A*, *176*(1), 211–225. doi:10.1111/j.1467-985X.2012.01038.x

West, B. T. (2013b). The effects of errors in paradata on weighting class adjustments: a simulation study. In F. Kreuter (Ed.), *Improving surveys with paradata. Making use of process information* (pp. 361–387). New York: Wiley.

West, B. T., & Groves, R. M. (2013). The PAIP score: A propensity-adjusted interviewer performance indicator. *Public Opinion Quarterly*. doi:10.1093/poq/nft002

West, B. T., & Kreuter, F. (2013). Factors impacting the accuracy of interviewer observations: evidence from the National Survey of Family Growth (NSFG). *Public Opinion Quarterly*. 77(2), 522–548. doi:10.1093/poq/nft016

West, B. T., & Sinibaldi, J. (2013). The quality of paradata: a literature review. In F. Kreuter (Ed.), *Improving surveys with paradata. Making use of process information* (pp. 339–356). New York: Wiley.

Willis, G. (2005). *Cognitive interviewing: a tool for improving questionnaire design*. Thousand Oaks: Sage.

Yan, T., & Olson, K. (2013). Analyzing paradata to investigate measurement error. In F. Kreuter (Ed.), *Improving surveys with paradata. Making use of process information* (pp. 73–90). New York: Wiley.

Part VII

Coping with Nonresponse

26

Coping with Nonresponse

Overview and Introduction

Peter Lynn

Surveys are carried out by a wide variety of organizations and for a vast range of purposes, but ultimately the objective is nearly always to enable estimation of some characteristics of a study population of interest. Those characteristics may be simple means or proportions, or differences in means between subgroups, or something rather more complex, such as the influence of a particular set of variables on a certain outcome, conditional on the presence or absence of some other characteristics. In any case, the inference from sample to population relies on the sample having been generated by a known probabilistic mechanism. For this reason, serious social and economic surveys employ probability sampling methods.

However, the desirable properties of the selected sample can be upset if the survey suffers from nonresponse, which pretty much all surveys do. Nonresponse will not necessarily bias survey estimates, but it will do so if the nonrespondents are systematically different from the respondents. Over the past couple of decades, almost all countries have experienced falling response rates and/or greater and costlier efforts required in order to maintain response rates (Curtin, Presser, & Singer, 2005; De Leeuw & de Heer, 2002). A lower response rate does not necessarily imply greater nonresponse bias (Groves & Peytcheva, 2008; Peytchev, 2013), but it certainly provides greater opportunity for bias: if the response rate is high then the nonrespondents, had they responded, would have contributed only a small part to the survey estimates. The bias in the estimates would therefore be small, even if the nonrespondents were quite distinctive in character. For this reason, falling response rates are a concern.

The reaction of researchers to the increased difficulty of obtaining high response rates has taken two forms (Massey & Tourangeau, 2013). One has been to search for better ways of persuading people to take part in surveys.

The other has been to search for better ways of making estimates in the situation where considerable nonresponse has affected the data. At the extreme, the latter of these reactions has led some to question the fundamental paradigm of probability-based statistical inference. Unfortunately, the essential qualities of survey nonresponse have remained a somewhat elusive beast. Despite a huge amount of research effort, response rates are still falling and the costs of maintaining response are still increasing. Yes, we now know quite a lot about the mechanisms that invoke nonresponse, but we are still not well able to extrapolate this knowledge to new situations or to exploit it to turn the tide.

The three chapters in this section offer different perspectives on the search for better ways of persuading people to take part in surveys.

Most aspects of survey design and implementation are highly standardized across sample members: Each sample member receives the same advance letter, the same incentive, identical survey materials and the same set of arguments for taking part. Considering that surveys have been highly successful in spotlighting diversity in society it is perhaps surprising that survey design does little to recognize this diversity. Chapter 27 champions the idea that surveys may benefit from offering a less standardized approach to the task of persuading respondents to take part in surveys. Some response-inducing strategies may work better for some sample members than others, so if we could target strategies at particular sample members, response may be improved. Longitudinal surveys provide a particularly promising context for such targeting due to the wealth of information known about each sample member prior to the start of each wave.

One response-inducing strategy with a strong track record of improving response rates is the administration of an incentive to each sample member. Incentives can take various forms. Notably they can be prepaid or postpaid, monetary or non-monetary and can vary in value. Also, their effect may depend on the survey mode or other features of the survey. Chapter 28 reviews the effects of all these features of incentives, firstly based on published meta-analyses of mail, telephone and face-to-face surveys, and secondly based on the rapidly expanding set of studies carried out on web surveys. The findings regarding web surveys are consistent with those of Singer and Ye (2013) who concluded that, "a search for more effective incentives [in web surveys] is needed."

A cross-national perspective on nonresponse is provided in Chapter 29, which presents an overview of nonresponse in the European Social Survey, involving more than 30 countries. The chapter discusses reasons why response rates may differ between countries, and how the appropriate use of auxiliary data can help to interpret these differences. The challenges

as in the adaptive designs of Wagner (2008). A broad distinction can be made between targeted and tailored strategies. Targeted strategies involve treating each of a limited number of sample subgroups in different ways, where the subgroups are defined by relevant common characteristics. Tailored strategies involve treating each individual sample member differently, depending on that person's characteristics and behavior (Couper & Wagner, 2011). At the margins, the distinction is difficult to pin down, but this paper focuses on targeting rather than tailoring.

The distinction between responsive and adaptive designs is not clear and Couper and Wagner (2011) have argued that the two lie at different points on a continuum of possible design variants. Schouten, Calinescu, and Luiten (2013) additionally include designs in which features are targeted at subgroups from the start—rather than only as fieldwork progresses—under the rubric of adaptive designs. It is designs of this kind with which we are concerned in this paper—and specifically those in which the relevant quality indicators are either response rate or response balance.

We review both theory and practice regarding targeted strategies to improve response rate or response balance. We define targeted strategies broadly, and in Section 27.4 below we outline the different ways in which strategies can be targeted, and identify three main categories of targeted strategy.

27.2 RESPONSE INDUCEMENT

Survey researchers have long been concerned with how best to obtain good response rates and have developed many elements of the survey process in ways intended to increase response rates. Such elements include, amongst others, the design of survey materials, the substantive content of survey communications, the nature and intensity of field effort and the provision of direct incentives such as money, gifts or lottery tickets. At every step in the survey design and implementation process, survey researchers consider carefully the likely implications of each possible decision for survey nonresponse. Often these considerations conflict with other objectives such as cost-efficiency, timeliness and parsimony. For this reason, the efficacy of measures to reduce nonresponse must be well-established in order for researchers to be able to justify incorporating a measure that costs more or delays completion of fieldwork, for example.

Large research literatures address some of the survey design features that affect response rates. Features found to affect response rates include the form and value of monetary incentives offered to respondents (Church, 1993; Singer, van Hoewyk, Gebler, Raghunathan, & McGonagle, 1999; Singer, 2002; VanGeest, Johnson, & Welch, 2007), the content and design of prenotification and invitation letters (De Leeuw, Callegaro, Hox, Korendijk, & Lensvelt-Mulders, 2007; Dillman, 2007; Hembroff, Rusz, Rafferty, McGee, & Ehrlich, 2005; Kaplowitz, Lupi, Couper, & Thorp, 2012), mode of prenotification (Bosnjak, Neubarth, Couper, Bandilla, & Kaczmirek, 2008; Kaplowitz, Hadlock, & Levine, 2004), interviewer calling patterns (Bennett & Steel, 2000; Campanelli, Sturgis, & Purdon, 1997; Weeks, Kulka, & Pierson, 1987), survey topic and sponsorship (Groves, Presser, & Dipko, 2004; Sheehan, 2006; Van Kenhove, Wijnen, & De Wulf, 2002), respondent burden (Crawford, Couper, & Lamias, 2001; Galesic & Bosnjak, 2009) and interviewer characteristics (Beerten, 1999; Durrant, Groves, Staetsky, & Steele, 2010; Jäckle, Lynn, Sinibaldi, & Tipping, 2013). Some of these features appear to be relevant for all survey modes, while others are specific to certain modes.

However, all of these findings relate to sample mean effects. On average, each of these features tends to affect response rates, so choice of the most effective option will tend to increase response rates, but this is not uniformly true for all sample subgroups. Indeed, such heterogeneity of effect may explain some of the inconsistencies in the methodological literature. If a particular feature improves response amongst older people, but not amongst younger people, for example, you would expect to observe a sample mean effect on a study of the total population, a stronger effect on a study of retired people, and no effect on a study of students. And there is plenty of evidence in the literature of heterogenous effects on response propensity. For example, Kaplowitz et al. (2012) found that the length of the invitation letter affected response rates to a web survey for staff and faculty of a university but not for students, while information about how long the survey would take to complete affected response rates for students, but not for faculty or staff. Similarly, Lynn (2012a) found that a monetary incentive improved response rates for older people but not for younger people. But rather than being viewed as a limitation of existing research, this heterogeneity of effects can be considered as an opportunity to achieve positive effects that are even stronger than observed sample mean effects. In principle, this can be achieved by targeting strategies to the sample subgroups where they are most effective.

Such targeting could have either of two objectives. One possible objective would be to maximize the survey response rate. An alternative would be to achieve balanced response across important covariates (for example, maximizing an R-indicator in the manner of Schouten, Cobben, & Bethlehem, 2009). In either case, this should be achieved in a cost-effective way. The two objectives can have different implications for the nature of the targeting, but in either case the basic strategy is the same.

In practice, targeted response inducement strategies are not often used. There are a number of reasons for this:

- There is a lack of information about how treatment effects vary over sample subgroups. Many articles reporting the effects of features designed to boost survey response report only the sample mean effects, with no information provided regarding the heterogeneity of the effects.
- Methodological studies define subgroups inconsistently. Where effects on subgroups are reported, the subgroups are defined differently in different studies, making it difficult to combine information to inform a strategy involving multiple design features.
- Often, subgroup membership is not known in advance. Many sampling frames contain little or no information that can be used to target response inducement strategies. This is particularly true for address-based sampling, where geographical location is typically the only characteristic known in advance. If the subgroup membership of a sample member is not known in advance, response inducement strategies cannot be targeted.
- Subgroups to be targeted may not correspond to subgroups for whom effect estimates are available. Even when a sampling frame is informative, the available variables may not be ones which any previous methodological study has investigated.
- The features available for manipulation are limited. The opportunities to influence the participation decision are typically limited to one or two brief communications. When these communications are written rather than interviewer-administered, and especially in the case of address-based sampling and similar situations in which the respondent is not yet identified, the communication may not be seen at all by some sample members.

Happily, some of these barriers to the use of targeted response inducement strategies are reduced in the case of longitudinal surveys. In the next section we discuss why this is the case and how we can take advantage of the opportunities provided by longitudinal surveys for the implementation of targeted strategies.

27.3 LONGITUDINAL SURVEYS

A strength of longitudinal surveys is the availability, once the recruitment wave has been completed, of a wide range of pertinent measures for each sample member. These rich data provide an opportunity to identify a multitude of alternative subgroups at whom response inducement strategies can be targeted. This opportunity is enjoyed only by longitudinal surveys. Even the most informative of sampling frames, such as population registers and administrative databases, typically include only a few variables, and not in as much detail as can be collected in a survey. Additionally, the richness of the information available in a longitudinal survey often means that measures can be constructed that correspond closely to the subgroup definitions used in earlier methodological studies, enabling direct projection of methodological findings to the survey sample.

A further difference between longitudinal surveys and cross-sectional surveys is that there are typically more features available for manipulation in the case of longitudinal surveys. This too makes the context for targeted response inducement strategies more promising in the longitudinal case. With a cross-sectional telephone survey, manipulable features are limited to the prenotification letter and the interviewer introduction. With a cross-sectional face-to-face survey, there may also be materials designed for the interviewer to hand over or show to the respondent. And with a mail survey the design of the questionnaire itself can also be manipulated. All of those possibilities apply to the longitudinal case too, but additionally there may be various kinds of between-wave interventions, including post-wave thank you letters, between-wave motivational mailings of findings or other information, keep-in-touch mailings or phone calls, birthday cards, change-of-address cards and so on. Additionally, longitudinal surveys are increasingly developing participant websites where sample members can log in, read information of various kinds and take part in various activities. The nature of these web-based interactions could also be targeted.

It could also be noted that there is perhaps a greater justification in the case of longitudinal surveys for the implementation of measures such as targeted inducement strategies that can improve overall response rates. This is simply because response rates are in some sense more important for longitudinal surveys than for other surveys. In addition to being a contributing factor to nonresponse bias (and a rather crude indicator of the likelihood of bias; Groves & Peytcheva, 2008), as for any survey, the continuing value and utility of a longitudinal survey relies on the continued participation of a high proportion of the sample members.

Unlike the cross-sectional case, a loss of sample numbers cannot be compensated for by simply adding more sample, as the historical longitudinal data will be missing and cannot be fully recreated retrospectively. There is therefore a particular imperative for high wave-on-wave response rates for longitudinal surveys. Without them, the whole survey becomes unviable.

27.4 THE TARGETED INDUCEMENT DESIGN

There are a number of ways in which inducements could be targeted. It may be useful to distinguish between three main categories:

- A design feature is applied only to one group. This could be done because the feature is believed to be effective only for that group, because it is only appropriate for that group or simply because that group is otherwise expected to have a lower response rate than other groups;
- A different design feature is offered to each group. Such a design may be chosen because it is believed that the optimum feature differs between groups, for example, where there is a choice between two incompatible features such as two different types of incentive;
- A group-specific variant of the same design feature is offered to each group. An example would be a prenotification letter in which the wording is varied between groups.

In any of these three cases, the tasks facing a researcher who wishes to introduce such a design consist of the following components:

1. Defining the subgroups to be targeted;
2. Identifying the inducement strategy to be applied to each subgroup;
3. Allocating sample units to subgroups;
4. Implementing the design.

Note that we refer here specifically to targeting that takes place before a wave of data collection begins, based on prior characteristics. This is distinct from the practice of adapting design features in response to respondent behavior during the course of a wave of data collection. For example, on the American Panel Study of Income Dynamics (PSID; McGonagle,

Schoeni, Sastry, & Freedman, 2012), respondents who are interviewed on their cell phone and who complain about the cost to them of the cell phone minutes are offered an additional $10 payment in compensation (McGonagle, 2013). Although this additional payment goes to only a subset of sample members, we do not consider this a targeted design as the payment would be offered to any sample member who complains about the cost of receiving a call on their cell phone. Similarly, the Household, Income and Labour Dynamics in Australia Survey (Watson & Wooden, 2012) sends a letter to households who have not participated by the end of the first fieldwork period within each wave (Watson, 2013). There are different versions of the letter, depending on the reason for not yet participating. Again, however, we do not consider this a targeted design as any sample household would receive the same treatment if they had the same outcome at the end of the first field period. Many other examples of such reactive adaptation on the part of the survey organization can be found. One can even think of the persuasion strategies used by interviewers and the choice of when to make the next call attempt to a sample member (whether that be determined by an interviewer or by a call scheduling algorithm) as examples of this.

We now outline in turn the requirements for each of the four components of a targeted inducement design.

Defining the Subgroups

The subgroups must be ones for which distinctive and effective inducement strategies can be identified. In practice this means that the first two components of the design listed above cannot be carried out independently. Simultaneous consideration of the two issues is needed.

If the objective is not only to increase response rate but also to improve response balance, then each subgroup should be relatively homogeneous both in terms of survey response propensity and in terms of key survey variables. In other words, the subgroups should be ones that are likely to differ from one another in terms of response rate in the absence of any targeted design and there should also be variation between the subgroups in the means, distributions and associations of key variables. These requirements are somewhat analogous to the requirements for successful cell-weighting for nonresponse adjustment. This is not surprising if we consider that in both cases the objective is to reduce nonresponse bias. The difference is that targeted inducement designs aim to reduce bias at the source during the data collection stage, whereas weighting adjustments aim to reduce bias post hoc at the estimation stage.

However, there are also two important differences between the requirements for subgroup definition for targeted inducement designs and the requirements for effective weight-adjustment cells. The first is the need to be able to develop distinctive and effective inducement strategies, as mentioned above. Second, there is no particular need to avoid small subgroup sample sizes, as the approach does not involve estimation for subgroups (though designing targeted materials for very small numbers of sample cases may be considered inefficient and researchers may prefer to avoid small groups for that reason).

Identifying Targeted Inducement Strategies

The optimum strategy for each subgroup is the one that maximizes the expected response rate, subject to budget constraints. However, a desire to achieve balanced response would suggest that resources for response inducement should be devoted disproportionately to those subgroups that have the lowest predicted response rates in the absence of a targeted strategy (Calinescu, Bhulai, & Schouten, 2013). Thus, strategies with a higher unit cost of implementation can be considered for the lowest response propensity groups if this is likely to produce a larger response rate gain for those groups than for other groups. Methodological experimentation is needed in order to establish the relative effectiveness of possible response inducement strategies for different subgroups. Previously published studies of design features that influence response propensity can therefore be used to inform the choice of targeted strategy, but only if those studies have included subgroup analysis. Alternatively, researchers may wish to carry out their own methodological tests. In many ways longitudinal surveys are ideal vehicles for this, as an experiment mounted at one wave can inform the design at the next wave. For example, a particular design feature could be implemented for a random half of the sample units at one wave. Analysis of the outcomes at that wave should reveal the subgroups for which the feature was most effective. At the following wave, this feature could then be implemented only for those subgroups. Assuming that there is a resource cost associated with implementing the feature, this should be more cost-effective than simply implementing the feature for the whole sample.

In the absence of information about differences in performance of features across subgroups, a targeted design can still be implemented, either by drawing upon nonresponse theory or through selective use of design features that have been shown to have a mean effect. For example, if a costly design feature (such as a large respondent incentive, for example) is known or believed to have a positive effect on response for all subgroups, this could be applied just to subgroups expected to have low response propensity, even in the absence of any evidence that it would be any more effective for those subgroups than for others.

Allocating Sample Units to Subgroups

The subgroup definitions must be applied to sample units based on information available either from the sampling frame or, more likely, from data collected at previous waves of the survey. This can be a very straightforward process if variables defining the subgroups are available for all sample units (no missing data) and if these measures are accurate (no measurement or processing errors). More often it may be the case that the available variables only provide approximations to the ideal definition of the subgroups and that there is item-missing data to deal with. In this situation the distinction is important between design features that are subgroup-specific and those which are generally applicable but applied selectively. If the design features under consideration are all of the generally applicable type, then a degree of misclassification of sample units to subgroups may not be of great importance. But if subgroup-specific features are to be used, care should be taken to avoid upsetting or annoying sample members by providing information, materials or persuasive messages that are inappropriate. For example, if a prenotification letter includes messaging that is specific to sample members with dependent children, a person without children may be upset at the implication that the survey organization believes they have children. The targeted features could then damage cooperation propensity rather than enhance it.

Implementing the Design

The additional complications of implementing a targeted design are unlikely to be substantial but should not be underestimated. Care must be taken to ensure that the correct treatments are applied to the correct sample members. The derived indicator of subgroup membership will determine the treatment applied and should therefore be subject to rigorous quality control checking. Similarly, the programming of treatments depending on this indicator—such as the generation of mailings or the appearance on screen of scripts for interviewers—needs to be carefully tested. Where interviewers are involved in delivering the treatment, appropriate briefing is required to ensure that interviewers are aware that the treatment will vary between sample members and of the importance of delivering the allocated treatment.

27.5 CURRENT PRACTICE AND METHODOLOGICAL RESEARCH

McGonagle, Couper, and Schoeni (2011) provide an example of a methodological experiment carried out on the PSID in which a heterogeneous effect on field outcomes is observed. Specifically, they show that two features of a between-wave mailing reduce the number of calls needed at the following wave, but only for sample members who had indicated at the previous wave that they were likely to move in the next couple of years.[1] The two features in question were offering an unconditional rather than conditional incentive to reply to a contact information request and using a traditional rather than new design for the mailing. These results may appear to suggest a targeted design in which the unconditional incentive and traditional design are used only for sample members with a high likelihood of moving. However, for the rest of the sample these features are no less effective than the alternatives. In such a situation, the organizational simplicity of having a standard rather than a targeted mailing may suggest this to be the most efficient option, particularly if the cost differential between the alternative treatments is modest. PSID has not adopted a targeted strategy for between-wave mailings. There are few examples of targeted inducement designs being used in practice. We describe here four examples.

Example 1: Prioritizing Contact on Wave 5 of the UK Millennium Cohort Study

At wave 5 of the UK Millennium Cohort Study (Hansen, 2012), sample households that were predicted to have the highest propensity to be not contacted (including not located) were issued to field first in order to maximize the time available in field and therefore hopefully increase the contact rate. These households were identified by fitting models predicting contact propensity at wave 4 based on outcome history at previous waves of the survey, household and neighborhood characteristics (Calderwood, Cleary, Flore, & Wiggins, 2012): the top 10% in rank order of predicted propensity to be not contacted were identified for the targeted treatment, along with any households known to have moved since the previous wave.

Example 2: Targeted Between-Wave Mailings on Understanding Society: the UK Household Longitudinal Study

In *Understanding Society*, each sample member receives a mailing approximately six months after each annual interview. This mailing includes a 'thank you' letter, a leaflet highlighting some survey findings, and a change-of-address card. For the post-wave 2 mailing, six versions of the leaflet were utilized: five versions which were each aimed at a target subgroup (young people, employed people, older people, ethnic minorities and people who had previously been members of the British Household Panel Survey sample and therefore had a much longer association with the survey than others) and a general version sent to all other sample members. This approach was introduced following methodological experimentation which suggested that the targeted approach could improve response rates (Fumagalli, Laurie & Lynn, 2013). This experimentation focused on two subgroups, younger people and work-busy people, and the main findings are summarized in Table 27.1. It can be seen that the targeted version of the leaflet seems to encourage young people to complete a full face-to-face interview rather than a shorter telephone interview, and encourages work-busy

TABLE 27.1

Effect of a targeted leaflet on response for two subgroups

	Young			Work-busy		
	Standard %	Targeted %	P	Standard %	Targeted %	P
Full face-to-face interview	91.6	93.2	.106	90.1	90.3	.435
Short telephone interview	2.6	0.8	.002	6.5	7.2	.250
Nonresponse	5.8	5.9	.465	3.5	2.5	.077
n	856	843		1,157	1,205	

Notes: The base consists of all sample members issued to field for BHPS wave 18. This includes all those enumerated at wave 17, aside from any known to have died subsequently, plus wave 17 non-respondents who had responded at wave 16. Short telephone interviews are offered as a last resort, only when all usual efforts to achieve a full face-to-face interview have been made. Young people are those who were aged 16–24 years at the start of wave 18 field work. Work-busy people are those who reported working more than 40 hours per week, or commuting for more than 10 hours per week in addition to working full time, or being self-employed. For more details of the experimental design, see Fumagalli et al. (2013).

people to at least complete the shorter telephone interview rather than not participate at all.

Example 3: Extra Keeping-in-Touch Mailings Between Waves 4 and 5 of Understanding Society: The UK Household Longitudinal Study

An additional between-wave mailing, asking sample members to notify any recent changes of addresses or imminent moves, was sent to those predicted to be at highest risk of moving and remaining untraced at wave 5. Predictions were based on wave 4 responses, using a model of wave 2 outcome based on wave 1 responses (Lynn 2012b). High risk was defined as a predicted probability of greater than 7.5%, a criterion that applied to 8.1% of sample members (so 91.9% of sample members did not receive this extra mailing). Figure 27.1 shows that this cut-off point represents a turning point in the distribution of predicted probabilities, so one should expect the targeted group to be somewhat distinctive. During the period of approximately 11 months between the wave 4 interview and the wave

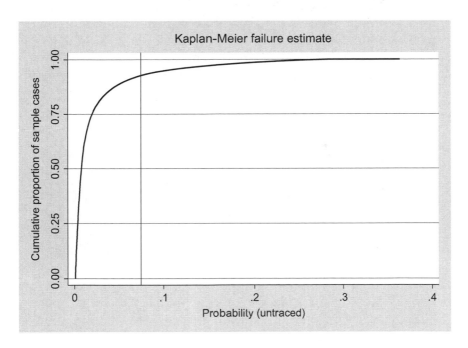

FIGURE 27.1
Predicted probabilities of remaining untraced at UKHLS wave 5

5 prenotification letter, the majority of sample members received just one mailing (as described in Example 2), while the targeted group received two. Thus, the mean interval between contacts was reduced from 5.5 months to 3.7 months for this group, increasing the chances of a change of address being identified before it was too late.

Example 4: Targeted Prenotification Letters on the Understanding Society Innovation Panel

An experiment is being carried out at wave 6 of the *Understanding Society* Innovation Panel (Uhrig, 2011), in which targeted versions of the prenotification letter are being sent to a random half of the sample. The five target groups are younger people, people with dependent children, work-busy people, people of pensionable age and people living in London and southeast England. Each version of the letter mentions reasons why the survey is particularly important for the respective subgroup. A sixth version of the letter is sent to residual sample members who do not belong to any of the five target groups. With this design—as with Example 2—it is necessary to define the subgroups based on a hierarchy of criteria. For example, sample members who have dependent children and are also work-busy are placed in the work-busy subgroup rather than the dependent children subgroup. This is based on the observation that re-interview rates are lower overall for work-busy people than for people with children, so arguments for participation by work-busy people may be more important for this group.

27.6 LOOKING FORWARD

Targeted response inducement strategies seem not to be common in longitudinal surveys, though they have been discussed in international forums, including the International Panel Survey Methods Workshop in both 2010[2] and 2012.[3] There are several possible reasons for this. One is that they add extra complexity to the administration of surveys that are invariably already complex. This is undoubtedly true, though for many of the types of design features that are likely to be manipulated with such strategies, the extra work involved may be fairly minimal. Another concern could be the cost of implementation, but if designed well, a targeted strategy could significantly improve cost-effectiveness. Even a simple mailing to sample members can be quite costly for surveys with large sample sizes. But if the mailing could be targeted just to the subgroup for whom it is effective, or where the effect is most needed, considerable efficiency savings could accrue. More expensive design features, such as large incentives or gifts, might be ruled out for the whole sample, but could become affordable (and remain effective) if well targeted.

Ethical considerations may be a barrier to some kinds of targeted strategies. Review boards and ethics committees may not take kindly to the idea of different sample members receiving different kinds of rewards for participating in a study. This could affect the use of targeted respondent incentives, though it is hard to imagine the argument being applied to letters, leaflets or booklets. In any case, researchers should certainly consider carefully the ethical implications of any proposed targeted strategy.

But in reality the main barrier to the introduction of targeted response inducement strategies may simply be a lack of experience with them. As more experience is gained, and more evidence is gathered regarding the types of designs that can be effective, and the circumstances in which they are more likely to be effective, the popularity of such designs is likely to grow. For this reason, the experimental introduction of such designs—as in Example 4 above and as in Fumagalli et al. (2013)—is to be encouraged. Experiments of this kind allow the research community to learn a lot about how to improve the trade-off between survey costs, on the one hand, and response rates and nonresponse bias, on the other hand. In the future, targeted strategies may become the norm for longitudinal surveys.

NOTES

1. The PSID between-wave interval is two years.
2. www1.mzes.uni-mannheim.de/konf/psmw2010/.
3. http://melbourneinstitute.com/miaesr/events/workshops/workshop_panel_2012.html.

BIBLIOGRAPHY

Beerten, R. (1999). The effect of interviewer and area characteristics on survey response rates: An exploratory analysis. *Survey Methodology Bulletin 45*, 7–15.
Bennett, D. J., & Steel, D. (2000). An evaluation of a large-scale CATI household survey using random digit dialing. *Australian and New Zealand Journal of Statistics, 42*(3), 255–270. doi:10.1111/1467-842X.00126
Bosnjak, M., Neubarth, W., Couper, M. P., Bandilla, W., & Kaczmirek, L. (2008). Prenotification in web-based access panel surveys: The influence of mobile text messaging versus E-mail on response rates and sample composition. *Social Science Computer Review, 26*, 213–223. doi:10.1177/0894439307305895

Calderwood, L., Cleary, A., Flore, G., & Wiggins, R. D. (2012, July). *Using response propensity models to inform fieldwork practice on the 5th wave of the Millennium Cohort Study.* Paper presented at the International Panel Survey Methods Workshop, Melbourne, Australia.

Calinescu, M., Bhulai, S., & Schouten, B. (2013). Optimal resource allocation in survey designs. *European Journal of Operational Research, 226*, 115–121. doi:10.1016/j.ejor.2012.10.046

Campanelli, P., Sturgis, P., & Purdon, S. (1997). *Can you hear me knocking? An investigation into the impact of interviewers on survey response rates.* The Survey Methods Centre at SCPR, London, UK. Retrieved from http://eprints.soton.ac.uk/80198/

Church, A. H. (1993). Estimating the effect of incentives on mail survey response rates: A meta-analysis. *Public Opinion Quarterly, 57*(1), 62–79. doi:10.1086/269355

Couper, M. P., & Wagner, J. (2011). Using paradata and responsive design to manage survey nonresponse. *Proceedings of the 58th World Statistical Congress, Dublin*, 542–548. Retrieved from http://2011.isiproceedings.org/papers/450080.pdf

Crawford, S. D., Couper, M. P., & Lamias, M. J. (2001). Web surveys: perceptions of burden. *Social Science Computer Review 19*(2), 146–162. doi:10.1177/089443930101900202

De Leeuw, E. D., Callegaro, M., Hox, J. J., Korendijk, E., & Lensvelt-Mulders, G. (2007). The influence of advance letters on response in telephone surveys: A meta-analysis. *Public Opinion Quarterly, 71*, 1–31. doi:10.1093/poq/nfm014

Dillman, D. A. (2007). *Mail and Internet Surveys: The Tailored Design Method* (2nd ed.). New York, NY: Wiley.

Durrant, G. B., Groves, R. M., Staetsky, L., & Steele, F. (2010). Effects of interviewer attitudes and behaviors on refusal in household surveys. *Public Opinion Quarterly 74*(1), 1–36. doi:10.1093/poq/nfp098

Fumagalli, L., Laurie, H., & Lynn, P. (2013). Experiments with methods to reduce attrition in longitudinal surveys. *Journal of the Royal Statistical Society Series A (Statistics in Society) 176*(2), 499–519. doi:10.1111/j.1467-985X.2012.01051.x

Galesic, M., & Bosnjak, M. (2009). Effects of questionnaire length on participation and indicators of response quality in a web survey. *Public Opinion Quarterly, 73*(2), 349–360. doi:10.1093/poq/nfp031

Groves, R. M., Cialdini, R. B., & Couper, M. P. (1992). Understanding the decision to participate in a survey. *Public Opinion Quarterly, 56*(4), 475–495. doi:10.1086/269338

Groves, R. M., & Heeringa, S. G. (2006). Responsive design for household surveys: tools for actively controlling survey nonresponse and costs. *Journal of the Royal Statistical Society: Series A (Statistics in Society), 169*(3), 439–457. doi:10.1111/j.1467-985X.2006.00423.x

Groves, R. M., & Peytcheva, E. (2008). The impact of nonresponse rates on nonresponse bias: A meta-analysis. *Public Opinion Quarterly, 72*(2), 167–189. doi:10.1093/poq/nfn011

Groves, R. M., Presser, S., & Dipko, S. (2004). The role of topic interest in survey participation decisions. *Public Opinion Quarterly, 68*(1), 2–31. doi:10.1093/poq/nfh002

Hansen, K. (Ed.). (2012). *Millenium Cohort Study first, second, third and fourth surveys: A guide to the datasets* (7th ed.). London: Centre for Longitudinal Studies.

Hembroff, L. A., Rusz, D., Rafferty, A., McGee, H., & Ehrlich, N. (2005). The cost-effectiveness of alternative advance mailings in a telephone survey. *Public Opinion Quarterly, 69*(2), 232–245. doi:10.1093/poq/nfi021

Jäckle, A., Lynn, P., Sinibaldi, J., & Tipping, S. (2013). The effect of interviewer experience, attitudes, personality and skills on respondent co-operation with face-to-face surveys. *Survey Research Methods*, 7(1), 1–15.

Kaplowitz, M. D., Hadlock, T. D., & Levine, R. (2004). A comparison of web and mail survey response rates. *Public Opinion Quarterly*, 68(1), 94–101. doi:10.1093/poq/nfh006

Kaplowitz, M. D., Lupi, F., Couper, M. P., & Thorp, L. (2012). The effect of invitation design on web survey response rates. *Social Science Computer Review*, 30(3), 339–349. doi:10.1177/0894439311419084

Laurie, H., & Lynn, P. (2009). The use of respondent incentives in longitudinal surveys. In P. Lynn (Ed.), *Methodology of Longitudinal Surveys*, Chichester: Wiley.

Lynn, P. (2012a). The propensity of older respondents to participate in a general purpose survey. Understanding Society Working Paper 2012–03, Colchester: University of Essex. Retrieved from www.understandingsociety.ac.uk/research/publications/working-paper/ understanding-society/2012-03

Lynn (2012b, September). *Failing to locate panel sample members: Minimising the risk.* Paper presented at the International Workshop on Household Survey Nonresponse, Ottawa, Canada.

McGonagle, K. (2013). Personal communication. February 17, 2013.

McGonagle, K., Couper, M. P., & Schoeni, R. F. (2011). Keeping track of panel members: An experimental test of a between-wave contact strategy. *Journal of Official Statistics*, 27(2), 319–338.

McGonagle, K., Schoeni, R. F., Sastry, N., & Freedman, V. A. (2012). The Panel Study of Income Dynamics: overview, recent innovations, and potential for lifecourse research. *Longitudinal and Life Course Studies*, 3(2), 268–284.

Morton-Williams, J. (1993). *Interviewer Approaches*. Aldershot: Dartmouth.

Schouten, B., Calinescu, M., & Luiten, A. (2013). Optimizing quality of response through adaptive survey designs. *Survey Methodology*, 39(1), 29–58.

Schouten, B., Cobben, F., & Bethlehem, J. (2009). Indicators for the representativeness of survey response. *Survey Methodology*, 35(1), 101–113.

Sheehan, K. B. (2006). Email survey response rates: A review. *Journal of Computer-Mediated Communication*, 6(2).

Singer, E. (2002). The use of incentives to reduce nonresponse in household surveys. In R. M. Groves, D. A. Dillman, J. L. Eltinge, & R.J.A. Litle (Eds.), *Survey nonresponse* (pp.163–177). New York, NY: Wiley.

Singer, E., van Hoewyk, J., Gebler, N., Raghunathan, T., & McGonagle, K. (1999). The effect of incentives on response rates in interviewer-mediated surveys. *Journal of Official Statistics*, 15(2), 217–230.

Uhrig, S.C.N. (2011). Using experiments to guide decision making. In S. L. McFall & C. Garrington (Eds.), *Understanding society: Early findings from the first wave of the UK's Household Longitudinal Study*. Colchester: University of Essex. Retrieved from http://research.understandingsociety.org.uk/findings/early-findings

VanGeest, J. B., Johnson, T. P., & Welch, V. L. (2007). Methodologies for improving response rates in surveys of physicians: A systematic review. *Evaluation and the Health Professions*, 30(4), 303–321.

Van Kenhove, P., Wijnen, K., & De Wulf, K. (2002). The influence of topic involvement on mail survey response behavior. *Psychology & Marketing*, 19(3), 293–301.

Wagner, J. (2008). *Adaptive survey design to reduce nonresponse bias*. Doctoral dissertation, University of Michigan. Retrieved from http://deepblue.lib.umich.edu/bitstream/handle/2027.42/60831/jameswag_1.pdf

Watson, N. (2013). Personal communication. February 19, 2013.

Watson, N., & Wooden, M. (2012). The HILDA survey: A case study in the design and development of a successful household panel study. *Longitudinal and Life Course Studies, 3*(3), 369–381.

Weeks, M. F., Kulka, R. A., & Pierson, S. A. (1987). Optimal call scheduling for a telephone survey. *Public Opinion Quarterly, 51*(4), 540–549.

28

Incentive Effects

Anja S. Göritz

28.1 INTRODUCTION

There are many methods to enhance survey participation. The most popular methods are incentives, prenotification, assurances of anonymity, personalization, stating a deadline, social-utility and help-the-researcher appeals as well as follow-ups. Participation-enhancing methods are employed in the hope of collecting more data and/or higher-quality data. Data quality is a multifaceted construct (cf. Bailar, 1984; De Leeuw, 1992). It pertains to the signal-to-noise ratio in the data. High-quality data enable researchers to draw valid conclusions about the subject matter under study. Meta-analyses show that in traditional survey modes incentives have a larger impact than other response-enhancing methods (Edwards et al., 2002; Kanuk & Berensen, 1975; Yammarino, Skinner, & Childers, 1991; Yu & Cooper, 1983). In the following we will describe the impact of incentives on data quantity and quality with a focus on empirical evidence rather than on theory.

Sample facets of *data quantity* are the response rate, the retention rate and the completion rate. The response rate refers to the number of people who start participating in a study of all those who were invited to participate in this study or were cognizant of the study. The retention rate refers to the share of respondents who stay until the end of the study. Instead of retention, some people refer to dropout, which is the complement of retention. The completion rate is the number of people who stay until the end of the study of all those who were invited to participate in this study or were cognizant of the study. Sample facets of *data quality* are item-nonresponse, length of answers to open-ended questions, acquiescence, nondifferentiation, heaping, completion time, composition bias, picking the endpoints or picking the middle category of response scales disproportionally often,

340 • Anja Göritz

the percentage of no-opinion responses, the consistency and reliability of responses and the magnitude of category effects.

Incentives can be classified along different dimensions. With regard to timing, one distinguishes between prepaid and postpaid incentives. Prepaid incentives are given to potential respondents before their participation, whereas postpaid (i.e., promised) incentives are awarded after responses have been collected. With regard to the certainty of receiving the incentive, one distinguishes between per-capita and lottery-type incentives. With per-capita incentives each eligible person receives a reward, whereas with a lottery only a few winners receive an incentive. With regard to the character of the incentive, one widespread distinction pertains to monetary versus nonmonetary incentives. Examples of monetary incentives are cash, checks, electronic payments and vouchers or loyalty points that can be redeemed against money. Examples of nonmonetary incentives are token gifts (e.g., pens, mouse pads, turkeys, trips, computer equipment), donations to charity, study results and vouchers or loyalty points that can be redeemed against tangible items. A crossing of these three dichotomous dimensions results in eight classes of incentives.

Next, we will summarize the effects of incentives in traditional data collection modes (i.e., mail, telephone and face-to-face) and in the newer web mode separately. Because of the wealth of incentive experiments pertaining to traditional data collection modes, we rely on meta-analyses as they provide more robust guidelines than individual studies. Meta-analyses rely on a summary of different yet comparable primary studies. Because the web mode has not been around for as long as traditional modes, the review of the effectiveness of incentives in web surveys is based on only two meta-analyses and complemented by individual experiments.

28.2 EFFECTIVENESS OF INCENTIVES IN MAIL, TELEPHONE AND FACE-TO-FACE SURVEYS

We condense the outcome of ten meta-analyses on five questions: (1) Which survey mode was studied? (2) How effective are prepaid versus postpaid incentives? (3) How effective are monetary versus nonmonetary incentives? (4) How effective are per-capita incentives versus lotteries? (5) What is the dose-effect relationship of incentives, and what was the range of incentive values studied? Table 28.1 lists in chronological order the results of this review on those questions on which at least one meta-analysis has something to say.

TABLE 28.1

Review of ten meta-analyses on the effectiveness of incentives in traditional data collection modes

Yu and Cooper (1983)	
mode	mail, telephone, face-to-face
prepaid vs. postpaid	prepaid monetary vs. control: $r = .16$, +15.6% response, $k = 55$
	postpaid monetary vs. control: $r = .05$, +5.8% response, $k = 20$
monetary vs. nonmonetary	monetary vs. control: $r = .15$, +15.3% response, $k = 79$
	nonmonetary (w/o survey results, with lotteries) vs. control: $r = .09$, +9.2% response, $k = 10$
	survey results vs. control: -2.6% response (n.s.), $k = 24$
dose-effect and range	positive linear $r = .61$ (only monetary incentives) across $0.1 - $50
Fox, Crask, and Kim (1988)	
mode	mail
prepaid vs. postpaid	prepaid monetary vs. control: +14.8% response (sig.), $k = 30$
dose-effect and range	diminishing returns y = 100*.031*$\sqrt{x}$ across $0.1 – $1: at $.25 +16% response, while at $1 +31%
Yammarino, Skinner, and Childers (1991)	
mode	mail
monetary vs. nonmonetary	monetary vs. control: $r = .16$, $k = 25$
	nonmonetary vs. control: $r = .08$, $k = 12$
dose-effect and range	$\leq$ $.5: $r = .18$, $k = 15$
	> $.5 – $\leq$ $1: $r = .12$, $k = 4$
	> $1: $r = .12$, $k = 6$
	=> no positive effect
Hopkins and Gullickson (1992)	
mode	mail
prepaid vs. postpaid	prepaid monetary vs. control: +19.2% response, $k = 73$
	postpaid monetary vs. control: +7.3% response, $k = 12$
dose-effect and range	< $.51: +13,3% response, $k = 26$
	$.51 – $.99: +19,4% response, $k = 15$
	$1 – $1.99: +22,1% response, $k = 24$
	> $1.99: +29,4% response, $k = 8$
	=> positive linear (only prepaid monetary incentives)

(Continued)

TABLE 28.1

(Continued)

Church (1993)

mode	mail
prepaid vs. postpaid/ monetary vs. nonmonetary	prepaid monetary vs. control: $d = .35$, +19.1% response, $k = 43$ prepaid nonmonetary vs. control: $d = .14$, +7.9% response, $k = 12$ postpaid monetary vs. control: $d = .09$, +4.5% response, $k = 9$ postpaid nonmonetary (with lottery and donations to charity; w/o survey results) vs. control: $d = .02$, +1.2% response, $k = 10$
dose-effect and range	positive linear $r = .45$ across $0.1 – $5

Singer, Van Hoewyk, Gebler, Raghunathan, and McGonagle (1999)

mode	telephone, face-to-face
prepaid vs. postpaid	prepaid vs. control: sign. positive impact postpaid vs. control: sign. positive impact prepaid vs. postpaid: prepaid more effective than postpaid, $\beta = 0.60$ (n.s.), $k = 55$; in all within-study comparisons ($k = 5$) prepaid yields higher response than postpaid
monetary vs. nonmonetary	monetary (including one lottery) vs. nonmonetary: $\beta = 4.37$
dose-effect and range	positive linear $\beta = .22$ across $1 – $100

Edwards et al. (2002)

mode	mail
prepaid vs. postpaid	prepaid vs. postpaid: odds ratio (OR) = 1.71, $k = 10$
monetary vs. nonmonetary	monetary vs. control: OR = 2.02, $k = 49$ nonmonetary vs. control: OR = 1.19, $k = 45$
dose-effect relation	diminishing returns Ln(OR) = 0.69 + 0.084 * Ln(Amount in $): at $1 odds of response are doubled, while at $15 odds of response are 2.5-fold

Engel, Pötschke, Schnabel, and Simonson (2004)

mode	mail, telephone, face-to-face
prepaid vs. postpaid	prepaid vs. postpaid (w/o lotteries): $d = 0.22$, $k = 107$
monetary vs. nonmonetary	monetary vs. nonmonetary: $d = 0.14$, $k = 119$ monetary postpaid to respondent ($k1 = 31$) vs. monetary postpaid to charity ($k2 = 8$): $d = 0.10$
per-capita vs. lottery	per-capita postpaid ($k1 = 34$) vs. lottery postpaid ($k2 = 12$): $d = -0.04$ (n.s.)
dose-effect and range	medium value vs. small value: $d = 0.13$ high value vs. small value: $d = 0.22$ => positive monotonous relationship in within-study comparisons ($k = 41$) across $1 – $16 (prepaid) and $16 – $103 (postpaid)

Jobber, Saunders, and Mitchell (2004)

mode	mail
prepaid vs. postpaid	prepaid monetary vs. control: +15.2% response, $k = 42$
dose-effect and range	positive linear B = .02 across $0.25 – $1

Edwards et al. (2007)

mode	mail
prepaid vs. postpaid	prepaid vs. postpaid: OR = 1.61, $k = 15$
monetary vs. nonmonetary	monetary vs. control: OR = 1.99, $k = 69$
	nonmonetary (w/o survey results) vs. control: OR = 1.13, $k = 72$
	survey results vs. control: OR = 0.92 (n.s.), $k = 10$
dose-effect relation	high value vs. small value: OR = 1.37, $k = 28$ => positive relationship

Note: OR stands for odds ratio, r is the correlation coefficient, d is the standardized mean difference, B is the unstandardized regression coefficient, β is the standardized regression coefficient, k pertains to the number of comparisons/studies integrated.

The meta-analyses partly overlap in terms of primary studies; in part they complement each other in that they examine different survey modes and different classes of incentives. The meta-analysis by Yu and Cooper (1983) not only summarizes controlled studies (that is, studies with a no-incentive control condition alongside one or more incentive conditions) but also uncontrolled studies. Because a summary of controlled studies is more conclusive, we omit results from uncontrolled studies.

With regard to effectiveness as a function of the timing of the incentive, prepaid incentives are clearly more effective than postpaid ones. Monetary prepaid incentives increase the response rate by about 15 to 19 percentage points, whereas monetary postpaid incentives increase the response rate by about six to eight percentage points. In terms of a ratio, monetary prepaid incentives are about two to three times as effective as monetary postpaid incentives. One meta-analysis (Church, 1993) has looked into the prepaid-postpaid difference with nonmonetary incentives. Nonmonetary prepaid incentives increase response by about eight percentage points, whereas nonmonetary postpaid incentives increase response by only one percentage point. Thus, the prepaid-postpaid difference is larger with nonmonetary than with monetary incentives.

How effective are monetary incentives compared to nonmonetary ones? Monetary incentives have been consistently shown to be more effective than nonmonetary incentives. Monetary incentives increase response by about 15 to 17 percentage points, whereas nonmonetary incentives increase response by about three to nine percentage points. In terms of a ratio, monetary incentives are about two to five times as effective as nonmonetary incentives. There is tentative evidence that the monetary-nonmonetary contrast is larger in mail surveys than in telephone or face-to-face surveys.

There is scant direct evidence on the effectiveness of per-capita versus lottery-type incentives. According to Engel et al. (2004) there is no effectiveness difference between postpaid per-capita and postpaid lottery incentives.

What is the dose-effect relationship of incentives? Only one of the ten meta-analyses, one which ranks among the analyses with the fewest primary studies (Yammarino, Skinner, & Childers, 1991), found more valuable incentives to decrease response. The remaining nine analyses found at least a positive monotonous relationship between incentive dose and effectiveness: the more valuable the incentive, the more strongly it increases the response rate. Five of these nine analyses find evidence of a linear dose-effect relationship. Taken together, with regard to the response rate but disregarding costs it is useful to offer a more valuable incentive. However, one cannot expect an incentive that is x-times as valuable as another to pay out in a proportional increase in response. Consequently, with regard to both the response rate as well as to costs it is the safer bet to use a small incentive.

If we look at the effectiveness of offering survey results and donations to charity, we find that offering survey results tends to somewhat decrease the response rate (Edwards et al., 2007; Yu & Cooper, 1983). Similarly, monetary incentives postpaid to charity lessen the response rate as compared to monetary incentives postpaid to respondents (Engel et al., 2004).

Some caution needs to be exercised in this review of meta-analyses. All meta-analyses purport to examine incentive effects on the response rate. Depending on the survey mode (e.g., mail) it is often impractical to distinguish people who start participating (i.e., respondents) and those who complete the entire survey (i.e., completes). Thus, although all analyses state that they pertain to response, slightly different facets of data quantity are implied across analyses, which limits the comparability of findings. In a similar vein, the analyses span several decades of research. Due to inflation, the value of the incentives used is not comparable across analyses. Moreover, the commensurability of findings is impaired by different classifications of incentives across analyses. For example, lotteries are sometimes counted as monetary incentives (e.g., Singer et al., 1999), whereas at times they are classified as nonmonetary (e.g., Yu & Cooper, 1983). Likewise, survey results are usually included in the group of nonmonetary incentives (e.g., Yu & Cooper, 1983); sometimes, however, they are excluded (Church, 1993).

Furthermore, the conclusiveness of the findings is reduced by several confounding factors. Usually, timing and value of the incentive are confounded in that prepaid incentives tend to be smaller than postpaid ones (Engel et al., 2004). Only Singer et al. (1999) have controlled for value of incentive when comparing prepaid and postpaid incentives. Moreover, response burden is likely confounded with incentive value, because long surveys often try to compensate for their high burden with a more valuable incentive. Furthermore, monetary incentives tend to be higher in value than nonmonetary incentives (Singer et al., 1999). Finally, survey mode and timing of the incentive tend to be confounded. For logistical reasons, mail surveys rely on a prepaid incentive more often than telephone surveys. In short, these meta-analytically derived findings have the methodological status of observational but not experimental data because third variables can influence the relationship between incentives and the response rate.

28.3 EFFECTIVENESS OF INCENTIVES IN WEB SURVEYS

Two meta-analyses review the overall effectiveness of incentives in web studies. The first analysis (Göritz, 2006a) summarizes 32 experiments on the impact of material incentives on response: Material incentives motivate people to start a web survey (OR = 1.19). The second analysis (Göritz, 2006a) comprises 26 experiments on the impact of material incentives on retention: Once people have accessed a survey for whatever reason, they are more likely to finish if a material incentive is offered (OR = 1.27).

Since these meta-analyses were published, new primary studies have been released that could not be included in them. First, we look at lotteries. Lotteries are widespread in web-based research. Compared to per-capita incentives, lotteries are easy to implement and usually cap the costs because most lotteries cost the same regardless of the number of respondents. The savings compared to a per-capita incentive rise with sample size. If in a lottery one prize or just a few big prizes are raffled instead of many smaller prizes, transaction costs are lower because fewer people need to be contacted and prizes delivered. Therefore, lotteries certainly are an attractive incentive for researchers; but are they attractive to potential survey respondents?

With regard to new experiments on lotteries that have not been incorporated in the meta-analyses, in five experiments in a nonprofit online panel (Göritz, 2006b, Experiments 2 to 6), response and retention did not differ between groups that were offered a cash win or no incentive. Furthermore, Göritz and Luthe (2013a) conducted five experiments in a nonprofit online panel in which they offered either a cash lottery, a voucher lottery or a lottery of surprise gifts. None of the lotteries significantly increased response, retention or response quality compared to a control group. Göritz and Luthe (2013b) conducted two experiments in a nonprofit online panel. Experiment 1 examined effects of a lottery per se and of the lottery's splitting into multiple prizes. Two cash lotteries and a control group were compared. One lottery was announced to be paid out in one lump sum, whereas the other lottery was split into multiple smaller prizes. The lottery and its splitting did not significantly affect response, retention, nondifferentiation and item nonresponse. However, in terms of effect sizes, splitting the lottery mildly decreased response and retention. In Experiment 2, a cash lottery enhanced response (OR = 1.39), retention (OR = 1.67) and nondifferentiation (d = 0.21), whereas splitting the lottery tended to decrease response and retention. Moreover, in a commercial online panel, Göritz and Luthe (2013) implemented three cash lotteries that differed in payout and were raffled either in one lump sum or split into multiple smaller prizes. Response was higher with a lottery than in the control group (OR = 1.18) when raffling the payout in a lump sum (OR = 1.30) and with higher single prize size (OR = 1.02 per €10). Item nonresponse was smaller with higher payouts (β = –0.07). Moreover, in a four-wave experiment, a lottery of vouchers increased the response rate (i.e., 68% with the lottery compared to 55% in the control group), but only in Wave 1 (Göritz & Wolff, 2007).

In Heerwegh (2006), a lottery of vouchers reduced response (OR = 0.92). In a commercial panel, Tuten, Galešić, and Bošnjak (2008) tested three cash lotteries (125, 500 and 2000 kuna) against a control group and observed higher response with 500 (OR = 1.77) and 2000 kuna (OR = 1.32) and somewhat higher retention with 2000 kuna (OR = 1.17), but also more item nonresponders with the lotteries. Furthermore, in Marcus, Bošnjak, Lindner, Pilischenko, and Schütz (2007) a lottery of two vouchers each worth €25 was ineffective. Finally, Sauermann and Roach's (2013) five lotteries had the same payout but differed in single prize size (100 × $5, 50 × $10, 20 × $25, 10 × $50 and 5 × $100). With regard to the dose-effect relationship, although not following a perfectly linear pattern, the larger the single prize the higher the response and retention. The overall effect of a lottery vs. none amounted to OR = 1.15.

To sum up, lotteries are usually mildly effective, which was also the outcome of the meta-analyses. The new experiments have added insight in that they revealed that when lotteries are used repeatedly on the same sample, they lose their effectiveness—except if single prizes are large.

Next, we look at postpaid per-capita monetary incentives. Because it is difficult to pay online respondents cash, incentive money is paid using online intermediaries such as PayPal. Consequently, our review of studies on postpaid per-capita monetary incentives is limited to studies that have used PayPal as an intermediary, thereby severely restricting generalizability to postpaid per-capita monetary incentives per se. In PayPal, an option called mass payment makes it possible to pay many recipients simultaneously. However, each transaction as well as the mass payment costs a fee.

Only one new primary study has been published since the meta-analyses: In a three-wave experiment in a nonprofit online panel, Göritz, Wolff, and Goldstein (2008) promised one group of participants €1.50 to be paid via PayPal for their participation at each wave. This was the first time that these people were offered a payment via PayPal in this panel. The control group was not offered any incentive. The promise of payment reduced response in Wave 1 compared to the control group (36% vs. 45%), but increased response in Wave 2 compared to the control group (80% vs. 60%). The reversal of the effect can be explained by the fact that only those people who took part in Wave 1 were invited to participate Wave 2.

To sum up the results that have been incorporated in the meta-analyses (i.e., Bošnjak & Tuten, 2003) as well as the new experiment on postpaid per-capita monetary incentives, paying respondents via PayPal after survey completion does not work initially, but is effective with respondents who are used to being paid via that intermediary. On account of the sparse data available, these results are preliminary.

What is the situation with postpaid per-capita nonmonetary incentives? There is only one experiment, and this experiment has already been incorporated in the meta-analyses; therefore results are tentative and restricted to the particular type of token gift tested: Cobanoglu and Cobanoglu (2003) promised a luggage tag and obtained a higher response rate than without an incentive (OR = 1.45).

Study results are a nonmaterial postpaid per-capita incentive whose standalone effects have not yet been the topic of a meta-analysis. Under most circumstances study results are the least expensive type of incentive.

Batinić and Moser (2005) conducted a review of several uncontrolled studies carried out in online panels: On average, studies in which results were offered elicited a lower response (65%) than studies with no such offer (72%). In the same vein, in a commercial online panel, Göritz and Luthe (in press) examined the effects of study results on response, retention and item nonresponse. Offering study results decreased response (OR = 0.88) and increased item nonresponse (OR = 0.89). By contrast, in Göritz and Luthe's (2013b) Experiment 2, which was conducted in a nonprofit panel, study results had no impact on response, retention and nondifferentiation, either as a standalone incentive or in combination with a lottery. Likewise, in Scherpenzeel and Toepoel (in press) various implementations of feedbacking survey results had no or inconsistent effects on participation behaviour in a probabilistic online panel. However, if topic salience is high (Tuten, Galešić, & Bošnjak, 2004: OR = 1.55) or if study results are tailored to each participant (Marcus et al., 2007: OR = 1.54) study results enhance completion.

Taken together, study results seem to have no effect or even a deleterious effect. The recommendation to date is that study results should not be offered unless they are tailored to the respondent and the study's topic is salient.

So far, we have dwelled upon postpaid incentives as they are easier to administer in web surveys. The evidence on prepaid incentives is sparser as prepaid incentives are usually more expensive and logistically more challenging. To date, only two publications have appeared, of which Bošnjak and Tuten (2003) has already been incorporated in the meta-analyses. The second publication is Göritz (2008): In a five-wave experiment, she sent a mouse pad as a prepaid nonmonetary incentive to one half of the new members of a commercial online panel; the other half did not get an incentive. The prepaid token gift significantly increased participation in the first ensuing study (OR = 1.51), but this effect dwindled linearly throughout further studies. To sum up on prepaid incentives, the lack of experiments that have looked at a variety of prepaid incentives means that it is too early to say anything on their general effectiveness.

Since there has been a lot of research on the effectiveness of lotteries in web-based surveys we can be relatively certain about the reliability of lottery effects. There is less or no research on the other types of incentives and on combinations of incentives; consequently, many more experiments are needed here, including ones on boundary conditions such as type of sample, type of study, length and topic of study. To conduct a comprehensive review of the effect of incentives in web surveys a new meta-analysis is planned. Readers are invited to contribute their own study results by filling out the form at www.göritz.net/incentives.htm.

Comparisons of the effectiveness of different types of incentives in traditional data collection modes and in the web remain preliminary due to sparse results on many types of incentives when they are used in the web.

What can be said across all data collection modes is that the effectiveness of lotteries is small and that study results are ineffective or even detrimental unless they are tailored to the respondent. This latter finding in particular reminds us that it is useful to heed research results when it comes to incentivizing respondents.

BIBLIOGRAPHY

Bailar, B. (1984). The quality of survey data. Proceedings of the Survey Research Methods Section, American Statistical Association, 43–52.

Batinić, B., & Moser, K. (2005). Determinanten der Ruecklaufquoten in Online-Panels [Determinants of response rates in online panels]. *Zeitschrift fuer Medienpsychologie, 17*(2), 64–74. doi:10.1026/1617-6383.17.2.64

Bošnjak, M., & Tuten, T. L. (2003). Prepaid and promised incentives in web surveys— An experiment. *Social Science Computer Review, 21,* 208–217. doi:10.1177/0894439303021002006

Church, A. H. (1993). Estimating the effect of incentives on mail survey response rates: A meta-analysis. *Public Opinion Quarterly, 57,* 26–79. doi: 10.1086/269355

Cobanoglu, C., & Cobanoglu, N. (2003). The effect of incentives in web surveys: Application and ethical considerations. *International Journal of Market Research, 45*(4), 1–14.

De Leeuw, E. D. (1992). *Data quality in mail, telephone, and face to face surveys.* TT-publikaties, Amsterdam.

Edwards, P. J., Roberts, I. G., Clarke, M. J., DiGuiseppi, C., Pratap, S., Wentz, R., & Kwan, I. (2002). Increasing response rates to postal questionnaires: systematic review. *British Medical Journal, 324,* 1183–1185. doi:10.1136/bmj.324.7347.1183

Edwards, P. J., Roberts, I. G., Clarke, M. J., DiGuiseppi, C., Wentz, R., Kwan, I., Cooper, R., Felix, L., & Pratap, S. (2007). Methods to increase response rates to postal questionnaires. *Cochrane Database of Systematic Reviews 2007,* Issue 2. Art. No.: MR000008. doi.10.1002/14651858.MR000008.pub3

Engel, U., Pötschke, M., Schnabel, C., & Simonson, J. (2004). *Nonresponse und Stichprobenqualitaet. Ausschoepfung in Umfragen der Markt- und Sozialforschung.* Frankfurt am Main: Deutscher Fachverlag HORIZONT productions.

Fox, R. J., Crask, M. R., & Kim, J. (1988). Mail survey response rates: A meta-analysis of selected techniques for inducing response. *Public Opinion Quarterly, 52,* 467–491. doi:10.1086/269125

Göritz, A. S. (2006a). Incentives in web studies: Methodological issues and a review. *International Journal of Internet Science, 1*(1), 58–70.

Göritz, A. S. (2006b). Cash lotteries as incentives in online panels. *Social Science Computer Review, 24*(4), 445–459. doi:10.1177/0894439305286127

Göritz, A. S. (2008). The long-term effect of material incentives on participation in online panels. *Field Methods, 20*(3), 211–225. doi:10.1177/1525822X08317069

Göritz, A. S., & Luthe, S. C. (2013a). Effects of lotteries on response behavior in online panels. *Field Methods, 25*(3), 219–237. doi:10.1177/1525822X12472876

Göritz, A. S., & Luthe, S. C. (2013b). How do lotteries and study results influence response behavior in online panels? *Social Science Computer Review, 31*(3), 371–385. doi:10.1177/0894439312458760

Göritz, A. S., & Luthe, S. C. (2013). Lotteries and study results in market research online panels. *International Journal of Market Research, 55*(5), 611–626. doi:10.2501/ IJMR-2013-016

Göritz, A. S., & Wolff, H.-G. (2007). Lotteries as incentives in longitudinal web studies. *Social Science Computer Review, 25*(1), 99–110. doi:10.1177/0894439306292268

Göritz, A. S., Wolff, H.-G., & Goldstein, D. G. (2008). Individual payments as a longer-term incentive in online panels. *Behavior Research Methods, 40*(4), 1144–1149. doi:10.3758/BRM.40.4.1144

Heerwegh, D. (2006). An investigation of the effect of lotteries on web survey response rates. *Field Methods, 18*(2), 205–220. doi:10.1177/1525822X05285781

Hopkins, K. D., & Gullickson, A. R. (1992). Response rates in survey research: A meta-analysis of the effects of monetary gratuities. *Journal of Experimental Education, 61*, 52–62. doi:10.1080/00220973.1992.9943849

Jobber, D., Saunders, J., & Mitchell, V.-W. (2004). Prepaid monetary incentive effects on mail survey response. *Journal of Business Research, 57*, 21–25. doi:10.1016/ S0148-2963(02)00280-1

Kanuk, L., & Berensen C. (1975). Mail surveys and response rates: A literature review. *Journal of Marketing Research, 12*, 440–453.

Marcus, B., Bošnjak, M., Lindner, S., Pilischenko, S., & Schütz, A. (2007). Compensating for low topic interest and long surveys: A field experiment on nonresponse in web surveys. *Social Science Computer Review, 25*(3), 372–383. doi:10.1177/0894439307297606

Sauermann, H., & Roach, M. (2013). Increasing web survey response rates in innovation research: An experimental study of static and dynamic contact design features. *Research Policy, 42*(1), 273–286. doi:10.1016/j.respol.2012.05.003

Scherpenzeel, A., & Toepoel, V. (2014). Informing panel members about study results. In M. Callegaro, R. Baker, J. Bethlehem, A. S. Göritz, J. A. Krosnick, & P. J. Lavrakas (Eds.), *Online panel research: A data quality perspective* (pp. 192–213). Chichester: Wiley. doi:10.1002/9781118763520.ch9

Singer, E., Van Hoewyk, J., Gebler, N., Raghunathan, T., & McGonagle, K. (1999). The effect of incentives on response rates in interviewer-mediated surveys. *Journal of Official Statistics, 15*, 217–230.

Tuten, T. L., Galešić, M., & Bošnjak, M. (2004). Effects of immediate versus delayed notification of prize draw results on response behavior in web surveys: An experiment. *Social Science Computer Review, 22*, 377–384. doi:10.1177/0894439304265640

Tuten, T. L, Galešić, M., & Bošnjak, M. (2008). Optimizing response rates and data quality in web surveys: The immediacy effect and prize values. In L. O. Petrieff & R. V. Miller (Eds.), *Public Opinion Research Focus* (pp 149–157). Hauppauge: Nova Science Publishers.

Yammarino, F. J., Skinner, S. J., & Childers, T. L. (1991). Understanding mail survey response behavior: A meta-analysis. *Public Opinion Quarterly, 55*(4), 613–639. doi:10.1086/269284

Yu, J., & Cooper, H. (1983). A quantitative review of research design effects on response rates to questionnaires. *Journal of Marketing Research, 20*, 36–44.

29

Nonresponse in Comparative Studies

Enhancing Response Rates and Detecting and Minimizing Nonresponse Bias

Ineke Stoop

29.1 INTRODUCTION

High response rates are difficult to achieve in national surveys (Peytchev, 2013), but they are even more challenging in cross-national studies where the need for optimal comparability across countries and over time can stand in the way of tailoring fieldwork and response efforts to national traditions and contexts. Minimizing, or even measuring, nonresponse bias may even be more difficult, especially in studies on values and attitudes where no external evidence on population outcomes is available.

Methodological studies based on the European Social Survey (ESS) can illustrate the nonresponse problem in cross-national attitude surveys, both because the ESS sets high methodological targets and because of the detailed documentation and availability of process data. This paper will give some basic information on the ESS, outline response-enhancing efforts, and provide an overview of different strategies to detect nonresponse bias. It will also discuss the present focus on overall response rates and suggest alternative approaches to reduce nonresponse bias.

29.2 ENHANCING AND MONITORING RESPONSE RATES

Peytchev (2013) lists a number of adverse consequences of the decrease in response rates in recent decades and of the struggle to maintain high response rates. Decreasing response rates may result in higher nonresponse bias, at least when survey outcomes are related to response behavior. Pursuing high response rates will increase survey costs and extend fieldwork periods. Complex designs aimed at enhancing response rates, such as mixed-mode interviewing, can seriously complicate fieldwork logistics, increase the need for careful monitoring, and will have to be incorporated in the analysis. This section will illustrate how difficult it is to achieve high response rates in many European countries. It will also describe efforts to treat data collection as a scientific process which, among other things, implies that detailed monitoring of fieldwork is required (see Stoop & Koch, 2013).

The European Social Survey (ESS) is a biennial face-to-face survey of attitudes, beliefs, and behavioral patterns, in which approximately 2,000 interviews are conducted in each of the 30+ participating countries (Jowell, Kaase, Fitzgerald, & Eva, 2007). Input harmonization (Körner & Meyer, 2005) has been implemented to pursue optimal comparability across countries. From the beginning, the ESS has sought to pursue high response rates, acknowledging the need for face-to-face interviewing, sufficient budgets, considerable field efforts, and long fieldwork periods to achieve this. It specifies a target response rate of 70%, and a target maximum noncontact rate of 3%. Koch, Blom, Stoop, and Kappelhof (2009) present a detailed overview of fieldwork specifications, requirements, efforts, and outcomes.

During preparation for the biennial fieldwork, each country reports its target response rate to the ESS Core Scientific Team (CST) fieldwork team. This target response rate is then discussed in relation to the response rate in the previous round (why is it lower? how do you envisage obtaining a higher rate than before?), in relation to efforts deployed in the previous round and outcomes of the analyses of paradata (why so few contact attempts? why so many contact attempts when nobody is at home?), and to the ESS target response rate. The resulting national target response is used in the design of the sample and in the calculation of the gross sample size.

The ESS prescribes face-to-face interviews and in-person recruitment. Only if the country's sample is one of named individuals with telephone numbers may the first contact be made by telephone in order to make an appointment to visit the respondent. Sampled individuals without a listed phone number should still be contacted face-to-face. Where those with telephone numbers cannot be contacted by phone, the same number of in-person visits is still required. Interviews may not, under any circumstances, be conducted over the telephone.

To pursue the 70% response rate, interviewers are required to make at least four visits to each sample unit before it is abandoned as non-productive, on different days of the week and at different times of day, of which at least one must be at the weekend and one in the evening. These visits should be spread over at least two different weeks, and the entire fieldwork period should not be less than 30 days. A wide range of measures have been implemented to enhance the response rate, such as close fieldwork monitoring, respondent incentives, interviewer bonuses, advance letters (and brochures), toll-free telephone numbers for potential respondents to contact, training of interviewers in response-maximization techniques and doorstep interactions, re-issuing noncontacts, and converting refusals.

Figure 29.1 presents the ESS response rates for those countries that participated in each of the first five rounds. Clearly, a 70% response rate is an ambitious target for most countries (though some countries that did not participate in every round exceeded the 70% target). A number of countries improve over time, others do worse, and still other countries did better in Round 5 after a steady decline in previous rounds.

Detailed process data (also called paradata, see Couper, 2000; Stoop, Matsuo, Koch, & Billiet, 2010) are collected in the ESS to monitor fieldwork progress, to check whether fieldwork has been carried out according to specifications, and to calculate response rates according to accepted standards (see American Association for Public Opinion Research, 2011). Paradata and other auxiliary variables are also used to analyze nonresponse.

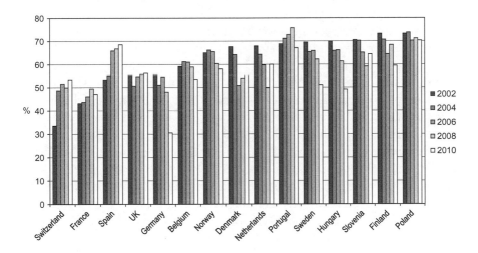

FIGURE 29.1

Response rates ESS in countries participating in Wave 1-5 (Source: European Social Survey, 2010, 2012)

Note: This information is partly based on the contact forms and partly on country reports, as not all countries provided complete call records.

Paradata comprise detailed information on respondent selection within households, and the timing and outcomes of each visit. In the ESS these data are collected manually (mostly on paper forms, sometimes electronically) using detailed *contact forms* (see Stoop, Devacht, Billiet, Loosveldt, & Philippens, 2003; Blom, Lynn, & Jäckle, 2008; Stoop, Billiet, Koch, & Fitzgerald, 2010), comparable to the Contact History Instrument (CHI) described by Bates, Dahlhamer, and Singer (2008). For each refusal, the interviewer is expected to record the reasons for refusal, a judgment on the likelihood of cooperation at future calls, and sex and age of doorstep contact. For each sample unit, the interviewer is required to observe and record information on the type of dwelling, the physical state of the building and neighborhood, and the presence of litter, vandalism and graffiti in the neighborhood.

A special feature of these ESS contact forms is that the resultant anonymized file is publicly available for secondary analysis, as are the ESS survey data. This means that researchers all over the world can—and do—use this information to analyze nonresponse (e.g. Kreuter & Kohler, 2009).

Based on the paradata, a detailed overview of response outcomes can be calculated (Stoop, Billiet et al., 2010). These results show not only that response rates differ substantially across countries, but also that there are substantial differences in noncontact rates, reasons for refusal, and efforts at refusal conversion. There are several reasons for these differences. First, they may be due to the type of sampling frame used. Although every national survey is based on strict probability sampling, samples vary from individual samples (e.g. from population registers) to household samples and address samples (see Häder & Lynn, 2007). When an individual sampling frame is used, the sample unit may have moved to an unknown address, and thus be a nonrespondent. In an address sample, the household presently living at a particular address is always the target household. In this case, the need to select a person within a household may be an additional barrier to achieving response. Alternatively, interviewer discretion in selecting a respondent within households may have unwanted consequences. Koch (personal communication) found that women are (sometimes seriously) overrepresented in countries that use address and household samples—where the interviewer selects the respondent—whereas the gender distribution is fairly equal in countries with individual sampling frames.

A second reason for differences in response outcomes could be differences in recruitment mode. In countries that use an individual sampling frame with telephone numbers, recruitment (though not interviewing) by telephone is allowed. This means, for instance, that an interview can never be conducted at the first call. Third, differences in response outcomes could be due to differences in operational procedures and interpretations of guidelines and sample unit behavior by national survey agencies and interviewers. Stoop, Billiet et al. (2010), for instance, show large differences in reasons for refusal across countries.

Differences in response rates can also be due to the type of survey agency (national statistical agency, university, market research agency), the use and type of incentives, the attractiveness of the topic (and of Europe) in different countries, national survey traditions, interviewer position, remuneration, experience and training, the likelihood of finding at least one household member at home during the day (Stoop, 2007), fieldwork efforts, and available funds (see Koch et al., 2009; Stoop, Billiet et al., 2010). Survey scarcity is an additional factor underlying differences in response (or rather cooperation) rates. Anecdotal evidence shows, for instance, that people in Albania were really thrilled that an ESS interviewer came by to talk with them about their views and opinions, something that had rarely happened before.

Despite standardization of fieldwork and paradata, a lot of variance in cross-national differences in response rates and nonresponse composition remains unexplained.

29.3 DETECTING NONRESPONSE BIAS

The response rate of a survey sets a maximum boundary to the size of the nonresponse bias, but there is no linear relationship between response rates and nonresponse bias *across* surveys, if only because the response rate is a characteristic of a survey, and nonresponse bias of a survey variable (Groves, 2006). One of the main concerns of survey researchers is that response behavior is related to the topic of a survey (Bethlehem, 2002): Are people who are interested in politics and current affairs more likely to participate in the ESS? An additional concern would be that this relationship differs across countries: Could it be that those who are not interested in politics cooperate in countries where social surveys are a relatively new phenomenon but not in countries where survey requests abound?

Assessing nonresponse bias in a cross-national study of values, attitudes and opinions is far from simple, as there is no gold standard, no true value, no external information with which to gauge the survey outcomes. ESS results can be compared with results from national surveys, but differences in question formulation, response rates in those national surveys, and other survey quality issues will stand in the way and it will not be clear which survey yields the best or most plausible outcome. Stoop, Billiet et al. (2010) presented four standard methods to estimate nonresponse bias and to suggest ways of adjusting for it. *First*, the final sample composition in terms of background variables (sex, age, and education) was weighted with population statistics (*post-stratification*). Weighted results could then be compared with unweighted results, helping to identify those variables that might be particularly prone to bias (see also Vehovar, 2007; Billiet, Philippens, Fitzgerald, & Stoop, 2007). In the ESS these variables were media use, political interest, attitudes towards immigrants, and voluntary work.

Second, low-level neighborhood data can be used as auxiliary variables (see Smith, 2011). These data can come from different sources such as statistical agencies or commercial organizations. In the ESS, in which many different countries participate, neighborhood data are based on *interviewer observations* (see Section 29.1). An analysis of these data is presented in Billiet, Matsuo, Beullens, and Vehovar (2009) and Stoop, Billiet et al. (2010). The physical state of the buildings exhibited a negative relationship with the education level of target persons. Refusals and noncontacts were more likely in areas characterized by poor physical state of the buildings and the presence of litter and/or vandalism. This might reflect characteristics of the residents, but the possibility cannot be ruled out that the differences also to some degree reflect interviewers behaving differently in different areas. Observational data can in principle be collected for every sample unit in every country (although in practice privacy rules in a number of countries forbid this). A disadvantage is that the information relies mainly on the subjective assessment of the interviewers, and that this type of information is hard to standardize across countries. In the ESS, interviewers now use national photos of different types of dwellings and neighborhoods (and the physical state they are in) to pursue standardization.

A *third* type of data used to assess and analyze nonresponse bias in the ESS is *paradata* from the call records. Contactability (or the number of calls to first establish contact) could be one factor in nonresponse bias. Stoop, Billiet et al. (2010) showed that those respondents who required many calls (mainly because they were hard to catch at home) did differ substantially and systematically from those who were easy to contact in terms of age, labor market participation, and education, but differed relatively little, and unsystematically, in regard to core variables of the survey such as ethnocentrism, political interest, and social trust.

ESS paradata also make it possible to compare survey outcomes from cooperative respondents (those who participated at the first request) and reluctant respondents (those who refused at first but participated at a later request, usually by a new interviewer). Comparability across countries is a major problem here, too. There are vast differences in initial response rates (before refusal conversion) and different fieldwork strategies across countries (some countries do not re-approach any refusers at all, some countries almost all, and some only the promising cases). Consequently, there is substantial variation in how many people initially refuse, how many of those are re-approached by the same or a new interviewer, and how many of the latter finally participate (Matsuo, Billiet, & Loosveldt, 2010). Using paradata on refusal conversion as a means of studying nonresponse bias was therefore only feasible in a small number of countries where enough refusals had been converted. Billiet et al. (2007) found that converted refusers did differ on some attitudinal scales and background variables from cooperative respondents, and easy-to-convert initial refusers differed from hard-to-convert ones, but the patterns varied across countries. There are also indications that the process of refusal conversion can actually make the composition of the final sample worse: subgroups that were overrepresented before refusal conversion are more likely to be converted than underrepresented subgroups (Billiet et al., 2009; Stoop, Billiet et al., 2010).

A *fourth* method of analyzing nonresponse bias in the ESS is to compare respondents and nonrespondents after collecting core variables on the latter. Two approaches were implemented, the *doorstep* approach and the *follow-up* survey. In the *doorstep* approach, refusals are asked to answer at least a small number of questions; this approach is also called the Basic Question Approach of Kersten and Bethlehem (1984) or the Pre-Emptive Doorstep Administration of Key Survey Items (PEDAKSI) approach by Lynn (2003). In a *follow-up* survey, refusals and noncontacts are surveyed subsequent to the data collection in the original study, usually with a much shorter questionnaire. In order to control for context, mode, and timing effects, respondents are also surveyed. In the ESS, a *doorstep* questionnaire approach was implemented in Belgium, and a *follow-up* survey was conducted in Poland, Norway, and Switzerland. Results of these studies are presented in Billiet et al. (2009) and Stoop, Billiet et al. (2010). One outcome is that reluctant respondents are not similar to the final nonrespondents who answered the doorstep questionnaire or participated in the follow-up survey.

Given the practical constraints in a comparative study and the varying availability of auxiliary variables and paradata, it seems unlikely that any one approach is the most appropriate way to analyze nonresponse bias and adjust for nonresponse. The most promising approach is probably to select the best auxiliary variables for each country.

29.4 ALTERNATIVE RESPONSE STRATEGIES IN THE EUROPEAN SOCIAL SURVEY

Pros and Cons of the 70% Target Response Rate

Prescribing a high target response rate in a cross-national survey has a number of advantages. First, it is a goal that is easy to communicate and it is easy to check whether it has been reached. Second, the higher the response rates, the lower the maximum nonresponse bias that is theoretically possible (Wagner, 2008). The U.S. Office of Management and Budget (2006), for instance, sets a target response rate of 80% (even higher than the ESS, therefore). Only if this standard is not met is a nonresponse bias analysis conducted. Finally, setting a high target should act as a stimulus to less well-performing countries to increase their efforts and adapt their strategies in order to achieve these targets. As mentioned above, a number of ESS participant countries have made considerable progress over the past decade towards achieving the response targets. Other countries have maintained a consistently high level. In some other countries, though, response rates appear to be decreasing steadily.

Setting a fixed target response rate also has disadvantages. The first problem is that in some countries, a response rate of 60% or even 50% is the maximum that seems to be achievable in the ESS, which is a long face-to-face survey, not run by statistical organizations in most countries, based on strictly random sampling, and using a fairly restrictive definition of eligibility and response.

This brings us to another disadvantage of a high, fixed target response rate. While the maximum nonresponse bias decreases as the response rates go up, nonresponse bias depends on two factors: response rates and the differences between respondents and nonrespondents. If, for instance, increased efforts to achieve the target response rates result in very high response rates in rural areas, while the rate in large cities remains low, and if city-dwellers have different attitudes towards ethnic minority groups than those living in rural areas, nonresponse bias will not go down. Analyses of the effects of refusal conversion (see Stoop, Billiet et al., 2010) have shown that in some countries refusal conversion can substantially increase the response rate, but also that it does not improve the composition of the sample in terms of background variables (see previous section). It is possible that at present most of the efforts made in the ESS to increase the response rates are most effective in converting those target persons who are quite similar to those who are immediately cooperative, and that these efforts would therefore not be effective in minimizing nonresponse bias.

Third, pursuing a high response rate is expensive, extends the duration of the fieldwork period and may have an effect on measurement error. This could be due to the fact that 'unwilling' respondents may be less motivated to answer questions conscientiously (see Peytchev, 2013), or to the fact that successful interviewers may be given very large assignments, resulting in large interviewer effects.

Finally, placing too much emphasis on achieving high response rates may have adverse effects. Might it not, for example, be tempting for interviewers to use the little leeway they have—given that they are paid for successful interviews only, and that they have to select a respondent within the household according to a random scheme—when it turns out that the selected person is not present, not able, or not willing to be interviewed whereas the doorstep contact who helps them with selection would love to be interviewed? And would a survey agency closely monitor this when there are financial sanctions in place that are imposed when the response rate is too low?

As we have seen, achieving a high response rate is very difficult in most countries that participate in the European Social Survey. In addition, it is not certain that increasing the response rates by a few percentage points will have an effect on nonresponse bias. What could be done is to shift the focus away from a blind pursuit of high response rates to an informed pursuit of high response rates (Groves, 2006), i.e. not trying to obtain response rates but rather to minimize nonresponse bias. This would mean less focus on the target response rate of 70% and more focus on the execution of fieldwork and attention to those groups that might be underrepresented.

Informed Pursuit of High Response Rates

What alternative is there to setting a fixed target response rate that appears in practice not to be achievable in many of the participating countries and that may not help reduce nonresponse bias? Alternatives that directly focus on nonresponse bias are not unproblematic. One serious problem is that the response rate is a characteristic of a survey, while nonresponse bias is a characteristic of a survey variable. Specifying target values for nonresponse bias for all ESS variables—or even for a small selection—would be impracticable.

A practical alternative for a survey quality indicator that reflects nonresponse might be the so-called 'representativity indicators' (Schouten, Cobben, & Bethlehem, 2009). These indicators have a high value when response rates in different subgroups of the sample are equal and a low value when they are unequal. A national sample which overrepresents rural citizens and underrepresents residents of large cities would not be representative according to this criterion. There are two caveats to this solution. First, information on subgroup membership ideally has to be available for the entire sample, both respondents and nonrespondents. And second, if these subgroup variables are not related to core variables of the survey, representativity may not imply the absence of nonresponse bias.

A practical solution for the ESS would be not only to set a general response rate target, but also to highlight the importance of high (or at least equal) response rates in different subgroups. This issue has been stressed from the start of the ESS in the guidelines on 'Enhancing Response Rates' (Koch, Fitzgerald, Stoop, Widdop, & Halbherr, 2012). Striving for a *balanced* response rate means paying more attention to systematic monitoring of the contrast between respondents and nonrespondents during fieldwork. This brings us close to the responsive design proposed by Groves and Heeringa (2006). In practice this would mean that the need for post-stratification weighting would be minimized.

The question arises as to which variables might be candidates for pursuing a balanced response. Geographic identifiers (region, urbanicity) will presumably be the only auxiliary variables available in all ESS countries, irrespective of the sampling frame used. Some countries might also have access to demographic information like sex and age for all sample units, but more important background variables such as educational level are not likely to be available. Second, will balancing response according to these variables actually contribute to minimizing nonresponse bias in substantive variables? The results of a meta-analysis by Peytcheva and Groves (2009) cast doubt on this assumption.

In addition, making more efforts to balance response rates across subgroups is likely to make fieldwork more expensive. And finally, setting three potentially conflicting targets might also be difficult to manage and monitor for survey agencies: conducting a prescribed number of interviews, achieving a target response rate, and delivering a balanced sample (which means similar response rates in subgroups defined in advance).

What could be recommended is to pay more attention to what is happening nationally in the field. Paying more attention to national fieldwork, analyses of nonresponse bias, and tapping national knowledge on the fieldwork process from National Coordinators and field directors could help to ascertain how response rates can be enhanced and how nonresponse bias can be minimized.

A small expert group in the European Social Survey is currently considering issues such as target response rates, balanced response rates, paradata, fieldwork control, and nonresponse bias. This group has delivered its recommendations in 2013.

REFERENCES

American Association for Public Opinion Research (2011). *Standard Definitions: Final dispositions of case codes and outcome rates for surveys.* (7th ed.). AAPOR.

Bates, N., Dahlhamer, J., & Singer, E. (2008). Privacy concerns, too busy, or just not interested: Using doorstep concerns to predict survey nonresponse. *Journal of Official Statistics*, 24(4), 591–612.

Bethlehem, J. G. (2002). Weighting nonresponse adjustments based on auxiliary information. In R. M. Groves, D. A. Dillman, J. L. Eltinge, & R.J.A. Little (Eds.), *Survey nonresponse* (pp. 265–287). New York: Wiley.

Billiet, J., Matsuo, H., Beullens, K., & Vehovar, V. (2009). Non-response bias in cross-national surveys: Designs for detection and adjustment in the ESS. *ASK. Sociological Methods & Research, 18*, 3–43.

Billiet, J., Philippens, M., Fitzgerald R., & Stoop, I. (2007). Estimation of nonresponse bias in the European Social Survey: Using information from reluctant respondents. *Journal of Official Statistics, 23*(2), 135–162.

Blom, A. G., Lynn, P., & Jäckle, A. (2008). *Understanding cross-national differences in unit nonresponse: The role of contact data.* ISER Working paper 2008–01.

Couper, M. P. (2000). Usability evaluation of computer-assisted survey instruments. *Social Science Computer Review, 18*, 384–396. doi:10.1177/089443930001800402

European Social Survey (2010). *ESS4-2008 Documentation Report.* Edition 3.01. Bergen, European Social Survey Data Archive, Norwegian Social Science Data Services.

European Social Survey (2012). *ESS5-2010 Documentation Report.* Edition 2.0. Bergen, European Social Survey Data Archive, Norwegian Social Science Data Services.

Groves, R. M. (2006). Nonresponse rates and nonresponse bias in household surveys. *Public Opinion Quarterly, 70*, 646–675. doi:10.1093/poq/nfl033

Groves, R. M., & Heeringa S. (2006). Responsive design for household surveys: Tools for actively controlling survey errors and costs. *Journal of the Royal Statistical Society Series A: Statistics in Society, 169*, Part 3, 439–457. doi:10.1111/j.1467-985X.2006.00423.x

Häder, S., & Lynn, P. (2007). How representative can a multi-nation survey be? In R. Jowell, C. Roberts, R. Fitzgerald, & G. Eva (Eds.), *Measuring Attitudes Cross-Nationally. Lessons from the European Social Survey* (pp. 33–52). London: Sage.

Jowell, R., Kaase, M., Fitzgerald R., & Eva, G. (2007). The European Social Survey as a measurement model. In R. Jowell, C. Roberts, R. Fitzgerald, & G. Eva (Eds.), *Measuring attitudes cross-nationally. Lessons from the European Social Survey* (pp. 1–31). London: Sage.

Kersten, H.M.P., & Bethlehem J. G. (1984). Exploring and reducing the nonresponse bias by asking the basic question. *Statistical Journal of the U.N. Economic Commission for Europe, 2*, 369–380.

Koch, A., Blom, A. G., Stoop, I., & Kappelhof, J. (2009). Data collection quality assurance in cross-national surveys: The example of the ESS. *Methoden Daten Analysen. Zeitschrift für Empirische Sozialforschung, 3*(2), 219–247.

Koch, A., Fitzgerald, R., Stoop, I., Widdop, S., & Halbherr, V. (2012). *Field procedures in the European Social Survey Round 6: Enhancing response rates.* Mannheim: European Social Survey, GESIS.

Körner, T., & Meyer, I. (2005). Harmonising socio-demographic information in household surveys of official statistics: Experiences from the Federal Statistical Office Germany. In J.H.P. Hoffmeyer-Zlotnik, & J. A. Harkness (Eds.), *Methodological aspects in cross-national research* (pp. 149–162). Mannheim: ZUMA Nachrichten Spezial, Band 11.

Kreuter, F., & Kohler, U. (2009). Analyzing contact sequences in call record data. Potential and limitations of sequence indicators for nonresponse adjustments in the European Social Survey. *Journal of Official Statistics, 25*(2), 203–226.

Lynn, P. (2003). PEDAKSI: Methodology for collecting data about survey non-respondents. *Quality and Quantity, 37,* 239–261.

Matsuo, H., Billiet, J., & Loosveldt, G. (2010). *Response-based quality assessment of ESS Round 4: Results for 24 countries based on contact files.* Leuven: European Social Survey, University of Leuven.

Office of Management and Budget. (2006). *Standards and guidelines for statistical surveys.* Retrieved from www.whitehouse.gov/sites/default/files/omb/assets/omb/inforeg/statpolicy/standards_stat_surveys.pdf

Peytchev, A. (2013). Consequences of survey nonresponse. *The ANNALS of the American Academy of Political and Social Science, 645*(1), 88–111.

Peytcheva, E., & Groves, R. M. (2009). Using variation in response rates of demographic subgroups as evidence of nonresponse bias in survey estimates. *Journal of Official Statistics, 25*(2), 193–201.

Schouten, B., Cobben, F., & Bethlehem, J. (2009). Indicators of representativeness of survey nonresponse. *Survey Methodology, 35,* 101–113.

Smith, T. W. (2011). The report of the international workshop on using multi-level data from sample frames, auxiliary databases, paradata and related sources to detect and adjust for nonresponse bias in surveys. *International Journal of Public Opinion Research, 23*(3), 389–402. doi:10.1093/ijpor/edr035

Stoop, I. (2007). No time, too busy. Time strain and survey cooperation. In G. Loosveldt, M. Swyngedouw, & B. Cambré (Eds.), *Measuring meaningful data in social research* (pp. 301–314). Leuven: Acco.

Stoop, I., Billiet, J., Koch, A., & Fitzgerald, R. (2010). *Improving Survey Response. Lessons Learned from the European Social Survey.* Chichester: Wiley.

Stoop, I., Devacht, S., Billiet, J., Loosveldt, G., & Philippens, M. (2003). *The development of a uniform contact description form in the ESS.* Paper presented at the 14th International Workshop on Household Survey Nonresponse, Leuven, September 2003.

Stoop, I., & Koch, A. (2013). Data collection as a scientific process: Process control and process quality in the European Social Survey. In B. Kleiner, I. Renschler, B. Wernli, P. Farago, & D. Joye (Eds.), *Understanding research infrastructures in the social sciences* (pp. 145–157). Zürich: Seismo Press.

Stoop, I., Matsuo, H., Koch, A., & Billiet, J. (2010). *Paradata in the European Social Survey: Studying nonresponse and adjusting for bias.* 2010 JSM Proceeding. Section on Survey Research Methods, pp. 407–421.

Vehovar, V. (2007). Non-response bias in the European Social Survey. In G. Loosveldt, M. Swyngedouw, & B. Cambré (Eds.), *Measuring meaningful data in social research* (pp. 335–356). Leuven: Acco.

Wagner, J. (2008). *Adaptive survey design to reduce nonresponse bias.* PhD thesis, University of Michigan.

Part VIII

Handling Missing Data

30

Handling Missing Data

Overview and Introduction

Martin Spiess

Missing data occur in almost every survey dataset when participation is not mandatory. They occur either as missing items if not all information of otherwise observed units, like individuals or households, is observed, or as missing units when sampled objects are not observed at all. Depending on the mechanism that led to the missing data, the observed part of the dataset may not be a simple random subsample of the selected data values. Thus, standard inference methods that would have been applied to the complete sample, if applied to the observed subsample only, may fail to allow valid inferences. But even if the observed data can be interpreted as a simple random subsample from the complete sample, standard analysis tools may not be able to adequately handle incompletely observed units. Thus, methods to analyze incomplete datasets and to compensate for possible bias introduced by the missing mechanism are necessary. So-called ad hoc methods like ignoring the missing mechanism or imputing (conditional) means have been shown either not to work or to work only in very specific situations (e.g., Horton & Kleinman, 2007). On the other hand, methods that allow for valid inferences in the analysis of interest, like weighting (e.g., Wooldridge, 2002), mainly adopted to compensate for missing units, or multiple imputation (Rubin, 1987), usually used to compensate for missing items, are more demanding.

Weighting as a method to compensate for different selection probabilities has been proposed, e.g., by Horvitz and Thompson (1952). The difference between selecting units into the sample by a probability design and self-selection of units into or out of a sample is that in the latter case the selection mechanism is unknown. The idea of weighting to compensate for a possible bias due to missing units has therefore been adapted by estimating these probabilities (e.g., Wooldridge, 2002). Although weighting

366 • *Martin Spiess*

methods are easy to apply as long as they are used to compensate for missing units in regression models, they have also been proposed to compensate for missing items (e.g., Robins, Rotnitzky, & Zhao, 1995). However, standard software is not yet able to handle these situations.

Usually, researchers are not interested in solving missing data problems. Therefore, an optimal compensation method would be very easy to apply and at the same time should allow valid inferences in a great number of different situations. The method of multiple imputation (Rubin, 1987) has been developed to serve this purpose: The idea is that the imputer who generates several predictions or imputations for each missing value and the analyst are different entities. Given a multiply imputed dataset, the analyst applies his or her standard analysis several times and combines the results for the inference of scientific interest according to simple rules given, e.g., in Rubin (1987). Since the main burden of creating multiple imputations is not on the analyst, from the analyst's point of view the first requirement of an optimal compensation method is almost met. Furthermore, most of the available software packages enable users to easily generate multiple imputations. However, these imputation techniques are mainly based on standard parametric imputation models which may be too restrictive and thus not close to the true process that generated the data. Although the method of multiple imputation seems to be "self-correcting" (e.g., Rubin, 2003), i.e., a possible bias of the resulting estimators might be masked by a large variance, grossly misspecified imputation models may lead to invalid inferences. Misspecification of imputation models may be due to ignoring important variables, wrong distributional or independence assumptions or a misspecified relationship between variables to be imputed and all other variables. Thus, the second requirement may be harder to fulfill.

Ideas on how to compensate for missing data do not only apply to the above described standard missing data situation. Missing data may even be intended by the research design. For example, in matrix sampling only a subset of all items is administered to each interviewee, thereby reducing the burden on the surveyed units. Nevertheless, to simplify analyses of the dataset, the unobserved answers to the not-administered items may be multiply imputed. In these cases, the missing mechanism is usually known, which reduces the error-proneness due to a misspecified missing data mechanism.

In Chapter 31, Bahrami, Aßmann, Meinfelder, and Rässler propose a split questionnaire survey design, in which subsets of items are administered to subsamples of interviewees. Blocks of items are defined based on a pilot study such that within-block correlations are high and between-block correlations are low. Each subsample receives one complete item block and a random item sample, where items from blocks with high correlations are selected with lower probability than items from blocks with low correlations. Based on the complete-block information, imputations are generated using this item sample. Since the items from low-correlation blocks are administered with higher probability, the final analyses of interest may be expected to be more efficient. However, the first step is to demonstrate that this strategy works, which is done by simulations.

Up until now, there has not been one software solution for all practically relevant situations. Thus, in Chapter 32, Kleinke and Reinecke propose a function to be used with mice within the R package to generate imputations for count data based on a multilevel model, i.e., to allow for clustered data when generating imputations. This function, which is evaluated in a simulation study, extends the range of situations to generate imputations considerably, as these are either restricted to simple marginal univariate imputation models, or to very restrictive multivariate models.

To reduce the possibility of misspecifications of relationships in imputation models, de Jong and Spiess propose a new semiparametric imputation method in Chapter 33. Within this approach, it is only necessary to correctly model the conditional mean and variance—optionally the (conditional) shape too—of the imputation model. Simulation results imply that this method may be the better choice compared to existing imputation models in a wide range of situations.

REFERENCES

Horton, N. J., & Kleinman, K. P. (2007). Much ado about nothing: A comparison of missing data methods and software to fit incomplete data regression models. *The American Statistician, 61*(1), 79–90.

Horvitz, D. G., & Thompson, D. J. (1952). A generalization of sampling without replacement from a finite universe. *Journal of the American Statistical Association, 47,* 663–685.

Robins, J. M., Rotnitzky, A., & Zhao, L. P. (1995). Analysis of semiparametric regression models for repeated outcomes in the presence of missing data. *Journal of the American Statistical Association, 90*(429), 106–121.

Rubin, D. (1987). *Multiple imputation for nonresponse in surveys.* New York: Wiley.

Rubin, D. B. (2003). Discussion on multiple imputation. *International Statistical Review, 71*(3), 619–625.

Wooldridge, J. M. (2002). Inverse probability weighted M-estimation for sample selection, attrition, and stratification. *Portuguese Economic Journal, 1,* 117–139.

31

A Split Questionnaire Survey Design for Data with Block Structure Correlation Matrix

Sara Bahrami, Christian Aßmann,
Florian Meinfelder and Susanne Rässler

31.1 INTRODUCTION

In multipurpose surveys, there is often a need for increasing the number of questions in order to assure the coverage of all issues of interest. However, increasing the length of a questionnaire can increase respondent burden, see Sharp and Frankel (1983). This then has possibly a negative influence on the response rate as shown by Marcus, Bosnjak, Lindner, Pilischenko, and Schütz (2007), as well as the quality of the responses, see Herzog and Bachman (1981). One possibility to address this problem is to decrease the length of the questionnaire using multiple matrix sampling design or split questionnaire survey design. The latter, originally developed by Raghunathan and Grizzle (1995) can be considered as an extension of the multiple matrix sampling design described by Shoemaker (1973) and Munger and Loyd (1988). In matrix sampling, every surveyed individual answers a random set of items whereas in the split questionnaire survey design the questionnaire is divided into several components with roughly equal numbers of items, i.e., a core component containing items that are considered to be vitally important (e.g., sociodemographic items) and some split components. Apart from items in the core component, which are inquired of all individuals surveyed, only a fraction of the split components are administered to random subsamples of individuals. Assigning items to split components is based on the correlation coefficients between the items. Items with higher correlations are assigned to different components. Also, the branches of an item and items containing skip patterns are assigned to the same component, because then it can be avoided that items that explain each other very well are jointly missing for any observation. Following the split questionnaire design each sample individual receives a fraction of the long questionnaire. Data gathered from the whole sample are combined and missing data in the sample caused by the items that are not asked from sample individuals due to split design are completed using multiple imputation as discussed by Rubin (1987), see also Gelman, King, and Liu (1998), Rässler and Koller (2002) and Adiguezel and Wedel (2008).

In this paper we develop and evaluate a method for creating a split design by combining the matrix sampling and the split questionnaire designs in which a subset of items is administered to randomly selected respondents. This design is created in such a way that it includes items that are predictive of the excluded items, so that subsequent analysis based on multiple imputation can recover information about the excluded items more efficiently. Similar to the design introduced by Raghunathan and Grizzle (1995), it is based on the correlation between the variables. Therefore, in order to be able to design a split questionnaire, prior information about the correlation of the variables is needed. This information can be provided by data collected in surveys which are conducted on a regular basis with almost identical questions, like panels or the considered tracking surveys; another possibility is to use data collected by pilot studies. Pilot studies are conducted prior to the main data collection on a small subsample of the population of interest to test the instruments and the course of the main data collection.

For illustration, the German National Educational Panel Study (NEPS) conducted pilot studies one year before the main data collection. Pilot data from one of the NEPS stages tracking a cohort of new entrants into higher education are used to illustrate the suggested split questionnaire design. The relationship between questions in the instrument is reflected in a structured correlation matrix for the data. For example, there are five questions in the instrument about the academic self-concept and these five items are highly correlated. Moreover, there are five questions in relation to dropout intentions that are also highly correlated. Items that are highly correlated can be considered as a block. Hence, the correlation matrix structure of the pilot data features high within-block correlation and low between-block correlation for the data. Concerning the widespread use of these kinds of instruments in surveys, a split questionnaire for data with a blockwise correlation matrix structure is designed.

The design is described in detail in Section 31.2. For evaluation purposes, based on the correlation matrix structure of the pilot data, a dataset is simulated. The implementation of the design on the simulated dataset is described in Section 31.3, including a description of the data generating process in Subsection 31.3.1, the application of the design on the simulated dataset in Subsection 31.3.2 and the multiple imputation technique used to fill the missing values induced by the design, in Subsection 31.3.3. The procedure tries to conserve the correlation matrix structure of the pilot data provided by the higher education stage of the NEPS. Different regression analyses of interest are performed on the simulated data and the parameters are estimated for the data before and after implementing the design. The point and interval estimates of the regression coefficients as well as their variance estimates and the coverage of their 95% confidence intervals between the complete and the split dataset are compared and tabulated in Subsection 31.3.4. A further empirical illustration of our split design based on ALLBUS data is provided in Section 31.4. Section 31.5 concludes.

31.2 SPLIT QUESTIONNAIRE SURVEY DESIGN FOR DATA WITH A BLOCKWISE CORRELATION MATRIX

Pilot data provided by NEPS consists of blocks, with each block containing several items. An interesting feature of the correlation matrix of the pilot data implied by the survey instrument is that the correlations between the items inside the blocks (within-block correlations) are higher than the correlations between the items in different blocks (between-block correlations). Moreover, we consider the blocks with within-correlations of at least 0.35 as highly correlated blocks. The choice of 0.35 is based on experience and personal judgment regarding general associations among survey variables and can hence be adapted if necessary. On the basis of the correlation matrix structure, a split questionnaire was designed. The idea is to divide the sample into subsamples and assign a fraction of items of each block to a random subsample. To ensure that the items of each block are administered simultaneously to a subsample of individuals, each random subsample receives one of the blocks completely. In addition, each respondent receives a random set of items from the rest of the blocks, where the probability of choosing items from highly correlated blocks is lower than the probability of choosing items from the rest of the blocks. Applying this design to a complete dataset results in a dataset with missing values for items which are not administered to individuals. As expected, the design imposes a higher ratio of missing values on items in highly correlated blocks, which is reasonable because the information lost by eliminated items can be recovered from those items with which they are highly correlated by means of a subsequent multiple imputation process.

31.3 EVALUATION OF THE SPLIT DESIGN USING SIMULATION

In order to assess the properties of estimators based on split design data, we generated a data source that reflects typical features of the observed pilot data. This dataset should reflect the characteristics of the pilot data with regard to its correlation matrix structure. We orientated the data generating process towards the pilot data obtained from the NEPS student cohort. Hence, a dataset with 13 blocks and a total of 60 items from altogether 24 blocks of pilot data is considered. Five out of the 13 blocks were chosen as highly correlated blocks. The data generating process aims to preserve the correlation matrix structure of these 13 item blocks and is discussed in more detail in the following subsection.

Data Generating Process

The simulated dataset consists of 70 variables including 40 metric variables, 10 binary variables, 10 ordinal variables and 10 multinomial variables with three categories each. To simulate all the variables with the exception of multinomial variables we use the correlation matrix that we extracted from 13 blocks containing 60 variables of the pilot data. We start by simulating 60 variables from a multivariate normal distribution,

$$X = (X_1, X_2, \ldots, X_{60}), \; X \sim N(\mu, \Sigma), \tag{31.1}$$

where, for the first 40 elements of mean vector μ, arbitrary (nonzero) values are defined and the remaining 20 elements are considered 0. The covariance matrix Σ of the multivariate normal distribution is specified using the correlation matrix extracted from pilot data. The correlation matrix of the pilot data ρ_p was converted to the covariance matrix according to the following relation,

$$\Sigma = \rho_p \otimes (\sigma\sigma'), \tag{31.2}$$

where, σ denotes the vector of standard deviations and is defined as follows. We specify arbitrary values for standard deviations of the first 40 variables and 1 for the remaining 20 variables. In the next step, we consider the first 40 variables with arbitrary mean values and standard deviations as our metric variables,

$$Y^{\text{met}} = (X_1, X_2, \ldots, X_{40}), \tag{31.3}$$

the remaining 20 variables with mean 0 and standard deviation of 1 are used to create binary and ordinal variables. Using binary probit models, 10 binary variables are created. To create binary variables, 10 normally distributed latent variables are defined as follows,

$$Y_i^* = Z_i' \beta_i + \epsilon_i, \quad \epsilon_i \in (X_{41}, \ldots, X_{50}), \quad i = 41, \ldots, 50; \quad Z_i' \subseteq Y^{\text{met}}, \tag{31.4}$$

and the subsequent binary variables are given as,

$$Y_i^{bin} = \begin{cases} 1 & \text{if} \quad Y_i^* \geq 0, \\ 0 & \text{if} \quad Y_i^* < 0. \end{cases} \tag{31.5}$$

The explanatory variables in the linear predictor of the latent variables are chosen from our metric variables Y^{met} and the error terms were set to $(X_{41}, \ldots, X_{50})$. For example, to create the first latent variable Y_{41}^* the corresponding residual ϵ_{41} is set to X_{41}, while for Y_{42}^* the corresponding residual ϵ_{42} is set to X_{42}, etc. The regression coefficients β_i including an intercept are specified arbitrarily. The same procedure is used to create 10 ordinal variables using ordinal probit models as follows:

$$Y_i^* = Z_i' \beta_i + \epsilon_i, \quad \epsilon_i \in (X_{51}, \ldots, X_{60}), \quad i = 51, \ldots, 60; \quad Z_i' \subseteq Y^{\text{met}}, \tag{31.6}$$

$$Y_i^{ord} = \begin{cases} 1 & \text{if} \quad -\infty < Y_i^* \leq \mu_{i,1}, \\ 2 & \text{if} \quad \mu_{i,1} < Y_i^* \leq \mu_{i,2}, \\ 3 & \text{if} \quad \mu_{i,2} < Y_i^* < +\infty. \end{cases} \tag{31.7}$$

In this case, the error terms of the normal latent variables are set to $(X_{51}, \ldots, X_{60})$. Considering three levels for the ordinal variables, two cutpoints $\mu_{i,1}$ and $\mu_{i,2}$ for each variable are specified. The regression coefficients in β_i are again specified arbitrarily. The ordered probit model is identified either by setting $\mu_{i,1} = 0$ or $\beta_{i,0} = 0$, where we chose the latter.

Furthermore, to check the robustness of the suggested approach, 10 unordered categorical variables are generated using multinomial logit models. The multinomial variables we want to generate have three categories labeled 0, 1 and 2. The first value, here 0, is designated as the reference category. The probability of membership in other categories is compared to the probability of membership in the reference category. Hence,

$$\Pr(Y_i = k) = \begin{cases} \dfrac{\exp\left(z_{ki}\right)}{1+\sum_{h=1}^{K}\exp\left(z_{hi}\right)}, & k = 1,\ldots,K \\[2ex] \dfrac{1}{1+\sum_{h=1}^{K}\exp\left(z_{hi}\right)}, & k = 0 \end{cases} \tag{31.8}$$

with $z_{ki} = \beta_{0k} + \beta_{1k}X_{i1} + \beta_{2k}X_{i2}$. For a multinomial variable with $K = 3$ categories, calculation of $K - 1 = 2$ equations are needed to describe the relationship between the multinomial variable and the independent variables. So we need to define two equations for z_{1i} and z_{2i} in which X_{i1}, X_{i2} are chosen from metric variables and the two sets of coefficients $\beta_{01}, \beta_{11}, \beta_{21}$, and $\beta_{02}, \beta_{12}, \beta_{22}$, are defined arbitrarily. In the next step, for each observation an independent random number u is drawn from a standard uniform distribution, consequently Y_i takes values 0, 1 and 2 if u belongs to the ranges shown below,

$$Y_i^{\text{cat}} = \begin{cases} 0 & \text{if} \quad 0 < u \le Pr(Y_i = 0), \\ 1 & \text{if} \quad Pr(Y_i = 0) < u \le Pr(Y_i = 0) + Pr(Y_i = 1), \\ 2 & \text{if} \quad Pr(Y_i = 0) + Pr(Y_i = 1) < u \le 1 \end{cases} \tag{31.9}$$

with $i = 61, \ldots, 70$. Note that as opposed to metric, binary and ordinal variables, nominal variables depend on other variables only via a specified conditional mean function. This approach provides a dataset in which the correlation matrix structure of the pilot data is preserved. Using different measures of association like Tetrachoric Coefficient between binary variables, Polychoric Coefficient between ordinal variables, Biserial Coefficient between binary and metric variables and Spearman Rank Order Coefficient between metric and ordinal variables confirms the preservation of association between the variables of the generated dataset, although the considered measures of correlation are not directly designed for variables with nominal scales.

Application of the Design

In this subsection we explain how we applied the design to the simulated dataset. The 70 variables in the simulated dataset can be categorized into 15 blocks, each block containing four to five variables. In general, the correlations of variables inside the blocks are higher than the correlations of variables between different blocks. Furthermore, six blocks have higher within-correlations than the other nine blocks. In this study we want to simulate a case in which only half of the items are assigned to each individual, thus each individual should receive only 35 items. For this reason we divide the sample into as many subsamples as the number of blocks, in our case 15 subsamples. Each subsample receives one of the blocks completely. In addition to a complete block (four to five items), each individual randomly receives 30 to 31 items from the rest of the blocks, so that the probability of receiving items from blocks with higher within-correlations is lower than the corresponding probability for blocks with smaller within-correlations. In our design, we set the probability of missingness in highly correlated blocks to 0.55 and the probability of missingness in the rest of the blocks to 0.45.

Figure 31.1 shows the implementation of the design on the data schematically. The columns $b_1, \ldots, b_{15}$ are the blocks, where $b_1, \ldots, b_6$ are those with high within-correlations. The rows are the subsamples and the shaded diagonal squares represent the complete blocks received by each subsample. Applying the design to the complete dataset induces missing values in the data. The next step is to deal with the missing values.

	b_1	b_2	...	...	...	b_6	b_7	b_8	...	...	...	...	...	...	b_{15}
1	■														
2		■													
.			■												
.				■											
.					■										
6						■									
7							■								
.								■							
.									■						
.										■					
.											■				
.												■			
.													■		
.														■	
15															■

FIGURE 31.1
Design implementation on the simulated dataset

Multiple Imputation to Recover Missing Values Induced by Split Design

In order to analyze the split data, the missing values induced by the split design are treated using Multiple Imputation (MI) methods as discussed in detail by Rubin (1987). Multiple imputation is a general purpose procedure for analyzing incomplete datasets, where the uncertainty due to missingness is represented by different datasets that vary in the imputed part. The R package MICE by van Buuren and Groothuis-Oudshoorn (2011) implements multiple imputations via chained equations. The imputation method used for metric and binary variables is Predictive Mean Matching (PMM) as described by Rubin (1986) and Little (1988). PMM is the nearest-neighbor approach that automatically yields plausible values in the imputation process. To impute the ordinal and multinomial variables, the ordered logistic regression and polytomous logistic regression are used. Given the simulation setup, the PMM method for imputing the binary variables yields better MI-estimates for the binary probit model compared to the logistic regression method recommended by MICE for imputing binary variables. The missing values are imputed $m = 10$ times.

Simulation Results

The next step is to evaluate the design by means of the generated dataset. For this purpose three analytical models are selected, namely a binary probit model, an ordered probit model and a multinomial logit model. These models are chosen in anticipation of potential analysis objectives from the models used in the data generating process.

First, a sample of 50,000 was generated using the method described above. This sample is considered as the population. The regression coefficients of the analytical models were then estimated for this sample and considered as the true parameters as shown in Table 31.1. In the next step 1,000 samples, each of size 5,000, are drawn from the hypothetical population. The models are then estimated for these samples before and after design implementation and the following multiple imputation. Before the deletion model estimates and their estimated variances specified by BD in the table are the average model estimates and their estimated variances over all 1,000 samples before design implementation. In the table the average model estimates and their estimated variances among all 1,000 samples before design implementation are specified by BD. Multiple imputation estimates and their corresponding variances, which are specified by MI in the table, are calculated as follows: the design is applied to each sample and

TABLE 31.1

Comparison of split and complete data estimates of regression coefficients and their variances as well as the coverage of their 95% confidence intervals for three different models for a data set on 1,000 observations. Furthermore the fraction of missing information (γ) for the individual estimates are represented in this table.

	binary probit			ordered probit		multinomial logit					
	β_0	β_1	β_2	β_0	β_1	β_{01}	β_{11}	β_{21}	β_{02}	β_{12}	β_{22}
Parameter	.086	.209	−.211	.294	−.188	.960	.177	−.151	.982	.187	−.171
Estimate											
BD	.086	.210	−.212	.294	−.189	.961	.177	−.152	.982	.186	−.172
MI	.085	.198	−.198	.285	−.180	.886	.164	−.130	.918	.173	−.148
Variance											
BD	.00038	.00021	.00015	.00009	.00010	.00192	.00056	.00084	.00191	.00056	.00084
MI	.00067	.00060	.00044	.00022	.00025	.00268	.00111	.00191	.00243	.00102	.00170
Coverage											
BD	.95	.96	.96	.96	.95	.95	.97	.96	.97	.98	.96
MI	.96	.94	.94	.93	.92	.72	.95	.95	.75	.96	.95
γ	.44	.60	.58	.53	.55	.30	.50	.55	.25	.45	.50

missing values caused by the design are imputed using multiple imputation. In our case, multiple imputation produces $m = 10$ imputed datasets. The models are estimated for each imputed dataset $j, j = 1, \ldots, m$. The model estimates, $\hat{\beta}^{(j)}$, and their estimated variances, $\widehat{var}(\hat{\beta}^{(j)})$, of all $m = 10$ imputed datasets are combined using Rubin's combining rules, see Rubin (1987). According to Rubin's combining rules, the multiple imputation estimator is defined by $\hat{\beta}_{MI} = 1/m \sum_{j=1}^{m} \hat{\beta}^{(j)}$. The total estimated variance of $\hat{\beta}_{MI}$ is defined as $T = W + (1 + 1/m)B$, where $W = 1/m \sum_{j=1}^{m} \widehat{var}(\hat{\beta}^{(j)})$ is the variance within the imputed datasets and $B = 1/m-1 \sum_{j=1}^{m} (\hat{\beta}^{(j)} - \hat{\beta}_{MI})'(\hat{\beta}^{(j)} - \hat{\beta}_{MI})$ is the variance between the imputed datasets. *MI* variance in the table indicates the average total variances of $\hat{\beta}_{MI}$ over all 1,000 samples drawn from the population. Coverage indicates the proportion of samples for which the 95% confidence interval of the model estimates contains the true parameter. BD coverage indicates the 95% coverage before design implementation, and MI coverage indicates the 95% coverage after design implementation and the following multiple imputation. Furthermore, the fraction of missing information γ due to multiple imputation is calculated for each estimator, $\gamma = (1 + 1/m)\frac{B}{T}$.

The results presented in Table 31.1 reveal that all coverages meet the expected 95% level, except those for the intercepts of the multinomial logit model. We assume that these findings result from the data generating process used to create the simulated data, where the nominal variables depend on any other variable only via the specified conditional mean function. This provides less association with other variables to be exploited within the multiple imputation procedure. Further, the chosen correlation measure is not directly designed for variables with nominal scale. Given this, we consider the high coverage for the other parameters of the multinomial logit model as evidence in favor of the robustness of the suggested split design.

31.4 EMPIRICAL APPLICATION

The split design is also illustrated by means of survey data taken from the ALLBUS 2009 survey. The ALLBUS dataset resembles the correlation structure found in the NEPS pilot data. For this reason, 63 variables were selected from ALLBUS data and combined to create a smaller dataset. The dataset contains variables about personal characteristics, political participation and attitudes towards the political system, world view and value orientations as well as attitudes to different ethnic groups in Germany, citizenship, national identity, social inequality and religion.

The variables are divided into 12 blocks, each containing five to six variables. The within-block correlations are in general higher than between-block correlations, four blocks have higher within-correlations than the other blocks. In this study we use two empirical models to evaluate the design, a binary probit model and a multinomial logit model. In the multinomial logit model, we specify the respondents' opinion on ethnically mixed neighborhoods with three values, yes, no and no preferences, as the dependent variable. As explanatory variables, we use opinion on intermarriage and how agreeable it is to have foreign neighbors. Both explanatory variables are ordinal and take six values. In the binary probit model, we specify opinion about dual citizenship as the dependent variable, and the variables importance of law and order and self-classification in left-right political spectrum as explanatory variables. Both explanatory variables are again ordinal with five and ten values respectively.

The ALLBUS dataset includes approximately 3,000 observations. For simulation purposes, this sample is considered as the population and model estimates for this sample are considered as true parameters. One thousand samples of 1,000 each were drawn from the population; the models were estimated for each sample before implementing the design (BD) and after implementing the design and the following multiple imputation (MI). Their associated variances, the 95% coverage and the fraction of missing information (γ) due to multiple imputation are provided in Table 31.2. The

TABLE 31.2

Comparison of split and complete data estimates of regression coefficients and their variances as well as the coverage of their 95% confidence intervals for two different models for Allbus Data on 1,000 observations. Furthermore the fraction of missing information (γ) for the individual estimates are represented in this table.

	binary probit			multinomial logit					
	β_0	β_1	β_2	β_{01}	β_{11}	β_{21}	β_{02}	β_{12}	β_{22}
Parameter	−.073	−.116	.099	1.670	−.310	−.530	.940	−.120	−.270
Estimate									
BD	−.078	−.116	.101	1.666	−.316	−.532	.932	−.120	−.267
MI	−.117	−.101	.099	.962	−.189	−.367	1.000	−.100	−.247
Variance									
BD	.026	.0006	.0015	.27	.0066	.0085	.1166	.0023	.0031
MI	.063	.0015	.0032	.49	.0133	.0147	.2869	.0071	.0076
Coverage									
BD	.97	.97	.96	.98	.98	.97	.99	.96	.98
MI	.97	.97	.97	.87	.86	.77	.95	.95	.95
γ	.62	.72	.50	.66	.68	.62	.60	.59	.62

results suggest that the model estimates are quite unbiased and the coverages are quite high, which meet our expectations regarding the application of split questionnaire design for long questionnaires. Again, some caveats apply concerning the coefficients of the multinomial logit model, where again for the given choice of correlation measure we interpret the results in favor of robustness of the suggested approach. Future research could address the effects of correlation measures directly designed for variables with nominal scale.

31.5 DISCUSSION

In this study we have explained how we designed a particular kind of split questionnaire for items with a particular correlation matrix structure available from a pilot study. Due to the fact that the small number of observations in the empirical data would lead to inaccurate multiple imputation estimates, generating a dataset with a sufficient sample size that could reproduce the correlation matrix structure of the pilot data could help us to evaluate our design.

The results shown in Table 31.1 illustrate how using this design could affect the regression coefficient estimates of the analytical models. The estimates are unbiased and the coverages are high, although further improvements may be gained via consideration of richer dependence structures for the variables with nominal scale and other measure of dependence between the variables. By implementing the design on a dataset extracted from ALLBUS data, we demonstrated that this design could work very well for data with this particular correlation matrix structure.

REFERENCES

Adiguezel, F., & Wedel, M. (2008). Questionnaire survey design for massive surveys. *Journal of Marketing Research, XLV*, 608–617.

Gelman, A., King, G., & Liu, C. (1998). Not asked and not answered: Multiple imputation for multiple surveys. *Journal of the American Statistical Association, 93*(443), 846–857.

Herzog, A. R., & Bachman, J. G. (1981). Effects of questionnaire length on response quality. *Public Opinion Quarterly, 45*, 549–559.

Little, R. (1988). Missing-data adjustments in large surveys. *Journal of Business and Economic Statistics, 6*(3).

Marcus, B., Bosnjak, M., Lindner, S., Pilischenko, S., & Schütz, A. (2007). Compensating for low topic interest and long surveys: A field experiment on nonresponse in web surveys. *Social Science Computer Review, 25*(3), 372–383.

Munger, G. F., & Loyd, B. H. (1988). The use of multiple matrix sampling for survey research. *The Journal of Experimental Education, 56*(4), 187–191. Retrieved from www.jstor. org/stable/20151742

Raghunathan, T. E., & Grizzle, J. E. (1995). A split questionnaire survey design. *Journal of the American Statistical Association, 90*(429), 54–63.

Rässler, S., & Koller, F. (2002). A split questionnaire survey design applied to German media and consumer surveys. *Proceedings of the International Conference on Improving Surveys, ICIS.*

Rubin, D. (1986). Statistical matching using file concatenation with adjusted weights and multiple imputation. *Journal of Economic and Business Statistics, 4*, 87–94.

Rubin, D. (1987). *Multiple imputation for nonresponse in surveys.* New York: Wiley.

Sharp, L., & Frankel, J. (1983). Respondent burden: A test of some common assumptions. *Public Opinion Quarterly, 47*, 36–53.

Shoemaker, D. M. (1973). *Principles and procedures of multiple matrix sampling.* Cambridge: Ballinger.

van Buuren, S., & Groothuis-Oudshoorn, K. (2011). mice: Multivariate imputation by chained equations in R. *Journal of Statistical Software, 45*(3), 1–67.

32

Multiple Imputation of Multilevel Count Data

Kristian Kleinke and Jost Reinecke

Throughout the last couple of years, multiple imputation has become a popular and widely accepted technique to handle missing data. Although various multiple imputation procedures have been implemented in all major statistical packages, currently available software is still highly limited regarding the imputation of incomplete count data. As count data analysis typically makes it necessary to fit statistical models that are suited for count data like Poisson or negative binomial models, also imputation procedures should be specially tailored to the statistical specialities of count data. We present a flexible and easy-to-use solution to create multiple imputations of incomplete multilevel count data, based on a generalized linear mixed-effects Poisson model with multivariate normal random effects, using penalized quasi-likelihood. Our procedure works as an add-on for the popular and powerful multiple imputation package MICE (van Buuren & Groothuis-Oudshoorn, 2011) for the R language and environment for statistical computing

32.1 INTRODUCTION AND OVERVIEW

Missing data pose a threat to the validity of statistical inferences when they are numerous and not missing completely at random (Little & Rubin, 1987; Schafer, 1997a). In this case, multiple imputation (MI; e.g. Schafer, 1997a; van Buuren & Groothuis-Oudshoorn, 2011) is a state-of-the-art procedure to address the missing data problem, as it allows the use of all available information in the dataset to predict missing information. In comparison to simple solutions like case deletion, unconditional mean imputation, or last value carried forward, MI typically yields far better and mostly unbiased parameter estimates and standard errors (Schafer & Graham, 2002; Graham, 2009; Kleinke, Stemmler, Reinecke, & Lösel, 2011).

Based on theoretical work by Rubin (1987), Schafer (1997a,b) introduced MI software for continuous data (**norm**), categorical data (**cat**), incomplete datasets containing both continuous and categorical data (**mix**), and for continuous clustered or panel data (**pan**). Today, most statistical packages have implemented some kind of multiple imputation routine. For an overview, see Horton and Lipsitz (2001), Horton and Kleinman (2007), or www.multiple-imputation.com.

It is, however, quite unfortunate that most statistical packages provide no or only very basic support for incomplete count data imputation, and to our best knowledge, MI software for multilevel count data does not yet exist: Imputation solutions that allow the imputation of missing count data using a regression-based Poisson or negative binomial approach include the **mi** package in R (Su, Gelman, Hill, & Yajima, 2009), **IVEware** in SAS (available from www.isr.umich.edu/src/smp/ive/), or **ice** in STATA (Royston, 2009). However, zero-inflated or multilevel count data are not supported.

To remedy this lack of support regarding important count data models, Kleinke and Reinecke (2011, 2013a) introduced a comprehensive count data imputation package for the R language and environment for statistical computing, called **countimp**.[1] This package supports imputation of ordinary, overdispersed, zero-inflated, and multilevel count data.

In this paper, we focus solely on multilevel count data imputation. Our solution predicts and imputes missing data on the basis of a generalized linear mixed effects Poisson model with penalized quasi-likelihood within a sequential-regression-based MI framework (cf. Raghunathan, Lepkowski, van Hoewyk, & Solenberger, 2001; van Buuren & Groothuis-Oudshoorn, 2011). We begin by giving a brief introduction to count data models and by outlining why count data require special analysis and imputation procedures (Section 32.2). We then give background information regarding multiple imputation, the software MICE, and introduce our multilevel count data imputation procedure (Section 32.3). Several Monte Carlo simulations were run to test the quality of this procedure (Section 32.4). We conclude with a discussion of our results and outline fruitful avenues for future research and software development (Section 32.5).

32.2 COUNT DATA ANALYSIS AND IMPUTATION

A comprehensive introduction to count data modeling is given in Zeileis, Kleiber, and Jackman (2008). Counts are non-negative integer numbers and represent the number of occurrences of a certain event within a given period of time, like the number of times a patient visits a medical doctor within one year. The distribution of the count data is typically not normal. Therefore it may not be too surprising that traditional solutions to analyze and to impute count data that rely on the normal model yield suboptimal results (cf. Yu, Burton, & Rivero-Arias, 2007). First, applying some kind of normalizing transformation like a square-root transformation and then using ordinary least squares (OLS) regression will work only as a very rough approximation in most scenarios and will yield parameter estimates that are (a) hard to interpret and (b) not optimal. Second, instead of using a normalizing transformation, count data are very often treated as if they were normal, i.e. the fact that their distribution is usually not normal is simply ignored. Imputations obtained by Bayesian normal model MI—a procedure intended to be used for multivariate normal continuous data— is known to produce suboptimal results, especially when the distribution of the count data is skewed and has an excess number of zeros (Yu et al., 2007). A more robust procedure in this regard is predictive mean matching. Although it also imputes missing data based on a linear regression model, it fills in an actual observed value and can thus better preserve the original distribution of the data and can so buffer some of the effects of the misspecified imputation model (Yu et al., 2007). Furthermore, using imputation procedures for categorical data like polytomous regression can only be recommended as a quick proxy if the number of categories is quite small. The larger the number of categories, the more likely it is that there are empty cell problems and the greater the probability that the algorithm runs into estimation problems (cf. van Buuren & Groothuis-Oudshoorn, 2011). Yu et al. (2007) argue that using "MI methods with inappropriate distributional assumptions should be avoided when the data depart considerably from these assumptions" (p. 255). Kleinke and Reinecke (2013b) have also demonstrated that when the count data imputation model fits the data well, imputations are plausible and parameter estimates are unbiased. We therefore argue in favor of using imputation procedures that are tailored to the specialities of count data: Instead of using a normal model, the distribution of count data can usually be better described by the Poisson (32.1) or negative binomial (NB) model (32.2).[2] Consequently, instead of using OLS regression, the better solution is to fit a generalized linear model using the Poisson family (Nelder & Wedderburn, 1972), or to fit a negative binomial regression model (Hilbe, 2011) to analyze or to impute count data.

$$f(y;\mu) = \frac{e^{-\mu_i}\mu_i^{y_i}}{y_i!} \tag{32.1}$$

$$f(y;\mu,\alpha) = \begin{pmatrix} y_i + \dfrac{1}{\alpha} - 1 \\ \dfrac{1}{\alpha} - 1 \end{pmatrix} \left(\dfrac{1}{1+\alpha\mu_i} \right)^{\frac{1}{\alpha}} \left(\dfrac{\alpha\mu_i}{1+\alpha\mu_i} \right)^{y_i} \qquad (32.2)$$

The difference between the Poisson and the NB model is that the former assumes equidispersion, which means that the variance $VAR(\mu)$ is equal to the mean μ, while the latter does not make this assumption. NB models estimate an additional heterogeneity or overdispersion parameter α. What the models have in common is that they stem from the same family. The negative binomial model, as a Poisson-gamma mixture model, can be derived from an otherwise Poisson model where the overdispersion takes the form of a gamma distribution (for details see Hilbe, 2011, Chapter 8).

One typical way to analyze clustered or panel count data is to fit a generalized linear mixed effects Poisson model or a mixed effects NB model (cf. Venables & Ripley, 2002; Hilbe, 2011). The advantage of mixed effects modeling is that unlike ordinary generalized linear models, they do not have to assume that intercepts and slopes are constant across clusters. Instead, intercept and slope variation and covariation across groups can be estimated, and predictors can be added to explain why different groups or individuals differ in their intercepts and slopes. This is, for example, of interest in the analysis of change to explain why different individuals have different starting levels and exhibit different change patterns over time.

The imputation functions in the **countimp** package use various count data models to impute different kinds of incomplete count data within a sequential-regression-based MI framework: ordinary count data are, for example, predicted by a classical Poisson model, and clustered or panel count data can be imputed by a two-level Poisson model—which is the focus of this paper. Functions for overdispersed, zero-inflated and two-level zero-inflated, and overdispersed count data are also available.

In the next section, we discuss the concept and theory of multiple imputation and introduce our two-level Poisson imputation procedure.

32.3 MULTIPLE IMPUTATION OF MULTILEVEL COUNT DATA

The term imputation refers to a class of procedures that replace missing values with plausible values so that the completed dataset may be analyzed by standard complete-data techniques. An overview and review of various simple and more sophisticated imputation approaches is given in Kleinke et al. (2011). The problem with single imputation procedures (e.g. single-regression- or expectation-maximization-based imputation) is that—regardless of how sophisticated they are and even if imputations are properly generated—they tend to yield biased standard errors unless some correction procedure like a bootstrap (Efron, 1982, 1994) or jackknife (Rao & Shao, 1992) is applied (see also Little & Rubin, 1987; Schafer & Graham, 2002; Graham, Cumsille, & Elek-Fisk, 2003). This is because imputations are uncertain predictions of the unknown true values and this estimation uncertainty due to missing data has to be adequately taken into account. The most common and computationally feasible procedure today to address this estimation uncertainty is to generate multiple imputations following Rubin's theory (Rubin, 1987). The idea here is to replace each missing value m times with a different, but equally plausible value. Typically, between 5 and 20 imputations are sufficient. The resulting m complete datasets are then analyzed separately, and the m statistical results are combined into an overall result using Rubin's (1987) rules for MI inference: the combined parameter estimate is the mean of the m estimates. The combined standard error incorporates both between and within imputation variability to address the extra estimation uncertainty due to missing data.

The most commonly used frameworks that are being used today to create multiple imputations are the Bayesian joint modeling approach (JM, e.g. Schafer, 1997a,b) and sequential regressions MI (e.g. Raghunathan et al., 2001; van Buuren, Brand, Groothuis-Oudshoorn, & Rubin, 2006; van Buuren, 2007). Introductions to JM may be found in Allison (2001); Graham (2009); Graham et al. (2003); Schafer (1997a); Schafer and Graham (2002); an introduction to the sequential regressions framework is given in van Buuren and Groothuis-Oudshoorn (2011). Both frameworks assume that values are missing at random in the sense of Rubin (1976). Simplistically speaking, that means that missing information can be predicted by observed information in the dataset. The main difference between these two approaches is that JM makes it necessary to specify a joint probability model for the dataset as a whole, which can be highly unfeasible or even impossible to specify for large and complex datasets, whereas the sequential regressions approach allows to impute data on a variable-to-variable basis and is thus more flexible.

Due to this great modeling flexibility, we use the sequential regressions framework as the basis for our count data imputation procedures. Our functions work as add-on functions to the popular and powerful MICE package (van Buuren & Groothuis-Oudshoorn, 2011) for the R language and environment for statistical computing. This has several reasons:

(a) both MICE and R are open source and available free of charge from www.r-project.org, (b) R is enjoying increasing popularity among (social) scientists, and is increasingly being used for data analysis, (c) MICE already offers lots of helpful imputation functionalities as well as diagnostic tools for assessing imputation quality, and most importantly, (d) MICE very easily allows us to call user-written imputation functions such as ours. The apparent advantage herein is that missing data researchers do not have to "re-invent the wheel", i.e. come up with yet another new statistical software when developing new missing data imputation solutions, and data analysts can work with the software they are already familiar with.

Readers who are not yet familiar with MICE may find a detailed introduction, an overview of all its functionalities, and practical examples in the user's manual (van Buuren & Groothuis-Oudshoorn, 2011). An introduction to R is given in Adler (2010). Here, we review only the most basic MICE essentials.

Since our proposed multiple imputation solution for two-level count data works as an add-on to the MICE package, the `mice()` function is used to specify the imputation model(s), the respective imputation procedure(s), and to create the multiple imputations. During the imputation stage, `mice()` automatically calls our add-on function, and passes all necessary information to this function. Practitioners who are already familiar with the MICE package do not have to learn anything new and can work with MICE as they are accustomed to. When calling the main function `mice()` to multiply impute incomplete data, the user [. . .] can specify certain arguments, e.g. `method` and `predictorMatrix`. The argument `method` is used to specify the imputation procedure for imputing missing data in a certain variable. The argument `method` must thus be a character vector of length equal to the number of variables in the dataset. The first entry in `method` specifies the imputation procedure for the first variable in the dataset, the second entry the method for the second variable, and so on. Variables that need not be imputed have method " ". MICE already comes with a variety of imputation functions (for an overview, see van Buuren & Groothuis-Oudshoorn, 2011). The information provided in the `method` entry is used by MICE to call the respective imputation subfunction. These are called `mice.impute.name()`, where name identifies the respective function and can be any combination of characters. Specifying "`2l.poisson`" for a certain variable, for example, would call our proposed two-level Poisson imputation function `mice.impute.2l.poisson()`.

The imputation model, i.e. the subset of predictors that is used to predict missing information in the respective incomplete variable, is specified via the `predictorMatrix` argument: `predictorMatrix` must be a rectangular matrix of dimensions equal to the number of variables in the dataset. An example is given in van Buuren and Groothuis-Oudshoorn (2011). Each row i in that matrix denotes the imputation model of variable V_i. Zeros and ones indicate (0 = no; 1 = yes), if the respective variable V_j is used to predict missing data in V_i. Note that two-level imputation models in MICE (i.e. when the imputation function starts with `mice.impute.21.`) allow additional entries in the respective row of the `predictorMatrix` (e.g. codes 2 and –2), which will be explained later.

Our proposed function `mice.impute.21.poisson()` imputes missing data based on a two-level generalized linear mixed effects regression model. The function requires MICE version 2.6 or newer and the R package MASS (Venables & Ripley, 2002). It fits a Poisson glmmPQL model (generalized linear mixed effects model with multivariate normal random effects, using penalized quasi-likelihood). An introduction and discussions of PQL models may be found in Venables and Ripley (2002), Schall (1991), Breslow and Clayton (1993), or Wolfinger and O'Connell (1993).

We now describe the function in detail. R code is listed in Function 32.1. The argument `.21.` before the function name is necessary and tells MICE that a two-level model is being fitted. It enables certain functionalities that are needed to specify the imputation model. The argument `intercept = TRUE` in the function header means that by default, the imputation model automatically includes the intercept as a fixed and random effect. If models are to be fitted without a random intercept, the **countimp** package provides a function `mice.impute.21.poisson.noint()`, which is identical to `mice.impute.21.poisson()`, but sets `intercept = FALSE` in the function header. Additional fixed and random effects are defined via the `predictorMatrix` argument as described below. Four arguments are passed on by the main `mice()` function: y, ry, x, and type. The argument y is the incomplete variable to be imputed, a vector of length n, while ry is the corresponding response indicator, informing whether a value in y is observed (ry = TRUE) or missing (ry = FALSE). The argument x is an $n \times p$ matrix of complete or completed covariates that are used to model y: which variables are included in x is determined by the `predictorMatrix`. The argument type is a vector of length equal to the number of columns in x, identifying the fixed effects, both fixed and random effects, and the class variable: type is also extracted from the `predictorMatrix`.[3] Variables to be treated only as a fixed (but not random) effect are coded '1' in the respective row of the `predictorMatrix`. Random variables have the code '2', and they also include the fixed effect. The class variable is identified by a '-2'. The current version supports only two-level models and thus allows only one class variable. If more than one

```
mice.impute.2l.poisson <- function (y, ry, x, type, intercept = TRUE)
{
    Y <- y[ry]
    X <- x[ry, ]
    nam <- paste("V", 1:ncol(X), sep = "")
    colnames(X) <- nam
    if (sum(type == -2) > 1) {
        stop("only one class allowed!")
    }
    grp <- which(type == -2)
    fixedeff <- paste("+", paste(nam[-grp], collapse = "+"),
        sep = "")
    if (any(type == 2)) {
        ran <- which(type == 2)
        randeff <- paste("+", paste(nam[ran], collapse = "+"),
            sep = "")
        if (!intercept) {
            randeff <- paste("~0", randeff, "|", paste(nam[grp]),
                sep = "")
        }
        else {
            randeff <- paste("~1", randeff, "|", paste(nam[grp]),
                sep = "")
        }
    }
    else {
        if (!intercept) {
            randeff <- paste("~0", "|", paste(nam[grp]), sep = "")
        }
        else {
            randeff <- paste("~1", "|", paste(nam[grp]), sep = "")
        }
    }
    randeff <- as.formula(randeff)
    fixedeff <- as.formula(paste("Y", "~", fixedeff, sep = ""))
    dat <- data.frame(Y, X)
    fit <- glmmPQL(fixed = fixedeff, data = dat, random = randeff,
        family = "poisson", control = list(opt = "optim"), na.action = na.omit)
    fit.sum <- summary(fit)
    beta <- fit$coefficients$fixed
    rv <- t(chol(vcov(fit)))
    b.star <- beta + rv %*% rnorm(ncol(rv))
    fitmis <- fit
    fitmis$coefficients$fixed <- b.star
    newdatamis <- data.frame(X = x[!ry, ])
    colnames(newdatamis) <- nam
    yhatmis <- predict(fitmis, newdata = newdatamis, type = "response",
        na.action = na.pass)
    yhatmis <- rpois(length(yhatmis), yhatmis)
    return(yhatmis)
}
```

FUNCTION 32.1

Multilevel Poisson Imputation

class is specified, the function aborts with an error message. An example and hands-on instructions regarding how to specify a two-level imputation model and how to set the respective entries of the `predictorMatrix` is given in van Buuren and Groothuis-Oudshoorn (2011).

With the information stored in `y`, `x`, `ry`, and `type`, we then fit a glmmPQL model, using the `glmmPQL()` function from the R package **MASS** using the `poisson` family with a log-link. We then follow the classical Bayesian regression steps (Rubin, 1987), i.e. we apply a stochastic imputation approach to ensure a plausible variability of imputations: First, model parameters θ are estimated. Second, new parameters θ^* are simulated from $N(\hat{\theta}, VAR(\hat{\theta}))$, where $\hat{\theta}$ and $VAR(\hat{\theta})$ are the posterior mean and variance of model parameters θ. As done by other Bayesian regression imputation functions in MICE, θ are obtained by a matrix multiplication of the transpose of the Choleski factorized unscaled estimated covariance matrix of the estimated coefficients and a vector of $N(0,1)$ random values and adding this result to θ. In the third step, counts are predicted for each case with missing `y`, using the model from step one and new parameters θ^*. These predicted values are then returned to the main `mice()` function.

For a brief discussion of Bayesian regression and the assumed normal distribution of parameters $N(\hat{\theta}, VAR(\hat{\theta}))$, see Rubin (1987). As an alternative, we also provide a bootstrap regression variant which fits the count regression model to different bootstrap samples respectively to ensure a plausible variability of imputations (for details, see Kleinke & Reinecke, 2013a).

Section 32.4 presents several Monte Carlo simulations that were run to evaluate the quality of our approach.

32.4 MONTE CARLO SIMULATIONS

To evaluate our imputation solution for multilevel count data, we ran different Monte Carlo simulations with models of varying complexity (models with individual level predictors, group level predictors, models with and without quadratic terms), varying missing data mechanisms (missing data e.g. dependent on individual level or group level predictors), and varying sample sizes. Each simulation was replicated 200 times.

Simulation 1

In our first Monte Carlo study, we simulated datasets containing data from 100 different groups and varied the number of observational units per group. We chose three scenarios: In the small dataset condition, each group contained only 100 observational units, whereas in the large dataset condition, we had a constant size of 1000 units per group. In the third condition, we allowed for varying group sizes. Here, the number of observational units per group was chosen randomly and ranged between 382 and 1981 (M = 1210.84, SD = 470.15). For data generation, data imputation, and data analysis we used a rather simple model with the dependent count variable y, only one individual level predictor x, and no group level predictor. The intercept as well as the slope of x were allowed to vary in each group (random effects). Using typical multilevel notation (cf. Bryk & Raudenbush, 1992), the data generation process for the Poisson variable y for each group g was

$$
\begin{aligned}
y_{ig} &\sim \text{POIS}(\exp(\beta_{0g} + \beta_{1g}x_{ig} + e_{ig})) \\
\beta_{0g} &= \gamma_{00} + u_{0g} = 1 + u_0 \\
\beta_{1g} &= \gamma_{10} + u_{1g} = .75 + u_1 \\
x_{ig} &\sim N(0, 1) \\
u_{0g} &\sim N(0, \sigma_{00} = .5) \\
u_{1g} &\sim N(0, \sigma_{11} = .3) \\
\sigma_{01} &= 0 \\
e_{ig} &\sim N(0, 1),
\end{aligned}
\tag{32.3}
$$

where u_{0g}, u_{1g}, and e_{ig} represent intercept and slope variability and the individual level error terms respectively. Subscripts i and g are the individual and group identifiers, σ_{00} and σ_{11} are the random effects standard deviations of the intercept term and slope respectively, and σ_{01} denotes the random effects correlation. The data of the g groups were finally stacked upon each other to get a multilevel dataset in "long format".

In this simulation, data were only missing in y. Predictor x was fully observed. We introduced missing data according to the following rule, where p_{ig} denotes the probability that y_{ig} will be missing, and NA is the missing data indicator (i.e. "not available"):

$$
\begin{aligned}
p_{ig} &= \text{invlogit}(-1 + x_{ig}) \\
u_{ig} &\sim U(0,1) \\
y_{ig} &= \text{NA, if } u_{ig} < p_{ig}
\end{aligned}
\tag{32.4}
$$

This generated an average percentage of missing data in y of 30.3%. Note that missing data in y were dependent on x and were thus missing at random (MAR, Rubin, 1976, 1987). Data were then imputed m = 5 times using the MICE package with our `mice.impute.21.poisson()` add-on function. We fitted the glmmPQL model described above to each of the five completed datasets and combined results according to Rubin's formula (Rubin, 1987). As Monte Carlo quality statistics we report (a) the average combined parameter estimate across the 200 replications $\hat{Q}$, (b) the standard deviation of the combined parameter estimates across the 200 replications $SD_{\hat{Q}}$, (c) bias in parameter estimation, which is quantified as BIAS = $Q - \hat{Q}$, and (d) the coverage rate, CR, which denotes the percentage of 95% confidence intervals that cover the true parameter.[4] $\hat{Q}$ should be close to the simulated "true" population parameters Q, which translates to a near-zero bias, $SD_{\hat{Q}}$ should be small and coverage rates should be well above 90%. If these criteria are met, parameter estimates are precise, consistent across replications, and measures of uncertainty are estimated well enough so that true parameters are included in the confidence intervals most of the time. For a more thorough discussion of Monte Carlo quality statistics, see Schafer and Graham (2002) or Kleinke et al. (2011). Results of the first simulation are displayed in Table 32.1.

As can be seen in the table, estimates are very close to the simulated "true" parameter values, bias is negligible and coverage is very good, which means that the standard error estimates are also reasonable.

TABLE 32.1

Simulation 1

	β_0	β_1	σ_{00}	σ_{11}	σ_{01}
Q	1.000	0.750	0.500	0.300	0
			1000 observational units		
$\hat{Q}$	0.999	0.753	0.496	0.279	−0.003
$SD_{\hat{Q}}$	0.054	0.034	0.033	0.021	0.094
BIAS	0.001	−0.003	0.004	0.003	0.003
CR	96.689	98.657			
			Varying group sizes		
$\hat{Q}$	0.998	0.748	0.504	0.294	−0.012
$SD_{\hat{Q}}$	0.047	0.030	0.036	0.021	0.093
BIAS	0.002	0.002	−0.004	0.006	0.012
CR	98.171	98.171			
			100 observational units		
$\hat{Q}$	1.007	0.747	0.493	0.294	−0.014
$SD_{\hat{Q}}$	0.048	0.034	0.036	0.024	0.115
BIAS	−0.007	0.003	0.007	0.006	0.014
CR	97.191	96.629			

Note: β denote the fixed effects estimates, σ the random effects standard deviations and correlation. Q is the simulated parameter value, $\hat{Q}$ the Monte Carlo estimate of Q, $SD_{\hat{Q}}$ the standard deviation of $\hat{Q}$ across the 200 replications, BIAS = $Q - \hat{Q}$, CR = coverage rate.

Simulation 2

The data generating process was identical to the one used in Simulation 1, except that this time we included the quadratic term x^2 in addition to the linear predictor x. Group size did not vary. Each of the 100 groups had a sample size of $n_g = 1000$. The intercept term and the linear slope of x were allowed to vary across groups (random effects). The fixed effects coefficients of the intercept term, the linear slope, and the quadratic term were set to $\beta_0 = 1$, $\beta_1 = 0.75$, and $\beta_2 = 0.5$ respectively. Missing data were introduced in the same way as in Simulation 1. This created an average percentage of missing data of 30.3%. Results are displayed in the top part of Table 32.2. As in Simulation 1, estimates were very close to the simulated "true" parameter values, with negligible bias and very good coverage. Also the quadratic term (β_2) was unbiased.

Simulation 3

Again, the data generating process was the same as in Simulation 1—with the following differences: in the third simulation, we included a group level predictor z in addition to the individual level predictor x, which we simulated from $z \sim N(0,1)$. Group sizes of the 100 groups ranged from 300 to 1960 (M = 1198.6, SD = 468.18). The fixed effects coefficients of the intercept term, the individual level predictor x and the group level predictor z

TABLE 32.2

Results of Simulations 2 and 3

	β_0	β_1	β_2	σ_{00}	σ_{11}	σ_{01}
Q	1.000	0.750	0.500	0.500	0.300	0
			Simulation 1			
$\hat{Q}$	0.997	0.740	0.504	0.508	0.300	−0.003
$SD_{\hat{Q}}$	0.088	0.057	0.026	0.121	0.030	0.087
BIAS	0.003	0.010	−0.004	−0.008	−0.000	0.003
CR	96.154	96.154	98.077			
			Simulation 2			
$\hat{Q}$	1.000	0.747	0.492	0.503	0.293	−0.005
$SD_{\hat{Q}}$	0.046	0.028	0.056	0.037	0.020	0.097
BIAS	−0.000	0.003	0.008	−0.003	0.007	0.005
CR	96.732	96.732	95.425			

Note: β denote the fixed effects estimates, σ the random effects standard deviations and correlation. Q is the simulated parameter value, $\hat{Q}$ the Monte Carlo estimate of Q, $SD_{\hat{Q}}$ the standard deviation of $\hat{Q}$ across the 200 replications, BIAS = $Q - \hat{Q}$, CR=coverage rate.

were set to $\beta_0 = 1$, $\beta_1 = 0.75$, and $\beta_2 = 0.5$ respectively. Missing data in y were introduced in the same way as in Simulation 1. However, this time missingness was dependent on z. This created an average percentage of missing data of 30.5%. Results are displayed in the bottom part of Table 32.2. We see that the group level predictor was as well estimated as the individual level predictor. Bias was always negligibly small and coverage was excellent.

32.5 DISCUSSION

We have proposed an imputation procedure for multilevel count data within a sequential regressions MI framework, using a Bayesian regression generalized linear mixed effects Poisson model to create the multiple imputations. Three Monte Carlo simulations, where we varied the number of observational units per group, the complexity of the model, and the missing data mechanism, have shown that our procedure is able to produce unbiased parameter estimates as well as standard errors—when the imputation model fits the data. We have also demonstrated that the proposed procedure is able to handle unbalanced group sizes. We would not suggest using this procedure to impute zero-inflated and/or overdispersed multilevel count data: the ordinary Poisson model would both impute fewer zeros than necessary and would underestimate the degree of dispersion and would thus impute the "wrong" counts. These issues are better handled by other functions from the **countimp** package: `mice.impute.2l.nb2()`: multiple imputation of incomplete overdispersed two-level count data; and `mice.impute.2l.zihnb()`: multiple imputation of zero-inflated two-level count data, based on a hurdle model.

Practitioners need also bear in mind that our proposed imputation procedure requires certain assumptions to be met, for example that missing data are MAR, and that the assumptions of the underlying regression model like multivariate normal random effects and normally distributed individual level error terms are met. If the MAR assumption is thought to be violated, the general recommendation is to look for good auxiliary variables and include them in the imputation model to make the MAR assumption more plausible and to buffer possible bias in parameter estimation due to violations of the MAR assumption (cf. Collins, Schafer, & Kam, 2001). If, on the other hand, violations of the Bayesian regression model have to be assumed, one might in future consider using a more robust semi- or nonparametric imputation procedure, like the one currently being developed by de Jong (2011) and de Jong, van Buuren, and Spiess (2013). Future research should also address typical multilevel/growth modeling issues like heteroscedasticity or autocorrelation in the within-group errors, i.e. future versions of the proposed imputation function should allow to model these issues as well.

NOTES

1. The package, along with detailed documentation and practical examples, is available from http://uni-bielefeld.de/soz/kds/software.html.
2. The interested reader may find details about these models and different ways to parametrize the NB model in Hilbe (2011).
3. This is only done automatically when the function name starts with `mice.impute.21.`, and when a **mice** version ≥ 2.6 is used.
4. Note that the multilevel functions in R do not produce standard error estimates or confidence intervals for random effects. Coverage rates are thus reported only for the fixed part of the model.

REFERENCES

Adler, J. (2010). *R in a nutshell*. Beijing: O'Reilly.

Allison, P. D. (2001). *Missing data*. Thousand Oaks, CA: Sage.

Breslow, N., & Clayton, D. (1993). Approximate inference in generalized linear mixed models. *Journal of the American Statistical Association, 88*(421), 9–25. doi:10.1080/01621459.1993.10594284

Bryk, A. S., & Raudenbush, S. W. (1992). *Hierarchical linear models*. Newbury Park, CA: Sage.

Collins, L. M., Schafer, J. L., & Kam, C. M. (2001). A comparison of inclusive and restrictive missing-data strategies in modern missing-data procedures. *Psychological Methods, 6*(4), 330–351. doi:10.1037/1082–989X.6.4.330

de Jong, R. (2011). Robust multiple imputation (Technical Report). Hamburg: University of Hamburg, Department of Psychology.

de Jong, R., van Buuren, S., & Spiess, M. (2013). *Multiple imputation of predictor variables using generalized additive models*. Manuscript submitted for publication.

Efron, B. (1982). *The jackknife, the bootstrap, and other resampling plans*. Philadelphia, PA: Society for Industrial and Applied Mathematics.

Efron, B. (1994). Missing data, imputation, and the bootstrap. *Journal of the American Statistical Association, 89*(26), 463–475. doi:10.1080/01621459.1994.10476768

Graham, J. W. (2009). Missing data analysis: Making it work in the real world. *Annual Review of Psychology, 60*, 549–576. doi:10.1146/annurev.psych.58.110405.085530

Graham, J. W., Cumsille, P. E., & Elek-Fisk, E. (2003). Methods for handling missing data. In J. A. Schinka & W. F. Velicer (Eds.), *Handbook of psychology: Volume 2. Research methods in psychology* (pp. 87–114). Hoboken, NJ: Wiley.

Hilbe, J. M. (2011). *Negative binomial regression* (2nd ed.). Cambridge: Cambridge University Press.

Horton, N. J., & Kleinman, K. P. (2007). Much ado about nothing: A comparison of missing data methods and software to fit incomplete data regression models. *American Statistician, 61*(1), 79–90. doi:10.1198/000313007X172556

Horton, N. J., & Lipsitz, S. R. (2001). Multiple imputation in practice: Comparison of software packages for regression models with missing variables. *American Statistician, 55*(3), 244–254. doi:10.1198/000313001317098266

Kleinke, K., & Reinecke, J. (2011). *countimp – A multiple imputation package for incomplete count data* (Technical Report). Bielefeld: University of Bielefeld, Faculty of Sociology.

Kleinke, K., & Reinecke, J. (2013a). *countimp 1.0 – A multiple imputation package for incomplete count data* (Technical Report). Bielefeld: University of Bielefeld, Faculty of Sociology. Retrieved from www.uni-bielefeld.de/soz/kds/pdf/countimp.pdf

Kleinke, K., & Reinecke, J. (2013b). Multiple imputation of incomplete zero-inflated count data. *Statistica Neerlandica.* Advance online publication. doi:10.1111/stan.12009

Kleinke, K., Stemmler, M., Reinecke, J., & Lösel, F. (2011). Efficient ways to impute incomplete panel data. *Advances in Statistical Analysis, 95*(4), 351–373. doi:10.1007/s10182–011–0179–9

Little, R.J.A., & Rubin, D. B. (1987). *Statistical analysis with missing data.* New York: Wiley.

Nelder, J. A., & Wedderburn, R.W.M. (1972). Generalized linear models. *Journal of the Royal Statistical Society A, 135,* 370–384.

Raghunathan, T. E., Lepkowski, J. M., van Hoewyk, J., & Solenberger, P. (2001). A multivariate technique for multiply imputing missing values using a sequence of regression models. *Survey Methodology, 27*(1), 85–95.

Rao, J.N.K., & Shao, J. (1992). Jackknife variance estimation with survey data under hot deck imputation. *Biometrika, 79*(4), 811–822. doi:10.1093/biomet/79.4.811

Royston, P. (2009). Multiple imputation of missing values: Further update of ICE, with an emphasis on categorical variables. *Stata Journal, 9*(3), 466–477.

Rubin, D. B. (1976). Inference and missing data. *Biometrika, 63*(3), 581–592. doi:10.1093/biomet/63.3.581

Rubin, D. B. (1987). *Multiple imputation for nonresponse in surveys.* New York: Wiley.

Schafer, J. L. (1997a). *Analysis of incomplete multivariate data.* London: Chapman & Hall.

Schafer, J. L. (1997b). *Imputation of missing covariates under a general linear mixed model* (Technical Report 97–10). University Park: Pennsylvania State University, The Methodology Center.

Schafer, J. L., & Graham, J. W. (2002). Missing data: Our view of the state of the art. *Psychological Methods, 7*(2), 147–177. doi:10.1037/1082–989X.7.2.147

Schall, R. (1991). Estimation in generalized linear models with random effects. *Biometrika, 78*(4), 719–727. doi:10.1093/biomet/78.4.719

Su, Y.-S., Gelman, A., Hill, J., & Yajima, M. (2009). Multiple imputation with diagnostics (mi) in R: Opening windows into the black box. *Journal of Statistical Software, 20*(1), 1–27.

van Buuren, S. (2007). Multiple imputation of discrete and continuous data by fully conditional specification. *Statistical Methods in Medical Research, 16*(3), 219–242. doi:10.1177/0962280206074463

van Buuren, S., Brand, J.P.L., Groothuis-Oudshoorn, C.G.M., & Rubin, D. B. (2006). Fully conditional specification in multivariate imputation. *Journal of Statistical Computation and Simulation, 76*(12), 1049–1064. doi:10.1080/10629360600810434

van Buuren, S., & Groothuis-Oudshoorn, K. (2011). MICE: Multivariate imputation by chained equations in R. *Journal of Statistical Software, 45*(3), 1–67.

Venables, W. N., & Ripley, B. D. (2002). *Modern applied statistics with S* (4th ed.). New York: Springer.

Wolfinger, R., & O'Connell, M. (1993). Generalized linear mixed models a pseudo-likelihood approach. *Journal of Statistical Computation and Simulation, 48*(3), 233–243. doi:10.1080/00949659308811554

Yu, L. M., Burton, A., & Rivero-Arias, O. (2007). Evaluation of software for multiple imputation of semi-continuous data. *Statistical Methods in Medical Research, 16*(3), 243–258. doi:10.1177/0962280206074464

Zeileis, A., Kleiber, C., & Jackman, S. (2008). Regression models for count data in R. *Journal of Statistical Software, 27*(8), 1–25.

33

Robust Multiple Imputation

Roel de Jong and Martin Spiess

33.1 INTRODUCTION

Statistical inference is used to draw conclusions from data that are subject to random variation to population quantities of interest and requires assumptions about the Data Generating Process (DGP). When empirical studies are affected by missing data, as is often the case, analysts also need to make assumptions about the process that caused the missing data (Missing Data Mechanism, MDM), either explicitly by extending the DGP to formalize knowledge about the MDM, or implicitly by omitting such specification. Statistical inference based on incomplete data is only valid when the specified DGP, including the MDM, is sufficiently in concordance with the unknown true DGP.

A frequently posited DGP in the social sciences is the linear regression model for an observed response variable y:

$$y = \alpha + \mathbf{x}^T\beta + u, \tag{33.1}$$

where α is the intercept, x is a $(k \times 1)$ vector with predictors, β is a $k \times 1$ vector with the associated regression coefficients and u is a latent error variable with $E(u|\mathbf{x}) = E(u) = 0$. It is assumed that the u's are independent and identically distributed (IID). Since we are solely interested in features of the distribution of y conditional on $\mathbf{x}$, properties of $\mathbf{x}$ are omitted from the model specification. The parameter of scientific interest is β with elements β_i, where each β_i represents the expected change in y when the corresponding predictor x_i has increased with one unit.

When there are missing data, then in addition to y and $\mathbf{x}$, a random selection indicator s is observed, with $s = 1$ indicating that $\{\mathbf{x}, y\}$ is observed, and $s = 0$ indicating that at least one element of $\mathbf{x}$ or y has a missing value. In the presence of missing values, one simple and widely used approach, called listwise deletion or Complete Case Analysis (CCA), is to discard all units with missing values. After removal of all units for which $s = 0$, the analysis is performed unmodified as if there were no missing values: the MDM is assumed to be "neutral", and is ignored. It is important to realize that the ability to ignore the MDM ("ignorability") is not solely a property of the MDM, but also depends on the estimator utilized for estimating the parameters of scientific interest; an MDM might be ignorable for a maximum likelihood estimator, but not ignorable for a GEE-estimator (Liang & Zeger, 1986). Two major advantages of CCA are that it allows the use of standard statistical software which the user is familiar with, and that no additional modeling effort is required. Of course, the applicability of CCA hinges on the assumption that the MDM is ignorable and the completely observed units are a non-selective sample from the corresponding population.

In general, if the probability for $s = 1$ does not depend on $\{\mathbf{x}, y\}$, then the missing values are said to be Missing Completely At Random (MCAR), which is a sufficient condition for ignorability of the MDM in general. If this probability depends on observed values of $\{\mathbf{x}, y\}$ but is independent of those $\{\mathbf{x}, y\}$'s whose values are not observed, then the missing values are said to be Missing At Random (MAR). In this case the MDM may be ignorable, depending on the situation. For example, if the missing data are MAR, then the MDM is generally ignorable if inference is based on the direct-likelihood principle and if in addition the parameters of the interesting model and the MDM are distinct (Rubin, 1976). On the other hand, this is not true if standard errors in a regression model are calculated based on the usual expected information and if a frequentist view is adopted (cf. Laird, 1988). Finally, if the probability that $s = 1$ depends on unobserved values, then the missing data are said to be Missing Not At Random (MNAR) and the MDM is generally not ignorable (Rubin, 1976, 1987).

Table 33.1 indicates for the possible types of MDMs if the CCA is valid or if a strategy like multiple imputation to compensate for missing values should be adopted. Without loss of generality, we limit ourselves to missing values in a single variable. The predictor affected by missing values is denoted by x_1 (the first element of $\mathbf{x}$), and the completely observed predictors by $\mathbf{x}_{-1}$ (all elements of $\mathbf{x}$ except the first one). Note that CCA is valid in Class 4, when there are missing values in x_1 but the MDM is (conditionally) independent of y given $\mathbf{x}$, a fact which is often overlooked. The ignorability with respect to CCA is due to the fact that the conditional distribution of those y's whose x_1-values are missing, integrates out when the conditional distribution of the observed y's given the observed values $\mathbf{x}$ is derived. In Class 2 and Class 5 the MDM is not ignorable and CCA is invalid.

TABLE 33.1

Table exhaustively categorizing all classes of MDM in terms of the nomenclature in Rubin (1976, 1987). For each class it is indicated if the CCA is valid, or that an alternative strategy such as imputation is recommended, considerations of statistical efficiency aside and without using external information.

Class	Missings in	$\Pr(s \mid \cdot)$	Rubin's term	CCA valid	Impute
1	y	$\mathbf{x}$	MCAR, MAR	Yes	No
2	y or x_1	$y, \mathbf{x}$	MNAR	No	No
3	x_1	$\mathbf{x}_{-1}$	MCAR, MAR	Yes	No
4	x_1	$\mathbf{x}$	MNAR	Yes	No
5	x_1	$y, \mathbf{x}_{-1}$	MAR	No	Yes

33.2 MULTIPLE IMPUTATION

Multiple Imputation (MI; Rubin, 1987) is envisioned as a statistical mode of inference to draw conclusions from incomplete datasets. It involves generating plausible values, called imputations, for each missing datum in the dataset. These imputations are generated by an imputation method, and are based on the incomplete dataset and assumptions formulated in a separate DGP for the variables to be imputed. The resulting imputed dataset, which is free of missing data, combined with the specified DGP necessary for the analysis of scientific interest is used for inferences about the parameters of interest. In the MI framework, an analyst is never confronted with incomplete data, and always specifies the DGP as if there were no missing data: the MDM is ignored for analysis. Although the MDM is always ignorable for the analysis of multiply imputed data sets, the DGP for generating the imputations might contain the explicit specification of a hypothesized MDM; more often, the MDM is also ignored for imputation.

Unfortunately, treating observed and imputed data on equal footing generally leads to invalid inference, since the analysis does not take into account the additional uncertainty about the imputed data. MI is designed to solve this deficit; in contrast to single imputation, MI requires the imputation and analysis step to be performed at least two times, after which the resulting estimates are pooled to form the final multiple imputation inference using combining rules given, e.g. in Rubin (1987). Because the multiple imputations are random draws from the (approximative) predictive distribution implied by the specified DGP for the variables to be imputed, the point estimates vary; this variance between the multiple point estimates represents the uncertainty about the imputed data, and is incorporated by the combining rules.

The principal merit of MI is the separation of the missing data problem from the data analysis procedure. As a consequence, the entity which produces the imputed dataset, called imputer, and the entity which analyzes it, called analyst, need not be the same. Data analysts who lack the necessary skills and knowledge to correctly handle the missing data problem themselves can thus continue to perform the data analysis using the methods and computer programs they are familiar with. One minor caveat is the need to apply the combining rules; fortunately, there also exists software which handles this quite conveniently.

MI effectively delegates the task of solving the missing data problem to the imputer, who needs to specify a DGP of the random variables with missing values that may contain a hypothesized MDM. Given that the analysis procedure when applied to a completely observed data set has favorable frequentist properties, a necessary condition for validity of the inference based on the multiply imputed data set is compatibility of the DGP of the variables to be imputed with the analysis procedure (see Nielsen, 2003).

Although the missing data problem is separated from the analysis of the imputed data at the procedural level, at the modeling level both remain tightly coupled because compatibility of the DGP of the variables to be imputed depends on the data analysis chosen by the analyst. Incompatibility of this DGP may arise when analyst and imputer insufficiently communicate or when the same set of imputed datasets is analyzed multiple times by possibly different analysts to obtain unique inferences, each with its own analysis. In this case, the inferences are valid only when the DGP of the variables to be imputed is compatible with all analysis procedures. Absolutely speaking, however, there exists no regular parametric DGP of the variables to be imputed which encapsulates the collection of all parametric DGPs that can be adopted at the analysis stage. On the other hand, nonparametric imputation methods may not be a general solution, as they suffer from the curse of dimensionality, and typically exhibit poorer finite-sample performance. Creating ultimate imputations which allow valid inferences for all possible DGPs at the analysis stage is therefore likely to be an impossible goal.

A modeling approach for specifying the DGP of the variables to be imputed which has become increasingly popular in recent years is MI by sequential regression models (Raghunathan, Lepkowski, van Hoewyk, & Solenberger, 2001), which is also known as the fully conditional specification approach (van Buuren, 2007). This approach was conceived primarily due to a lack of multivariate imputation models when facing missing values in a mix of categorical, continuous, and count data. Using this framework, the imputer specifies for each variable with missing values an imputation model conditional on the other variables.

However, the great flexibility of the fully conditional specification approach allows for the possibility that the joint distribution implied by the specified conditional models does not exist, in which case they are said to be incompatible. The specified conditional models are compatible when the implied joint distribution does exist. An example of a compatible model is when all conditional distributions are normal with the mean linearly dependent on all other variables and constant variance, which implies a multivariate normal distribution. Incompatible models may arise easily due to the great flexibility when specifying the conditional models, especially when these vary in complexity and richness. Up until recently, the limited simulation study of van Buuren, Brand, Groothuis-Oudshoorn, and Rubin (2006) provided the only insight into the consequences of incompatibility. However, recent work of Liu, Gelman, Hill, Su, and Kropko (2012) provides an analysis of the characteristics of the Markov Chain when the conditional models are compatible and the consequences of incompatibility; they also prove consistency of the MI inference for the class of incompatible families of conditional distributions that contain the true marginal distributions. Consistency of the variance estimator could not be proven.

A model to generate imputations for x_1 is

$$x_1 = E(x_1 \mid \mathbf{w}) + \sigma(\mathbf{w})v, \qquad (33.2)$$

adopting the same assumptions as in (33.2), where $\mathbf{w} = [y \quad \mathbf{x}_{-1}{}^T]^T$, $E(v \mid \mathbf{w}) = 0$, and $\sigma^2(\mathbf{w})$ is the error variance. Note that $E(x_1 \mid \mathbf{w})$ and $\sigma(\mathbf{w})$ may be nonlinear local functions of $\mathbf{w}$. A special case of (33.1) is the reverse linear regression imputation model with a linear conditional expectation and constant error variance.

The conditional expectation and variance of $x_1 \mid \mathbf{w}$ are estimated using the observed data, which is valid when $s \perp x_1 \mid \mathbf{w}$ and thus $s \perp v \mid \mathbf{w}$, i.e. when the missing data are MAR. Let $\hat{\mu}(\mathbf{w})$ and $\hat{\sigma}^2(\mathbf{w})$ be estimators of $E(x_1 \mid \mathbf{w})$ and $\sigma^2(\mathbf{w})$, respectively. Imputations for x_1 are then generated as

$$\tilde{x}_1 = \hat{\mu}(\mathbf{w}) + \hat{\sigma}^2(\mathbf{w})\tilde{v}, \qquad (33.3)$$

where $\tilde{v}$ follows some distribution with $E(\tilde{v}) = 0$ and $\text{Var}(\tilde{v}) = 1$; out of convenience, $\tilde{v}$ is often taken to be distributed standard normal.

Since the fully conditional specification framework allows the splitting of a high dimensional imputation model into multiple one-dimensional problems and thus allows for the application of a wealth of existing univariate statistical models to generate imputations, this is the general strategy adopted in this paper.

Although various implementations of the fully conditional specification framework exist, we will only consider those made available for the open-source statistical environment and programming language R (R Development Core Team, 2011) to safeguard scientific reproducibility, transparency, and practical relevance. R packages considered are MICE (van Buuren & Groothuis-Oudshoorn, 2010) version 2.10 and Hmisc (aregImpute; Harrell, 2010) version 3.9–0.

The main goal of this work is to assess the robustness of inferences based on multiply imputed datasets for the parameters of the linear model using simulation, the results of which are presented in the results section. Further, to improve upon existing imputation methods with respect to robustness and generalizability, a new semiparametric imputation method is proposed in the section detailing GAMLSS. The next section describes the imputation methods considered.

33.3 IMPUTATION METHODS

Global Linear Regression

Global Linear Regression (GLR) is the most basic member of imputation methods. This method is implemented in all imputation software, and together with Predictive Mean Matching (PMM) remains one of the most widely used methods for the imputation of continuous data. Apart from availability, another advantage is the relative numerical robustness of the imputation method. A generalization of the GLR is generalized GLR (McCullagh & Nelder, 1989), which allows the generation of continuous as well as non-continuous imputations. A disadvantage of the method is the restriction on the functional form of the conditional mean and variance of x_1, which may lead to inconsistent estimation of the conditional expectation and variance, and ultimately to invalid inferences based on multiple imputations.

Predictive Mean Matching

Predictive Mean Matching was first proposed in Rubin (1987) and in Little (1988). To the best of our knowledge, the large-sample properties of the method have not been derived yet. Nevertheless, the method has been found to work well in simulation studies (e.g. Schenker & Taylor, 1996;

Andridge & Little, 2010; Yu, Burton & Rivero-Arias, 2007) and is currently adopted as the standard method in the widely used MICE package for multiple imputation inference with respect to β.

PMM can be seen as a type of random k-nearest-neighbor method. Given a metric and a query point for which x_1 is missing, the p nearest neighbors of the query point are sought to obtain a set of p donor values from which an imputation is randomly drawn. What differentiates PMM from nearest neighbor methods is the metric used, which is defined in terms of the linear predictor of the reverse linear regression:

$$d_{PMM}(\mathbf{a}, \mathbf{b}) = |\mathbf{a}\dot{\boldsymbol{\beta}} - \mathbf{b}\dot{\boldsymbol{\beta}}| = |(\mathbf{a} - \mathbf{b})\dot{\boldsymbol{\beta}}|, \tag{33.4}$$

where $\mathbf{a}$ and $\mathbf{b}$ are realizations of $\mathbf{w}$, and $\dot{\boldsymbol{\beta}}$ are (approximated) draws from the posterior distribution of the parameters of the reverse regression. Since matching is done using the linear predictor and imputed values are observed values, the method can also be used for imputing non-continuous data.

Problems may occur when regions of the sample space are sparsely populated, possibly due to the MDM. For example, certain regions of y may be affected by a lot of missing values in x_1. Because of the low number of observed values of x_1, the same donors are considered for each missing value and imputation, which might result in underestimation of the variance of the MI-estimator. Further, PMM is unable to extrapolate correctly from the observed values to a truncated region, leading to a biased estimate of the regression slope. Although often heralded for imputing "realistic" values, this can be a serious weakness of the method, especially when the MDM is selective.

AregImpute

The function aregImpute in package Hmisc is another readily available alternative. However, there are no large-sample results available, and the method has not been evaluated using simulations. The only source of information, apart from the program code itself, is the documentation contained in Harrell (2010).

First, the algorithm finds those transformations of the predictors $f_j(\mathbf{w}_j)$ which lead to optimal prediction of a linear transformation of x_1 in the following additive model:

$$\tilde{c} + x_1\tilde{d} = \tilde{\alpha} + \sum_{j=1}^{J} f_j(\mathbf{w}_j)\tilde{\beta}_j + \nu, \tag{33.5}$$

where the $f_j(\cdot)$ are restricted cubic spline basis functions with a fixed number of knots. After estimation of (33.5), a variant of PMM using weighted probability sampling of donor values is used to generate imputations, where the weights are inversely proportional to the following distance function:

$$d_{areg}(\mathbf{a},\mathbf{b}) = \sum_{j=1}^{J} |(f_j(\mathbf{a}_j) - f_j(\mathbf{b}_j))\tilde{\beta}_j|, \qquad (33.6)$$

and where $\mathbf{a}$ and $\mathbf{b}$ are realizations of $\mathbf{w}$. The method uses the simple non-parametric bootstrap to approximate draws from the Bayesian posterior distribution of the parameters of the imputation model. Since the final imputed values are produced using PMM, aregImpute can also be used for the imputation of non-continuous data.

Generalized Additive Models for Location, Scale and Shape

As shown in Spanos (1995), $E(x_1 \mid \mathbf{w})$ is nonlinear when x_1 and y are not distributed bivariate normal given $\mathbf{x}_{-1}$. The (generalized) GLR method imposes restrictions to the functional form of the conditional mean and variance of x_1, and may therefore fail to consistently estimate (33.2). PMM may run into problems when regions of the sample space are sparsely populated. To be robust against possible nonlinearities, a non-parametric technique can be used to estimate $E(x_1 \mid \mathbf{w})$. Thus, in this section, we propose an imputation method based on Generalized Additive Models for Location, Scale and Shape (GAMLSS; Rigby & Stasinopoulos, 2005).

To generate imputations based on GAMLSS, up to four parameters of a specified conditional distribution $\mathcal{D}$ of $x_1 \mid \mathbf{w}$ are modeled using additive terms, i.e.

$$\text{mean and dispersion: } g_1(\mu) = \tilde{\alpha}_1 + \sum_{j=1}^{k_1} h_{1j}(\mathbf{w}_j) \quad g_2(\sigma) = \tilde{\alpha}_2 + \sum_{j=1}^{k_2} h_{2j}(\mathbf{w}_j), \quad (33.7)$$

$$\text{shape: } \quad g_3(\nu) = \tilde{\alpha}_3 + \sum_{j=1}^{k_3} h_{3j}(\mathbf{w}_j) \quad g_4(\tau) = \tilde{\alpha}_4 + \sum_{j=1}^{k_4} h_{4j}(\mathbf{w}_j), \quad (33.8)$$

where $g_i(\cdot)$ are monotonic link functions which relate the parameters μ (mean), σ (dispersion), and (ν, τ) (shape) of the conditional distribution $\mathcal{D}$ to the predictor variables $\mathbf{w}$, and h_{ij} are smoother terms (Rigby & Stasinopoulos, 1996, 2005). The distribution, which we denote by $\mathcal{D}$, defaults to normal for continuous data, but alternatives can be chosen from a broad range of alternatives. This enables users in combination with a suitable link function to restrict the drawn imputations to a certain range by specifying, for example, a truncated normal distribution, and allows for easy generalization of the method to discrete and count data. Although this modeling approach is less restrictive than the GLR, a misspecification of D may lead to invalid inferences. However, this is not necessarily the case (see the results under the skew-normal condition).

If the sample size is relatively large, we can extend (33.7) by modeling the additional shape parameters (33.8). Since this extended model portrays the conditional distribution $f(x_1 \mid \mathbf{w})$ more accurately, the resulting imputations may be of higher quality compared to those whose DGP solely consists of (33.7).

Our implementation uses the R package GAMLSS to fit model (33.4). Implemented smoother terms include cubic smoothing splines, penalized splines, and local regression. In principle, any smoother can be used; however, penalized B-splines (Eilers & Marx, 1996) turned out to be the most computationally stable and thus are chosen for this simulation study. We use 20 knots, a piecewise polynomial of the second degree, a second order penalty, and the Local Maximum Likelihood criterion for selecting the smoothing parameter. This smoother has the attractive property that for high amounts of smoothing, the fit approaches linearity.

The package GAMLSS does not support Bayesian inference. Therefore, it is impossible to obtain multiple imputations by drawing from the posterior predictive distribution. Therefore we approximate draws from the posterior predictive distribution by the bootstrap predictive distribution (Harris, 1989). An advantage compared to a fully Bayesian approach is that no prior information—which we typically lack—needs to be specified.

33.4 THE SIMULATION STUDY

Since we are interested in consequences of a possibly mis-specified relationship between the predictor variable to be imputed and other variables, two variables are sufficient to capture the main features of the problem (but see de Jong, 2012, for models with more than two variables). Hence, for simplicity but without loss of generality, we consider the case with one predictor x. The three simulation parameters we varied in our study design are the distribution of the predictor x, the coefficient of determination R^2, and the sample size n. All studies are based on 1000 replications and $m = 10$ imputations, and a normal error distribution for the error u in (33.1). A very important factor is the distribution of the predictor x. In this study, we consider the normal and the skew-normal distributions for all combinations of the factor levels $R^2 \in \{.25,.50,.75\}$ and $n \in \{200,500,1000\}$; see de Jong (2012) for more extended studies.

For all studies, the following MDM is imposed:

$$
\Pr(s = 1 \mid y) = \begin{cases} (\varphi_1)^{1-s}(1-\varphi_1)^s & \text{if } y < \tilde{y} \\ (\varphi_2)^{1-s}(1-\varphi_2)^s & \text{if } y \geq \tilde{y}, \end{cases}
\tag{33.9}
$$

where $\tilde{y}$ is the sample median. Letting $\varphi_1 = 0.1$ and $\varphi_2 = 0.7$ results in 40% missing data in x, $\Pr(s = 1 \mid y < \tilde{y}) = 0.1$ and $\Pr(s = 1 \mid y \geq \tilde{y}) = 0.7$. While holding the MDM constant at (33.9), the coefficient of determination determines the extent to which the missing values are MAR, with R^2 approaching 0 implying the missing data are in fact MCAR and evenly spread, and a high value of R^2 giving rise to a strongly systematic MDM with the potential of thinning out selected regions of the sample space.

The results reported in the next section are based on different methods, which can be compared with a "gold standard", i.e. analysis based on the complete data, before any cases are deleted (Complete Data Analysis; COM). Complete Case Analysis (CCA), on the other hand, represents the analysis on the completely observed cases. All other entries are multiple imputation inferences using the indicated imputation model.

The criteria on which the imputation methods are compared are: Number of simulations which failed due to computational problems; Bias, comparing the mean of the estimates over simulations with the true value, which is 1.0; Efficiency, as indicated by the mean standard errors; and Coverage, based on 95% confidence interval estimates across the 1000 replications. Due to space restrictions only results for the simple linear regression model with one covariate (x) and based on the normal and the skew-normal distribution are presented, but see de Jong (2012) for studies using other distributions and more covariates.

33.5 RESULTS

Normal Condition

The first simulation scenario features a normal distribution for the predictor variable x, implying that x and y are distributed bivariate normal. Results of the simulation study for $n = 500$ are presented in Table 33.2 (see de Jong, 2012, for results based on $n = 200$ and $n = 1000$).

TABLE 33.2

Normal distribution, number of failed simulations (Failed), mean of estimates ($\hat{\beta}$), mean estimated standard errors ($\hat{\sigma}(\hat{\beta})$), and actual coverage rate (cover($\hat{\beta}$)) based on different imputation techniques over 1000 simulations.

	Method	Failed	$\hat{\beta}$	$\hat{\sigma}(\hat{\beta})$	cover($\hat{\beta}$)
	COM	0	1.002	0.078	0.940
	CCA	0	0.874	0.096	0.717
$n = 500$	GLR	0	0.993	0.097	0.943
$R^2 = 0.25$	PMM	0	0.992	0.094	0.903
	AREGIMPUTE	0	0.996	0.088	0.899
	GAMLSS	0	1.003	0.106	0.944
	COM	0	1.001	0.045	0.941
	CCA	0	0.912	0.058	0.649
$n = 500$	GLR	0	0.998	0.053	0.953
$R^2 = 0.50$	PMM	0	1.000	0.050	0.912
	AREGIMPUTE	0	0.995	0.050	0.904
	GAMLSS	0	1.005	0.059	0.939
	COM	0	1.000	0.026	0.952
	CCA	0	0.954	0.035	0.732
$n = 500$	GLR	0	0.999	0.032	0.957
$R^2 = 0.75$	PMM	0	1.005	0.031	0.922
	AREGIMPUTE	0	0.999	0.030	0.881
	GAMLSS	0	1.002	0.035	0.953

Since the probability of a missing datum in x depends on y, the CCA is biased, which leads to under-coverage. The under-coverage of CCA seems unaffected by the coefficient of determination, but becomes worse with increasing sample size

Since x and y are distributed bivariate normal, both the direct and reverse regression are linear, and the GLR method is expected to be perfectly adequate, which is confirmed in the simulation results, where the GLR is virtually unbiased and has nominal coverage. As is to be expected, the aggregated standard errors are larger than those of the gold standard set by the COM. This loss of precision is due to the missing values.

Since the reverse regression is linear, PMM is more flexible than needed in this scenario. Moreover, it may suffer from the theoretical issues described in the section "Predictive mean matching" since the sample space is thinned for large values of y. Indeed, the method suffers from mild to moderate under-coverage, with coverage rates between 0.892 ($n = 200$ and $R^2 = 0.75$, not shown) and 0.922 (Table 33.2, $n = 500$ and $R^2 = 0.75$). With respect to bias, PMM performs roughly equal to GLR, which means very limited empirical bias. On the other hand, the standard errors are slightly smaller than those of the GLR model, which is coun-terintuitive since PMM is more flexible and uses less information than the GLR method. This indicates that although PMM tracks the data well, it underestimates the variance, which leads to under-coverage. The fact that PMM produces confidence intervals which are too short leads to an increase in erroneous rejections of the null hypothesis.

The unsatisfactory performance of PMM did not arise in the simulation studies of He and Raghunathan (2009), probably because they simulated an MCAR MDM which does not attrite the sample space as selectively as the MDM (33.9). Indeed, if the missing values in x are MCAR instead of MAR and all other scenario parameters are held constant, the coverage rates of PMM are close to being acceptable and range from 0.921 to 0.940.

GAMLSS is expected to give unbiased results, albeit with some loss of efficiency compared to GLR. The conditional distribution $\mathcal{D}$ is specified to be normal. And in fact, the bias is comparable to that of GLR and thus negligible, although the standard errors are moderately larger than those of GLR; this is the price to pay because of the additional model uncertainty and great flexibility of the model. For larger sample sizes, the difference in efficiency diminishes. GAMLSS unfortunately fails to converge in a total of three cases for the lowest sample size condition; however, in the larger sample conditions no problems arise.

Skew-Normal Condition

He and Raghunathan (2009) investigated the robustness of imputation methods to violations of the normality assumption of the error distribution in the conditional imputation models. They conclude that with respect to the estimation of regression coefficients, GLR and PMM can have poor performance when the error distribution is strongly heavy tailed. They considered a setting with three variables, and presupposed that the missing data were MCAR, demonstrating that currently used MI procedures can in fact give worse performance than CCA under seemingly innocuous deviations from standard simulation conditions.

Therefore, the second simulation study featured a marginal skew-normal distribution for the predictor variable x, with density $f(x) = 2\phi(x)\Phi(5x)$, where $\phi(x)$ and $\Phi(x)$ are the standard normal density and distribution function, respectively. Results for $n = 500$ are given in Table 33.3. Results for $n = 200$ and $n = 1000$ can be found in de Jong (2012). Because it can be shown that the reverse regression of x given y is nonlinear and heterosce-dastic, the GLR method is expected to fail. Indeed, the GLR method breaks down with coverages ranging between 0.472 ($n = 1000$, $R^2 = 0.75$) and 0.916

TABLE 33.3

Skew-Normal distribution, number of failed simulations (Failed), mean of estimates ($\hat{\beta}$), mean estimated standard errors ($\hat{\sigma}(\hat{\beta})$), and actual coverage rate (cover($\hat{\beta}$)) based on different imputation techniques over 1000 simulations.

	Method	Failed	$\hat{\beta}$	$\hat{\sigma}(\hat{\beta})$	cover($\hat{\beta}$)
	COM	0	1.000	0.078	0.950
	CCA	0	0.922	0.103	0.851
$n = 500$	GLR	0	1.065	0.105	0.885
$R_2 = 0.25$	PMM	0	0.991	0.094	0.907
	AREGIMPUTE	0	0.988	0.088	0.881
	GAMLSS	0	0.971	0.122	0.960
	COM	0	1.000	0.045	0.946
	CCA	0	0.958	0.062	0.873
$n = 500$	GLR	0	1.075	0.057	0.745
$R_2 = 0.50$	PMM	0	1.008	0.052	0.884
	AREGIMPUTE	0	0.994	0.051	0.873
	GAMLSS	3	1.012	0.068	0.934
	COM	0	1.001	0.026	0.959
	CCA	0	0.977	0.037	0.906
$n = 500$	GLR	0	1.053	0.034	0.694
$R_2 = 0.75$	PMM	0	1.012	0.033	0.884
	AREGIMPUTE	0	0.999	0.031	0.862
	GAMLSS	9	1.013	0.040	0.928

($n = 200$, $R^2 = 0.25$; see de Jong, 2012). The under-coverage seems primarily due to empirical biases ranging from 0.051 to 0.075, which are comparable to those of the CCA. Although PMM and aregImpute have negligible bias, their coverage rates are equal to those of the normal study, and remain poor. The performance of PMM and aregImpute continue to be substandard, irrespective of the conditional distribution of x (de Jong, 2012).

For the GAMLSS approach, the conditional distribution $\mathcal{D}$ of x is specified as normal. Since u is simulated from a normal distribution, and $\mathcal{D}$ is specified as the family of normal distributions, it follows that x and y are assumed to be bivariate normally distributed. However, this implies that the conditional expectation of x given y should be linear, which is not true. Despite this, the conditional distribution of x given y is roughly symmetrical in form, and only the first two moments need to be correct for consistency. Moreover, the skew-normal distribution has full support, so there is no need to restrict the imputed values via the conditional distribution; all in all, the normal distribution does not seem an unreasonable choice.

Since the conditional mean is not restricted to being a linear function of the predictors, and the conditional variance is not restricted to being constant, the GAMLSS approach is expected to offer robust performance in the skew-normal scenario. Generally speaking, these expectations are fulfilled, although for $R^2 = 0.25$ the method has a substantially larger empirical bias than PMM. For the case with $n = 500$ and $R^2 = 0.75$ the coverage is good, but the number of failures is relatively high. Since GAMLSS is the only method with adequate coverages, any comparison of confidence interval lengths is meaningless.

33.6 CONCLUSION

Imputation by reverse regression DGPs such as the GLR are based on parametric regression models and pose restrictions on the functional form of the conditional mean and variance of the variable with missing values. These restrictions may lead to inconsistent estimation of the parameters of scientific interest, and ultimately to invalid multiple imputation inferences; therefore, it was expected that imputation methods which jointly estimate the conditional expectation and conditional variance using non-parametric techniques offer better performance. The proposed GAMLSS method models parameters of a specified distribution $\mathcal{D}$ using additive smoother terms, which in combination with a suitable link allows for easy generalization of the method to discrete and count data.

Simulations have been performed where data are generated based on a linear regression model with missing values in a single predictor variable, and a strongly systematic MAR mechanism. Although the PMM and aregImpute imputation methods are virtually unbiased, they suffer from mild to moderate under-coverage in all conducted experiments, including the experiment where all variables are jointly normally distributed. The GLR method performs excellently when the variables are jointly normally distributed, but breaks down when the distribution of the predictor deviates from normality, and the reverse regression becomes nonlinear. In contrast, the GAMLSS method features better coverage than currently available methods.

REFERENCES

Andridge, R. R., & Little, R.J.A. (2010). A review of hot deck imputation for survey non-response. *International Statistical Review, 78,* 40–64. doi:10.1111/j.1751-5823.2010.00103.x

de Jong, R. (2012). Robust multiple imputation. PhD thesis, University of Hamburg. Retrieved from http://ediss.sub.uni-hamburg.de/volltexte/2012/5971/

Eilers, P.H.C., & Marx, B. D. (1996). Flexible smoothing with B-splines and penalties. *Statistical Science, 11(2),* 89–121. doi:10.1214/ss/1038425655

Harrell, F. E. (2010). *Hmisc: Harrell Miscellaneous.* R package version 3.8–3.

Harris, I. (1989). Predictive fit for natural exponential families. *Biometrika, 76*(4), 675–684. doi:10.1093/biomet/76.4.675

He, Y., & Raghunathan, T. (2009). On the performance of sequential regression multiple imputation methods with non normal error distributions. *Communications in Statistics-Simulation and Computation, 38*(4), 856–883.

Laird, N. M. (1988). Missing data in longitudinal studies. *Statistics in Medicine, 7,* 305–315. doi:10.1080/03610910802677191

Liang, K.-Y., & Zeger, S. L. (1986). Longitudinal data analysis using generalized linear models. *Biometrika, 73*(1), 13–22. doi:10.1093/biomet/73.1.13

Little, R. (1988). Missing data adjustments in large surveys. *Journal of Business & Economic Statistics, 6*(3), 287–296. doi:10.1080/07350015.1988.10509663

Liu, J., Gelman, A., Hill, J., Su, Y.-S., & Kropko, J. (2012). *On the stationary distribution of iterative imputations.* Retrieved from www.stat.columbia.edu/~gelman/research/unpublished/mi_theory4.pdf

McCullagh, P., & Nelder, J. (1989). *Generalized Linear Models* (2nd ed.). London: Chapman and Hall.

Nielsen, S. (2003). Proper and improper multiple imputation. *International Statistical Review, 71*(3), 593–627. doi:10.1111/j.1751-5823.2003.tb00214.x

R Development Core Team (2011). *R: A Language and Environment for Statistical Computing.* R Foundation for Statistical Computing, Vienna, Austria. ISBN 3–900051¬07–0.

Raghunathan, T., Lepkowski, J. M., van Hoewyk, J., & Solenberger, P. (2001). A multivariate technique for multiply imputing missing values using a sequence of regression models. *Survey Methodology, 27*(1), 85–95.

Rigby, R. A., & Stasinopoulos, D. M. (1996). A semi-parametric additive model for variance heterogeneity. *Statistics and Computing, 6*(1), 57–65.

Rigby, R. A., & Stasinopoulos, D. M. (2005). Generalized additive models for location, scale and shape (with discussion). *Journal of the Royal Statistical Society: Series C (Applied Statistics), 54*(3), 507–554. doi:10.1111/j.1467-9876.2005.00510.x

Rubin, D. B. (1976). Inference and missing data. *Biometrika, 63*(3), 581–592. doi:10.1093/biomet/63.3.581

Rubin, D. (1987). *Multiple imputation for nonresponse in surveys.* New York: Wiley.

Schenker, N., & Taylor, J.M.G. (1996). Partially parametric techniques for multiple imputation. *Computational Statistics & Data Analysis, 22,* 425–446. doi:10.1016/0167-9473(95)00057-7

Spanos, A. (1995). On normality and the linear regression model. *Econometric Reviews, 14*(2), 195–203. doi:10.1080/07474939508800314

van Buuren, S. (2007). Multiple imputation of discrete and continuous data by fully conditional specification. *Statistical Methods in Medical Research, 16*(3), 219–242. doi:10.1177/0962280206074463

van Buuren, S., Brand, J., Groothuis-Oudshoorn, C., & Rubin, D. B. (2006). Fully conditional specification in multivariate imputation. *Journal of Statistical Computation and Simulation, 76(12),* 1049–1064. doi:10.1080/10629360600810434

van Buuren, S., & Groothuis-Oudshoorn, K. (2010). *MICE: Multivariate Imputation by Chained Equations in R.* R package version 2.10.

Yu, L.-M., Burton, A., & Rivero-Arias, O. (2007). Evaluation of software for multiple imputation of semicontinuous data. *Statistical Methods in Medical Research, 16,* 243–258. doi:10.1177/0962280206074464

Author Index

Subject Index